PUBLIC BUDGETING
USING 1-2-3

Keith G. Baker

MIS: PRESS

MANAGEMENT INFORMATION SOURCE, INC.

COPYRIGHT

DEDICATION

To my mother, Jessie Glosson Baker, and in loving memory of my father, Maurice Dewitt Baker.

TABLE OF CONTENTS

DISK ORDER FORM
ON LAST PAGE OF BOOK

PREFACE

Public Budgeting Using 1-2-3 is a hands-on approach to budget construction and data manipulation. If you are interested in simplifying and strengthening many of the functions that are essential to the craft of budgeting, this book is for you.

The worksheet application presented in this book requires 512 kilobytes of RAM and is driven by the Lotus 1-2-3 (Release 2.0 or higher). The application is quite sophisticated. It addresses the needs of advanced users, but computer and budget novices can take heart. The book does not assume that you have mastered Lotus 1-2-3 or the techniques of creating electronic spreedsheets. The needs of both beginners and more seasoned users are taken into account. The instructions in this book follow a steep, yet manageable, learning curve.

The relationships among individual spreadsheets, data tables, and macros are systemic, so even if you are a more experienced user of 1-2-3, it is important that you follow instructions in the order in which they are presented. Once budget/spreadsheet techniques have been presented in detail, they are not fully delineated again in later chapters that use the same techniques.

Complete cell listings of the various worksheet components are included in each chapter in which instructions appear for their construction. If you prefer a more direct access to the data instead of or in addition to the "learn-by-doing" approach provided in this book, you can order the entire application on floppy disk (MS/PC-DOS format) by using the order form at the back of the book.

Most books on budgeting first define what budgeting is and then examine "ideal systems" for doing it. The typical course on public sector budgeting deals with the advantages and disadvantages of various theories of budgeting and presents several approaches to budgeting: line-item, program, performance, management-by-objectives, and zero-based budgeting. Instructors often spend most of their time exploring the politics of the budgetary process.

Many books stress the use of advanced management techniques to promote and ease the process of budgeting. Few, however, emphasize the "hands-on" techniques that improve the practice of budgeting. Faced with a widening gap between theory and practice, some practitioners express frustration, confessing "a sense of shame for their self-perceived failure to attain the holy grail of sophisticated, modern budgeting as described by observers" (from *Effective Budgetary Presentations: The Cutting Edge*, Chicago: Municipal Finance Officers Association, 1982).

Public Budgeting Using 1-2-3 aims to bridge this gap between budget theory and practice by focusing on the tools and techniques of budgeting. It demonstrates how to construct a series of interrelated, electronic spreadsheets and supporting data tables that automate many of the tasks of budget construction and data manipulation. All of the spreadsheeting functions are menu- or macro-driven for ease of use.

The application greatly improves the speed and technical accuracy of "what-if" budget analysis. Moreover, the package enhances overall the decision-making and analysis capabilities of nontechnical budget participants as well as budget specialists. It does so largely by improving budget time frame and spatial construction requirements that would otherwise be more time-consuming and burdensome.

This book incorporates the most basic and pervasively used form of budget expenditure classifications — the objective of expenditures, or line-item format. This particular format was selected (the application easily can be adapted to other formats and circumstances) for two major reasons, one conceptual and the other practical. First, listing expenditures by object class is the basic building block for budget classification. Second, because the line-item format serves as the basic structure for all budget classifications and is widely used, worksheet applications that rely on it will have the broadest user appeal.

This book focuses on budgeting from a biennial perspective. Focusing on two years rather than just one year into the future enriches for demonstration purposes both the budget construction process and the usefulness of the application.

Pertinent summary budget schedules are included in the book along with several special schedules and tables pertaining to budget ratios, trend analysis, and forecasting. Because forms of budget presentation (e.g., schedules, tables, etc.) can vary widely across types and levels of government, in this book a spreadsheet format is used that can easily be adapted to other levels and contexts of budgeting. The format has been effectively tested on students in the classroom and on experienced practitioners at the local, state, regional, and federal levels of government. With slight modification, the application may also be applied to a variety of public-related or private, nonprofit budgeting contexts.

The speed, ease of use, and technical accuracy of the budget worksheet application have been noted in general terms. More specific is the example of a public agency (local, state, regional, federal, etc.) Department Director or Director of Finance who has been mandated by his or her chief executive (city/county manager, governor, etc.) to cut travel within a department by eight percent over the next two years. The Director may choose to use the convenient and commonly prescribed meat-ax approach and make an eight percent across-the-board cut or alternately allow, where feasible, variations above and below the eight percent requirement within divisions. If the Director is granted the luxury of choice (e.g., having lower information costs resulting from fewer time constraints, lower energy/manpower requirements, etc.), it may make sense to cut travel expenses more in some divisions and less in others.

If budget worksheet applications are patterned after the one presented in this book, budget analysts and presenters of budget data will be assisted in several important respects. These applications will (1) help them carry out the steps and calculations necessary to produce justifiable program requests, (2) provide them with more manageable tools for checking linkages between justifications and requests, (3) present them with a more accurate way of checking budget trends, departures from the past, and forecasting, and (4) present them with much needed improvements in the ease of use and speed with which budget outputs can be prepared and effectively presented.

With the budget technology provided in *Public Budgeting Using 1-2-3,* budget officials can easily perform multiple what-if analyses, taking into account the varying needs of multiple agencies. With minor adaptations to the application, division-level expenditure objects can be experimentally juggled so users will know instantly (and without exorbitant information costs) the relative impacts expenditure variances at that level will have on department-level budget requests. This marks a substantial improvement over the "rule of thumb calculus" that budget officials typically must use due to time/energy and other resource constraints.

This book begins by focusing on the multiple components of the worksheet application and the process of constructing a working model. In Chapter 1, the conceptual and physical layout of the spreadsheets and data tables found in the overall worksheet application are presented. Chapter 2 reviews the major functions contained in the worksheet application. Chapters 3-9 consist of step-by-step explanations describing the construction and use of fourteen (14) interrelated budget schedules: Schedules A, B (six), C, R, DA, DC, DR, T and F.

Chapter 7 deals with the construction of three deflator schedules and a macro for automating the calculation and application of alternate deflators to expenditure requests. Chapters 8-9 explain how to develop budget trend and forecasting models. Beginning with Chapter 8, the first of sixteen (16) data tables appearing in the worksheet application, Schedules T and F Data Table, is reviewed. Other data tables include Tables A, DA, C, DC, R (three), T (five), and F (three). These tables support the manipulation and calculation of budget data among the interrelated spreadsheets and graphics functions.

Chapters 10 and 11 are devoted to the development of a user-defined, macro-driven menu system for customizing several important worksheet functions. Menus are presented to facilitate moving around within the worksheet and automating 1-2-3's horizontal and vertical screen division capabilities. Chapters 12-19 discuss how to develop additional menu systems and how to automate the generation of spreadsheet graphics. Finally, Chapters 20-28 explain how to menu-drive the printing of spreadsheets in a variety of printing pitches and the printing to file of spreadsheets.

CONVENTIONS USED IN THIS BOOK

The Lotus 1-2-3 conventions used in this book will help you construct the worksheet application. It is recommended that you consistently follow the examples below, which appear in the narrative of the text, and those that appear in 1-2-3 macros.

The first letter of each command from 1-2-3's menu system appears in uppercase and boldface: e.g., /**W**orksheet **G**lobal /**F**ormat. To enter this series of commands, you manually type the letters "w," "g," and "f."

Words appearing in uppercase include range names (e.g., END), functions (e.g., @SUM), modes (e.g., READY), cell references (e.g., BT1..BU5), and worksheet application menu options (e.g., 1TOTDA).

Macro names (Alt/character combinations) are accompanied with the backslash (\) and appear as single character names, such as \w. The backslash in this example indicates that you press and hold down the Alt key while simultaneously pressing the w key.

In macros, the following elements appear in uppercase and are surrounded by curly brackets: commands from Lotus release 2's command language, e.g., {WAIT}; cursor key representations, e.g., {UP}; editing keys, e.g., {DEL}; and function keys, e.g., {CALC}.

1-2-3 menu keystrokes appearing in macro lines are in lowercase (e.g., /rnc), whereas range names appearing in macro lines are in uppercase (e.g., /rncHERE).

"Enter" or "Return" is represented in macros by the tilde (~) character. <**Return**> means to press the Return key on the keyboard.

The spreadsheet border character that appears as ¦ on your Lotus screen and in dot matrix printouts will appear as | in the cell listings in this book.

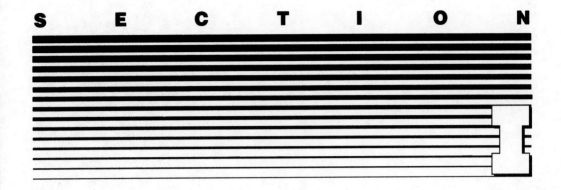

BUDGET WORKSHEET APPLICATION DESIGN AND OPERATION

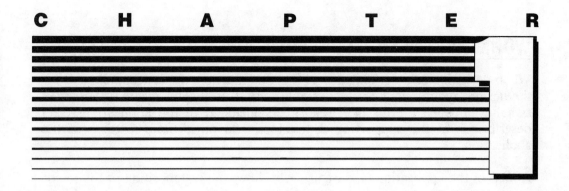

C H A P T E R 1

WORKSHEET DESIGN CONTENT

WORKSHEET DESIGN CONCEPT

When designing or describing a worksheet application, the conceptual basis for the design layout must be firmly established. This chapter includes thumbnail sketches of each of the 14 spreadsheets included in the application, brief descriptions of the supporting data tables, and other basic features of the application.

A map of the application (see Figure 1.1) shows the juxtaposition of the major worksheet areas. You will gain a better perspective on individual spreadsheet construction requirements if you keep in mind the scale characteristics of the map as you proceed. You will understand the more subtle systemic relationships of the various worksheet components as you create the individual spreadsheets.

Keep the map in mind for reference purposes not only during but after the worksheet construction process to help avoid accidental extended deletions or insertions that may occur if you invoke the /Worksheet Insert and /Worksheet Delete commands. The map also serves as a reminder of available space if you need to expand the worksheet beyond the features presented in this book or need to otherwise modify the worksheet.

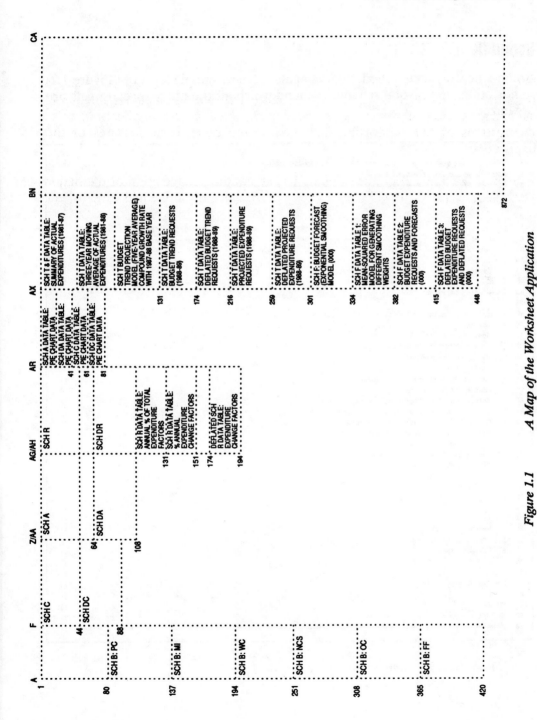

Figure 1.1   *A Map of the Worksheet Application*

Schedule A

Among the worksheet schedules, **Schedule A** (see a sample layout in Figure 1.2) stands out as the pivotal schedule around which all the other spreadsheets are organized.

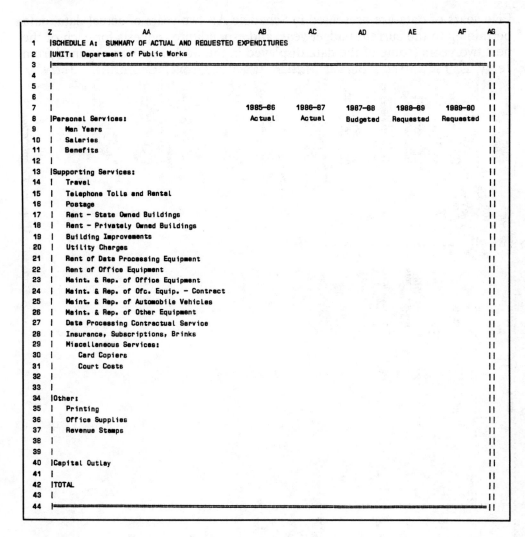

Figure 1.2   Sample Layout of Schedule A

The line-item expenditures included in Schedule A are divided into two of the most fundamental and pervasive categories of current expenditures — Personal Services and Supporting Expenses — and the noncurrent expenditure category — Capital Outlays.

Five years of data are presented in Schedule A: two years of actual data, data pertaining to the current budget year, and expenditure requests for each of the next two years (some of the data displayed in the worksheet was obtained from Jerry L. McCaffery, *Budget Master*, [Pacific Grove, California: Jerry L. McCaffery, 1987], pp. 3-53). The first three columns consist of actual budget data. The first two columns of expenditure data are only for historical comparison; the third column — current budget year — serves also as the base period for the biennial expenditure requests. The last two columns of data consist of formulas dependent in part on data posted from the Schedules B, as will be explained in Chapter 2.

Schedules B

Spreadsheet A is directly dependent on the data entered on the six **Schedules B** (see sample layout in Figure 1.3) for its ongoing biennial development. Data entered on Schedules B pertain to individual line-item requests for projected increases or decreases in expenditures since the most previous budget period (i.e., current budget year).

```
                     A                 B      C      D      E
81
82  SCHEDULE B:  BUDGET CHANGE DESCRIPTION
83
84  UNIT:  Department of Public Works
85
86  1. Categories of Budget Change:
87
88      -X-Price Change                 ——New and Changed Services
89
90      ——Methods Improvement           ——Other Continuing
91
92      ——Workload Change               ——Full Financing
93
94  2. Fiscal Effect:
95
96                                  1988-89  1989-90
97      MAJOR OBJECT EXPENDITURES   AMOUNT REQUESTED      REFERENCE
98
99
100
101
102
103 TOTAL AMOUNT EACH YEAR
104
105 3. EXPLANATION:
106
107
108
109
110
111
112
113
114
115
116
117
118
119
120
```

Figure 1.3　　　*Sample Layout of Schedules B*

Note that each of the six Schedules B is organized to explain, compare, and justify why line-item requests for the next two years differ from those allocated for the current budget year. The six Schedule B categories (also obtained from *Budget Master*, pp. 3-53) are as follows:

- **Price Changes**: Changes in expenditure requests that result from changes in line-item costs that have occurred since the last budget period.

- **Methods Improvements**: Expenditure increases or decreases that result from improved management methods, innovations, or procedures.

- **Workload Changes**: Cost changes necessary for extending the current budget year's level of services to the same percentage of the client population currently served.

- **New and Changed Services**: Cost changes that result from proposing services currently not provided, improving the quality or frequency of an existing service, or serving a larger percentage of clientele.

- **Other Continuing**: Cost changes that do not fall into other Schedule B categories but are required to provide the same level of goods for the same client population.

- **Full Financing**: Cost increases required to maintain services for a full budget period, which most recently were for a partial budget period.

Schedule C

The layout of **Schedule C** is shown in Figure 1.4. This schedule is a budget matrix of summary categories of budget items included in the Schedules B. All expenditure requests above or below those budgeted for the current budget year and entered on the Schedules B are subsequently posted to Schedule C. They are organized on that schedule next to their respective line-item categories and compiled for each biennium in each of the six budget change categories.

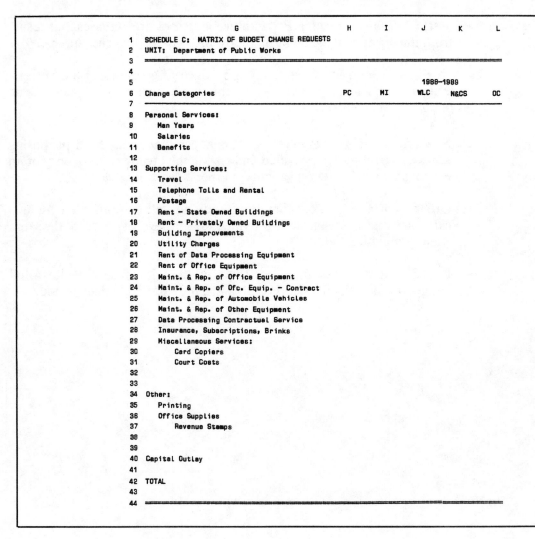

Figure 1.4   Sample Layout of Schedule C

	M	N	O	P	Q	R	S	T	U	V	W	X	YZ

FF		TOTAL		PC	MI	1989–1990 WLC	N&CS	OC	FF		TOTAL	

Schedule R

The **Schedule R** layout illustrated in Figure 1.5 includes each of the objects of expenditure in terms of its percentage of total expenditures over the five-year period. It also includes first-differenced percentages on each object of expenditure for between-year comparisons.

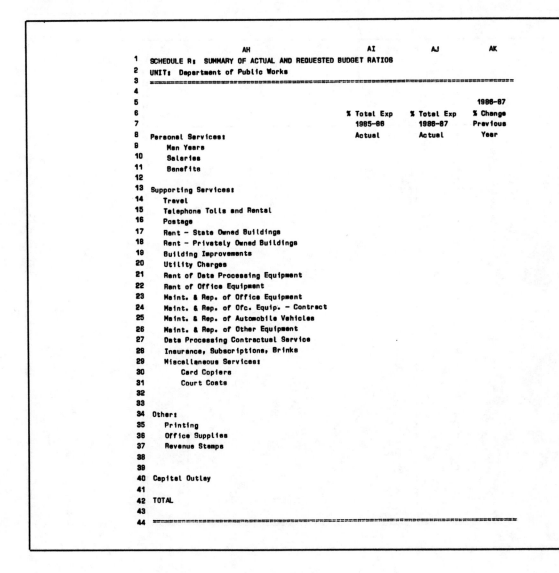

Figure 1.5   Sample Layout of Schedule R

```
        AL          AM          AN          AO          AP          AQ    AR
                                                                          ||
                                                                          ||
==========================================================================||
                                                                          ||
                    1987-88                 1988-89                 1989-90||
        % Total Exp % Change    % Total Exp % Change    % Total Exp % Change  ||
        1987-88     From Previous 1988-89    From Previous 1989-90    From Previous||
        Budgeted    Year        Requested   Year        Requested   Year   ||
                                                                          ||
                                                                          ||
                                                                          ||
                                                                          ||
                                                                          ||
                                                                          ||
                                                                          ||
                                                                          ||
                                                                          ||
                                                                          ||
                                                                          ||
                                                                          ||
                                                                          ||
                                                                          ||
                                                                          ||
                                                                          ||
                                                                          ||
                                                                          ||
                                                                          ||
                                                                          ||
                                                                          ||
                                                                          ||
                                                                          ||
                                                                          ||
                                                                          ||
                                                                          ||
                                                                          ||
                                                                          ||
                                                                          ||
                                                                          ||
                                                                          ||
                                                                          ||
                                                                          ||
                                                                          ||
==========================================================================||
```

Schedule T

Schedule T (see Figure 1.6) includes budget trend data based on five-year averages of objects of expenditure. The model is based on a compounded growth rate factor applied to actual expenditure items for computing projected line-item budget requests over the biennium period. Projected expenditure requests are compared to actual expenditures and calculated percent differences.

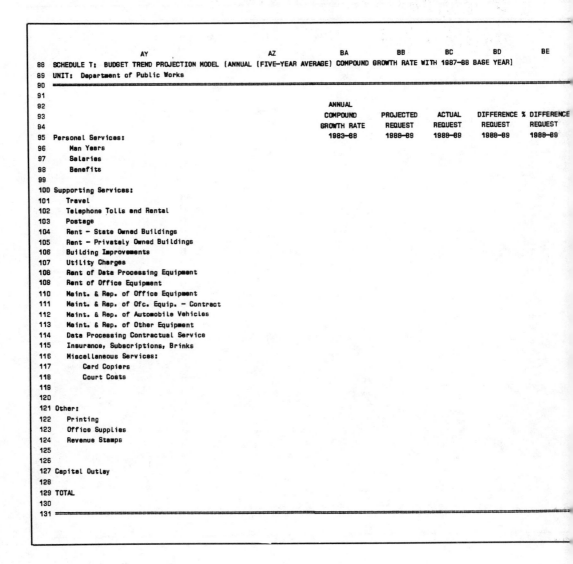

	AY	AZ	BA	BB	BC	BD	BE
88	SCHEDULE T: BUDGET TREND PROJECTION MODEL [ANNUAL [FIVE-YEAR AVERAGE] COMPOUND GROWTH RATE WITH 1987-88 BASE YEAR]						
89	UNIT: Department of Public Works						
90							
91							
92			ANNUAL				
93			COMPOUND	PROJECTED	ACTUAL	DIFFERENCE	% DIFFERENCE
94			GROWTH RATE	REQUEST	REQUEST	REQUEST	REQUEST
95	Personal Services:		1983-88	1988-89	1988-89	1988-89	1988-89
96	Man Years						
97	Salaries						
98	Benefits						
99							
100	Supporting Services:						
101	Travel						
102	Telephone Tolls and Rental						
103	Postage						
104	Rent - State Owned Buildings						
105	Rent - Privately Owned Buildings						
106	Building Improvements						
107	Utility Charges						
108	Rent of Data Processing Equipment						
109	Rent of Office Equipment						
110	Maint. & Rep. of Office Equipment						
111	Maint. & Rep. of Ofc. Equip. - Contract						
112	Maint. & Rep. of Automobile Vehicles						
113	Maint. & Rep. of Other Equipment						
114	Data Processing Contractual Service						
115	Insurance, Subscriptions, Brinks						
116	Miscellaneous Services:						
117	Card Copiers						
118	Court Costs						
119							
120							
121	Other:						
122	Printing						
123	Office Supplies						
124	Revenue Stamps						
125							
126							
127	Capital Outlay						
128							
129	TOTAL						
130							
131							

Figure 1.6   Sample Layout of Schedule T

8F	8G	8H	8I	8J	8K	8L	8M	8N	8O	8P	8Q
											PRINT=
PROJECTED	ACTUAL	DIFFERENCE	% DIFFERENCE								
REQUEST	REQUEST	REQUEST	REQUEST								
1989-90	1989-90	1989-90	1989-90								

Schedule F

Schedule F (Figure 1.7) is a budget forecast model based on the weighting of data (exponential smoothing technique) over a seven-year period.

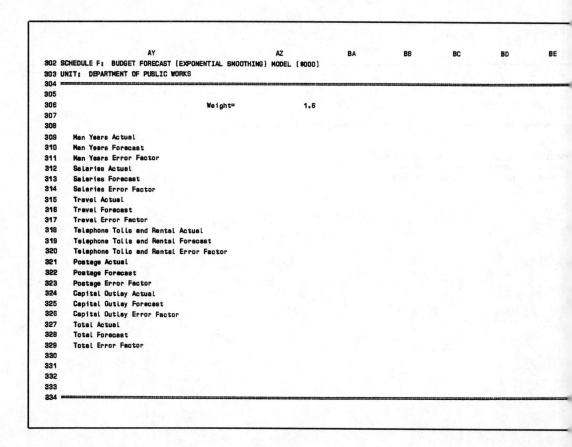

	AY	AZ	BA	BB	BC	BD	BE
302	SCHEDULE F: BUDGET FORECAST (EXPONENTIAL SMOOTHING) MODEL ($000)						
303	UNIT: DEPARTMENT OF PUBLIC WORKS						
304							
305							
306	Weight=	1.6					
307							
308							
309	Man Years Actual						
310	Man Years Forecast						
311	Man Years Error Factor						
312	Salaries Actual						
313	Salaries Forecast						
314	Salaries Error Factor						
315	Travel Actual						
316	Travel Forecast						
317	Travel Error Factor						
318	Telephone Tolls and Rental Actual						
319	Telephone Tolls and Rental Forecast						
320	Telephone Tolls and Rental Error Factor						
321	Postage Actual						
322	Postage Forecast						
323	Postage Error Factor						
324	Capital Outlay Actual						
325	Capital Outlay Forecast						
326	Capital Outlay Error Factor						
327	Total Actual						
328	Total Forecast						
329	Total Error Factor						
330							
331							
332							
333							
334							

Figure 1.7   *Sample Layout of Schedule F*

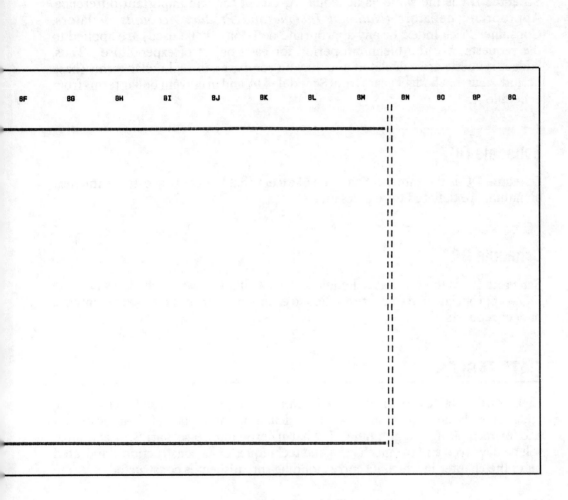

Schedule DA

Schedule DA is the same as Schedule A, except for one important difference. Appropriate deflators (*National Income and Product Accounts* deflators, Consumer Price Index, or any appropriate deflator may be used) are applied to the requests over the biennium period for each object of expenditure. Thus, budget requests are calculated and may be compared in real dollar terms (base period = current budget year) from Schedule DA and in current dollar terms from Schedule A.

Schedule DC

Schedule DC is the same as Schedule C except that budget requests for the next biennium are deflated to real dollars.

Schedule DR

Schedule DR is the same as Schedule R except that — as with Schedules DA and DC — appropriate deflators are applied to each expenditure in the next biennium's budget requests.

DATA TABLES

Eighteen data tables are included in the worksheet. Some are used for calculating budget trends, and others are used for calculating forecasts and deflator effects and/or facilitating the graphing of "what-if" expenditure scenarios. Each table will be displayed and the mechanics and techniques of its construction elaborated on in the chapter in which its corresponding spreadsheet is constructed.

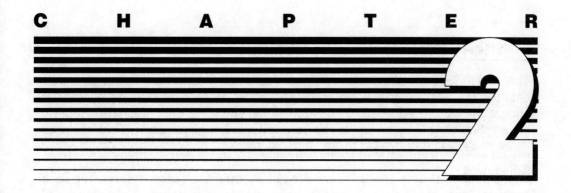

MAJOR WORKSHEET APPLICATION FUNCTIONS AND RELATIONSHIPS

CURRENT (NONDEFLATED) DOLLAR SCHEDULES

The **Schedules B** are the starting point for data entry. Enter expenditure request data for the next biennium, where appropriate, on each of the six Schedule B budget change spreadsheets. Justify individual entries in the Explanation section of each Schedule B according to the expenditure change requested (i.e., above or below the amount budgeted for the current year).

Post Schedule B data entries manually to **Schedule C** by cross-referencing each entry on Schedule C according to its Schedule B cell location. The Schedule C cell reference data are then automatically totalled in their respective line-item categories within each of the six budget change categories and within the biennial period for which they are requested. The automatic posting and/or tabulation of worksheet data is accomplished through the application of appropriate 1-2-3 formulas by pressing the F9 key, which sets 1-2-3's calculation mode to manual (this topic will be fully explained in later chapters). For example, all postage expenditure changes for each biennial period (i.e., those that occur due to price changes, methods improvements, workload changes, etc.) are totalled on the Schedule C into summary postage change expenditure categories in each biennium and each column of line items totalled.

After all Schedule C calculations have been made, the totals of all expenditure change categories for each biennial period are transferred to **Schedule A**, where they are summed with each line-item category for the current budget year and posted to the two budget request columns.

Enter the first three columns of Schedule A — budget years 1985-86, 1986-87, and 1987-88 — as numerical data. Enter all other Schedule A data as formulas. Once the postage change request totals have been posted from Schedule C (with other line-item totals posted from Schedule C) and summed on Schedule A, all line-item categories are totalled in their respective columns. All data from Schedule A are then automatically posted to **Schedule R**.

The data posted from Schedule C to Schedule R are automatically converted and displayed between budget years' percentage differences in Schedule R as line-item percentages of total expenditures. All Schedule R column totals are automatically summed.

Schedule T obtains its data from Schedule A and from a Schedule T and F data table. Note that the Schedule T and F data table depends on Schedule A for some of its data. Cross-reference the Schedule T data from Schedule A cell location entries. The Schedule T and F data table data includes postings to Schedule T of seven years of actual line-item expenditure data between the years 1981-82 and 1987-88. Enter the postings as formulas for computing a compounded growth rate factor for each line item. That factor is used to compute projected line-item budget requests for the years 1988-89 and 1989-90. Percent differences between actual requests and projected requests are then computed and displayed, and all line-item percentage totals are displayed in the appropriate columns.

Schedule F — a budget forecast model — contains actual, forecast, and error factor data. Schedule F depends on the Schedule T and F data table for actual expenditure data. The schedule obtains one particular item of data — an exponential smoothing weight. It obtains that weight from a macro that, after calculating the weight for select expenditure objects, posts that weight to Schedule F. You can activate this macro by pressing the Alt/W key combination and responding to self-explanatory prompts that appear on the 1-2-3 command line. (The Alt/W macro and other macros upon which the worksheet depends will be fully explained in subsequent chapters.) All of this spreadsheet's other calculations are performed by using forecast and error factor formulas.

You may determine subjectively or objectively the appropriate weight to use for exponential smoothing. For the latter approach, the worksheet application includes a special data table — **Schedule F Data Table 1** — which is macro-driven. When you press the Alt/E key combination, Data Table 1 objectively calculates the appropriate weights for the exponential smoothing of individual objects of expenditures. After invoking the macro by pressing the Alt/E key combination, you activate it by responding to prompts that appear on the 1-2-3 command line. Once these calculations are made, the mean-squared errors (MSEs) of data are arrayed alongside their respective weighting factors, so you can choose the most appropriate factor (i.e., the one with the lowest MSE in association with the particular line-item budget request you want to forecast). After the appropriate weight has been determined, activate the Alt/W macro.

REAL (DEFLATED) DOLLAR SCHEDULES

As noted in Chapter 1, the data in Schedules DA, DC, and DR are deflated to real dollar terms. The deflated schedules are located in the worksheet application alongside their nondeflated counterpart worksheets and are identical to them except that two years of budget requests have been deflated to real dollar terms. The current deflator is the one entered most recently.

Each of the deflated schedules obtains its data from its nondeflated counterpart schedule. Data posting occurs automatically because each entry in the deflated schedules is associated with a cell location in the respective nondeflated schedules. The formulas appearing in each entry of the two budget request columns call the nondeflated data, which then are multiplied by a deflator factor.

To select the deflator factor, begin by pressing the Alt/D key combination. This command activates a deflator macro, which, in turn, prompts you from the command line to "Enter Deflator Factor." You should enter an inflation rate percentage appropriate to project deflated budget requests for the next biennium. As soon as you enter the inflation percentage on the command line, the deflator macro automatically converts that percentage to a deflator factor. It is then entered in a macro location. From this location, it is posted to each expenditure object cell and immediately multiplied by each nondeflated expenditure object that previously was posted from Schedules A, C, and R, respectively. As the deflator factor calculations are performed, all spreadsheets and data tables are recalculated to reflect data changes since the worksheet application was last recalculated.

You can enter new deflator factors at any time and recalculate the entire worksheet by pressing the Alt/D deflator macro key combination and entering the appropriate inflation percentage.

GRAPHICS

The worksheet application provides for the automatic, menu-driven graphing of data from each of the budget schedules. More than 100 combinations of individual expenditure objects can be graphed in the application you will create, and others can be programmed. Also, the deflator and weighting features provided allow you to develop and graph an infinite number of "what-if" scenarios.

Graphing is simple. The multiple settings normally required by 1-2-3 for graphing are programmed and menu/macro-driven by the application. For example, to graph the results of the calculations, simply choose the graph option from the main menu, and choose expenditure categories to be graphed from submenus. From then on, all graphing functions are performed automatically with macros.

PRINTING/PRINTING TO FILE

The application provides for the automated printing and printing to file of budget schedules. It currently is geared for printing with a C.Itoh ProWriter 8510 printer, but print codes for other popular printers (IBM, Epson, etc.) may be substituted. The number and type of printing options available vary according to the type of printer used. (See Appendix A for how to make the application compatible with other printers.)

Menu-driven options are available in the worksheet application for printing in pica, elite, compress, or proportional pitches. To print, after choosing the print option from the main menu, select from submenu(s) the expenditure category you want to print and the pitch that you prefer. Printing begins immediately when you toggle the preferred pitch option.

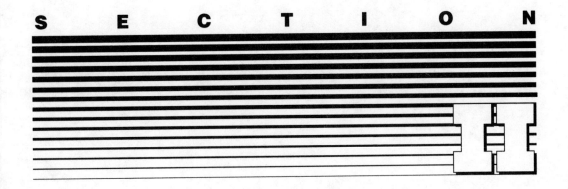

S E C T I O N

II

BUDGET WORKSHEET
APPLICATION CONSTRUCTION

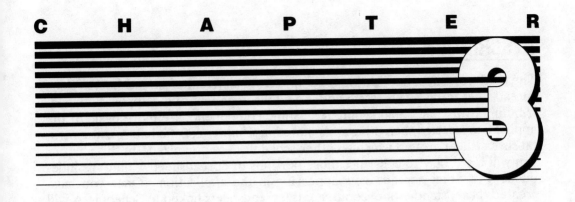

C H A P T E R

3

SCHEDULE A

DESCRIPTION

The total worksheet application is comprised of a system of spreadsheets. Each spreadsheet forms a subsystem and is a vital component of the application, contributing to its functional symmetry. Some components are more basic to the application's design than others. As noted in Chapter 1, Schedule A is the pivotal spreadsheet around which all other schedules are organized. In this chapter you will learn how to construct those portions of Spreadsheet A that are independent of other spreadsheets appearing in the application. Once you have created these "stand-alone" components, spreadsheets linked to Schedule A will be discussed.

CONSTRUCTING SCHEDULE A

The first step in building Schedule A is to clear the worksheet by entering the command sequence, /Worksheet Erase Yes (see Figure 3.1).

Next, format the worksheet for commas inserted with no decimal places:

/Worksheet Global Format ,(Commas inserted) 0 <**Return**>

Z	AA	AB	AC	AD	AE	AF	AG
1	SCHEDULE A: SUMMARY OF ACTUAL AND REQUESTED EXPENDITURES						II
2	UNIT: Department of Public Works						II
3	==						II
4							II
5							II
6							II
7		1985-66	1986-67	1987-88	1988-89	1989-90	II
8	Personal Services:	Actual	Actual	Budgeted	Requested	Requested	II
9	Man Years	98	100	101	104	106	II
10	Salaries	1,352,400	1,380,000	1,393,800	1,449,839	1,553,500	II
11	Benefits	0	0	0	12,500	17,500	II
12							II
13	Supporting Services:						II
14	Travel	70,000	70,000	64,000	64,960	74,500	II
15	Telephone Tolls and Rental	14,000	14,857	15,754	15,754	15,754	II
16	Postage	60,000	69,000	70,000	75,560	75,607	II
17	Rent - State Owned Buildings	10,000	10,000	10,000	14,400	14,400	II
18	Rent - Privately Owned Buildings	6,600	6,600	6,600	12,600	13,600	II
19	Building Improvements	100	100	400	400	400	II
20	Utility Charges	250	250	500	500	500	II
21	Rent of Data Processing Equipment	40,100	45,200	46,000	46,000	46,000	II
22	Rent of Office Equipment	4,000	4,100	4,000	4,400	4,400	II
23	Maint. & Rep. of Office Equipment	0	0	0	0	0	II
24	Maint. & Rep. of Ofc. Equip. - Contract	8,000	8,100	8,000	5,000	5,000	II
25	Maint. & Rep. of Automobile Vehicles	0	0	0	0	0	II
26	Maint. & Rep. of Other Equipment	0	0	0	0	0	II
27	Data Processing Contractual Service	80,000	82,000	84,000	89,000	94,000	II
28	Insurance, Subscriptions, Brinks	500	500	600	600	600	II
29	Miscellaneous Services:						II
30	Card Copiers	0	0	0	0	0	II
31	Court Costs	0	0	0	0	0	II
32							II
33							II
34	Other:						II
35	Printing	89,000	92,000	94,000	96,700	96,745	II
36	Office Supplies	24,000	24,000	36,000	30,000	30,000	II
37	Revenue Stamps	0	0	0	0	0	II
38							II
39							II
40	Capital Outlay	7,306	12,097	34,523	56,523	34,523	II
41		-------	-------	-------	-------	-------	II
42	TOTAL	$1,766,256	$1,818,604	$1,869,177	1,974,736	$2,077,029	II
43							II
44	==						II

Figure 3.1   Schedule A

Set the width of column Z to 1, the width of column A to 45, and the width of columns AB..AF to 12, each with the **/W**orksheet **C**olumn **S**et-Width command sequence.

Make the following Label and Value entries:

1. Enter Label \| in Z1.
2. Copy Label in Z1 to Z2..Z43.
3. Enter and left-align as Labels all entries found in the range AA1..AA44.
4. Enter Label \= in AA3.
5. Copy Label in AA3 to AB3..AF3
6. Enter and center-align as Labels all entries displayed in AB7..AF and AB8..AF.
7. Enter as Values all numerical entries listed in the range AB9..AD40.
8. Enter Formula { @SUM(AB10..AB40) } in AB43.
9. Copy Formula in AB43 to AC43..AD43.
10. Enter as Values the two numerical entries in AE9 and AF9.
11. Enter Value ^---------- in AB41.
12. Copy Label in AB41 to AC42..AF41.
13. Enter Label ^========== in AB43.
14. Copy Label in AB43 to AC43..AF43.
15. Enter Label \= in AA44.
16. Copy Label in AA44 to AB44..AG44.

Steps 1-2, 4-6, and 12-16 construct the spreadsheet borders, dividers, and column underscores, respectively. Steps 3 and 7 result in the entering of a variety of labels: those specifying the type of spreadsheet, the agency to which the spreadsheet applies, major categories of expenditure objects, individual expenditure objects, and column headings designating the fiscal years to which expenditure data pertain and the currency of the period. Steps 8 and 11 enter actual expenditure data. Step 9 defines cell AB43 as the sum of cells AB10..AB40. When the formula is copied in Step 10 to cells AC43..AD43, 1-2-3 uses relative addresses so that the formulas in cells AC43 and AD43 result in the sums of their respective columns.

The independent components of Schedule A have been constructed. (The entries for columns AE and AF depend on data to be posted from other schedules and will be developed in subsequent chapters.) As you will see in the next two chapters, although Schedule A is the master spreadsheet of the application, its functional viability depends on the contributions of up to seven other spreadsheets: six Schedules B and one Schedule C.

Cell Listing: Figure 3.1

```
Z1:  [W1] '|
AA1: [W45] ^SCHEDULE A:   SUMMARY OF ACTUAL AND REQUESTED
            EXPENDITURES
AG1: [W2] ^||
Z2:  [W1] '|
AA2: [W45] 'UNIT:   Department of Public Works
AG2: [W2] ^||
Z3:  [W1] ^|
AA3: [W45] '\=
AB3: [W12] ^\=
AC3: [W12] ^\=
AD3: [W12] ^\=
AE3: [W12] ^\=
AF3: [W12] ^\=
AG3: [W2] ^||
AG4: [W2] |||
Z5:  [W1] ^|
AG5: [W2] ^||
Z6:  [W1] ^|
AG6: [W2] ^||
Z7:  [W1] ^|
AB7: [W12] ^1985-86
AC7: [W12] ^1986-87
AD7: [W12] ^1987-88
AE7: [W12] ^1988-89
AF7: [W12] ^1989-90
AG7: [W2] ^||
Z8:  [W1] ^|
AA8: [W45] 'Personal Services:
AB8: [W12] ^Actual
AC8: [W12] ^Actual
AD8: [W12] ^Budgeted
AE8: [W12] ^Requested
AF8: [W12] ^Requested
AG8: [W2] ^||
Z9:  [W1] ^|
AA9: [W45] '    Man Years
AB9: (F0) U [W12] 98
AC9: (F0) U [W12] 100
AD9: (F0) U [W12] 101
```

continued...

...from previous page

```
AE9:  [W12] 104
AF9:  [W12] 106
AG9:  [W2] ^||
Z10:  [W1] ^|
AA10: [W45] '    Salaries
AB10: (,0) U [W12] 1352400
AC10: (,0) U [W12] 1380000
AD10: (,0) U [W12] 1393800
AE10: [W12] +AD10+O10
AF10: [W12] +AD10+X10
AG10: [W2] ^||
Z11:  [W1] ^|
AA11: [W45] '    Benefits
AB11: (,0) U [W12] 0
AC11: (,0) U [W12] 0
AD11: U [W12] 0
AE11: [W12] +AD11+O11
AF11: [W12] +AD11+X11
AG11: [W2] ^||
Z12:  [W1] ^|
AG12: [W2] ^||
Z13:  [W1] ^|
AA13: [W45] 'Supporting Services:
AG13: [W2] ^||
Z14:  [W1] ^|
AA14: [W45] '    Travel
AB14: (,0) U [W12] 70000
AC14: (,0) U [W12] 70000
AD14: (,0) U [W12] 64000
AE14: [W12] +AD14+O14
AF14: [W12] +AD14+X14
AG14: [W2] ^||
Z15:  [W1] ^|
AA15: [W45] '    Telephone Tolls and Rental
AB15: (,0) U [W12] 14000
AC15: (,0) U [W12] 14657
AD15: (,0) U [W12] 15754
AE15: [W12] +AD15+O15
AF15: [W12] +AD15+X15
```

continued...

...from previous page

```
AG15: [W2] ^||
Z16: [W1] ^|
AA16: [W45] '    Postage
AB16: (,0) U [W12] 60000
AC16: (,0) U [W12] 69000
AD16: (,0) U [W12] 70000
AE16: [W12] +AD16+O16
AF16: [W12] +AD16+X16
AG16: [W2] ^||
Z17: [W1] ^|
AA17: [W45] '    Rent - State Owned Buildings
AB17: (,0) U [W12] 10000
AC17: (,0) U [W12] 10000
AD17: (,0) U [W12] 10000
AE17: [W12] +AD17+O17
AF17: [W12] +AD17+X17
AG17: [W2] ^||
Z18: [W1] ^|
AA18: [W45] '    Rent - Privately Owned Buildings
AB18: (,0) U [W12] 6600
AC18: (,0) U [W12] 6600
AD18: (,0) U [W12] 6600
AE18: [W12] +AD18+O18
AF18: [W12] +AD18+X18
AG18: [W2] ^||
Z19: [W1] ^|
AA19: [W45] '    Building Improvements
AB19: (,0) U [W12] 100
AC19: (,0) U [W12] 100
AD19: (,0) U [W12] 400
AE19: [W12] +AD19+O19
AF19: [W12] +AD19+X19
AG19: [W2] ^||
Z20: [W1] ^|
AA20: [W45] '    Utility Charges
AB20: (,0) U [W12] 250
AC20: (,0) U [W12] 250
AD20: (,0) U [W12] 500
AE20: [W12] +AD20+O20
```

continued...

...from previous page

```
AF20: [W12] +AD20+X20
AG20: [W2] ^||
Z21: [W1] ^|
AA21: [W45] '    Rent of Data Processing Equipment
AB21: (,0) U [W12] 40100
AC21: (,0) U [W12] 45200
AD21: (,0) U [W12] 46000
AE21: [W12] +AD21+O21
AF21: [W12] +AD21+X21
AG21: [W2] ^||
Z22: [W1] ^|
AA22: [W45] '    Rent of Office Equipment
AB22: (,0) U [W12] 4000
AC22: (,0) U [W12] 4100
AD22: (,0) U [W12] 4000
AE22: [W12] +AD22+O22
AF22: [W12] +AD22+X22
AG22: [W2] ^||
Z23: [W1] ^|
AA23: [W45] '    Maint. & Rep. of Office Equipment
AB23: (,0) U [W12] 0
AC23: (,0) U [W12] 0
AD23: (,0) U [W12] 0
AE23: [W12] +AD23+O23
AF23: [W12] +AD23+X23
AG23: [W2] ^||
Z24: [W1] ^|
AA24: [W45] '    Maint. & Rep. of Ofc. Equip. - Contract
AB24: (,0) U [W12] 8000
AC24: (,0) U [W12] 8100
AD24: (,0) U [W12] 8000
AE24: [W12] +AD24+O24
AF24: [W12] +AD24+X24
AG24: [W2] ^||
Z25: [W1] ^|
AA25: [W45] '    Maint. & Rep. of Automobile Vehicles
AB25: (,0) U [W12] 0
AC25: (,0) U [W12] 0
AD25: (,0) U [W12] 0
```

continued...

...from previous page

```
AE25: [W12] +AD25+O25
AF25: [W12] +AD25+X25
AG25: [W2] ^||
Z26: [W1] ^|
AA26: [W45] '   Maint. & Rep. of Other Equipment
AB26: (,0) U [W12] 0
AC26: (,0) U [W12] 0
AD26: (,0) U [W12] 0
AE26: [W12] +AD26+O26
AF26: [W12] +AD26+X26
AG26: [W2] ^||
Z27: [W1] ^|
AA27: [W45] '   Data Processing Contractual Service
AB27: (,0) U [W12] 80000
AC27: (,0) U [W12] 82000
AD27: (,0) U [W12] 84000
AE27: [W12] +AD27+O27
AF27: [W12] +AD27+X27
AG27: [W2] ^||
Z28: [W1] ^|
AA28: [W45] '   Insurance, Subscriptions, Brinks
AB28: (,0) U [W12] 500
AC28: (,0) U [W12] 500
AD28: (,0) U [W12] 600
AE28: [W12] +AD28+O28
AF28: [W12] +AD28+X28
AG28: [W2] ^||
Z29: [W1] ^|
AA29: [W45] '   Miscellaneous Services:
AG29: [W2] ^||
Z30: [W1] ^|
AA30: [W45] '     Card Copiers
AB30: (,0) U [W12] 0
AC30: (,0) U [W12] 0
AD30: (,0) U [W12] 0
AE30: [W12] +AD30+O30
AF30: [W12] +AD30+X30
AG30: [W2] ^||
Z31: [W1] ^|
```

continued...

...from previous page

```
AA31: [W45] '       Court Costs
AB31: (,0) U [W12] 0
AC31: (,0) U [W12] 0
AD31: (,0) U [W12] 0
AE31: [W12] +AD31+O31
AF31: [W12] +AD31+X31
AG31: [W2] ^||
Z32: [W1] ^|
AG32: [W2] ^||
Z33: [W1] ^|
AG33: [W2] ^||
Z34: [W1] ^|
AA34: [W45] 'Other:
AG34: [W2] ^||
Z35: [W1] ^|
AA35: [W45] '   Printing
AB35: (,0) U [W12] 89000
AC35: (,0) U [W12] 92000
AD35: (,0) U [W12] 94000
AE35: [W12] +AD35+O35
AF35: [W12] +AD35+X35
AG35: [W2] ^||
Z36: [W1] ^|
AA36: [W45] '   Office Supplies
AB36: (,0) U [W12] 24000
AC36: (,0) U [W12] 24000
AD36: (,0) U [W12] 36000
AE36: [W12] +AD36+O36
AF36: [W12] +AD36+X36
AG36: [W2] ^||
Z37: [W1] ^|
AA37: [W45] '   Revenue Stamps
AB37: (,0) U [W12] 0
AC37: (,0) U [W12] 0
AD37: (,0) U [W12] 0
AE37: [W12] +AD37+O37
AF7: [W12] +AD37+X37
AG37: [W2] ^||
Z38: [W1] ^|
```

continued...

...from previous page

```
AG38: [W2] ^||
Z39: [W1] ^|
AG39: [W2] ^||
Z40: [W1] ^|
AA40: [W45] 'Capital Outlay
AB40: (,0) U [W12] 7306
AC40: (,0) U [W12] 12097
AD40: (,0) U [W12] 34523
AE40: [W12] +AD40+O40
AF40: [W12] +AD40+X40
AG40: [W2] ^||
Z41: [W1] ^|
AB41: U [W12] ^-----------
AC41: U [W12] ^-----------
AD41: U [W12] ^-----------
AE41: [W12] ^-----------
AF41: [W12] ^-----------
AG41: [W2] |||
Z42: [W1] ^|
AA42: [W45] 'TOTAL
AB42: (C0) U [W12] @SUM(AB10..AB40)
AC42: (C0) U [W12] @SUM(AC10..AC40)
AD42: (C0) U [W12] @SUM(AD10..AD40)
AE42: [W12] +AD42+O42
AF42: (C0) [W12] +AD42+X42
AG42: [W2] ^||
Z43: [W1] ^|
AB43: U [W12] ^==========
AC43: U [W12] ^==========
AD43: U [W12] ^==========
AE43: [W12] ^==========
AF43: [W12] ^==========
AG43: [W2] ^||
Z44: [W1] ^|
AA44: [W45] \=
AB44: [W12] \=
AC44: [W12] \=
AD44: [W12] \=
AE44: [W12] \=
AF44: [W12] \=
AG44: [W2] ^||
```

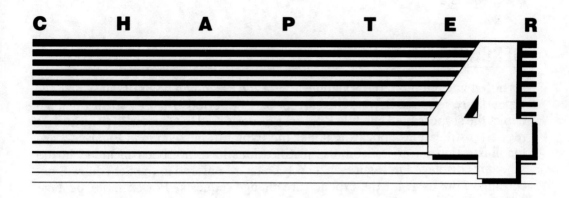

CHAPTER 4

SCHEDULES B

DESCRIPTION

As noted in Chapter 1, the Schedules B are the beginning point of data entry for expenditure requests beyond the current budget period. Figures 4.1 through 4.6 depict the six possible Schedule B categories described in Chapter 1. (The budget request justifications appearing under the Explorations section in Figure 4.1 are for illustration purposes. Similar justifications have not been included in the schedules displayed in Figures 4.2-2.6.) Data are entered in the Schedules B according to the basis for the expenditure change requests. For example, postage expenses may increase or decrease during one or both of the next two years for a variety of reasons. If you anticipate that these rate fluctuations will result from changes in the per unit cost of mailings, you would enter such changes in the Price Change Schedule B. Projected postage expense changes occurring from improvements in work or production methods would be reported in the Methods Improvements Schedule B. Anticipated changes in an output function related to postage — such as clientele services — would be reported in the Workload Changes Schedule B. Changes resulting from additions or changes in public goods or services rendered would be reported in the New and Changed Services Schedule B. Any changes resulting from the financing of current services at the same level — but over a more complete fiscal period — would be listed under Full Financing Schedule B. Those changes that do not fall into any of the above categories would be entered in the Other Continuing Schedule B category.

CONSTRUCTING SCHEDULES B

You will learn how to construct Schedules B through the step-by-step creation of just one of the six Schedules, the Price Change spreadsheet. You can construct the remaining five schedules by replicating with minor adjustments the steps required in building the Price Change spreadsheet.

```
                    A              B        C        D        E
 82  SCHEDULE B:  BUDGET CHANGE DESCRIPTION
 83
 84  UNIT:  Department of Public Works
 85
 86  1. Categories of Budget Change:
 87
 88     —X—Price Change                  ——New and Changed Services
 89
 90     ——Methods Improvement            ——Other Continuing
 91
 92     ——Workload Change                ——Full Financing
 93
 94  2. Fiscal Effect:
 95
 96                                  1988—89  1989—90
 97     MAJOR OBJECT EXPENDITURES     AMOUNT  REQUESTED        REFERENCE
 98
 99     Postage                       4,000    4,000            (1)
100     Rent — State Owned Buildings  4,400    4,400            (2)
101     Data Processing Contr. Service 5,000  10,000            (3)
102                                   ——————   ——————
103  TOTAL AMOUNT EACH YEAR          $13,400  $18,400
104                                  ═══════  ═══════
105  3. EXPLANATION:
106
107     (1) The postal budget should be increased by $4,000.
108         This is needed because of a penny change in the postal
109         rate.  (0.01 x 4000,000 = $4,000)
110
111     (2) Present rent is based on $3.60  per sq. ft., totally
112         $7,200 per year.  Rent is being increased to $5.80
113         per sq. ft. on 2,000 sq. ft. used by the Department.
114         This would bring the price up to $11,600, a difference
115         of $4,400 per year.
116
117     (3) The Department of Administration has increased data
118         processing contractual service charges by $5,000 each
119         year.  This will result in an increase of $10,000 over
120         the biennium.
121
122
123
124
125
126
127
128
129
130
131
132
133
134
135
136
137 ═════════════════════════════════════════════════════════
```

Figure 4.1   *Schedule B: Price Changes*

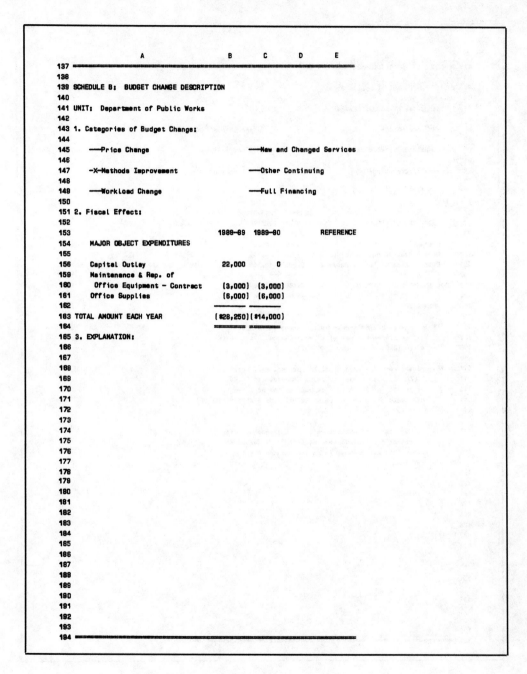

```
                    A                    B       C       D        E
137 ================================================================
138
139 SCHEDULE B:  BUDGET CHANGE DESCRIPTION
140
141 UNIT:  Department of Public Works
142
143 1. Categories of Budget Change:
144
145      ——Price Change                    ——New and Changed Services
146
147      -X-Methods Improvement            ——Other Continuing
148
149      ——Workload Change                 ——Full Financing
150
151 2. Fiscal Effect:
152
153                              1988-89  1989-90          REFERENCE
154      MAJOR OBJECT EXPENDITURES
155
156      Capital Outlay             22,000      0
159      Maintenance & Rep. of
160        Office Equipment - Contract  (3,000) (3,000)
161      Office Supplies              (6,000) (6,000)
162                                  ———————  ———————
163 TOTAL AMOUNT EACH YEAR          [$28,250][$14,000]
164                                  ======== ========
165 3. EXPLANATION:
166
167
168
169
170
171
172
173
174
175
176
177
178
179
180
181
182
183
184
185
186
187
188
189
190
191
192
193
194 ================================================================
```

Figure 4.2   Schedule B: Methods Improvements

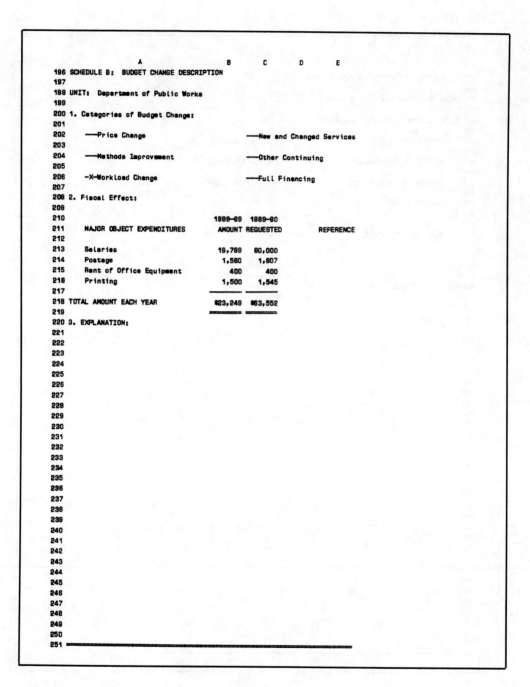

```
                    A              B      C      D      E
196 SCHEDULE B:  BUDGET CHANGE DESCRIPTION
197
198 UNIT:  Department of Public Works
199
200 1. Categories of Budget Change:
201
202       ——Price Change                ——New and Changed Services
203
204       ——Methods Improvement          ——Other Continuing
205
206       -X-Workload Change             ——Full Financing
207
208 2. Fiscal Effect:
209
210                              1988-89  1989-90
211       MAJOR OBJECT EXPENDITURES  AMOUNT REQUESTED      REFERENCE
212
213       Salaries              19,789   60,000
214       Postage                1,560    1,607
215       Rent of Office Equipment  400      400
216       Printing               1,500    1,545
217                             --------  --------
218 TOTAL AMOUNT EACH YEAR       $23,249  $63,552
219                             ========  ========
220 3. EXPLANATION:
221
222
223
224
225
226
227
228
229
230
231
232
233
234
235
236
237
238
239
240
241
242
243
244
245
246
247
248
249
250
251 ====================================================
```

Figure 4.3   *Schedule B: Workload Changes*

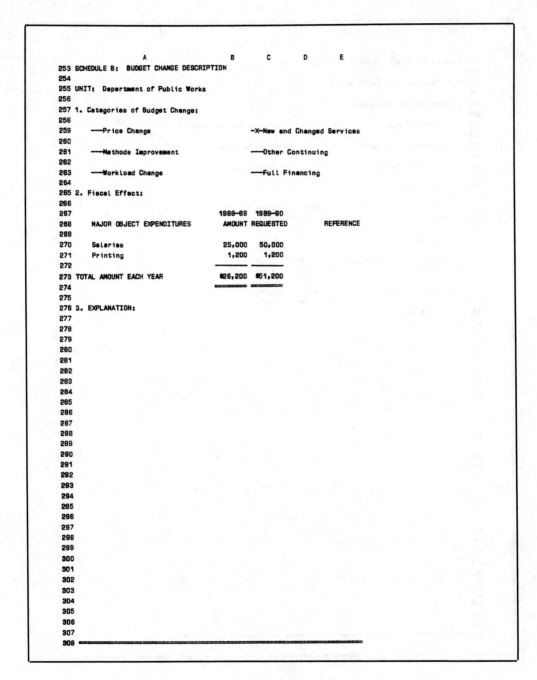

```
                        A                    B         C         D         E
253 SCHEDULE B:   BUDGET CHANGE DESCRIPTION
254
255 UNIT:  Department of Public Works
256
257 1. Categories of Budget Change:
258
259      ——Price Change                    -X-New and Changed Services
260
261      ——Methods Improvement             ——Other Continuing
262
263      ——Workload Change                 ——Full Financing
264
265 2. Fiscal Effect:
266
267                                   1988-89   1989-90
268      MAJOR OBJECT EXPENDITURES    AMOUNT REQUESTED         REFERENCE
269
270      Salaries                     25,000    50,000
271      Printing                      1,200     1,200
272                                 ————————  ————————
273 TOTAL AMOUNT EACH YEAR           $26,200   $51,200
274                                 ════════  ════════
275
276 3. EXPLANATION:
277
278
279
280
281
282
283
284
285
286
287
288
289
290
291
292
293
294
295
296
297
298
299
300
301
302
303
304
305
306
307
308 ════════════════════════════════════════════════════════════════════
```

Figure 4.4   Schedule B: New and Changed Services

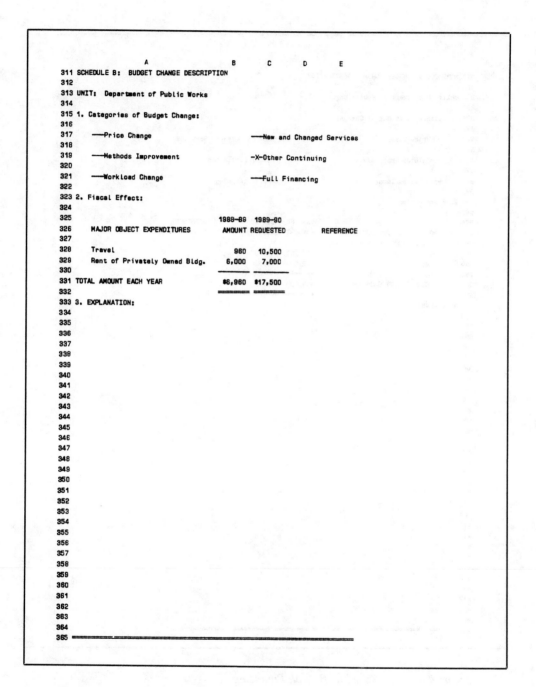

```
                        A                    B       C       D       E
311 SCHEDULE B:  BUDGET CHANGE DESCRIPTION
312
313 UNIT:  Department of Public Works
314
315 1. Categories of Budget Change:
316
317      ——Price Change                    ——New and Changed Services
318
319      ——Methods Improvement             -X-Other Continuing
320
321      ——Workload Change                 ——Full Financing
322
323 2. Fiscal Effect:
324
325                                   1988-89  1989-90
326      MAJOR OBJECT EXPENDITURES    AMOUNT REQUESTED        REFERENCE
327
328      Travel                          960   10,500
329      Rent of Privately Owned Bldg. 6,000    7,000
330                                   ————————  ————————
331 TOTAL AMOUNT EACH YEAR            $6,960  $17,500
332                                   ========  ========
333 3. EXPLANATION:
334
335
336
337
338
339
340
341
342
343
344
345
346
347
348
349
350
351
352
353
354
355
356
357
358
359
360
361
362
363
364
365 ===================================================================
```

Figure 4.5   *Schedule B: Other Continuing*

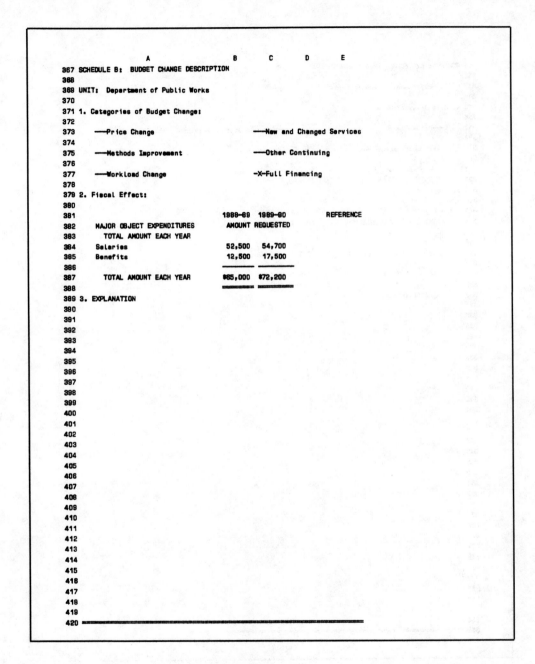

	A	B	C	D	E
367	SCHEDULE B: BUDGET CHANGE DESCRIPTION				
368					
369	UNIT: Department of Public Works				
370					
371	1. Categories of Budget Change:				
372					
373	——Price Change		——New and Changed Services		
374					
375	——Methods Improvement		——Other Continuing		
376					
377	——Workload Change		-X-Full Financing		
378					
379	2. Fiscal Effect:				
380					
381		1988-89	1989-90		REFERENCE
382	MAJOR OBJECT EXPENDITURES	AMOUNT	REQUESTED		
383	TOTAL AMOUNT EACH YEAR				
384	Salaries	52,500	54,700		
385	Benefits	12,500	17,500		
386					
387	TOTAL AMOUNT EACH YEAR	$65,000	$72,200		
388					
389	3. EXPLANATION				
390					
391					
392					
393					
394					
395					
396					
397					
398					
399					
400					
401					
402					
403					
404					
405					
406					
407					
408					
409					
410					
411					
412					
413					
414					
415					
416					
417					
418					
419					
420					

Figure 4.6   Schedule B: Full Financing

Begin constructing the Price Change Schedule B by setting the width of column A to 35 and the width of column F to 2. Next, make the following entries:

1. Enter Label \= in A80.
2. Copy Label in A80 to B80..E80.
3. Copy range A80..E80 to range A137..E137.
4. Enter Label \| in F80.
5. Copy Label in F80 to range F81..F193.
6. Enter and left-align as Labels all entries in the range A82..A120.
7. Enter and left-align as Labels all entries in the range C88..C92.
8. Enter and center-align as Labels all entries displayed in B96 and C96.
9. Enter and right-align as a Label the entry in B97.
10. Enter and center-align as a Label the entry in C97.
11. Enter and center-align as Labels all entries in the range E96..E101.
12. Enter as Values all numerical entries listed in the range B99..C101.
13. Enter Formula { @SUM(B99..B101) } in B103.
14. Copy Formula in B103 to C103.
15. Enter Value ^-------- in B162 and C162.
16. Enter Value ^======== in B164 and C164.

Steps 1-5 and 15-16 result in the construction of worksheet borders, dividers, and underscores. Spreadsheet labels are entered using steps 6-11; numerical data are entered in step 12. Steps 13-14 cause the numerical entries in each year of the biennium to be totalled.

The construction of the remaining Schedules B is facilitated because major sections of the Price Change Schedule B now can serve as a template for constructing the remaining Schedules B. Instead of entering individual labels in the range A82..A97, you can copy all labels in the range A82..E97 into the remaining Schedules B in one step: copy range A82..E97 to range A139..E154.

Next, edit (press the F2 key) cells A145 and A147 to specify "Methods Improvements" rather than "Price Change" in the schedule heading.

You can construct the Methods Improvement Schedule B and each of the remaining Schedules B by using as templates (whenever possible) all standardized features of the schedules or by otherwise replicating steps from the previous list of entries. You should construct these schedules before proceeding to Chapter 5.

Cell Listing: Figure 4.1

```
F82: PR [W2] ^||
F83: PR [W2] ^||
A82: PR [W35] ^SCHEDULE B:  BUDGET CHANGE DESCRIPTION
A84: PR [W35] 'UNIT:  Department of Public Works
F84: PR [W2] ^||
F85: PR [W2] ^||
A86: PR [W35] '1. Categories of Budget Change:
F86: PR [W2] ^||
F87: PR [W2] ^||
A88: PR [W35] '    -X-Price Change                        ---Other
          Continuing
C88: PR '---New and Changed Services
F88: PR [W2] ^||
F89: PR [W2] ^||
A90: PR [W35] '     ---Methods Improvement
C90: PR '---Other Continuing
F90: PR [W2] ^||
F91: PR [W2] ^||
A92: PR [W35] '     ---Workload Change
C92: PR '---Full Financing
F92: PR [W2] ^||
F93: PR [W2] ^||
A94: PR [W35] '2. Fiscal Effect:
F94: PR [W2] ^||
F95: PR [W2] ^||
B96: PR ^1988-89
C96: PR ^1989-90
F96: PR [W2] ^||
A97: PR [W35] '    MAJOR OBJECT EXPENDITURES      AMOUNT
          REQUESTED          REFERENCE
F97: PR [W2] ^||
F98: PR [W2] ^||
A99: PR [W35] '   Postage                        4,120
          4,244          A
B99: U 4000
C99: U 4000
E99: PR ^(1)
F99: PR [W2] ^||
A100: PR [W35] '   Rent - State Owned Buildings
```

continued...

...from previous page

```
B100: U 4400
C100: U 4400
E100: PR ^(2)
F100: PR [W2] ^||
A101: PR [W35] '    Data Processing Contr. Service
B101: U 5000
C101: U 10000
E101: PR ^(3)
F101: PR [W2] ^||
A102: PR [W35] '
B102: PR '--------
C102: PR '--------
F102: PR [W2] ^||
A103: PR [W35] 'TOTAL AMOUNT EACH YEAR                9,120
              9,244
B103: (C0) PR @SUM(B99..B101)
C103: (C0) PR @SUM(C99..C101)
F103: PR [W2] ^||
B104: PR ^========
C104: PR ^========
F104: PR [W2] ^||
A105: PR [W35] '3. EXPLANATION:
F105: PR [W2] ^||
A106: PR [W35] '
F106: PR [W2] ^||
A107: PR [W35] '    (1) The postal budget should be increased by
              $4,000.
F107: PR [W2] ^||
A108: PR [W35] '        This is needed because of a penny change in
              the postal
F108: PR [W2] ^||
A109: PR [W35] '        rate.  (0.01 x 4000,000 = $4,000)
F109: PR [W2] ^||
F110: PR [W2] ^||
A111: PR [W35] '    (2) Present rent is based on $3.60  per sq. ft.,
              totally
F111: PR [W2] ^||
A112: PR [W35] '        $7,200 per year.  Rent is being increased to
              $5.80
F112: PR [W2] ^||
```

continued...

...from previous page

```
A113: PR [W35] '         per sq. ft. on 2,000 sq. ft. used by the
                Department.
F113: PR [W2] ^||
A114: PR [W35] '         This would bring the price up to $11,600, a
                difference
F114: PR [W2] ^||
A115: PR [W35] '         of $4,400 per year.
F115: PR [W2] ^||
F116: PR [W2] ^||
A117: PR [W35] '    (3) The Department of Administration has
                increased data
F117: PR [W2] ^||
A118: PR [W35] '         processing contractual service charges by
                $5,000 each
F118: PR [W2] ^||
A119: PR [W35] '         year.  This will result in an increase of
                $10,000 over
F119: PR [W2] ^||
A120: PR [W35] '         the biennium.
F120: PR [W2] ^||
F121: PR [W2] ^||
F122: PR [W2] ^||
F123: PR [W2] ^||
F124: PR [W2] ^||
F125: PR [W2] ^||
F126: PR [W2] ^||
F127: PR [W2] ^||
F128: PR [W2] ^||
F129: PR [W2] ^||
F130: PR [W2] ^||
F131: PR [W2] ^||
F132: PR [W2] ^||
F133: PR [W2] ^||
F134: PR [W2] ^||
F135: PR [W2] ^||
F136: PR [W2] ^||
A137: PR [W35] ^\=
B137: PR ^=========
C137: PR ^=========
D137: PR ^=========
E137: PR ^=========
F137: PR [W2] ^||
```

Cell Listing: Figure 4.2

F138: PR [W2] ^||
A139: PR [W35] ^SCHEDULE B: BUDGET CHANGE DESCRIPTION
F139: PR [W2] ^||
F140: PR [W2] ^||
A141: PR [W35] 'UNIT: Department of Public Works
F141: PR [W2] ^||
F142: PR [W2] ^||
A143: PR [W35] '1. Categories of Budget Change:
F143: PR [W2] ^||
F144: PR [W2] ^||
A145: PR [W35] '   ---Price Change   ---Other
               Continuing
C145: PR '---New and Changed Services
F145: PR [W2] ^||
F146: PR [W2] ^||
A147: PR [W35] '   -X-Methods Improvement
C147: PR '---Other Continuing
F147: PR [W2] ^||
F148: PR [W2] ^||
A149: PR [W35] '   ---Workload Change
C149: PR '---Full Financing
F149: PR [W2] ^||
F150: PR [W2] ^||
A151: PR [W35] '2. Fiscal Effect:
F151: PR [W2] ^||
F152: PR [W2] ^||
A153: PR [W35] '   1987-88   1988-89
B153: PR ^1988-89
C153: PR ^1989-90
E153: PR ^REFERENCE
F153: PR [W2] ^||
A154: PR [W35] '   MAJOR OBJECT EXPENDITURES   AMOUNT
               REQUESTED   REFERENCE
F154: PR [W2] ^||
A155: PR [W35] '
F155: PR [W2] ^||
A156: PR [W35] '   Capital Outlay   12,000
               0   A
B156: U 22000
C156: U 0

continued...

...from previous page

```
F156: PR [W2] ^||
A157: PR [W35] '      Salaries                         (21,200)
             (21,200)              A&B
B157: (,0) U -41250
C157: (,0) U -5000
F157: PR [W2] ^||
A158: PR [W35] '
F158: PR [W2] ^||
A159: PR [W35] '      Maintenance & Rep. of
F159: PR [W2] ^||
A160: PR [W35] '       Office Equipment - Contract      (3,000)
             (3,000)              C
B160: (,0) U -3000
C160: (,0) U -3000
F160: PR [W2] ^||
A161: PR [W35] '      Office Supplies                   (6,000)
             (6,000)              D
B161: (,0) U -6000
C161: (,0) U -6000
F161: PR [W2] ^||
B162: (,0) PR '--------
C162: PR '--------
F162: PR [W2] ^||
A163: PR [W35] 'TOTAL AMOUNT EACH YEAR                  (18,200)
             (30,200)
B163: (C0) PR @SUM(B156..B161)
C163: (C0) PR @SUM(C156..C161)
F163: PR [W2] ^||
B164: (,0) PR ^========
C164: PR ^========
F164: PR [W2] ^||
A165: PR [W35] '3. EXPLANATION:
F165: PR [W2] ^||
F166: PR [W2] ^||
F167: PR [W2] ^||
F168: PR [W2] ^||
F169: PR [W2] ^||
F170: PR [W2] ^||
F171: PR [W2] ^||
```

continued...

...from previous page

```
F172: PR [W2] ^||
F173: PR [W2] ^||
F174: PR [W2] ^||
F175: PR [W2] ^||
F176: PR [W2] ^||
F177: PR [W2] ^||
F178: PR [W2] ^||
F179: PR [W2] ^||
F180: PR [W2] ^||
F181: PR [W2] ^||
F182: PR [W2] ^||
F183: PR [W2] ^||
F184: PR [W2] ^||
F185: PR [W2] ^||
F186: PR [W2] ^||
F187: PR [W2] ^||
F188: PR [W2] ^||
F189: PR [W2] ^||
F190: PR [W2] ^||
F191: PR [W2] ^||
F192: PR [W2] ^||
F193: PR [W2] ^||
A194: PR [W35] ^\=
B194: PR ^=========
C194: PR ^=========
D194: PR ^=========
E194: PR ^=========
AF194: PR [W2] ^||
```

Cell Listing: Figure 4.3

```
F195: PR [W2] ^||
A196: PR [W35] ^SCHEDULE B:   BUDGET CHANGE DESCRIPTION
B196: PR 'ION
F196: PR [W2] ^||
F197: PR [W2] ^||
A198: PR [W35] 'UNIT:   Department of Public Works
F198: PR [W2] ^||
A199: PR [W35] '
F199: PR [W2] ^||
A200: PR [W35] '1. Categories of Budget Change:
F200: PR [W2] ^||
A201: PR [W35] '
F201: PR [W2] ^||
A202: PR [W35] '      ---Price Change                         ---Other
           Continuing
C202: PR '---New and Changed Services
F202: PR [W2] ^||
F203: PR [W2] ^||
A204: PR [W35] '      ---Methods Improvement
C204: PR '---Other Continuing
F204: PR [W2] ^||
F205: PR [W2] ^||
A206: PR [W35] '     -X-Workload Change
C206: PR '---Full Financing
F206: PR [W2] ^||
F207: PR [W2] ^||
A208: PR [W35] '2. Fiscal Effect:
F208: PR [W2] ^||
A209: PR [W35] '
F209: PR [W2] ^||
A210: PR [W35] '                                      1987-88   1988-89
B210: PR ^1988-89
C210: PR ^1989-90
F210: PR [W2] ^||
A211: PR [W35] '      MAJOR OBJECT EXPENDITURES        AMOUNT
           REQUESTED            REFERENCE
F211: PR [W2] ^||
A212: PR [W35] '
F212: PR [W2] ^||
```

continued...

...from previous page

```
A213: PR [W35] '      Salaries                        19,789
              39,573                A
B213: U 19789
C213: U 60000
F213: PR [W2] ^||
A214: PR [W35] '      Postage                          1,560
              1,607                B
B214: (,0) U 1560
C214: (,0) U 1607
F214: PR [W2] ^||
A215: PR [W35] '      Rent of Office Equipment           400
              400                  C
B215: (,0) U 400
C215: (,0) U 400
F215: PR [W2] ^||
A216: PR [W35] '      Printing                         1,500
              1,545                D
B216: (,0) U 1500
C216: (,0) U 1545
F216: PR [W2] ^||
A217: PR [W35] '
B217: PR '---------
C217: PR '---------
F217: PR [W2] ^||
A218: PR [W35] 'TOTAL AMOUNT EACH YEAR                23,249
              43,125
B218: (C0) PR @SUM(B213..B216)
C218: (C0) PR @SUM(C213..C216)
F218: PR [W2] ^||
B219: PR ^=========
C219: PR ^=========
F219: PR [W2] ^||
A220: PR [W35] '3. EXPLANATION:
F220: PR [W2] ^||
F221: PR [W2] ^||
F222: PR [W2] ^||
F223: PR [W2] ^||
F224: PR [W2] ^||
F225: PR [W2] ^||
```

continued...

...from previous page

```
F226:  PR [W2]  ^||
F227:  PR [W2]  ^||
F228:  PR [W2]  ^||
F229:  PR [W2]  ^||
F230:  PR [W2]  ^||
F231:  PR [W2]  ^||
F232:  PR [W2]  ^||
F233:  PR [W2]  ^||
F234:  PR [W2]  ^||
F235:  PR [W2]  ^||
F236:  PR [W2]  ^||
F237:  PR [W2]  ^||
F238:  PR [W2]  ^||
F239:  PR [W2]  ^||
F240:  PR [W2]  ^||
F241:  PR [W2]  ^||
F242:  PR [W2]  ^||
F243:  PR [W2]  ^||
F244:  PR [W2]  ^||
F245:  PR [W2]  ^||
F246:  PR [W2]  ^||
F247:  PR [W2]  ^||
F248:  PR [W2]  ^||
F249:  PR [W2]  ^||
F250:  PR [W2]  ^||
A251:  PR [W35] ^\=
B251:  PR ^=========
C251:  PR ^=========
D251:  PR ^=========
E251:  PR ^=========
F251:  PR [W2]  ^||
```

Cell Listing: Figure 4.4

```
F252: PR [W2] ^||
A253: PR [W35] ^SCHEDULE B:  BUDGET CHANGE DESCRIPTION
F253: PR [W2] ^||
F254: PR [W2] ^||
A255: PR [W35] 'UNIT:  Department of Public Works
F255: PR [W2] ^||
F256: PR [W2] ^||
A257: PR [W35] '1. Categories of Budget Change:
F257: PR [W2] ^||
F258: PR [W2] ^||
A259: PR [W35] '     ---Price Change                    ---Other
             Continuing
C259: PR '-X-New and Changed Services
F259: PR [W2] ^||
F260: PR [W2] ^||
A261: PR [W35] '     ---Methods Improvement
C261: PR '---Other Continuing
F261: PR [W2] ^||
F262: PR [W2] ^||
A263: PR [W35] '     ---Workload Change
C263: PR '---Full Financing
F263: PR [W2] ^||
F264: PR [W2] ^||
A265: PR [W35] '2. Fiscal Effect:
F265: PR [W2] ^||
F266: PR [W2] ^||
B267: PR ^1988-89
C267: PR ^1989-90
F267: PR [W2] ^||
A268: PR [W35] '     MAJOR OBJECT EXPENDITURES         AMOUNT
             REQUESTED          REFERENCE
F268: PR [W2] ^||
F269: PR [W2] ^||
A270: PR [W35] '   Salaries                          12,179

             11,882              A&B
B270: U 25000
C270: U 50000
F270: PR [W2] ^||
```

continued...

...from previous page

```
A271: PR [W35] '     Printing
B271: (,0) U 1200
C271: (,0) U 1200
F271: PR [W2] ^||
A272: PR [W35] ^
B272: PR '--------
C272: PR '--------
F272: PR [W2] ^||
A273: PR [W35] 'TOTAL AMOUNT EACH YEAR
B273: (C0) PR @SUM(B270..B271)
C273: (C0) PR @SUM(C270..C271)
F273: PR [W2] ^||
A274: PR [W35] ^
B274: PR ^========
C274: PR ^========
F274: PR [W2] ^||
F275: PR [W2] ^||
A276: PR [W35] '3. EXPLANATION:
F276: PR [W2] ^||
F277: PR [W2] ^||
F278: PR [W2] ^||
F279: PR [W2] ^||
F280: PR [W2] ^||
F281: PR [W2] ^||
F282: PR [W2] ^||
F283: PR [W2] ^||
F284: PR [W2] ^||
F285: PR [W2] ^||
F286: PR [W2] ^||
F287: PR [W2] ^||
F288: PR [W2] ^||
F289: PR [W2] ^||
F290: PR [W2] ^||
F291: PR [W2] ^||
F292: PR [W2] ^||
F293: PR [W2] ^||
F294: PR [W2] ^||
F295: PR [W2] ^||
F296: PR [W2] ^||
```

continued...

...from previous page

```
F297: PR [W2] ^||
F298: PR [W2] ^||
F299: PR [W2] ^||
F300: PR [W2] ^||
F301: PR [W2] ^||
F302: PR [W2] ^||
F303: PR [W2] ^||
F304: PR [W2] ^||
F305: PR [W2] ^||
F306: PR [W2] ^||
F307: PR [W2] ^||
A308: PR [W35] ^\=
B308: PR ^=========
C308: PR ^=========
D308: PR ^=========
E308: PR ^=========
F308: PR [W2] ^||
```

Cell Listing: Figure 4.5

```
F309: PR [W2] ^||
F310: PR [W2] ^||
A311: PR [W35] ^SCHEDULE B:   BUDGET CHANGE DESCRIPTION
F311: PR [W2] ^||
F312: PR [W2] ^||
A313: PR [W35] 'UNIT:  Department of Public Works
F313: PR [W2] ^||
F314: PR [W2] ^||
A315: PR [W35] '1. Categories of Budget Change:
F315: PR [W2] ^||
F316: PR [W2] ^||
A317: PR [W35] '     ---Price Change              ---Other
               Continuing
C317: PR '---New and Changed Services
F317: PR [W2] ^||
F318: PR [W2] ^||
A319: PR [W35] '     ---Methods Improvement
```

continued...

...from previous page

```
C319: PR '-X-Other Continuing
F319: PR [W2] ^||
F320: PR [W2] ^||
A321: PR [W35] '      ---Workload Change
C321: PR '---Full Financing
F321: PR [W2] ^||
F322: PR [W2] ^||
A323: PR [W35] '2. Fiscal Effect:
F323: PR [W2] ^||
F324: PR [W2] ^||
B325: PR ^1988-89
C325: PR ^1989-90
F325: PR [W2] ^||
A326: PR [W35] '      MAJOR OBJECT EXPENDITURES        AMOUNT
              REQUESTED            REFERENCE
F326: PR [W2] ^||
F327: PR [W2] ^||
A328: PR [W35] '     Travel                               960
              0             A
B328: U 960
C328: U 10500
F328: PR [W2] ^||
A329: PR [W35] '     Rent of Privately Owned Bldg.      6,000
              6,000           B
B329: (,0) U 6000
C329: (,0) U 7000
F329: PR [W2] ^||
B330: PR ^ ----------
C330: PR ^ ----------
F330: PR [W2] ^||
A331: PR [W35] 'TOTAL AMOUNT EACH YEAR                  6,960
              6,000
B331: (C0) PR @SUM(B328..B329)
C331: (C0) PR @SUM(C328..C329)
F331: PR [W2] ^||
A332: PR [W35] '
B332: PR ^ ========
C332: PR ^ ========
F332: PR [W2] ^||
```

continued...

...from previous page

```
A333: PR [W35] '3. EXPLANATION:
F333: PR [W2] ^||
F334: PR [W2] ^||
F335: PR [W2] ^||
F336: PR [W2] ^||
F337: PR [W2] ^||
F338: PR [W2] ^||
F339: PR [W2] ^||
F340: PR [W2] ^||
F341: PR [W2] ^||
F342: PR [W2] ^||
F343: PR [W2] ^||
F344: PR [W2] ^||
F345: PR [W2] ^||
F346: PR [W2] ^||
F347: PR [W2] ^||
F348: PR [W2] ^||
F349: PR [W2] ^||
F350: PR [W2] ^||
F351: PR [W2] ^||
F352: PR [W2] ^||
F353: PR [W2] ^||
F354: PR [W2] ^||
F355: PR [W2] ^||
F356: PR [W2] ^||
F357: PR [W2] ^||
F358: PR [W2] ^||
F359: PR [W2] ^||
F360: PR [W2] ^||
F361: PR [W2] ^||
F362: PR [W2] ^||
F363: PR [W2] ^||
F364: PR [W2] ^||
A365: PR [W35] ^\=
B365: PR ^=========
C365: PR ^=========
D365: PR ^=========
E365: PR ^=========
F365: PR [W2] ^||
```

Cell Listing: Figure 4.6

```
F366:  PR [W2] ^||
A367:  PR [W35] ^SCHEDULE B:   BUDGET CHANGE DESCRIPTION
F367:  PR [W2] ^||
F368:  PR [W2] ^||
A369:  PR [W35] 'UNIT:   Department of Public Works
F369:  PR [W2] ^||
F370:  PR [W2] ^||
A371:  PR [W35] '1. Categories of Budget Change:
F371:  PR [W2] ^||
F372:  PR [W2] ^||
A373:  PR [W35] '      ---Price Change                        ---Other
               Continuing
C373:  PR '---New and Changed Services
F373:  PR [W2] ^||
F374:  PR [W2] ^||
A375:  PR [W35] '     ---Methods Improvement
C375:  PR '---Other Continuing
F375:  PR [W2] ^||
F376:  PR [W2] ^||
A377:  PR [W35] '     ---Workload Change
C377:  PR '-X-Full Financing
F377:  PR [W2] ^||
F378:  PR [W2] ^||
A379:  PR [W35] '2. Fiscal Effect:
F379:  PR [W2] ^||
F380:  PR [W2] ^||
B381:  PR ^1988-89
C381:  PR ^1989-90
E381:  PR ^REFERENCE
F381:  PR [W2] ^||
A382:  PR [W35] '     MAJOR OBJECT EXPENDITURES          AMOUNT
               REQUESTED          REFERENCE
F382:  PR [W2] ^||
A383:  PR [W35] ^TOTAL AMOUNT EACH YEAR
F383:  PR [W2] ^||
A384:  PR [W35] '    Salaries
B384:  U 52500
C384:  U 54700
F384:  PR [W2] ^||
```

continued...

...from previous page

```
A385: PR [W35] '      Benefits
B385: U 12500
C385: U 17500
F385: PR [W2] ^||
B386: PR ^ ---------
C386: PR ^ ---------
F386: PR [W2] ^||
A387: PR [W35] ^TOTAL AMOUNT EACH YEAR
B387: (C0) PR @SUM(B384..B385)
C387: (C0) PR @SUM(C384..C385)
F387: PR [W2] ^||
B388: PR ^ =========
C388: PR ^ =========
F388: PR [W2] ^||
A389: PR [W35] '3. EXPLANATION
F389: PR [W2] ^||
F390: PR [W2] ^||
F391: PR [W2] ^||
F392: PR [W2] ^||
F393: PR [W2] ^||
F394: PR [W2] ^||
F395: PR [W2] ^||
F396: PR [W2] ^||
F397: PR [W2] ^||
F398: PR [W2] ^||
F399: PR [W2] ^||
F400: PR [W2] ^||
F401: PR [W2] ^||
F402: PR [W2] ^||
F403: PR [W2] ^||
F404: PR [W2] ^||
F405: PR [W2] ^||
F406: PR [W2] ^||
F407: PR [W2] ^||
F408: PR [W2] ^||
F409: PR [W2] ^||
F410: PR [W2] ^||
F411: PR [W2] ^||
F412: PR [W2] ^||
F413: PR [W2] ^||
```

continued...

...from previous page

```
F414: PR [W2] ^||
F415: PR [W2] ^||
F416: PR [W2] ^||
F417: PR [W2] ^||
F418: PR [W2] ^||
F419: PR [W2] ^||
A420: PR [W35] \=
B420: PR \=
C420: PR \=
D420: PR \=
E420: PR \=
F420: PR [W2] ^||
```

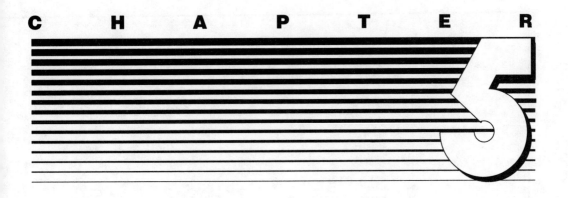

SCHEDULE C

5 Schedule C

	G	H	I	J	K	L
1	SCHEDULE C: MATRIX OF BUDGET CHANGE REQUESTS					
2	UNIT: Department of Public Works					
3						
4						
5				1988-1989		
6	Change Categories	PC	MI	WLC	N&CS	OC
7						
8	Personal Services:					
9	Man Years					
10	Salaries		[41,250]	19,789	25,000	
11	Benefits					
12						
13	Supporting Services:					
14	Travel					960
15	Telephone Tolls and Rental					
16	Postage	4,000		1,560		
17	Rent - State Owned Buildings	4,400				
18	Rent - Privately Owned Buildings					6,000
19	Building Improvements					
20	Utility Charges					
21	Rent of Data Processing Equipment					
22	Rent of Office Equipment			400		
23	Maint. & Rep. of Office Equipment					
24	Maint. & Rep. of Ofc. Equip. - Contract		[3,000]			
25	Maint. & Rep. of Automobile Vehicles					
26	Maint. & Rep. of Other Equipment					
27	Data Processing Contractual Service	5,000				
28	Insurance, Subscriptions, Brinks					
29	Miscellaneous Services:					
30	Card Copiers					
31	Court Costs					
32						
33						
34	Other:					
35	Printing			1,500	1,200	
36	Office Supplies		[6,000]			
37	Revenue Stamps					
38						
39						
40	Capital Outlay			22,000		
41						
42	TOTAL	$13,400	[$28,250]	$23,249	$26,200	$6,960
43						
44						

Figure 5.1   *Schedule C*

M	N	O	P	Q	R	S	T	U	V	W	X
FF	TOTAL		PC	MI	WLC	N&CS	OC	FF		TOTAL	
					1989–1990						
52,500	56,039			(5,000)	60,000	50,000		54,700		159,700	
12,500	12,500							17,500		17,500	
	960						10,500			10,500	
	0									0	
	5,560		4,000		1,607					5,607	
	4,400		4,400							4,400	
	6,000						7,000			7,000	
	0									0	
	0									0	
	400				400					400	
	0									0	
	(3,000)			(3,000)						(3,000)	
	0									0	
	0									0	
	5,000		10,000							10,000	
	0									0	
	0									0	
	0									0	
	0									0	
	2,700				1,545	1,200				2,745	
	(6,000)			(6,000)						(6,000)	
	0									0	
	22,000			0						0	
$65,000	$106,559		$18,400	(14,000)	$63,552	$51,200	$17,500	$72,200		$208,852	

DESCRIPTION

Schedule C (see Figure 5.1) includes in a matrix format the six categories of price changes represented in the Schedules B. The schedule serves two important functions. First, Schedule C totals the budget requests for each biennium within each of the Schedule B change categories, which enables analysts to easily determine, for example, the relative influence of changes in workload in comparison with price changes on overall expenditure requests or in comparison with other summary change categories. Second, Schedule C is the only schedule that summarizes total expenditure changes requested above or below expenditures allocated for the current budget period.

Equally important in terms of the systemic dynamics of the worksheet application is the matrix format that permits Schedule C to serve as a bridge between the Schedules B and Schedule A for calculation purposes. Data entered in the Schedules B must be posted to Schedule C and to the individual categories aggregated before the line-item calculation of budget requests on Schedule A for each of the biennial periods can be posted.

CONSTRUCTING SCHEDULE C

Begin constructing Schedule C by moving the cursor to cell F1. Set the width of column F to 2 and the width of column G to 45. Move to and, in turn, set columns N4, P4, W4, and Y4 each to a width of 1. The preceding entries and the setting of spreadsheet borders should be entered using the same techniques that were applied in constructing spreadsheet borders, dividers, and underscores in previous chapters.

Complete the remaining portions of the spreadsheet as follows:

1. Enter and left-align as Labels all entries in the range G1..G41.
2. Enter and right-align as Labels the entries displayed in cells J5 and S5.
3. Enter and left-align as Labels the entries displayed in cells K5 and T5.
4. Enter and center-align as Labels the entries displayed in the ranges H6..M6 and Q6..V6.

At this point, it is necessary to split the screen into two unsynchronized, horizontal parts, the top half containing Schedule C and the lower half containing Schedule B, Price Changes (see Figure 5.2). First, move the cursor to midpoint in the display and enter the following two command combinations:

/Worksheet Window Horizontal

/Worksheet Window Unsync

Now, move the cursor to the lower window by pressing the F6 key, and position the Price Change Schedule B in the lower window so that the line-item expenditures — Postage, Rent (State-Owned Buildings), and Data Processing Contr. Service entries — can be seen. Position the cursor on top of the $4000 postage expenditure entry in the first biennial period.

```
                        G                 H       I       J
    13  Supporting Services:
    14      Travel
    15      Telephone Tolls and Rental
    16      Postage                     4,000           1,560
    17      Rent - State Owned Buildings 4,400
    18      Rent - Privately Owned Buildings
    19      Building Improvements
    20      Utility Charges
    21      Rent of Data Processing Equipment
    22      Rent of Office Equipment                            400
                        A             B        C      D      E
    96                              1988-89  1989-90
    97      MAJOR OBJECT EXPENDITURES  AMOUNT REQUESTED    REFERENCE
    98
    99      Postage                   4,000    4,000        (1)
    100     Rent - State Owned Buildings 4,400  4,400       (2)
    101     Data Processing Contr. Service 5,000 10,000     (3)
    102                              --------- ---------
    103 TOTAL AMOUNT EACH YEAR       $13,400  $18,400
    104                              ========= =========
```

Figure 5.2   *Schedules C and B — Price Changes: Horizontally Split Screen*

The cell coordinates of the current cell (B99) are displayed in the upper left corner of 1-2-3's control panel. Once these cell coordinates are confirmed, move the cursor to the top window and place it in cell H16, immediately adjacent to the Postage expenditure object. Next, in cell H16, enter the cell coordinates previously identified from the lower window, +B99. The contents of cell B99 ($4000) will be displayed in cell H16.

Repeat the procedure just mentioned to automatically post to Schedule C the individual line-item expenditure change requests listed in each of the Schedules B to Schedule C. Repeat this procedure for each of the biennial periods.

Once the individual line-item expenditure postings have been made, the lines and columns of Schedule C need to be summed:

1. With the cursor in the top window, enter the formula { @SUM(H10..H40) } in cell, H42.
2. Copy Formula in H42 to range I42..M42.
3. Enter Formula { @SUM(H10..M10) } in O10.
4. Copy Formula in O10 to range O11..O40.
5. Copy Formula in M42 to O42.

Step 4 causes several zeros to appear in column O of the spreadsheet lines in which expenditure objects are not listed. Erase these zeros by using the **/R**ange Erase command.

Next, replicate the techniques used in the preceding steps to produce the second biennial period data for Schedule C. Once these data have been entered, check them against the display in Figure 5.1 for accuracy.

The final task for rounding out the systemic dependency requirements of Schedule C is to link it with Schedule A, but before you enter the required data, clear the two horizontal windows and replace them with vertical windows. Enter

/Worksheet Window Clear

Move the cursor to the middle of the screen, and enter

/Worksheet Window Vertical

Now, position Schedule C so that the Total column for the first biennium is displayed in the left window. Then, move Schedule A into the right window to display the Requested columns for the biennium. The two spreadsheets should now appear in the two windows as illustrated in Figure 5.3. Juxtaposing them in this way facilitates the cross-referencing and automatic posting of data from Schedule C to Schedule A.

	M	N	O	P		AD	AE	AF	AG
1				1					II
2				2					II
3	==================3					=================================			II
4		I		I4					II
5		I		I5					II
6	FF	I	TOTAL	I6					II
7	————	I——	———	I7		1987-88	1988-89	1989-90	II
8		I		I8		Budgeted	Requested	Requested	II
9		I		I9		101	104	106	II
10	52,500	I	56,039	I10		1,393,800	1,449,839	1,553,500	II
11	12,500	I	12,500	I11		0	12,500	17,500	II
12		I		I12					II
13		I		I13					II
14		I	980	I14		64,000	64,980	74,500	II
15		I	0	I15		15,754	15,754	15,754	II
16		I	5,560	I16		70,000	75,560	75,807	II
17		I	4,400	I17		10,000	14,400	14,400	II
18		I	6,000	I18		6,600	12,600	13,600	II
19		I	0	I19		400	400	400	II
20		I	0	I20		500	500	500	II

Figure 5.3   *Schedules A and C—First Biennium Data: Vertically Split Screen*

Begin automating the posting of data by moving the cursor to the right window and entering the values 104 and 106 into cells AE9 and AF9, respectively. Next, enter the formula AD10+010 into cell AE10. The value 1,449,839 should appear in cell AE10. Copy cell AE10 to the range AE11..AE42. Then, replace the ERR(OR) values that appear in cells AE41 and AE43 with underscores by copying the contents of cells AD41 and AD43 into AE42 and AE43, respectively. Erase all remaining ERR values that appear in column AE.

The formulas entered in column AE add each of the six budget change totals on the Schedules B in each expenditure category for which changes are requested in the next biennial period to the respective expenditure categories budgeted for the current year. This totalling of the current budget year expenditure categories with expenditure object increments for the next period of the biennium fleshes out line-item budget requests for the next fiscal period.

To automate the posting of second biennium data from Spreadsheet C to Spreadsheet A, realign the two spreadsheets as shown in Figure 5.4. Then, replicate the procedures used to automate the posting of first biennium data. Once this replication is performed, the construction and linking of Schedule C and Schedule A are complete.

	V	W	X	YZ	AD	AE	AF	AG
1	w			‖1				‖
2				‖2				‖
3	==================‖3				==========================‖			
4		‖		‖4				‖
5		‖		‖5				‖
6	FF	‖	TOTAL	‖6				‖
7	——————‖————‖7				1987–88	1988–89	1989–90	‖
8		‖		‖8	Budgeted			‖
9		‖		‖9	101			‖
10	54,700	‖	159,700	‖10	1,393,800			‖
11	17,500	‖	17,500	‖11	0			‖
12		‖		‖12				‖
13		‖		‖13				‖
14		‖	10,500	‖14	64,000			‖
15		‖	0	‖15	15,754			‖
16		‖	5,607	‖16	70,000			‖
17		‖	4,400	‖17	10,000			‖
18		‖	7,000	‖18	6,600			‖
19		‖	0	‖19	400			‖
20		‖	0	‖20	500			‖

Figure 5.4   Schedules A and C—Second Biennium Data: Vertically Split Screen

Cell Listing: Figure 5.1

```
G1: PR [W45] 'SCHEDULE C:  MATRIX OF BUDGET CHANGE REQUESTS
Y1: PR [W1] '|
G2: PR [W45] 'UNIT:  Department of Public Works
Y2: PR [W1] '|
G3: PR [W45] '\=
H3: PR '=========
I3: PR [W9] '=========
J3: PR '=========
K3: PR [W9] '=========
L3: PR '=========
M3: PR '=========
N3: PR [W1] '=
O3: PR '=========
P3: PR [W1] '=========
Q3: PR '=========
R3: PR [W9] '=========
S3: PR '=========
T3: PR [W9] '=========
U3: PR '=========
V3: PR '=========
W3: PR [W1] '=========
X3: PR '=========
Y3: PR [W1] ^|
G4: PR [W45] ^
N4: PR [W1] ||
P4: PR [W1] ||
W4: PR [W1] ||
Y4: PR [W1] |||
J5: PR ^     1988-
K5: PR [W9] '1989
N5: PR [W1] ||
P5: PR [W1] ^|
S5: PR ^     1989-
T5: PR [W9] '1990
W5: PR [W1] ||
Y5: PR [W1] ^|
G6: PR [W45] 'Change Categories
H6: PR ^PC
I6: PR [W9] ^MI
```

continued...

...from previous page

```
J6: PR ^WLC
K6: PR [W9] ^N&CS
L6: PR ^OC
M6: PR ^FF
N6: PR [W1] ||
O6: PR ^TOTAL
P6: PR [W1] ^|
Q6: PR ^PC
R6: PR [W9] ^MI
S6: PR ^WLC
T6: PR [W9] ^N&CS
U6: PR ^OC
V6: PR ^FF
W6: PR [W1] ||
X6: PR ^TOTAL
Y6: PR [W1] ^|
G7: PR [W45] '\-
H7: PR '---------
I7: PR [W9] '----------
J7: PR '---------
K7: PR [W9] '----------
L7: PR '---------
M7: PR '---------
N7: PR [W1] ||
O7: PR '---------
P7: PR [W1] ^|
Q7: PR '---------
R7: PR [W9] '----------
S7: PR '---------
T7: PR [W9] '----------
U7: PR '---------
V7: PR '---------
W7: PR [W1] ||
X7: PR '---------
Y7: PR [W1] ^|
G8: PR [W45] 'Personal Services:
N8: PR [W1] ^|
P8: PR [W1] ^|
W8: PR [W1] ^|
```

continued...

...from previous page

```
Y8: PR [W1] ^|
G9: PR [W45] '   Man Years
N9: PR [W1] ^|
P9: PR [W1] ^|
W9: PR [W1] ^|
Y9: PR [W1] ^|
G10: PR [W45] '   Salaries
I10: PR [W9] +B157
J10: PR +B213
K10: PR [W9] +B270
M10: PR (B384)
N10: PR [W1] ^|
O10: PR @SUM(H10..M10)
P10: PR [W1] ^|
R10: PR [W9] +C157
S10: PR +C213
T10: PR [W9] +C270
V10: PR +C384
W10: PR [W1] ^|
X10: PR @SUM(Q10..V10)
Y10: PR [W1] ^|
G11: PR [W45] '   Benefits
M11: PR +B385
N11: PR [W1] ^|
O11: PR @SUM(H11..M11)
P11: PR [W1] ^|
V11: PR +C385
W11: PR [W1] ^|
X11: PR @SUM(Q11..V11)
Y11: PR [W1] ^|
N12: PR [W1] ^|
P12: PR [W1] ^|
W12: PR [W1] ^|
Y12: PR [W1] ^|
G13: PR [W45] 'Supporting Services:
N13: PR [W1] ^|
P13: PR [W1] ^|
W13: PR [W1] ^|
Y13: PR [W1] ^|
```

continued...

...from previous page

```
G14: PR [W45] '    Travel
L14: PR +B328
N14: PR [W1] ^|
O14: PR @SUM(H14..M14)
P14: PR [W1] ^|
U14: PR +C328
W14: PR [W1] ^|
X14: PR @SUM(Q14..V14)
Y14: PR [W1] ^|
G15: PR [W45] '    Telephone Tolls and Rental
N15: PR [W1] ^|
O15: PR @SUM(H15..M15)
P15: PR [W1] ^|
W15: PR [W1] ^|
X15: PR @SUM(Q15..V15)
Y15: PR [W1] ^|
G16: PR [W45] '    Postage
H16: PR +B99
I16: PR [W9] '
J16: PR +B214
N16: PR [W1] ^|
O16: PR @SUM(H16..M16)
P16: PR [W1] ^|
Q16: PR +C99
S16: PR +C214
W16: PR [W1] ^|
X16: PR @SUM(Q16..V16)
Y16: PR [W1] ^|
G17: PR [W45] '    Rent - State Owned Buildings
H17: PR +B100
N17: PR [W1] ^|
O17: PR @SUM(H17..M17)
P17: PR [W1] ^|
Q17: PR +C100
W17: PR [W1] ^|
X17: PR @SUM(Q17..V17)
Y17: PR [W1] ^|
G18: PR [W45] '    Rent - Privately Owned Buildings
L18: PR +B329
```

continued...

...from previous page

```
N18: PR [W1] ^|
O18: PR @SUM(H18..M18)
P18: PR [W1] ^|
U18: PR +C329
W18: PR [W1] ^|
X18: PR @SUM(Q18..V18)
Y18: PR [W1] ^|
G19: PR [W45] '   Building Improvements
N19: PR [W1] ^|
O19: PR @SUM(H19..M19)
P19: PR [W1] ^|
W19: PR [W1] ^|
X19: PR @SUM(Q19..V19)
Y19: PR [W1] ^|
G20: PR [W45] '   Utility Charges
N20: PR [W1] ^|
O20: PR @SUM(H20..M20)
P20: PR [W1] ^|
W20: PR [W1] ^|
X20: PR @SUM(Q20..V20)
Y20: PR [W1] ^|
G21: PR [W45] '   Rent of Data Processing Equipment
N21: PR [W1] ^|
O21: PR @SUM(H21..M21)
P21: PR [W1] ^|
W21: PR [W1] ^|
X21: PR @SUM(Q21..V21)
Y21: PR [W1] ^|
G22: PR [W45] '   Rent of Office Equipment
J22: PR +B215
N22: PR [W1] ^|
O22: PR @SUM(H22..M22)
P22: PR [W1] ^|
S22: PR +C215
W22: PR [W1] ^|
X22: PR @SUM(Q22..V22)
Y22: PR [W1] ^|
G23: PR [W45] '   Maint. & Rep. of Office Equipment
N23: PR [W1] ^|
```

continued...

...from previous page

```
O23: PR @SUM(H23..M23)
P23: PR [W1] ^|
W23: PR [W1] ^|
X23: PR @SUM(Q23..V23)
Y23: PR [W1] ^|
G24: PR [W45] '   Maint. & Rep. of Ofc. Equip. - Contract
I24: PR [W9] +B160
N24: PR [W1] ^|
O24: PR @SUM(H24..M24)
P24: PR [W1] ^|
R24: PR [W9] +C160
W24: PR [W1] ^|
X24: PR @SUM(Q24..V24)
Y24: PR [W1] ^|
G25: PR [W45] '   Maint. & Rep. of Automobile Vehicles
N25: PR [W1] ^|
O25: PR @SUM(H25..M25)
P25: PR [W1] ^|
W25: PR [W1] ^|
X25: PR @SUM(Q25..V25)
Y25: PR [W1] ^|
G26: PR [W45] '   Maint. & Rep. of Other Equipment
N26: PR [W1] ^|
O26: PR @SUM(H26..M26)
P26: PR [W1] ^|
W26: PR [W1] ^|
X26: PR @SUM(Q26..V26)
Y26: PR [W1] ^|
G27: PR [W45] '   Data Processing Contractual Service
H27: PR +B101
N27: PR [W1] ^|
O27: PR @SUM(H27..M27)
P27: PR [W1] ^|
Q27: PR +C101
W27: PR [W1] ^|
X27: PR @SUM(Q27..V27)
Y27: PR [W1] ^|
G28: PR [W45] '   Insurance, Subscriptions, Brinks
N28: PR [W1] ^|
```

continued...

...from previous page

```
O28: PR @SUM(H28..M28)
P28: PR [W1] ^|
W28: PR [W1] ^|
X28: PR @SUM(Q28..V28)
Y28: PR [W1] ^|
G29: PR [W45] '    Miscellaneous Services:
N29: PR [W1] ^|
O29: PR @SUM(H29..M29)
P29: PR [W1] ^|
W29: PR [W1] ^|
Y29: PR [W1] ^|
G30: PR [W45] '        Card Copiers
N30: PR [W1] ^|
O30: PR @SUM(H30..M30)
P30: PR [W1] ^|
W30: PR [W1] ^|
X30: PR @SUM(Q30..V30)
Y30: PR [W1] ^|
G31: PR [W45] '        Court Costs
N31: PR [W1] ^|
O31: PR @SUM(H31..M31)
P31: PR [W1] ^|
W31: PR [W1] ^|
X31: PR @SUM(Q31..V31)
Y31: PR [W1] ^|
N32: PR [W1] ^|
P32: PR [W1] ^|
W32: PR [W1] ^|
X32: PR @SUM(Q32..V32)
Y32: PR [W1] ^|
N33: PR [W1] ^|
P33: PR [W1] ^|
W33: PR [W1] ^|
X33: PR @SUM(Q33..V33)
Y33: PR [W1] ^|
G34: PR [W45] 'Other:
N34: PR [W1] ^|
P34: PR [W1] ^|
W34: PR [W1] ^|
```

continued...

...from previous page

```
Y34: PR [W1] ^|
G35: PR [W45] '    Printing
J35: PR +B216
K35: PR [W9] +B271
N35: PR [W1] ^|
O35: PR @SUM(H35..M35)
P35: PR [W1] ^|
S35: PR +C216
T35: PR [W9] +C271
W35: PR [W1] ^|
X35: PR @SUM(Q35..V35)
Y35: PR [W1] ^|
G36: PR [W45] '    Office Supplies
I36: PR [W9] (B161)
N36: PR [W1] ^|
O36: PR @SUM(H36..M36)
P36: PR [W1] ^|
R36: PR [W9] +C161
W36: PR [W1] ^|
X36: PR @SUM(Q36..V36)
Y36: PR [W1] ^|
G37: PR [W45] '         Revenue Stamps
N37: PR [W1] ^|
O37: PR @SUM(H37..M37)
P37: PR [W1] ^|
W37: PR [W1] ^|
X37: PR @SUM(Q37..V37)
Y37: PR [W1] ^|
N38: PR [W1] ^|
P38: PR [W1] ^|
W38: PR [W1] ^|
Y38: PR [W1] ^|
N39: PR [W1] ^|
P39: PR [W1] ^|
W39: PR [W1] ^|
Y39: PR [W1] ^|
G40: PR [W45] 'Capital Outlay
I40: PR [W9] +B156
N40: PR [W1] ^|
O40: PR @SUM(H40..M40)
```

continued...

...from previous page

```
P40: PR [W1] ^|
R40: PR [W9] +C156
W40: PR [W1] ^|
X40: PR @SUM(Q40..V40)
Y40: PR [W1] ^|
G41: PR [W45] 'TOTAL
H41: (C0) PR @SUM(H10..H40)
I41: (C0) PR [W9] @SUM(I10..I40)
J41: (C0) PR @SUM(J10..J40)
K41: (C0) PR [W9] @SUM(K10..K40)
L41: (C0) PR @SUM(L10..L40)
M41: (C0) PR @SUM(M10..M40)
N41: (C0) PR [W1] ^|
O41: (C0) PR @SUM(O10..O40)
P41: PR [W1] ^|
Q41: (C0) PR @SUM(Q10..Q40)
R41: (C0) PR [W9] @SUM(R10..R40)
S41: (C0) PR @SUM(S10..S40)
T41: (C0) PR [W9] @SUM(T10..T40)
U41: (C0) PR @SUM(U10..U40)
V41: (C0) PR @SUM(V10..V40)
W41: (C0) PR [W1] ^|
X41: (C0) PR @SUM(Q41..V41)
Y41: PR [W1] ^|
H42: PR '========
I42: PR [W9] '========
J42: PR '========
K42: PR [W9] '========
L42: PR '========
M42: PR '========
N42: PR [W1] ^|
O42: PR '========
P42: PR [W1] ^|
Q42: PR '========
R42: PR [W9] '========
S42: PR '========
T42: PR [W9] '========
U42: PR '========
V42: PR '========
W42: PR [W1] ^|
```

continued...

...from previous page

```
X42: PR '========
Y42: PR [W1] ^|
N43: PR [W1] ^|
P43: PR [W1] ^|
W43: PR [W1] ^|
Y43: PR [W1] ^|
G44: PR [W45] '\=
H44: PR \=
I44: PR [W9] \=
J44: PR \=
K44: PR [W9] \=
L44: PR \=
M44: PR \=
N44: PR [W1] \=
O44: PR \=
P44: PR [W1] \=
Q44: PR \=
R44: PR [W9] \=
S44: PR \=
T44: PR [W9] \=
U44: PR \=
V44: PR \=
W44: PR [W1] \=
X44: PR \=
Y44: PR [W1] ^=
```

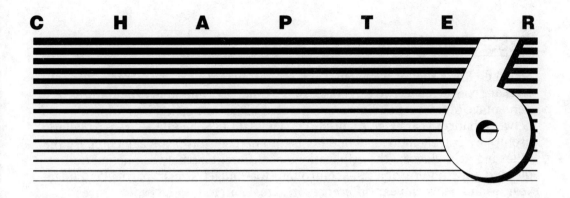

C H A P T E R

6

SCHEDULE R

DESCRIPTION

Schedule R is a summary of actual and requested budget ratios. Expenditure objects are converted to two categories of percentages: line-item expenditures as a percentage of total expenditures and percent difference in line-item expenditures between budget years (see Figure 6.1). The data in Schedule R are particularly useful. By putting individual line items into percent form, you can compare the following at a glance: the implications of differentials between actual and requested expenditure objects—controlling for budget size in particular budget years—and between-year differences in actual and requested expenditures.

		AH	AI	AJ	AK
1	SCHEDULE R: SUMMARY OF ACTUAL AND REQUESTED BUDGET RATIOS				
2	UNIT: Department of Public Works				
3					
4					
5					1986-87
6			% Total Exp	% Total Exp	% Change
7			1985-86	1986-87	Previous
8	Personal Services:		Actual	Actual	Year
9	Man Years				2.04%
10	Salaries		76.57%	75.88%	2.04%
11	Benefits		0.00%	0.00%	0.00%
12					
13	Supporting Services:				
14	Travel		3.96%	3.85%	0.00%
15	Telephone Tolls and Rental		0.79%	0.81%	4.69%
16	Postage		3.40%	3.79%	15.00%
17	Rent — State Owned Buildings		0.57%	0.55%	0.00%
18	Rent — Privately Owned Buildings		0.37%	0.36%	0.00%
19	Building Improvements		0.01%	0.01%	0.00%
20	Utility Charges		0.01%	0.01%	0.00%
21	Rent of Data Processing Equipment		2.27%	2.49%	12.72%
22	Rent of Office Equipment		0.23%	0.23%	2.50%
23	Maint. & Rep. of Office Equipment		0.00%	0.00%	0.00%
24	Maint. & Rep. of Ofc. Equip. — Contract		0.45%	0.45%	1.25%
25	Maint. & Rep. of Automobile Vehicles		0.00%	0.00%	0.00%
26	Maint. & Rep. of Other Equipment		0.00%	0.00%	0.00%
27	Data Processing Contractual Service		4.53%	4.51%	2.50%
28	Insurance, Subscriptions, Brinks		0.03%	0.03%	0.00%
29	Miscellaneous Services:				
30	Card Copiers		0.00%	0.00%	0.00%
31	Court Costs		0.00%	0.00%	0.00%
32					
33					
34	Other:				
35	Printing		5.04%	5.08%	3.37%
36	Office Supplies		1.36%	1.32%	0.00%
37	Revenue Stamps		0.00%	0.00%	0.00%
38					
39					
40	Capital Outlay		0.41%	0.67%	65.58%
41					
42	TOTAL		100.00%	100.00%	2.96%
43					
44					

Figure 6.1   Schedule R

AL	AM	AN	AO	AP	AQ	AR
						||
						||
						||
						||
	1987-88		1988-89		1989-90	||
% Total Exp	% Change	% Total Exp	% Change	% Total Exp	% Change	||
1987-88	From Previous	1988-89	From Previous	1989-90	From Previous	||
Budgeted	Year	Requested	Year	Requested	Year	||
	1.00%		2.97%		1.92%	||
74.61%	1.00%	73.42%	4.02%	74.79%	7.15%	||
0.00%	0.00%	0.63%	0.00%	0.84%	40.00%	||
						||
						||
3.43%	-8.57%	3.29%	1.50%	3.59%	14.69%	||
0.84%	7.48%	0.80%	0.00%	0.76%	0.00%	||
3.75%	1.45%	3.83%	7.94%	3.64%	0.06%	||
0.54%	0.00%	0.73%	44.00%	0.69%	0.00%	||
0.35%	0.00%	0.64%	90.91%	0.65%	7.94%	||
0.02%	300.00%	0.02%	0.00%	0.02%	0.00%	||
0.03%	100.00%	0.03%	0.00%	0.02%	0.00%	||
2.46%	1.77%	2.33%	0.00%	2.21%	0.00%	||
0.21%	-2.44%	0.22%	10.00%	0.21%	0.00%	||
0.00%	0.00%	0.00%	0.00%	0.00%	0.00%	||
0.43%	-1.23%	0.25%	-37.50%	0.24%	0.00%	||
0.00%	0.00%	0.00%	0.00%	0.00%	0.00%	||
0.00%	0.00%	0.00%	0.00%	0.00%	0.00%	||
4.50%	2.44%	4.51%	5.95%	4.53%	5.62%	||
0.03%	20.00%	0.03%	0.00%	0.03%	0.00%	||
						||
0.00%	0.00%	0.00%	0.00%	0.00%	0.00%	||
0.00%	0.00%	0.00%	0.00%	0.00%	0.00%	||
						||
						||
						||
5.03%	2.17%	4.90%	2.87%	4.66%	0.05%	||
1.93%	50.00%	1.52%	-16.67%	1.44%	0.00%	||
0.00%	0.00%	0.00%	0.00%	0.00%	0.00%	||
						||
						||
1.85%	185.38%	2.86%	63.73%	1.66%	-38.92%	||
						||
100.00%	2.73%	100.00%	5.70%	100.00%	5.18%	||
						||
						||

CONSTRUCTING SCHEDULE R

Begin constructing Schedule R by filling in the label and border entries using the data entry techniques and procedures discussed in previous chapters. Then, enter the following in cell AI10:

```
(AB10/$AB$42)
```

This formula divides the value of AB10 (1985-86 salary expenditures data located in Schedule A) by the value of AB42 (total expenditures, also located in Schedule A). The resulting quotient in cell AI10 means that salaries in budget year 1985-86 comprise 76.57% of total expenditures. The dollar sign ($) in the formula is needed to make the value of the denominator an absolute rather than a relative cell reference.

Enter the following formulas in cells AJ10, AL10, AN10, and AP10, respectively:

```
1. (AC10/$AC$42)
2. (ADC10/$AD$42)
3. (AE10/$AE$42)
4. (AF10/$AF$42)
```

Next, copy each formula in cells AI10, AJ10, AL10, AN10, and AP10 to the ranges AI11..AI42, AL11..AL42, AN11..AN4, and AP11..AP42, respectively; erase any resulting ERR messages.

Then, enter the following formulas in cells AK9, AM9, AO9, and AQ9, respectively:

```
1. @IF(ISERR((AC9-AB9)/AB9),0,(AC9-AB9)/AB9)
2. @IF(ISERR((AD9-AC9)/AC9),0,(AD9-AC9)/AC9)
3. @IF(ISERR((AE9-AD9)/AD9),0,(AE9-AD9)/AD9)
4. @IF(ISERR((AF9-AE9)/AE9),0,(AF9-AE9)/AE9)
```

Copy each of the above formulas, in turn, to the cell ranges AK10..AK4, AM10..AM42, AO10..AO42, and AQ10..AQ42. Again, erase any resulting ERR messages.

The formulas just listed compute percentage changes (increases or decreases) in each object expenditure between budget years. The @ISERR function keeps certain ERR messages from appearing in the worksheet. Without it, the value of ERR would appear in cells AB9..AE9 if the calculation of any cell within the range is blank or if it contains zeros or labels. For example, entry #1 says, "If the value of (AC9-AB9)/AB9 is ERR, enter a zero in this cell; otherwise, enter the quotient resulting from the division."

Complete the construction of Schedule R by entering the divider and underscore lines in ranges AI41..AQ41 and AI43..AQ43, respectively.

Cell Listing: Figure 6.1

```
AH1: PR [W45] 'SCHEDULE R:  SUMMARY OF ACTUAL AND REQUESTED BUDGET
     RATIOS
AH2: PR [W45] 'UNIT:  Department of Public Works
AH3: PR [W45] '\=
AI3: PR [W15] \=
AJ3: PR [W15] \=
AK3: PR [W13] \=
AL3: PR [W13] \=
AM3: PR [W13] \=
AN3: PR [W13] \=
AO3: PR [W13] \=
AP3: PR [W13] \=
AQ3: PR [W13] \=
AK5: (G) PR [W13] ^1986-87
AM5: PR [W13] ^1987-88
AO5: PR [W13] ^1988-89
AQ5: PR [W13] ^1989-90
AI6: PR [W15] ^% Total Exp
AJ6: PR [W15] ^% Total Exp
AK6: PR [W13] ^% Change
AL6: PR [W13] ^% Total Exp
AM6: PR [W13] ^% Change
AN6: PR [W13] ^% Total Exp
AO6: PR [W13] ^% Change
AP6: PR [W13] ^% Total Exp
AQ6: PR [W13] ^% Change
```

continued...

...from previous page

```
AI7:  PR [W15] ^1985-86
AJ7:  PR [W15] ^1986-87
AK7:  PR [W13] ^Previous
AL7:  PR [W13] ^1987-88
AM7:  PR [W13] ^From Previous
AN7:  PR [W13] ^1988-89
AO7:  PR [W13] ^From Previous
AP7:  PR [W13] ^1989-90
AQ7:  PR [W13] ^From Previous
AH8:  PR [W45] 'Personal Services:
AI8:  PR [W15] ^Actual
AJ8:  PR [W15] ^Actual
AK8:  PR [W13] ^Year
AL8:  PR [W13] ^Budgeted
AM8:  PR [W13] ^Year
AN8:  PR [W13] ^Requested
AO8:  PR [W13] ^Year
AP8:  PR [W13] ^Requested
AQ8:  PR [W13] ^Year
AH9:  PR [W45] '     Man Years
AK9:  (P2) U [W13] @IF(@ISERR((AC9-AB9)/AB9),0,(AC9-AB9)/AB9)
AM9:  (P2) U [W13] @IF(@ISERR((AD9-AC9)/AC9),0,(AD9-AC9)/AC9)
AO9:  (P2) U [W13] @IF(@ISERR((AE9-AD9)/AD9),0,(AE9-AD9)/AD9)
AQ9:  (P2) U [W13] @IF(@ISERR((AF9-AE9)/AE9),0,(AF9-AE9)/AE9)
AH10: PR [W45] '     Salaries
AI10: (P2) U [W15] (AB10/$SCHAT)
AJ10: (P2) U [W15] (AC10/$AC$42)
AK10: (P2) U [W13] @IF(@ISERR((AC10-AB10)/AB10),0,(AC10-AB10)/AB10)
AL10: (P2) U [W13] (AD10/$AD$42)
AM10: (P2) U [W13] @IF(@ISERR((AD10-AC10)/AC10),0,(AD10-AC10)/AC10)
AN10: (P2) U [W13] (AE10/$AE$42)
AO10: (P2) U [W13] @IF(@ISERR((AE10-AD10)/AD10),0,(AE10-AD10)/AD10)
AP10: (P2) U [W13] (AF10/$AF$42)
AQ10: (P2) U [W13] @IF(@ISERR((AF10-AE10)/AE10),0,(AF10-AE10)/AE10)
AH11: PR [W45] '     Benefits
AI11: (P2) U [W15] (AB11/$SCHAT)
AJ11: (P2) U [W15] (AC11/$AC$42)
AK11: (P2) U [W13] @IF(@ISERR((AC11-AB11)/AB11),0,(AC11-AB11)/AB11)
AL11: (P2) U [W13] (AD11/$AD$42)
```

continued...

...from previous page

```
AM11: (P2) U [W13] @IF(@ISERR((AD11-AC11)/AC11),0,(AD11-AC11)/AC11)
AN11: (P2) U [W13] (AE11/$AE$42)
AO11: (P2) U [W13] @IF(@ISERR((AE11-AD11)/AD11),0,(AE11-AD11)/AD11)
AP11: (P2) U [W13] (AF11/$AF$42)
AQ11: (P2) U [W13] @IF(@ISERR((AF11-AE11)/AE11),0,(AF11-AE11)/AE11)
AH13: PR [W45] 'Supporting Services:
AH14: PR [W45] '    Travel
AI14: (P2) U [W15] (AB14/SCHAT)
AJ14: (P2) U [W15] (AC14/$AC$42)
AK14: (P2) U [W13] @IF(@ISERR((AC14-AB14)/AB14),0,(AC14-AB14)/AB14)
AL14: (P2) U [W13] (AD14/$AD$42)
AM14: (P2) U [W13] @IF(@ISERR((AD14-AC14)/AC14),0,(AD14-AC14)/AC14)
AN14: (P2) U [W13] (AE14/$AE$42)
AO14: (P2) U [W13] @IF(@ISERR((AE14-AD14)/AD14),0,(AE14-AD14)/AD14)
AP14: (P2) U [W13] (AF14/$AF$42)
AQ14: (P2) U [W13] @IF(@ISERR((AF14-AE14)/AE14),0,(AF14-AE14)/AE14)
AH15: PR [W45] '    Telephone Tolls and Rental
AI15: (P2) U [W15] (AB15/$SCHAT)
AJ15: (P2) U [W15] (AC15/$AC$42)
AK15: (P2) U [W13] @IF(@ISERR((AC15-AB15)/AB15),0,(AC15-AB15)/AB15)
AL15: (P2) U [W13] (AD15/$AD$42)
AM15: (P2) U [W13] @IF(@ISERR((AD15-AC15)/AC15),0,(AD15-AC15)/AC15)
AN15: (P2) U [W13] (AE15/$AE$42)
AO15: (P2) U [W13] @IF(@ISERR((AE15-AD15)/AD15),0,(AE15-AD15)/AD15)
AP15: (P2) U [W13] (AF15/$AF$42)
AQ15: (P2) U [W13] @IF(@ISERR((AF15-AE15)/AE15),0,(AF15-AE15)/AE15)
AH16: PR [W45] '    Postage
AI16: (P2) U [W15] (AB16/$SCHAT)
AJ16: (P2) U [W15] (AC16/$AC$42)
AK16: (P2) U [W13] @IF(@ISERR((AC16-AB16)/AB16),0,(AC16-AB16)/AB16)
AL16: (P2) U [W13] (AD16/$AD$42)
AM16: (P2) U [W13] @IF(@ISERR((AD16-AC16)/AC16),0,(AD16-AC16)/AC16)
AN16: (P2) U [W13] (AE16/$AE$42)
AO16: (P2) U [W13] @IF(@ISERR((AE16-AD16)/AD16),0,(AE16-AD16)/AD16)
AP16: (P2) U [W13] (AF16/$AF$42)
AQ16: (P2) U [W13] @IF(@ISERR((AF16-AE16)/AE16),0,(AF16-AE16)/AE16)
AH17: PR [W45] '    Rent - State Owned Buildings
AI17: (P2) U [W15] (AB17/$SCHAT)
AJ17: (P2) U [W15] (AC17/$AC$42)
```

continued...

...from previous page

```
AK17: (P2) U [W13] @IF(@ISERR((AC17-AB17)/AB17),0,(AC17-AB17)/AB17)
AL17: (P2) U [W13] (AD17/$AD$42)
AM17: (P2) U [W13] @IF(@ISERR((AD17-AC17)/AC17),0,(AD17-AC17)/AC17)
AN17: (P2) U [W13] (AE17/$AE$42)
AO17: (P2) U [W13] @IF(@ISERR((AE17-AD17)/AD17),0,(AE17-AD17)/AD17)
AP17: (P2) U [W13] (AF17/$AF$42)
AQ17: (P2) U [W13] @IF(@ISERR((AF17-AE17)/AE17),0,(AF17-AE17)/AE17)
AH18: PR [W45] '    Rent - Privately Owned Buildings
AI18: (P2) U [W15] (AB18/$SCHAT)
AJ18: (P2) U [W15] (AC18/$AC$42)
AK18: (P2) U [W13] @IF(@ISERR((AC18-AB18)/AB18),0,(AC18-AB18)/AB18)
AL18: (P2) U [W13] (AD18/$AD$42)
AM18: (P2) U [W13] @IF(@ISERR((AD18-AC18)/AC18),0,(AD18-AC18)/AC18)
AN18: (P2) U [W13] (AE18/$AE$42)
AO18: (P2) U [W13] @IF(@ISERR((AE18-AD18)/AD18),0,(AE18-AD18)/AD18)
AP18: (P2) U [W13] (AF18/$AF$42)
AQ18: (P2) U [W13] @IF(@ISERR((AF18-AE18)/AE18),0,(AF18-AE18)/AE18)
AH19: PR [W45] '    Building Improvements
AI19: (P2) U [W15] (AB19/$SCHAT)
AJ19: (P2) U [W15] (AC19/$AC$42)
AK19: (P2) U [W13] @IF(@ISERR((AC19-AB19)/AB19),0,(AC19-AB19)/AB19)
AL19: (P2) U [W13] (AD19/$AD$42)
AM19: (P2) U [W13] @IF(@ISERR((AD19-AC19)/AC19),0,(AD19-AC19)/AC19)
AN19: (P2) U [W13] (AE19/$AE$42)
AO19: (P2) U [W13] @IF(@ISERR((AE19-AD19)/AD19),0,(AE19-AD19)/AD19)
AP19: (P2) U [W13] (AF19/$AF$42)
AQ19: (P2) U [W13] @IF(@ISERR((AF19-AE19)/AE19),0,(AF19-AE19)/AE19)
AH20: PR [W45] '    Utility Charges
AI20: (P2) U [W15] (AB20/$SCHAT)
AJ20: (P2) U [W15] (AC20/$AC$42)
AK20: (P2) U [W13] @IF(@ISERR((AC20-AB20)/AB20),0,(AC20-AB20)/AB20)
AL20: (P2) U [W13] (AD20/$AD$42)
AM20: (P2) U [W13] @IF(@ISERR((AD20-AC20)/AC20),0,(AD20-AC20)/AC20)
AN20: (P2) U [W13] (AE20/$AE$42)
AO20: (P2) U [W13] @IF(@ISERR((AE20-AD20)/AD20),0,(AE20-AD20)/AD20)
AP20: (P2) U [W13] (AF20/$AF$42)
AQ20: (P2) U [W13] @IF(@ISERR((AF20-AE20)/AE20),0,(AF20-AE20)/AE20)
AH21: PR [W45] '    Rent of Data Processing Equipment
AI21: (P2) U [W15] (AB21/$SCHAT)
```

continued...

...from previous page

```
AJ21: (P2) U [W15] (AC21/$AC$42)
AK21: (P2) U [W13] @IF(@ISERR((AC21-AB21)/AB21),0,(AC21-AB21)/AB21)
AL21: (P2) U [W13] (AD21/$AD$42)
AM21: (P2) U [W13] @IF(@ISERR((AD21-AC21)/AC21),0,(AD21-AC21)/AC21)
AN21: (P2) U [W13] (AE21/$AE$42)
AO21: (P2) U [W13] @IF(@ISERR((AE21-AD21)/AD21),0,(AE21-AD21)/AD21)
AP21: (P2) U [W13] (AF21/$AF$42)
AQ21: (P2) U [W13] @IF(@ISERR((AF21-AE21)/AE21),0,(AF21-AE21)/AE21)
AH22: PR [W45] '    Rent of Office Equipment
AI22: (P2) U [W15] (AB22/$SCHAT)
AJ22: (P2) U [W15] (AC22/$AC$42)
AK22: (P2) U [W13] @IF(@ISERR((AC22-AB22)/AB22),0,(AC22-AB22)/AB22)
AL22: (P2) U [W13] (AD22/$AD$42)
AM22: (P2) U [W13] @IF(@ISERR((AD22-AC22)/AC22),0,(AD22-AC22)/AC22)
AN22: (P2) U [W13] (AE22/$AE$42)
AO22: (P2) U [W13] @IF(@ISERR((AE22-AD22)/AD22),0,(AE22-AD22)/AD22)
AP22: (P2) U [W13] (AF22/$AF$42)
AQ22: (P2) U [W13] @IF(@ISERR((AF22-AE22)/AE22),0,(AF22-AE22)/AE22)
AH23: PR [W45] '    Maint. & Rep. of Office Equipment
AI23: (P2) U [W15] (AB23/$SCHAT)
AJ23: (P2) U [W15] (AC23/$AC$42)
AK23: (P2) U [W13] @IF(@ISERR((AC23-AB23)/AB23),0,(AC23-AB23)/AB23)
AL23: (P2) U [W13] (AD23/$AD$42)
AM23: (P2) U [W13] @IF(@ISERR((AD23-AC23)/AC23),0,(AD23-AC23)/AC23)
AN23: (P2) U [W13] (AE23/$AE$42)
AO23: (P2) U [W13] @IF(@ISERR((AE23-AD23)/AD23),0,(AE23-AD23)/AD23)
AP23: (P2) U [W13] (AF23/$AF$42)
AQ23: (P2) U [W13] @IF(@ISERR((AF23-AE23)/AE23),0,(AF23-AE23)/AE23)
AH24: PR [W45] '    Maint. & Rep. of Ofc. Equip. - Contract
AI24: (P2) U [W15] (AB24/$SCHAT)
AJ24: (P2) U [W15] (AC24/$AC$42)
AK24: (P2) U [W13] @IF(@ISERR((AC24-AB24)/AB24),0,(AC24-AB24)/AB24)
AL24: (P2) U [W13] (AD24/$AD$42)
AM24: (P2) U [W13] @IF(@ISERR((AD24-AC24)/AC24),0,(AD24-AC24)/AC24)
AN24: (P2) U [W13] (AE24/$AE$42)
AO24: (P2) U [W13] @IF(@ISERR((AE24-AD24)/AD24),0,(AE24-AD24)/AD24)
AP24: (P2) U [W13] (AF24/$AF$42)
AQ24: (P2) U [W13] @IF(@ISERR((AF24-AE24)/AE24),0,(AF24-AE24)/AE24)
AH25: PR [W45] '    Maint. & Rep. of Automobile Vehicles
```

continued...

...from previous page

```
AI25: (P2) U [W15] (AB25/$SCHAT)
AJ25: (P2) U [W15] (AC25/$AC$42)
AK25: (P2) U [W13] @IF(@ISERR((AC25-AB25)/AB25),0,(AC25-AB25)/AB25)
AL25: (P2) U [W13] (AD25/$AD$42)
AM25: (P2) U [W13] @IF(@ISERR((AD25-AC25)/AC25),0,(AD25-AC25)/AC25)
AN25: (P2) U [W13] (AE25/$AE$42)
AO25: (P2) U [W13] @IF(@ISERR((AE25-AD25)/AD25),0,(AE25-AD25)/AD25)
AP25: (P2) U [W13] (AF25/$AF$42)
AQ25: (P2) U [W13] @IF(@ISERR((AF25-AE25)/AE25),0,(AF25-AE25)/AE25)
AH26: PR [W45] '   Maint. & Rep. of Other Equipment
AI26: (P2) U [W15] (AB26/$SCHAT)
AJ26: (P2) U [W15] (AC26/$AC$42)
AK26: (P2) U [W13] @IF(@ISERR((AC26-AB26)/AB26),0,(AC26-AB26)/AB26)
AL26: (P2) U [W13] (AD26/$AD$42)
AM26: (P2) U [W13] @IF(@ISERR((AD26-AC26)/AC26),0,(AD26-AC26)/AC26)
AN26: (P2) U [W13] (AE26/$AE$42)
AO26: (P2) U [W13] @IF(@ISERR((AE26-AD26)/AD26),0,(AE26-AD26)/AD26)
AP26: (P2) U [W13] (AF26/$AF$42)
AQ26: (P2) U [W13] @IF(@ISERR((AF26-AE26)/AE26),0,(AF26-AE26)/AE26)
AH27: PR [W45] '   Data Processing Contractual Service
AI27: (P2) U [W15] (AB27/$SCHAT)
AJ27: (P2) U [W15] (AC27/$AC$42)
AK27: (P2) U [W13] @IF(@ISERR((AC27-AB27)/AB27),0,(AC27-AB27)/AB27)
AL27: (P2) U [W13] (AD27/$AD$42)
AM27: (P2) U [W13] @IF(@ISERR((AD27-AC27)/AC27),0,(AD27-AC27)/AC27)
AN27: (P2) U [W13] (AE27/$AE$42)
AO27: (P2) U [W13] @IF(@ISERR((AE27-AD27)/AD27),0,(AE27-AD27)/AD27)
AP27: (P2) U [W13] (AF27/$AF$42)
AQ27: (P2) U [W13] @IF(@ISERR((AF27-AE27)/AE27),0,(AF27-AE27)/AE27)
AH28: PR [W45] '   Insurance, Subscriptions, Brinks
AI28: (P2) U [W15] (AB28/$SCHAT)
AJ28: (P2) U [W15] (AC28/$AC$42)
AK28: (P2) U [W13] @IF(@ISERR((AC28-AB28)/AB28),0,(AC28-AB28)/AB28)
AL28: (P2) U [W13] (AD28/$AD$42)
AM28: (P2) U [W13] @IF(@ISERR((AD28-AC28)/AC28),0,(AD28-AC28)/AC28)
AN28: (P2) U [W13] (AE28/$AE$42)
AO28: (P2) U [W13] @IF(@ISERR((AE28-AD28)/AD28),0,(AE28-AD28)/AD28)
AP28: (P2) U [W13] (AF28/$AF$42)
AQ28: (P2) U [W13] @IF(@ISERR((AF28-AE28)/AE28),0,(AF28-AE28)/AE28)
```

continued...

...from previous page

```
AH29: PR [W45] '    Miscellaneous Services:
AH30: PR [W45] '         Card Copiers
AI30: (P2) U [W15] (AB30/$SCHAT)
AJ30: (P2) U [W15] (AC30/$AC$42)
AK30: (P2) U [W13] @IF(@ISERR((AC30-AB30)/AB30),0,(AC30-AB30)/AB30)
AL30: (P2) U [W13] (AD30/$AD$42)
AM30: (P2) U [W13] @IF(@ISERR((AD30-AC30)/AC30),0,(AD30-AC30)/AC30)
AN30: (P2) U [W13] (AE30/$AE$42)
AO30: (P2) U [W13] @IF(@ISERR((AE30-AD30)/AD30),0,(AE30-AD30)/AD30)
AP30: (P2) U [W13] (AF30/$AF$42)
AQ30: (P2) U [W13] @IF(@ISERR((AF30-AE30)/AE30),0,(AF30-AE30)/AE30)
AH31: PR [W45] '         Court Costs
AI31: (P2) U [W15] (AB31/$SCHAT)
AJ31: (P2) U [W15] (AC31/$AC$42)
AK31: (P2) U [W13] @IF(@ISERR((AC31-AB31)/AB31),0,(AC31-AB31)/AB31)
AL31: (P2) U [W13] (AD31/$AD$42)
AM31: (P2) U [W13] @IF(@ISERR((AD31-AC31)/AC31),0,(AD31-AC31)/AC31)
AN31: (P2) U [W13] (AE31/$AE$42)
AO31: (P2) U [W13] @IF(@ISERR((AE31-AD31)/AD31),0,(AE31-AD31)/AD31)
AP31: (P2) U [W13] (AF31/$AF$42)
AQ31: (P2) U [W13] @IF(@ISERR((AF31-AE31)/AE31),0,(AF31-AE31)/AE31)
AH34: PR [W45] 'Other:
AH35: PR [W45] '    Printing
AI35: (P2) U [W15] (AB35/$SCHAT)
AJ35: (P2) U [W15] (AC35/$AC$42)
AK35: (P2) U [W13] @IF(@ISERR((AC35-AB35)/AB35),0,(AC35-AB35)/AB35)
AL35: (P2) U [W13] (AD35/$AD$42)
AM35: (P2) U [W13] @IF(@ISERR((AD35-AC35)/AC35),0,(AD35-AC35)/AC35)
AN35: (P2) U [W13] (AE35/$AE$42)
AO35: (P2) U [W13] @IF(@ISERR((AE35-AD35)/AD35),0,(AE35-AD35)/AD35)
AP35: (P2) U [W13] (AF35/$AF$42)
AQ35: (P2) U [W13] @IF(@ISERR((AF35-AE35)/AE35),0,(AF35-AE35)/AE35)
AH36: PR [W45] '    Office Supplies
AI36: (P2) U [W15] (AB36/$SCHAT)
AJ36: (P2) U [W15] (AC36/$AC$42)
AK36: (P2) U [W13] @IF(@ISERR((AC36-AB36)/AB36),0,(AC36-AB36)/AB36)
AL36: (P2) U [W13] (AD36/$AD$42)
AM36: (P2) U [W13] @IF(@ISERR((AD36-AC36)/AC36),0,(AD36-AC36)/AC36)
AN36: (P2) U [W13] (AE36/$AE$42)
```

continued...

...from previous page

```
AO36: (P2) U [W13] @IF(@ISERR((AE36-AD36)/AD36),0,(AE36-AD36)/AD36)
AP36: (P2) U [W13] (AF36/$AF$42)
AQ36: (P2) U [W13] @IF(@ISERR((AF36-AE36)/AE36),0,(AF36-AE36)/AE36)
AH37: PR [W45] '    Revenue Stamps
AI37: (P2) U [W15] (AB37/$SCHAT)
AJ37: (P2) U [W15] (AC37/$AC$42)
AK37: (P2) U [W13] @IF(@ISERR((AC37-AB37)/AB37),0,(AC37-AB37)/AB37)
AL37: (P2) U [W13] (AD37/$AD$42)
AM37: (P2) U [W13] @IF(@ISERR((AD37-AC37)/AC37),0,(AD37-AC37)/AC37)
AN37: (P2) U [W13] (AE37/$AE$42)
AO37: (P2) U [W13] @IF(@ISERR((AE37-AD37)/AD37),0,(AE37-AD37)/AD37)
AP37: (P2) U [W13] (AF37/$AF$42)
AQ37: (P2) U [W13] @IF(@ISERR((AF37-AE37)/AE37),0,(AF37-AE37)/AE37)
AH40: PR [W45] 'Capital Outlay
AI40: (P2) U [W15] (AB40/$SCHAT)
AJ40: (P2) U [W15] (AC40/$AC$42)
AK40: (P2) U [W13] @IF(@ISERR((AC40-AB40)/AB40),0,(AC40-AB40)/AB40)
AL40: (P2) U [W13] (AD40/$AD$42)
AM40: (P2) U [W13] @IF(@ISERR((AD40-AC40)/AC40),0,(AD40-AC40)/AC40)
AN40: (P2) U [W13] (AE40/$AE$42)
AO40: (P2) U [W13] @IF(@ISERR((AE40-AD40)/AD40),0,(AE40-AD40)/AD40)
AP40: (P2) U [W13] (AF40/$AF$42)
AQ40: (P2) U [W13] @IF(@ISERR((AF40-AE40)/AE40),0,(AF40-AE40)/AE40)
AI41: (P2) U [W15] "----------
AJ41: (P2) U [W15] "----------
AK41: (P2) U [W13] "----------
AL41: (P2) U [W13] "----------
AM41: (P2) U [W13] "----------
AN41: (P2) U [W13] "----------
AO41: (P2) U [W13] "----------
AP41: (P2) U [W13] "----------
AQ41: (P2) U [W13] "----------
AH42: PR [W45] 'TOTAL
AI42: (P2) U [W15] (SCHAT/$SCHAT)
AJ42: (P2) U [W15] (AC42/$AC$42)
AK42: (P2) U [W13] @IF(@ISERR((AC42-SCHAT)/SCHAT),0,(AC42-SCHAT)
       /SCHAT)
AL42: (P2) U [W13] (AD42/$AD$42)
AM42: (P2) U [W13] @IF(@ISERR((AD42-AC42)/AC42),0,(AD42-AC42)/AC42)
```

continued...

...from previous page

```
AN42: (P2)  U  [W13]  (AE42/$AE$42)
AO42: (P2)  U  [W13]  @IF(@ISERR((AE42-AD42)/AD42),0,(AE42-AD42)/AD42)
AP42: (P2)  U  [W13]  (AF42/$AF$42)
AQ42: (P2)  U  [W13]  @IF(@ISERR((AF42-AE42)/AE42),0,(AF42-AE42)/AE42)
AI43: (P2)  U  [W15]  "=========
AJ43: (P2)  U  [W15]  "=========
AK43: (P2)  U  [W13]  "=========
AL43: (P2)  U  [W13]  "=========
AM43: (P2)  U  [W13]  "=========
AN43: (P2)  U  [W13]  "=========
AO43: (P2)  U  [W13]  "=========
AP43: (P2)  U  [W13]  "=========
AQ43: (P2)  U  [W13]  "=========
```

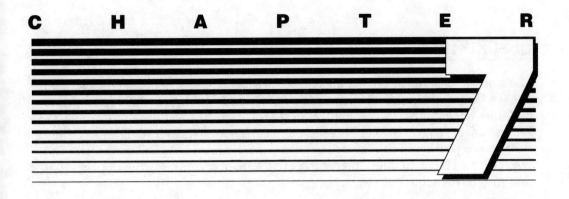

DEFLATED SCHEDULES

DESCRIPTION

The worksheet application includes three spreadsheets — Schedules DA, DC, and DR — which are similar to Schedules A, C, and R, except that appropriate deflators are applied to biennial requests for each of the expenditure objects. While budget request data are presented in current dollars in Schedules A, C, and R, they are presented in real dollar terms in Schedules DA, DC, and DR. The DA, DC, and DR schedules, therefore, are useful in considering the impact inflation may have on budget requests.

The applications of deflator factors to each of Schedules DA, DC, and DR are macro-driven. In the following sections, the three schedules will be constructed first, followed by the macros that drive them.

CONSTRUCTING SCHEDULE DA

Begin the construction of Schedule DA (Figure 7.1) by entering the schedule borders and then the labels appearing in range AA65..AA68. Enter 1.75 as a numerical value in cell AB68. Then, move to cell BZ13 and, after assigning it a fixed format with four decimal places, enter the numerical value 0.9824. (The numerical values in cells AB68 and BZ13 will be changed to formulas at a later time to automate the entry of alternate weights.)

	AA	AB	AC	AD	AE	AF	AG
65	SCHEDULE DA: SUMMARY OF ACTUAL AND DEFLATED REQUESTED EXPENDITURES						II
66	UNIT: Department of Public Works						II
67	===						II
68	Deflator Factor:	4.20					II
69							II
70							II
71		1985-86	1986-87	1987-88	1988-89	1989-90	II
72	Personal Services:	Actual	Actual	Budgeted	Requested	Requested	II
73	Man Years	98	100	101	104	106	II
74	Salaries	1,352,400	1,380,000	1,393,800	1,388,946	1,488,253	II
75	Benefits	0	0	0	11,975	16,765	II
76							II
77	Supporting Services:						II
78	Travel	70,000	70,000	64,000	62,232	71,371	II
79	Telephone Tolls and Rental	14,000	14,657	15,754	15,092	15,092	II
80	Postage	60,000	69,000	70,000	72,386	72,432	II
81	Rent - State Owned Buildings	10,000	10,000	10,000	13,795	13,795	II
82	Rent - Privately Owned Buildings	6,600	6,600	6,600	12,071	13,029	II
83	Building Improvements	100	100	400	383	383	II
84	Utility Charges	250	250	500	479	479	II
85	Rent of Data Processing Equipment	40,100	45,200	46,000	44,068	44,068	II
86	Rent of Office Equipment	4,000	4,100	4,000	4,215	4,215	II
87	Maint. & Rep. of Office Equipment	0	0	0	0	0	II
88	Maint. & Rep. of Ofc. Equip. - Contract	8,000	8,100	8,000	4,790	4,790	II
89	Maint. & Rep. of Automobile Vehicles	0	0	0	0	0	II
90	Maint. & Rep. of Other Equipment	0	0	0	0	0	II
91	Data Processing Contractual Service	80,000	82,000	84,000	85,262	90,052	II
92	Insurance, Subscriptions, Brinks	500	500	600	575	575	II
93	Miscellaneous Services:						II
94	Card Copiers	0	0	0	0	0	II
95	Court Costs	0	0	0	0	0	II
96							II
97							II
98	Other:						II
99	Printing	89,000	92,000	94,000	92,839	92,682	II
100	Office Supplies	24,000	24,000	36,000	28,740	28,740	II
101	Revenue Stamps	0	0	0	0	0	II
102							II
103							II
104	Capital Outlay	7,306	12,097	34,523	54,149	33,073	II
105		----------	----------	----------	----------	----------	II
106	TOTAL	$1,766,256	$1,818,604	$1,868,177	$1,891,797	$1,989,794	II
107		==========	==========	==========	==========	==========	II
108	===						II

Figure 7.1   *Schedule DA*

7 Deflated Schedules

Divide the screen horizontally (as in Figure 7.2), displaying Schedule A in the top window and Schedule DA in the bottom window. Next, copy the contents of range AA7..AD43 to range AA71..AD107 and the contents of range AE7..AF9 to range AE71..AF73.

Move the cursor to cell AE74, and enter the formula +AE10*($BZ$13). Copy this formula to the range AE74..AF107, and erase any ERR messages or errant zeros that appear in columns AE and AF. Finally, enter the missing line dividers and total underlines in cells AE105, AF105, AE107, and AF107.

The formulas in columns AE and AF take the budget request values for each of the expenditure objects in Schedule A and multiply them by an expenditure deflator. The process for automating the application of the deflator will be explained later.

	AA	AB	AC
7		1985-86	1986-87
8	Personal Services:	Actual	Actual
9	Man Years	98	100
10	Salaries	1,352,400	1,380,000
11	Benefits	0	0
12			
13	Supporting Services:		
14	Travel	70,000	70,000
15	Telephone Tolls and Rental	14,000	14,657
16	Postage	60,000	69,000
	AA	AB	AC
71		1985-86	1986-87
72	Personal Services:	Actual	Actual
73	Man Years	98	100
74	Salaries	1,352,400	1,380,000
75	Benefits	0	0
76			
77	Supporting Services:		
78	Travel	70,000	70,000
79	Telephone Tolls and Rental	14,000	14,657

Figure 7.2   *Schedules A and DA: Horizontally Split Screen*

100

CONSTRUCTING SCHEDULE DC

First, construct the borders of Schedule DC (see Figure 7.3) and enter the labels appearing in range G45..G48. Then, divide the screen horizontally (see Figure 7.4), with Schedule C appearing in the top window and Schedule DC in the bottom window. Copy the range G6..G42 to range G50..G85, and enter the numerical value 1.75 as the deflator factor in cell H48. (Later in this chapter, the numerical value in cell H48 will be changed to a formula to automate the entry of alternate deflator factors.) Next, copy the labels in the range H5..X6 to the range H49..X50.

Enter the following formula into cell H54, and then copy it to range H54..X86:

```
@IF(@ISERR(H10*$BZ$13),0,H10*$BZ$13)
```

Once the above range is copied, replace the * entries (these appear in columns N, P, and W, indicating where the entries exceed the specified column width) with the appropriate schedule divider entries, and erase any errant zeros. Finally, enter the total underlines for each expenditure object data column in the range H87..X87. Note that the large display of zeros in Schedule DC and throughout the worksheet application may be suppressed globally with 1-2-3's /Worksheet Global Zero command. If, however, you prefer to retain particular zero entries, the cell listing for a macro, \z, appears in Appendix C to facilitate this. Errant zeros appear in the empty cells of Schedule DC each time the automatic deflator macro is activated. The \z macro automatically removes them and reenters line-divider entries that it initially removes along with the zeros. Therefore, you may want to include the \z macro in the worksheet along with the other macros and invoke it after running the deflator macro.

	G	H	I	J	K	L
45	SCHEDULE DC: MATRIX OF DEFLATED BUDGET CHANGE REQUESTS					
46	UNIT: Department of Public Works					
47	══					
48	Deflator Factor:	4.20				
49				1988—1989		
50	Change Categories	PC	MI	WLC	N&CS	OC
51						
52	Personal Services:					
53	Man Years					
54	Salaries	0	(39,518)	18,958	23,950	0
55	Benefits	0	0	0	0	0
56		0	0	0	0	0
57	Supporting Services:	0	0	0	0	0
58	Travel	0	0	0	0	920
59	Telephone Tolls and Rental	0	0	0	0	0
60	Postage	3,832	0	1,494	0	0
61	Rent — State Owned Buildings	4,215	0	0	0	0
62	Rent — Privately Owned Buildings	0	0	0	0	5,748
63	Building Improvements	0	0	0	0	0
64	Utility Charges	0	0	0	0	0
65	Rent of Data Processing Equipment	0	0	0	0	0
66	Rent of Office Equipment	0	0	383	0	0
67	Maint. & Rep. of Office Equipment	0	0	0	0	0
68	Maint. & Rep. of Ofc. Equip. — Contract	0	(2,874)	0	0	0
69	Maint. & Rep. of Automobile Vehicles	0	0	0	0	0
70	Maint. & Rep. of Other Equipment	0	0	0	0	0
71	Data Processing Contractual Service	4,790	0	0	0	0
72	Insurance, Subscriptions, Brinks	0	0	0	0	0
73	Miscellaneous Services:	0	0	0	0	0
74	Card Copiers	0	0	0	0	0
75	Court Costs	0	0	0	0	0
76		0	0	0	0	0
77		0	0	0	0	0
78	Other:	0	0	0	0	0
79	Printing	0	0	1,437	1,150	0
80	Office Supplies	0	(5,748)	0	0	0
81	Revenue Stamps	0	0	0	0	0
82		0	0	0	0	0
83		0	0	0	0	0
84	Capital Outlay	0	21,076	0	0	0
85			0	0	0	0
86	TOTAL	12,837	(27,064)	22,273	25,100	6,668
87		═══════	═══════	═══════	═══════	═══════
88	══					

Figure 7.3   *Schedule DC*

M	N	O	P	Q	R	S	T	U	V	W	X	YZ
FF	TOTAL		PC	MI	WLC	N&CS	OC	FF	TOTAL			
					1989–1990							
50,295	53,685		0	(4,790)	57,480	47,800	0	52,403	152,993			
11,975	11,975		0	0	0	0	0	16,765	16,765			
0	0		0	0	0	0	0	0	0			
0	0		0	0	0	0	0	0	0			
0	920		0	0	0	0	10,059	0	10,059			
0	0		0	0	0	0	0	0	0			
0	5,326		3,832	0	1,540	0	0	0	5,372			
0	4,215		4,215	0	0	0	0	0	4,215			
0	5,748		0	0	0	0	6,706	0	6,706			
0	0		0	0	0	0	0	0	0			
0	0		0	0	0	0	0	0	0			
0	383		0	0	383	0	0	0	383			
0	0		0	0	0	0	0	0	0			
0	(2,874)		0	(2,874)	0	0	0	0	(2,874)			
0	0		0	0	0	0	0	0	0			
0	0		0	0	0	0	0	0	0			
0	4,790		9,580	0	0	0	0	0	9,580			
0	0		0	0	0	0	0	0	0			
0	0		0	0	0	0	0	0	0			
0	0		0	0	0	0	0	0	0			
0	0		0	0	0	0	0	0	0			
0	0		0	0	0	0	0	0	0			
0	0		0	0	0	0	0	0	0			
0	2,587		0	0	1,480	1,150	0	0	2,630			
0	(5,748)		0	(5,748)	0	0	0	0	(5,748)			
0	0		0	0	0	0	0	0	0			
0	0		0	0	0	0	0	0	0			
0	21,076		0	0	0	0	0	0	0			
0	0		0	0	0	0	0	0	0			
62,270	102,084		17,627	(13,412)	60,883	49,050	16,765	69,168	200,080			

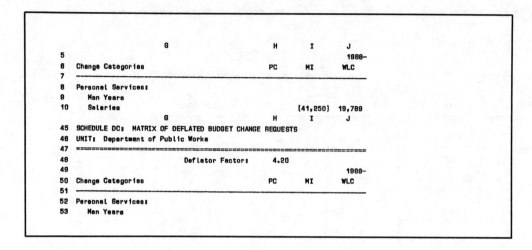

Figure 7.4   Schedules C and DC: Horizontally Split Screen

CONSTRUCTING SCHEDULE DR

Construct the borders of Schedule DR (see Figure 7.5), and enter the labels in range AH65..AH68. Divide the screen horizontally (see Figure 7.6), with Schedule DA displayed in the top window and Schedule DR in the bottom window. Copy the range AA72..AA106 to range AH72..AH106. Then, enter the value 4.20 in cell AI68. The numerical value in cell AI68 will be changed to a formula later to automate the entry of alternate deflator factors. Next, copy the range AI5..AQ8 from Schedule R to range AI69..AQ72 in Schedule DR.

Enter the following formulas, respectively, in cells AI74, AJ74, AK73, AL74, AM73, AN74, AO73, AP74, and AQ73:

1. `(AB74/$AB$106)`
2. `(AC74/$AC$106)`
3. `@IF(@ISERR((AC73-AB73)/AB73),0,(AC73-AB73)/AB73)`
4. `(AD74/$AD$106)`
5. `@IF(@ISERR((AD73-AC73)/AC73),0,(AD73-AC73)/AC73)`
6. `(AE74/$AE$106)`
7. `@IF(@ISERR((AE74-AD73)/AD73),0,(AE73-AD73)/AD73)`
8. `(AF74/$AF$74)`
9. `@IF(@ISERR((AF74-AE73)/AE73),0,(AF73-AE73)/AE73)`

Copy each of these formulas, in turn, to the following ranges: AI74..AI106, AJ74..AJ106, AK73..AK106, AL74..AL106, AM73..AM106, AN74..AN106, AO73..AO106, AP74..AP106, and AQ73..AQ106. Round out the construction of Schedule DR by erasing any errant zeros and ERR messages and entering the divider and underscore lines in columns AI-AQ.

The numerator values of the above formulas that were entered as items 1, 2, 4, 6, and 8 (columns AI, AJ, AL, AN, and AP) cause the posting of expenditure object entries from Schedule DA into counterpart cells of Schedule DR; as in Schedule R, the denominator cells result in the calculation of expenditure objects as a percentage of total expenditures. Formulas enter numbers 3, 5, 7, and 9 (cells AK, AM, AO, and AQ) and, in addition to entering zeros where ERR messages occur, calculate the between-year percentage differences in expenditures.

It should be noted that the posting of data to Schedule DR from Schedule DA results in deflated values appearing only in post-current budget year columns. In comparing the data in Schedule R with data in Schedule DR, the only notable expenditure object differences occur in column AO where deflated percentage changes in expenditure objects between budget years 1987-88 and 1988-89 are displayed. There are no differences in columns AN, AP, and AQ. This is because the deflator acts as a constant term in the calculation of percentages of total expenditures in columns AN and AP and in the calculation of percentage changes in expenditure objects between budget years 1988-89 and 1989-90 in column AQ.

		AH	AI	AJ	AK
65	SCHEDULE DR: SUMMARY OF ACTUAL AND DEFLATED REQUESTED BUDGET RATIOS				
66	UNIT: Department of Public Works				
67					
68		Deflator Factor:	4.20		
69					1986-87
70			% Total Exp	% Total Exp	% Change
71			1985-86	1986-87	Previous
72	Personal Services:		Actual	Actual	Year
73	Man Years				2.04%
74	Salaries		76.57%	75.88%	2.04%
75	Benefits		0.00%	0.00%	0.00%
76					
77	Supporting Services:				
78	Travel		3.96%	3.85%	0.00%
79	Telephone Tolls and Rental		0.79%	0.81%	4.69%
80	Postage		3.40%	3.79%	15.00%
81	Rent - State Owned Buildings		0.57%	0.55%	0.00%
82	Rent - Privately Owned Buildings		0.37%	0.36%	0.00%
83	Building Improvements		0.01%	0.01%	0.00%
84	Utility Charges		0.01%	0.01%	0.00%
85	Rent of Data Processing Equipment		2.27%	2.49%	12.72%
86	Rent of Office Equipment		0.23%	0.23%	2.50%
87	Maint. & Rep. of Office Equipment		0.00%	0.00%	0.00%
88	Maint. & Rep. of Ofc. Equip. - Contract		0.45%	0.45%	1.25%
89	Maint. & Rep. of Automobile Vehicles		0.00%	0.00%	0.00%
90	Maint. & Rep. of Other Equipment		0.00%	0.00%	0.00%
91	Data Processing Contractual Service		4.53%	4.51%	2.50%
92	Insurance, Subscriptions, Brinks		0.03%	0.03%	0.00%
93	Miscellaneous Services:				
94	Card Copiers		0.00%	0.00%	0.00%
95	Court Costs		0.00%	0.00%	0.00%
96					
97					
98	Other:				
99	Printing		5.04%	5.06%	3.37%
100	Office Supplies		1.36%	1.32%	0.00%
101	Revenue Stamps		0.00%	0.00%	0.00%
102					
103					
104	Capital Outlay		0.41%	0.67%	65.58%
105					
106	TOTAL		100.00%	100.00%	2.96%
107					
108					

Figure 7.5   *Schedule DR*

AL	AM	AN	AO	AP	AQ	AR
	1987-88		1988-89		1989-90	
% Total Exp	% Change	% Total Exp	% Change	% Total Exp	% Change	
1987-88	From Previous	1988-89	From Previous	1989-90	From Previous	
Budgeted	Year	Requested	Year	Requested	Year	
	1.00%		2.97%		1.92%	
74.61%	1.00%	73.42%	-0.35%	74.79%	7.15%	
0.00%	0.00%	0.63%	0.00%	0.84%	40.00%	
3.43%	-8.57%	3.29%	-2.76%	3.59%	14.69%	
0.84%	7.48%	0.80%	-4.20%	0.76%	0.00%	
3.75%	1.45%	3.83%	3.41%	3.64%	0.06%	
0.54%	0.00%	0.73%	37.95%	0.69%	0.00%	
0.35%	0.00%	0.64%	82.89%	0.65%	7.94%	
0.02%	300.00%	0.02%	-4.20%	0.02%	0.00%	
0.03%	100.00%	0.03%	-4.20%	0.02%	0.00%	
2.46%	1.77%	2.33%	-4.20%	2.21%	0.00%	
0.21%	-2.44%	0.22%	5.38%	0.21%	0.00%	
0.00%	0.00%	0.00%	0.00%	0.00%	0.00%	
0.43%	-1.23%	0.25%	-40.13%	0.24%	0.00%	
0.00%	0.00%	0.00%	0.00%	0.00%	0.00%	
0.00%	0.00%	0.00%	0.00%	0.00%	0.00%	
4.50%	2.44%	4.51%	1.50%	4.53%	5.62%	
0.03%	20.00%	0.03%	-4.20%	0.03%	0.00%	
0.00%	0.00%	0.00%	0.00%	0.00%	0.00%	
0.00%	0.00%	0.00%	0.00%	0.00%	0.00%	
5.03%	2.17%	4.90%	-1.45%	4.66%	0.05%	
1.93%	50.00%	1.52%	-20.17%	1.44%	0.00%	
0.00%	0.00%	0.00%	0.00%	0.00%	0.00%	
1.85%	185.38%	2.86%	56.85%	1.66%	-38.92%	
100.00%	2.73%	100.00%	1.26%	100.00%	5.18%	

107

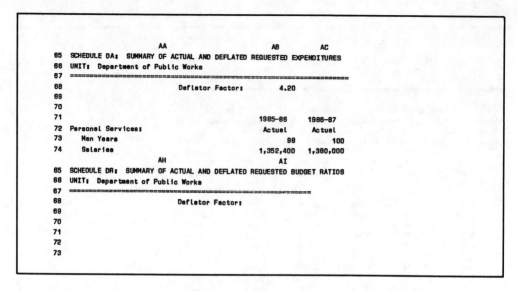

Figure 7.6   Schedules DA and DR: Horizontally Split Screen

SCHEDULES DA, DC, AND DR MACRO

Name the macro for automating the calculation and application of alternate deflators \d (name location = cell BZ17), and enter it in the designated cells as follows:

<u>**Cell**</u>   <u>**Macro Entry**</u>

```
BX12: Deflator Factor=
BZ12: (F2) U 1.75
BY13:  Deflator=
BZ13: (G) (100-BZ12)*0.01
BY15: \d=
BZ15: (WINDOWSOFF}{BEEP 0}{BEEP 3}{BEEP 0}{BEEP 3}{BEEP 0}{BEEP
      3 }{BEEP 0}{INDICATE ENTER}~
BZ16: {GETNUMBER "Enter Deflator Factor (rounds to 2 decimal places):
      ",BZ12}
BZ17: {INDICATE WAIT}{PANELOFF}
BZ18: {CALC}
BZ19: {INDICATE}{ESC}
BZ20: {BEEP 0}{BEEP 3}{BEEP 0}{BEEP 3}{BEEP 0}{BEEP 3}{BEEP 0}
BZ21: {GOTO}AA65~
BZ22: {WINDOWSON}{PANELON}
```

BX12 is the deflator factor reference cell, and BZ12 is the deflator factor location. Cell BY13 is the deflator reference, and cell BZ13 is the formula for converting the deflator factor into the deflator value. The deflator factor value is automatically entered into cell BZ12 by the macro command located in cell BZ16. Cell BY15 is the macro reference. As you did with the macros constructed in Chapter 7, be sure to place a single right apostrophe before the reverse slash in cell BZ15 so the entry will not be interpreted as the command to activate 1-2-3's menu system.

Cell BZ15 performs several tasks. It disengages the redrawing of the screen during the macro's execution, sounds the computer bell to attract the user's attention, and changes the entry in the status mode indicator box from "READY" to "ENTER." BZ16 prompts the user to enter on the command line the value of the deflator factor that will be applied to Schedules DA, DC, and DR.

The entry in cell BZ17 changes the status mode indicator entry from "ENTER" to "WAIT" so the user is aware that the calculation and application of the deflator to the worksheet has begun. Cell BZ18 recalculates the worksheet; BZ19 returns the status mode indicator entry to "READY"; and BZ20 sounds the computer bell to alert the user that the calculation and application are finished. BZ22 reactivates the screen and command line.

Cell Listing: Figure 7.1

```
AA65: PR [W45] ^SCHEDULE DA:   SUMMARY OF DEFLATED ACTUAL AND REQUESTED
          EXPENDITURES
AG65: PR [W2] ^||
AA66: PR [W45] 'UNIT:   Department of Public Works
AG66: PR [W2] ^||
AA67: PR [W45] '\=
AB67: PR [W12] ^============
AC67: PR [W12] ^============
AD67: PR [W12] ^============
AE67: PR [W12] ^============
AF67: PR [W12] ^============
AG67: PR [W2] |||
AA68: PR [W45] "Deflator Factor:
AB68: (P2) PR [W12] +BZ12*0.01
AG68: PR [W2] ^||
```

continued...

...from previous page

```
AG69: PR [W2] ^||
AG70: PR [W2] ^||
AB71: PR [W12] ^1985-86
AC71: PR [W12] ^1986-87
AD71: PR [W12] ^1987-88
AE71: PR [W12] ^1988-89
AF71: PR [W12] ^1989-90
AG71: PR [W2] ^||
AA72: PR [W45] 'Personal Services:
AB72: PR [W12] ^Actual
AC72: PR [W12] ^Actual
AD72: PR [W12] ^Budgeted
AE72: PR [W12] ^Requested
AF72: PR [W12] ^Requested
AG72: PR [W2] ^||
AA73: PR [W45] '    Man Years
AB73: (F0) U [W12] 98
AC73: (F0) U [W12] 100
AD73: (F0) U [W12] 101
AE73: U [W12] 104
AF73: U [W12] 106
AG73: PR [W2] ^||
AA74: PR [W45] '    Salaries
AB74: (,0) U [W12] +AB10
AC74: (,0) U [W12] +AC10
AD74: (,0) U [W12] +AD10
AE74: (,0) U [W12] +AE10*($BZ$13)
AF74: (,0) U [W12] +AF10*($BZ$13)
AG74: PR [W2] ^||
AA75: PR [W45] '    Benefits
AB75: (,0) U [W12] +AB11
AC75: (,0) U [W12] +AC11
AD75: (,0) U [W12] +AD11
AE75: (,0) U [W12] +AE11*($BZ$13)
AF75: (,0) U [W12] +AF11*($BZ$13)
AG75: PR [W2] ^||
AB76: (H) U [W12] +AB12
AC76: (H) U [W12] +AC12
AD76: (H) U [W12] +AD12
```

continued...

...from previous page

```
AE76: (H) U [W12] +AE12*($BZ$13)
AF76: (H) U [W12] +AF12*($BZ$13)
AG76: PR [W2] ^||
AA77: PR [W45] 'Supporting Services:
AB77: (H) U [W12] +AB13
AC77: (H) U [W12] +AC13
AD77: (H) U [W12] +AD13
AE77: (H) U [W12] +AE13*($BZ$13)
AF77: (H) U [W12] +AF13*($BZ$13)
AG77: PR [W2] ^||
AA78: PR [W45] '   Travel
AB78: (,0) U [W12] +AB14
AC78: (,0) U [W12] +AC14
AD78: (,0) U [W12] +AD14
AE78: (,0) U [W12] +AE14*($BZ$13)
AF78: (,0) U [W12] +AF14*($BZ$13)
AG78: PR [W2] ^||
AA79: PR [W45] '   Telephone Tolls and Rental
AB79: (,0) U [W12] +AB15
AC79: (,0) U [W12] +AC15
AD79: (,0) U [W12] +AD15
AE79: (,0) U [W12] +AE15*($BZ$13)
AF79: (,0) U [W12] +AF15*($BZ$13)
AG79: PR [W2] ^||
AA80: PR [W45] '   Postage
AB80: (,0) U [W12] +AB16
AC80: (,0) U [W12] +AC16
AD80: (,0) U [W12] +AD16
AE80: (,0) U [W12] +AE16*($BZ$13)
AF80: (,0) U [W12] +AF16*($BZ$13)
AG80: PR [W2] ^||
AA81: PR [W45] '   Rent - State Owned Buildings
AB81: (,0) U [W12] +AB17
AC81: (,0) U [W12] +AC17
AD81: (,0) U [W12] +AD17
AE81: (,0) U [W12] +AE17*($BZ$13)
AF81: (,0) U [W12] +AF17*($BZ$13)
AG81: PR [W2] ^||
AA82: PR [W45] '   Rent - Privately Owned Buildings
```

continued...

...from previous page

```
AB82: (,0) U [W12] +AB18
AC82: (,0) U [W12] +AC18
AD82: (,0) U [W12] +AD18
AE82: (,0) U [W12] +AE18*($BZ$13)
AF82: (,0) U [W12] +AF18*($BZ$13)
AG82: PR [W2] ^||
AA83: PR [W45] '    Building Improvements
AB83: (,0) U [W12] +AB19
AC83: (,0) U [W12] +AC19
AD83: (,0) U [W12] +AD19
AE83: (,0) U [W12] +AE19*($BZ$13)
AF83: (,0) U [W12] +AF19*($BZ$13)
AG83: PR [W2] ^||
AA84: PR [W45] '    Utility Charges
AB84: (,0) U [W12] +AB20
AC84: (,0) U [W12] +AC20
AD84: (,0) U [W12] +AD20
AE84: (,0) U [W12] +AE20*($BZ$13)
AF84: (,0) U [W12] +AF20*($BZ$13)
AG84: PR [W2] ^||
AA85: PR [W45] '    Rent of Data Processing Equipment
AB85: (,0) U [W12] +AB21
AC85: (,0) U [W12] +AC21
AD85: (,0) U [W12] +AD21
AE85: (,0) U [W12] +AE21*($BZ$13)
AG85: PR [W2] ^||
AA86: PR [W45] '    Rent of Office Equipment
AB86: (,0) U [W12] +AB22
AC86: (,0) U [W12] +AC22
AD86: (,0) U [W12] +AD22
AE86: (,0) U [W12] +AE22*($BZ$13)
AF86: (,0) U [W12] +AF22*($BZ$13)
AG86: PR [W2] ^||
AA87: PR [W45] '    Maint. & Rep. of Office Equipment
AB87: (,0) U [W12] +AB23
AC87: (,0) U [W12] +AC23
AD87: (,0) U [W12] +AD23
AE87: (,0) U [W12] +AE23*($BZ$13)
AF87: (,0) U [W12] +AF23*($BZ$13)
```

continued...

...from previous page

```
AG87: PR [W2] ^||
AA88: PR [W45] '   Maint. & Rep. of Ofc. Equip. - Contract
AB88: (,0) U [W12] +AB24
AC88: (,0) U [W12] +AC24
AD88: (,0) U [W12] +AD24
AE88: (,0) U [W12] +AE24*($BZ$13)
AF88: (,0) U [W12] +AF24*($BZ$13)
AG88: PR [W2] ^||
AA89: PR [W45] '   Maint. & Rep. of Automobile Vehicles
AB89: (,0) U [W12] +AB25
AC89: (,0) U [W12] +AC25
AD89: (,0) U [W12] +AD25
AE89: (,0) U [W12] +AE25*($BZ$13)
AF89: (,0) U [W12] +AF25*($BZ$13)
AG89: PR [W2] ^||
AA90: PR [W45] '   Maint. & Rep. of Other Equipment
AB90: (,0) U [W12] +AB26
AC90: (,0) U [W12] +AC26
AD90: (,0) U [W12] +AD26
AE90: (,0) U [W12] +AE26*($BZ$13)
AF90: (,0) U [W12] +AF26*($BZ$13)
AG90: PR [W2] ^||
AA91: PR [W45] '   Data Processing Contractual Service
AB91: (,0) U [W12] +AB27
AC91: (,0) U [W12] +AC27
AD91: (,0) U [W12] +AD27
AE91: (,0) U [W12] +AE27*($BZ$13)
AF91: (,0) U [W12] +AF27*($BZ$13)
AG91: PR [W2] ^||
AA92: PR [W45] '   Insurance, Subscriptions, Brinks
AB92: (,0) U [W12] +AB28
AC92: (,0) U [W12] +AC28
AD92: (,0) U [W12] +AD28
AE92: (,0) U [W12] +AE28*($BZ$13)
AF92: (,0) U [W12] +AF28*($BZ$13)
AG92: PR [W2] ^||
AA93: PR [W45] '   Miscellaneous Services:
AB93: (H) U [W12] +AB29
AC93: (H) U [W12] +AC29
```

continued...

...from previous page

```
AD93: (H) U [W12] +AD29
AE93: (H) U [W12] +AE29*($BZ$13)
AF93: (H) U [W12] +AF29*($BZ$13)
AG93: PR [W2] ^||
AA94: PR [W45] '        Card Copiers
AB94: (,0) U [W12] +AB30
AC94: (,0) U [W12] +AC30
AD94: (,0) U [W12] +AD30
AE94: (,0) U [W12] +AE30*($BZ$13)
AF94: (,0) U [W12] +AF30*($BZ$13)
AG94: PR [W2] ^||
AA95: PR [W45] '        Court Costs
AB95: (,0) U [W12] +AB31
AC95: (,0) U [W12] +AC31
AD95: (,0) U [W12] +AD31
AE95: (,0) U [W12] +AE31*($BZ$13)
AF95: (,0) U [W12] +AF31*($BZ$13)
AG95: PR [W2] ^||
AB96: (H) U [W12] +AB32
AC96: (H) U [W12] +AC32
AD96: (H) U [W12] +AD32
AE96: (H) U [W12] +AE32*($BZ$13)
AF96: (H) U [W12] +AF32*($BZ$13)
AG96: PR [W2] ^||
AB97: (H) U [W12] +AB33
AC97: (H) U [W12] +AC33
AD97: (H) U [W12] +AD33
AE97: (H) U [W12] +AE33*($BZ$13)
AF97: (H) U [W12] +AF33*($BZ$13)
AG97: PR [W2] ^||
AA98: PR [W45] 'Other:
AB98: (H) U [W12] +AB34
AC98: (H) U [W12] +AC34
AD98: (H) U [W12] +AD34
AE98: (H) U [W12] +AE34*($BZ$13)
AF98: (H) U [W12] +AF34*($BZ$13)
AG98: PR [W2] ^||
AA99: PR [W45] '   Printing
AB99: (,0) U [W12] +AB35
AC99: (,0) U [W12] +AC35
```

continued...

...from previous page

```
AD99: (,0) U [W12] +AD35
AE99: (,0) U [W12] +AE35*($BZ$13)
AF99: (,0) U [W12] +AF35*($BZ$13)
AG99: PR [W2] ^||
AA100: PR [W45] '    Office Supplies
AB100: (,0) U [W12] +AB36
AC100: (,0) U [W12] +AC36
AD100: (,0) U [W12] +AD36
AE100: (,0) U [W12] +AE36*($BZ$13)
AF100: (,0) U [W12] +AF36*($BZ$13)
AG100: PR [W2] ^||
AA101: PR [W45] '    Revenue Stamps
AB101: (,0) U [W12] +AB37
AC101: (,0) U [W12] +AC37
AD101: (,0) U [W12] +AD37
AE101: (,0) U [W12] +AE37*($BZ$13)
AF101: (,0) U [W12] +AF37*($BZ$13)
AG101: PR [W2] ^||
AB102: (H) U [W12] +AB38
AC102: (H) U [W12] +AC38
AD102: (H) U [W12] +AD38
AE102: (H) U [W12] +AE38*($BZ$13)
AF102: (H) U [W12] +AF38*($BZ$13)
AG102: PR [W2] ^||
AB103: (H) U [W12] +AB39
AC103: (H) U [W12] +AC39
AD103: (H) U [W12] +AD39
AE103: (H) U [W12] +AE39*($BZ$13)
AF103: (H) U [W12] +AF39*($BZ$13)
AG103: PR [W2] ^||
AA104: PR [W45] 'Capital Outlay
AB104: (,0) U [W12] +AB40
AC104: (,0) U [W12] +AC40
AD104: (,0) U [W12] +AD40
AE104: (,0) U [W12] +AE40*($BZ$13)
AF104: (,0) U [W12] +AF40*($BZ$13)
AG104: PR [W2] |||
AB105: (,0) U [W12] "----------
AC105: (,0) U [W12] "----------
```

continued...

...from previous page

```
AD105: (,0) U [W12] "-----------
AE105: (,0) U [W12] "-----------
AF105: (,0) U [W12] "-----------
AG105: PR [W2] ^||
AA106: PR [W45] 'TOTAL
AB106: (C0) U [W12] @SUM(AB74..AB104)
AC106: (C0) U [W12] @SUM(AC74..AC104)
AD106: (C0) U [W12] @SUM(AD74..AD104)
AE106: (,0) U [W12] +AE42*($BZ$13)
AF106: (,0) U [W12] +AF42*($BZ$13)
AG106: PR [W2] ^||
AB107: U [W12] ^==========
AC107: U [W12] ^==========
AD107: U [W12] ^==========
AE107: (,0) U [W12] "==========
AF107: (,0) U [W12] "==========
AG107: (,0) PR [W2] |||
AA108: PR [W45] \=
AB108: PR [W12] \=
AC108: PR [W12] \=
AD108: PR [W12] \=
AE108: PR [W12] \=
AF108: PR [W12] \=
AG108: PR [W2] \=
```

Cell Listing: Figure 7.3

```
G45: PR [W45] 'SCHEDULE DC:  MATRIX OF DEFLATED BUDGET CHANGE REQUESTS
Y45: PR [W1] '|
Z45: PR [W1] '|
G46: PR [W45] 'UNIT:  Department of Public Works
Y46: PR [W1] '|
Z46: PR [W1] '|
G47: PR [W45] '\=
H47: PR '=========
I47: PR [W9] '=========
J47: PR '=========
K47: PR [W9] '=========
L47: PR '=========
M47: PR '=========
N47: PR [W1] '=
O47: PR '=========
P47: PR [W1] '=========
Q47: PR '=========
R47: PR [W9] '=========
S47: PR '=========
T47: PR [W9] '=========
U47: PR '=========
V47: PR '=========
W47: PR [W1] '=========
X47: PR '=========
Y47: PR [W1] ^|
Z47: PR [W1] ^|
G48: PR [W45] "Deflator Factor:
H48: (P2) PR +$BZ$12*0.01
N48: PR [W1] ||
P48: PR [W1] ||
W48: PR [W1] ||
Y48: PR [W1] |||
G49: PR [W45] ^
J49: PR ^    1988-
K49: PR [W9] '1989
N49: PR [W1] ||
P49: PR [W1] ^|
S49: PR ^    1989-
T49: PR [W9] '1990
```

continued...

...from previous page

```
W49: PR [W1] ||
Y49: PR [W1] ^|
Z49: PR [W1] ^|
G50: PR [W45] 'Change Categories
H50: PR ^PC
I50: PR [W9] ^MI
J50: PR ^WLC
K50: PR [W9] ^N&CS
L50: PR ^OC
M50: PR ^FF
N50: PR [W1] ||
O50: PR ^TOTAL
P50: PR [W1] ^|
Q50: PR ^PC
R50: PR [W9] ^MI
S50: PR ^WLC
T50: PR [W9] ^N&CS
U50: PR ^OC
V50: PR ^FF
W50: PR [W1] ||
X50: PR ^TOTAL
Y50: PR [W1] ^|
Z50: PR [W1] ^|
G51: PR [W45] '\-
H51: PR '---------
I51: PR [W9] '---------
J51: PR '---------
K51: PR [W9] '---------
L51: PR '---------
M51: PR '---------
N51: PR [W1] ||
O51: PR '---------
P51: PR [W1] ||
Q51: PR '---------
R51: PR [W9] '---------
S51: PR '---------
T51: PR [W9] '---------
U51: PR '---------
V51: PR '---------
```

continued...

...from previous page

```
W51: PR [W1] ||
X51: PR '----------
Y51: PR [W1] ^|
Z51: PR [W1] ^|
G52: PR [W45] 'Personal Services:
N52: PR [W1] ||
P52: PR [W1] ||
W52: PR [W1] ||
Y52: PR [W1] ^|
Z52: PR [W1] ^|
G53: PR [W45] '    Man Years
N53: PR [W1] ||
P53: PR [W1] ||
W53: PR [W1] ||
Y53: PR [W1] ^|
Z53: PR [W1] ^|
G54: PR [W45] '    Salaries
H54: (,0) U @IF(@ISERR(H10*$BZ$13),0,H10*$BZ$13)
I54: (,0) U [W9] @IF(@ISERR(I10*$BZ$13),0,I10*$BZ$13)
J54: (,0) U @IF(@ISERR(J10*$BZ$13),0,J10*$BZ$13)
K54: (,0) U [W9] @IF(@ISERR(K10*$BZ$13),0,K10*$BZ$13)
L54: (,0) U @IF(@ISERR(L10*$BZ$13),0,L10*$BZ$13)
M54: (,0) U @IF(@ISERR(M10*$BZ$13),0,M10*$BZ$13)
N54: PR [W1] ||
O54: (,0) U @IF(@ISERR(O10*$BZ$13),0,O10*$BZ$13)
P54: PR [W1] ||
Q54: (,0) U @IF(@ISERR(Q10*$BZ$13),0,Q10*$BZ$13)
R54: (,0) U [W9] @IF(@ISERR(R10*$BZ$13),0,R10*$BZ$13)
S54: (,0) U @IF(@ISERR(S10*$BZ$13),0,S10*$BZ$13)
T54: (,0) U [W9] @IF(@ISERR(T10*$BZ$13),0,T10*$BZ$13)
U54: (,0) U @IF(@ISERR(U10*$BZ$13),0,U10*$BZ$13)
V54: (,0) U @IF(@ISERR(V10*$BZ$13),0,V10*$BZ$13)
W54: PR [W1] ||
X54: (,0) U @IF(@ISERR(X10*$BZ$13),0,X10*$BZ$13)
Y54: PR [W1] ^||
G55: PR [W45] '    Benefits
H55: (,0) U @IF(@ISERR(H11*$BZ$13),0,H11*$BZ$13
I55: (,0) U [W9] @IF(@ISERR(I11*$BZ$13),0,I11*$BZ$13)
J55: (,0) U @IF(@ISERR(J11*$BZ$13),0,J11*$BZ$13)
```

continued...

...from previous page

```
K55: (,0) U [W9] @IF(@ISERR(K11*$BZ$13),0,K11*$BZ$13)
L55: (,0) U @IF(@ISERR(L11*$BZ$13),0,L11*$BZ$13)
M55: (,0) U @IF(@ISERR(M11*$BZ$13),0,M11*$BZ$13)
N55: PR [W1] ||
O55: (,0) U @IF(@ISERR(O11*$BZ$13),0,O11*$BZ$13)
P55: PR [W1] ||
Q55: (,0) U @IF(@ISERR(Q11*$BZ$13),0,Q11*$BZ$13)
R55: (,0) U [W9] @IF(@ISERR(R11*$BZ$13),0,R11*$BZ$13)
S55: (,0) U @IF(@ISERR(S11*$BZ$13),0,S11*$BZ$13)
T55: (,0) U [W9] @IF(@ISERR(T11*$BZ$13),0,T11*$BZ$13)
U55: (,0) U @IF(@ISERR(U11*$BZ$13),0,U11*$BZ$13)
V55: (,0) U @IF(@ISERR(V11*$BZ$13),0,V11*$BZ$13)
W55: PR [W1] ||
X55: (,0) U @IF(@ISERR(X11*$BZ$13),0,X11*$BZ$13)
Y55: PR [W1] ^||
H56: (,0) U @IF(@ISERR(H12*$BZ$13),0,H12*$BZ$13)
I56: (,0) U [W9] @IF(@ISERR(I12*$BZ$13),0,I12*$BZ$13)
J56: (,0) U @IF(@ISERR(J12*$BZ$13),0,J12*$BZ$13)
K56: (,0) U [W9] @IF(@ISERR(K12*$BZ$13),0,K12*$BZ$13)
L56: (,0) U @IF(@ISERR(L12*$BZ$13),0,L12*$BZ$13)
M56: (,0) U @IF(@ISERR(M12*$BZ$13),0,M12*$BZ$13)
N56: PR [W1] ||
O56: (,0) U @IF(@ISERR(O12*$BZ$13),0,O12*$BZ$13)
P56: PR [W1] ||
Q56: (,0) U @IF(@ISERR(Q12*$BZ$13),0,Q12*$BZ$13)
R56: (,0) U [W9] @IF(@ISERR(R12*$BZ$13),0,R12*$BZ$13)
S56: (,0) U @IF(@ISERR(S12*$BZ$13),0,S12*$BZ$13)
T56: (,0) U [W9] @IF(@ISERR(T12*$BZ$13),0,T12*$BZ$13)
U56: (,0) U @IF(@ISERR(U12*$BZ$13),0,U12*$BZ$13)
V56: (,0) U @IF(@ISERR(V12*$BZ$13),0,V12*$BZ$13)
W56: PR [W1] ||
X56: (,0) U @IF(@ISERR(X12*$BZ$13),0,X12*$BZ$13)
Y56: PR [W1] ^||
G57: PR [W45] 'Supporting Services:
H57: (,0) U @IF(@ISERR(H13*$BZ$13),0,H13*$BZ$13)
I57: (,0) U [W9] @IF(@ISERR(I13*$BZ$13),0,I13*$BZ$13)
J57: (,0) U @IF(@ISERR(J13*$BZ$13),0,J13*$BZ$13)
K57: (,0) U [W9] @IF(@ISERR(K13*$BZ$13),0,K13*$BZ$13)
L57: (,0) U @IF(@ISERR(L13*$BZ$13),0,L13*$BZ$13)
```

continued...

...from previous page

```
M57: (,0) U @IF(@ISERR(M13*$BZ$13),0,M13*$BZ$13)
N57: PR [W1] ||
O57: (,0) U @IF(@ISERR(O13*$BZ$13),0,O13*$BZ$13)
P57: PR [W1] ||
Q57: (,0) U @IF(@ISERR(Q13*$BZ$13),0,Q13*$BZ$13)
R57: (,0) U [W9] @IF(@ISERR(R13*$BZ$13),0,R13*$BZ$13)
S57: (,0) U @IF(@ISERR(S13*$BZ$13),0,S13*$BZ$13)
T57: (,0) U [W9] @IF(@ISERR(T13*$BZ$13),0,T13*$BZ$13)
U57: (,0) U @IF(@ISERR(U13*$BZ$13),0,U13*$BZ$13)
V57: (,0) U @IF(@ISERR(V13*$BZ$13),0,V13*$BZ$13)
W57: PR [W1] ||
X57: (,0) U @IF(@ISERR(X13*$BZ$13),0,X13*$BZ$13)
Y57: PR [W1] ^||
G58: PR [W45] '    Travel
H58: (,0) U @IF(@ISERR(H14*$BZ$13),0,H14*$BZ$13)
I58: (,0) U [W9] @IF(@ISERR(I14*$BZ$13),0,I14*$BZ$13)
J58: (,0) U @IF(@ISERR(J14*$BZ$13),0,J14*$BZ$13)
K58: (,0) U [W9] @IF(@ISERR(K14*$BZ$13),0,K14*$BZ$13)
L58: (,0) U @IF(@ISERR(L14*$BZ$13),0,L14*$BZ$13)
M58: (,0) U @IF(@ISERR(M14*$BZ$13),0,M14*$BZ$13)
N58: PR [W1] ||
O58: (,0) U @IF(@ISERR(O14*$BZ$13),0,O14*$BZ$13)
P58: PR [W1] ||
Q58: (,0) U @IF(@ISERR(Q14*$BZ$13),0,Q14*$BZ$13)
R58: (,0) U [W9] @IF(@ISERR(R14*$BZ$13),0,R14*$BZ$13)
S58: (,0) U @IF(@ISERR(S14*$BZ$13),0,S14*$BZ$13)
T58: (,0) U [W9] @IF(@ISERR(T14*$BZ$13),0,T14*$BZ$13)
U58: (,0) U @IF(@ISERR(U14*$BZ$13),0,U14*$BZ$13)
V58: (,0) U @IF(@ISERR(V14*$BZ$13),0,V14*$BZ$13)
W58: PR [W1] ||
X58: (,0) U @IF(@ISERR(X14*$BZ$13),0,X14*$BZ$13)
Y58: PR [W1] ^||
G59: PR [W45] '    Telephone Tolls and Rental
H59: (,0) U @IF(@ISERR(H15*$BZ$13),0,H15*$BZ$13)
I59: (,0) U [W9] @IF(@ISERR(I15*$BZ$13),0,I15*$BZ$13)
J59: (,0) U @IF(@ISERR(J15*$BZ$13),0,J15*$BZ$13)
K59: (,0) U [W9] @IF(@ISERR(K15*$BZ$13),0,K15*$BZ$13)
L59: (,0) U @IF(@ISERR(L15*$BZ$13),0,L15*$BZ$13)
M59: (,0) U @IF(@ISERR(M15*$BZ$13),0,M15*$BZ$13)
```

continued...

...from previous page

```
N59: PR [W1] ||
O59: (,0) U @IF(@ISERR(O15*$BZ$13),0,O15*$BZ$13)
P59: PR [W1] ||
Q59: (,0) U @IF(@ISERR(Q15*$BZ$13),0,Q15*$BZ$13)
R59: (,0) U [W9] @IF(@ISERR(R15*$BZ$13),0,R15*$BZ$13)
S59: (,0) U @IF(@ISERR(S15*$BZ$13),0,S15*$BZ$13)
T59: (,0) U [W9] @IF(@ISERR(T15*$BZ$13),0,T15*$BZ$13)
U59: (,0) U @IF(@ISERR(U15*$BZ$13),0,U15*$BZ$13)
V59: (,0) U @IF(@ISERR(V15*$BZ$13),0,V15*$BZ$13)
W59: PR [W1] ||
X59: (,0) U @IF(@ISERR(X15*$BZ$13),0,X15*$BZ$13)
Y59: PR [W1] ^||
G60: PR [W45] '    Postage
H60: (,0) U @IF(@ISERR(H16*$BZ$13),0,H16*$BZ$13)
I60: (,0) U [W9] @IF(@ISERR(I16*$BZ$13),0,I16*$BZ$13)
J60: (,0) U @IF(@ISERR(J16*$BZ$13),0,J16*$BZ$13)
K60: (,0) U [W9] @IF(@ISERR(K16*$BZ$13),0,K16*$BZ$13)
L60: (,0) U @IF(@ISERR(L16*$BZ$13),0,L16*$BZ$13)
M60: (,0) U @IF(@ISERR(M16*$BZ$13),0,M16*$BZ$13)
N60: PR [W1] ||
O60: (,0) U @IF(@ISERR(O16*$BZ$13),0,O16*$BZ$13)
P60: PR [W1] ||
Q60: (,0) U @IF(@ISERR(Q16*$BZ$13),0,Q16*$BZ$13)
R60: (,0) U [W9] @IF(@ISERR(R16*$BZ$13),0,R16*$BZ$13)
S60: (,0) U @IF(@ISERR(S16*$BZ$13),0,S16*$BZ$13)
T60: (,0) U [W9] @IF(@ISERR(T16*$BZ$13),0,T16*$BZ$13)
U60: (,0) U @IF(@ISERR(U16*$BZ$13),0,U16*$BZ$13)
V60: (,0) U @IF(@ISERR(V16*$BZ$13),0,V16*$BZ$13)
W60: PR [W1] ||
X60: (,0) U @IF(@ISERR(X16*$BZ$13),0,X16*$BZ$13)
Y60: PR [W1] ^||
G61: PR [W45] '    Rent - State Owned Buildings
H61: (,0) U @IF(@ISERR(H17*$BZ$13),0,H17*$BZ$13)
I61: (,0) U [W9] @IF(@ISERR(I17*$BZ$13),0,I17*$BZ$13)
J61: (,0) U @IF(@ISERR(J17*$BZ$13),0,J17*$BZ$13)
K61: (,0) U [W9] @IF(@ISERR(K17*$BZ$13),0,K17*$BZ$13)
L61: (,0) U @IF(@ISERR(L17*$BZ$13),0,L17*$BZ$13)
M61: (,0) U @IF(@ISERR(M17*$BZ$13),0,M17*$BZ$13)
N61: PR [W1] ||
```

continued...

...from previous page

```
O61: (,0) U @IF(@ISERR(O17*$BZ$13),0,O17*$BZ$13)
P61: PR [W1] ||
Q61: (,0) U @IF(@ISERR(Q17*$BZ$13),0,Q17*$BZ$13)
R61: (,0) U [W9] @IF(@ISERR(R17*$BZ$13),0,R17*$BZ$13)
S61: (,0) U @IF(@ISERR(S17*$BZ$13),0,S17*$BZ$13)
T61: (,0) U [W9] @IF(@ISERR(T17*$BZ$13),0,T17*$BZ$13)
U61: (,0) U @IF(@ISERR(U17*$BZ$13),0,U17*$BZ$13)
V61: (,0) U @IF(@ISERR(V17*$BZ$13),0,V17*$BZ$13)
W61: PR [W1] ||
X61: (,0) U @IF(@ISERR(X17*$BZ$13),0,X17*$BZ$13)
Y61: PR [W1] ^||
G62: PR [W45] '    Rent - Privately Owned Buildings
H62: (,0) U @IF(@ISERR(H18*$BZ$13),0,H18*$BZ$13)
I62: (,0) U [W9] @IF(@ISERR(I18*$BZ$13),0,I18*$BZ$13)
J62: (,0) U @IF(@ISERR(J18*$BZ$13),0,J18*$BZ$13)
K62: (,0) U [W9] @IF(@ISERR(K18*$BZ$13),0,K18*$BZ$13)
L62: (,0) U @IF(@ISERR(L18*$BZ$13),0,L18*$BZ$13)
M62: (,0) U @IF(@ISERR(M18*$BZ$13),0,M18*$BZ$13)
N62: PR [W1] ||
O62: (,0) U @IF(@ISERR(O18*$BZ$13),0,O18*$BZ$13)
P62: PR [W1] ||
Q62: (,0) U @IF(@ISERR(Q18*$BZ$13),0,Q18*$BZ$13)
R62: (,0) U [W9] @IF(@ISERR(R18*$BZ$13),0,R18*$BZ$13)
S62: (,0) U @IF(@ISERR(S18*$BZ$13),0,S18*$BZ$13)
T62: (,0) U [W9] @IF(@ISERR(T18*$BZ$13),0,T18*$BZ$13)
U62: (,0) U @IF(@ISERR(U18*$BZ$13),0,U18*$BZ$13)
V62: (,0) U @IF(@ISERR(V18*$BZ$13),0,V18*$BZ$13)
W62: PR [W1] ||
X62: (,0) U @IF(@ISERR(X18*$BZ$13),0,X18*$BZ$13)
Y62: PR [W1] ^||
G63: PR [W45] '    Building Improvements
H63: (,0) U @IF(@ISERR(H19*$BZ$13),0,H19*$BZ$13)
I63: (,0) U [W9] @IF(@ISERR(I19*$BZ$13),0,I19*$BZ$13)
J63: (,0) U @IF(@ISERR(J19*$BZ$13),0,J19*$BZ$13)
K63: (,0) U [W9] @IF(@ISERR(K19*$BZ$13),0,K19*$BZ$13)
L63: (,0) U @IF(@ISERR(L19*$BZ$13),0,L19*$BZ$13)
M63: (,0) U @IF(@ISERR(M19*$BZ$13),0,M19*$BZ$13)
N63: PR [W1] ||
O63: (,0) U @IF(@ISERR(O19*$BZ$13),0,O19*$BZ$13)
```

continued...

...from previous page

```
P63: PR [W1] ||
Q63: (,0) U @IF(@ISERR(Q19*$BZ$13),0,Q19*$BZ$13)
R63: (,0) U [W9] @IF(@ISERR(R19*$BZ$13),0,R19*$BZ$13)
S63: (,0) U @IF(@ISERR(S19*$BZ$13),0,S19*$BZ$13)
T63: (,0) U [W9] @IF(@ISERR(T19*$BZ$13),0,T19*$BZ$13)
U63: (,0) U @IF(@ISERR(U19*$BZ$13),0,U19*$BZ$13)
V63: (,0) U @IF(@ISERR(V19*$BZ$13),0,V19*$BZ$13)
W63: PR [W1] ||
X63: (,0) U @IF(@ISERR(X19*$BZ$13),0,X19*$BZ$13)
Y63: PR [W1] ^||
G64: PR [W45] '    Utility Charges
H64: (,0) U @IF(@ISERR(H20*$BZ$13),0,H20*$BZ$13)
I64: (,0) U [W9] @IF(@ISERR(I20*$BZ$13),0,I20*$BZ$13)
J64: (,0) U @IF(@ISERR(J20*$BZ$13),0,J20*$BZ$13)
K64: (,0) U [W9] @IF(@ISERR(K20*$BZ$13),0,K20*$BZ$13)
L64: (,0) U @IF(@ISERR(L20*$BZ$13),0,L20*$BZ$13)
M64: (,0) U @IF(@ISERR(M20*$BZ$13),0,M20*$BZ$13)
N64: PR [W1] ||
O64: (,0) U @IF(@ISERR(O20*$BZ$13),0,O20*$BZ$13 20
P64: PR [W1] ||
Q64: (,0) U @IF(@ISERR(Q20*$BZ$13),0,Q20*$BZ$13)
R64: (,0) U [W9] @IF(@ISERR(R20*$BZ$13),0,R20*$BZ$13)
S64: (,0) U @IF(@ISERR(S20*$BZ$13),0,S20*$BZ$13)
T64: (,0) U [W9] @IF(@ISERR(T20*$BZ$13),0,T20*$BZ$13)
U64: (,0) U @IF(@ISERR(U20*$BZ$13),0,U20*$BZ$13)
V64: (,0) U @IF(@ISERR(V20*$BZ$13),0,V20*$BZ$13)
W64: PR [W1] ||
X64: (,0) U @IF(@ISERR(X20*$BZ$13),0,X20*$BZ$13)
Y64: PR [W1] ||
Z64: PR [W1] ||
G65: PR [W45] '    Rent of Data Processing Equipment
H65: (,0) U @IF(@ISERR(H21*$BZ$13),0,H21*$BZ$13)
I65: (,0) U [W9] @IF(@ISERR(I21*$BZ$13),0,I21*$BZ$13)
J65: (,0) U @IF(@ISERR(J21*$BZ$13),0,J21*$BZ$13)
K65: (,0) U [W9] @IF(@ISERR(K21*$BZ$13),0,K21*$BZ$13)
L65: (,0) U @IF(@ISERR(L21*$BZ$13),0,L21*$BZ$13)
M65: (,0) U @IF(@ISERR(M21*$BZ$13),0,M21*$BZ$13)
N65: PR [W1] ||
O65: (,0) U @IF(@ISERR(O21*$BZ$13),0,O21*$BZ$13)
```

continued...

...from previous page

```
P65: PR [W1] ||
Q65: (,0) U @IF(@ISERR(Q21*$BZ$13),0,Q21*$BZ$13)
R65: (,0) U [W9] @IF(@ISERR(R21*$BZ$13),0,R21*$BZ$13)
S65: (,0) U @IF(@ISERR(S21*$BZ$13),0,S21*$BZ$13)
T65: (,0) U [W9] @IF(@ISERR(T21*$BZ$13),0,T21*$BZ$13)
U65: (,0) U @IF(@ISERR(U21*$BZ$13),0,U21*$BZ$13)
V65: (,0) U @IF(@ISERR(V21*$BZ$13),0,V21*$BZ$13)
W65: PR [W1] ||
X65: (,0) U @IF(@ISERR(X21*$BZ$13),0,X21*$BZ$13)
Y65: PR [W1] ^||
Z65: PR [W1] '|
G66: PR [W45] '    Rent of Office Equipment
H66: (,0) U @IF(@ISERR(H22*$BZ$13),0,H22*$BZ$13)
I66: (,0) U [W9] @IF(@ISERR(I22*$BZ$13),0,I22*$BZ$13)
J66: (,0) U @IF(@ISERR(J22*$BZ$13),0,J22*$BZ$13)
K66: (,0) U [W9] @IF(@ISERR(K22*$BZ$13),0,K22*$BZ$13)
L66: (,0) U @IF(@ISERR(L22*$BZ$13),0,L22*$BZ$13)
M66: (,0) U @IF(@ISERR(M22*$BZ$13),0,M22*$BZ$13)
N66: PR [W1] ||
O66: (,0) U @IF(@ISERR(O22*$BZ$13),0,O22*$BZ$13)
P66: PR [W1] ||
Q66: (,0) U @IF(@ISERR(Q22*$BZ$13),0,Q22*$BZ$13)
R66: (,0) U [W9] @IF(@ISERR(R22*$BZ$13),0,R22*$BZ$13)
S66: (,0) U @IF(@ISERR(S22*$BZ$13),0,S22*$BZ$13)
T66: (,0) U [W9] @IF(@ISERR(T22*$BZ$13),0,T22*$BZ$13)
U66: (,0) U @IF(@ISERR(U22*$BZ$13),0,U22*$BZ$13)
V66: (,0) U @IF(@ISERR(V22*$BZ$13),0,V22*$BZ$13)
W66: PR [W1] ||
X66: (,0) U @IF(@ISERR(X22*$BZ$13),0,X22*$BZ$13)
Y66: PR [W1] ^||
Z66: PR [W1] '|
G67: PR [W45] '    Maint. & Rep. of Office Equipment
H67: (,0) U @IF(@ISERR(H23*$BZ$13),0,H23*$BZ$13)
I67: (,0) U [W9] @IF(@ISERR(I23*$BZ$13),0,I23*$BZ$13)
J67: (,0) U @IF(@ISERR(J23*$BZ$13),0,J23*$BZ$13)
K67: (,0) U [W9] @IF(@ISERR(K23*$BZ$13),0,K23*$BZ$13)
L67: (,0) U @IF(@ISERR(L23*$BZ$13),0,L23*$BZ$13)
M67: (,0) U @IF(@ISERR(M23*$BZ$13),0,M23*$BZ$13)
N67: PR [W1] ||
```

continued...

...from previous page

```
O67: (,0) U @IF(@ISERR(O23*$BZ$13),0,O23*$BZ$13)
P67: PR [W1] ||
Q67: (,0) U @IF(@ISERR(Q23*$BZ$13),0,Q23*$BZ$13)
R67: (,0) U [W9] @IF(@ISERR(R23*$BZ$13),0,R23*$BZ$13)
S67: (,0) U @IF(@ISERR(S23*$BZ$13),0,S23*$BZ$13)
T67: (,0) U [W9] @IF(@ISERR(T23*$BZ$13),0,T23*$BZ$13)
U67: (,0) U @IF(@ISERR(U23*$BZ$13),0,U23*$BZ$13)
V67: (,0) U @IF(@ISERR(V23*$BZ$13),0,V23*$BZ$13)
W67: PR [W1] ||
X67: (,0) U @IF(@ISERR(X23*$BZ$13),0,X23*$BZ$13)
Y67: PR [W1] ^||
Z67: PR [W1] ^|
G68: PR [W45] '   Maint. & Rep. of Ofc. Equip. - Contract
H68: (,0) U @IF(@ISERR(H24*$BZ$13),0,H24*$BZ$13)
I68: (,0) U [W9] @IF(@ISERR(I24*$BZ$13),0,I24*$BZ$13)
J68: (,0) U @IF(@ISERR(J24*$BZ$13),0,J24*$BZ$13)
K68: (,0) U [W9] @IF(@ISERR(K24*$BZ$13),0,K24*$BZ$13)
L68: (,0) U @IF(@ISERR(L24*$BZ$13),0,L24*$BZ$13)
M68: (,0) U @IF(@ISERR(M24*$BZ$13),0,M24*$BZ$13)
N68: PR [W1] ||
O68: (,0) U @IF(@ISERR(O24*$BZ$13),0,O24*$BZ$13)
P68: PR [W1] ||
Q68: (,0) U @IF(@ISERR(Q24*$BZ$13),0,Q24*$BZ$13)
R68: (,0) U [W9] IF(@ISERR(R24*$BZ$13),0,R24*$BZ$13)
S68: (,0) U @IF(@ISERR(S24*$BZ$13),0,S24*$BZ$13)
T68: (,0) U [W9] @IF(@ISERR(T24*$BZ$13),0,T24*$BZ$13)
U68: (,0) U @IF(@ISERR(U24*$BZ$13),0,U24*$BZ$13)
V68: (,0) U @IF(@ISERR(V24*$BZ$13),0,V24*$BZ$13)
W68: PR [W1] ||
X68: (,0) U @IF(@ISERR(X24*$BZ$13),0,X24*$BZ$13)
gY68: PR [W1] ^||
G69: PR [W45] '   Maint. & Rep. of Automobile Vehicles
H69: (,0) U @IF(@ISERR(H25*$BZ$13),0,H25*$BZ$13)
I69: (,0) U [W9] @IF(@ISERR(I25*$BZ$13),0,I25*$BZ$13)
J69: (,0) U @IF(@ISERR(J25*$BZ$13),0,J25*$BZ$13)
K69: (,0) U [W9] @IF(@ISERR(K25*$BZ$13),0,K25*$BZ$13)
L69: (,0) U @IF(@ISERR(L25*$BZ$13),0,L25*$BZ$13)
M69: (,0) U @IF(@ISERR(M25*$BZ$13),0,M25*$BZ$13)
N69: PR [W1] ||
```

continued...

...from previous page

```
O69: (,0) U @IF(@ISERR(O25*$BZ$13),0,O25*$BZ$13)
P69: PR [W1] ||
Q69: (,0) U @IF(@ISERR(Q25*$BZ$13),0,Q25*$BZ$13)
R69: (,0) U [W9] @IF(@ISERR(R25*$BZ$13),0,R25*$BZ$13)
S69: (,0) U @IF(@ISERR(S25*$BZ$13),0,S25*$BZ$13)
T69: (,0) U [W9] @IF(@ISERR(T25*$BZ$13),0,T25*$BZ$13)
U69: (,0) U @IF(@ISERR(U25*$BZ$13),0,U25*$BZ$13)
V69: (,0) U @IF(@ISERR(V25*$BZ$13),0,V25*$BZ$13)
W69: PR [W1] ||
X69: (,0) U @IF(@ISERR(X25*$BZ$13),0,X25*$BZ$13)
Y69: PR [W1] ^||
Z69: PR [W1] ^|
G70: PR [W45] '    Maint. & Rep. of Other Equipment
H70: (,0) U @IF(@ISERR(H26*$BZ$13),0,H26*$BZ$13)
I70: (,0) U [W9] @IF(@ISERR(I26*$BZ$13),0,I26*$BZ$13)
J70: (,0) U @IF(@ISERR(J26*$BZ$13),0,J26*$BZ$13)
K70: (,0) U [W9] @IF(@ISERR(K26*$BZ$13),0,K26*$BZ$13)
L70: (,0) U @IF(@ISERR(L26*$BZ$13),0,L26*$BZ$13)
M70: (,0) U @IF(@ISERR(M26*$BZ$13),0,M26*$BZ$13)
N70: PR [W1] ||
O70: (,0) U @IF(@ISERR(O26*$BZ$13),0,O26*$BZ$13)
P70: PR [W1] ||
Q70: (,0) U @IF(@ISERR(Q26*$BZ$13),0,Q26*$BZ$13)
R70: (,0) U [W9] @IF(@ISERR(R26*$BZ$13),0,R26*$BZ$13)
S70: (,0) U @IF(@ISERR(S26*$BZ$13),0,S26*$BZ$13)
T70: (,0) U [W9] @IF(@ISERR(T26*$BZ$13),0,T26*$BZ$13)
U70: (,0) U @IF(@ISERR(U26*$BZ$13),0,U26*$BZ$13)
V70: (,0) U @IF(@ISERR(V26*$BZ$13),0,V26*$BZ$13)
W70: PR [W1] ||
X70: (,0) U @IF(@ISERR(X26*$BZ$13),0,X26*$BZ$13)
Y70: PR [W1] ^||
Z70: PR [W1] ^|
G71: PR [W45] '    Data Processing Contractual Service
H71: (,0) U @IF(@ISERR(H27*$BZ$13),0,H27*$BZ$13)
I71: (,0) U [W9] @IF(@ISERR(I27*$BZ$13),0,I27*$BZ$13)
J71: (,0) U @IF(@ISERR(J27*$BZ$13),0,J27*$BZ$13)
K71: (,0) U [W9] @IF(@ISERR(K27*$BZ$13),0,K27*$BZ$13)
L71: (,0) U @IF(@ISERR(L27*$BZ$13),0,L27*$BZ$13)
M71: (,0) U @IF(@ISERR(M27*$BZ$13),0,M27*$BZ$13)
```

continued...

...from previous page

```
N71: PR [W1] ||
O71: (,0) U @IF(@ISERR(O27*$BZ$13),0,O27*$BZ$13)
P71: PR [W1] ||
Q71: (,0) U @IF(@ISERR(Q27*$BZ$13),0,Q27*$BZ$13)
R71: (,0) U [W9] @IF(@ISERR(R27*$BZ$13),0,R27*$BZ$13)
S71: (,0) U @IF(@ISERR(S27*$BZ$13),0,S27*$BZ$13)
T71: (,0) U [W9] @IF(@ISERR(T27*$BZ$13),0,T27*$BZ$13)
U71: (,0) U @IF(@ISERR(U27*$BZ$13),0,U27*$BZ$13)
V71: (,0) U @IF(@ISERR(V27*$BZ$13),0,V27*$BZ$13)
W71: PR [W1] ||
X71: (,0) U @IF(@ISERR(X27*$BZ$13),0,X27*$BZ$13)
Y71: PR [W1] ^||
Z71: PR [W1] ^|
G72: PR [W45] '    Insurance, Subscriptions, Brinks
H72: (,0) U @IF(@ISERR(H28*$BZ$13),0,H28*$BZ$13)
I72: (,0) U [W9] @IF(@ISERR(I28*$BZ$13),0,I28*$BZ$13)
J72: (,0) U @IF(@ISERR(J28*$BZ$13),0,J28*$BZ$13)
K72: (,0) U [W9] @IF(@ISERR(K28*$BZ$13),0,K28*$BZ$13)
L72: (,0) U @IF(@ISERR(L28*$BZ$13),0,L28*$BZ$13)
M72: (,0) U @IF(@ISERR(M28*$BZ$13),0,M28*$BZ$13)
N72: PR [W1] ||
O72: (,0) U @IF(@ISERR(O28*$BZ$13),0,O28*$BZ$13)
P72: PR [W1] ||
Q72: (,0) U @IF(@ISERR(Q28*$BZ$13),0,Q28*$BZ$13)
R72: (,0) U [W9] @IF(@ISERR(R28*$BZ$13),0,R28*$BZ$13)
S72: (,0) U @IF(@ISERR(S28*$BZ$13),0,S28*$BZ$13)
T72: (,0) U [W9] @IF(@ISERR(T28*$BZ$13),0,T28*$BZ$13)
U72: (,0) U @IF(@ISERR(U28*$BZ$13),0,U28*$BZ$13)
V72: (,0) U @IF(@ISERR(V28*$BZ$13),0,V28*$BZ$13)
W72: PR [W1] ||
X72: (,0) U @IF(@ISERR(X28*$BZ$13),0,X28*$BZ$13)
Y72: PR [W1] ^||
Z72: PR [W1] ^|
G73: PR [W45] '    Miscellaneous Services:
H73: (,0) U @IF(@ISERR(H29*$BZ$13),0,H29*$BZ$13)
I73: (,0) U [W9] @IF(@ISERR(I29*$BZ$13),0,I29*$BZ$13)
J73: (,0) U @IF(@ISERR(J29*$BZ$13),0,J29*$BZ$13)
K73: (,0) U [W9] @IF(@ISERR(K29*$BZ$13),0,K29*$BZ$13)
L73: (,0) U @IF(@ISERR(L29*$BZ$13),0,L29*$BZ$13)
```

continued...

...from previous page

```
M73: (,0) U @IF(@ISERR(M29*$BZ$13),0,M29*$BZ$13)
N73: PR [W1] ||
O73: (,0) U @IF(@ISERR(O29*$BZ$13),0,O29*$BZ$13)
P73: PR [W1] ||
Q73: (,0) U @IF(@ISERR(Q29*$BZ$13),0,Q29*$BZ$13)
R73: (,0) U [W9] @IF(@ISERR(R29*$BZ$13),0,R29*$BZ$13)
S73: (,0) U @IF(@ISERR(S29*$BZ$13),0,S29*$BZ$13)
T73: (,0) U [W9] @IF(@ISERR(T29*$BZ$13),0,T29*$BZ$13)
U73: (,0) U @IF(@ISERR(U29*$BZ$13),0,U29*$BZ$13)
V73: (,0) U @IF(@ISERR(V29*$BZ$13),0,V29*$BZ$13)
W73: PR [W1] ||
X73: (,0) U @IF(@ISERR(X29*$BZ$13),0,X29*$BZ$13)
Y73: PR [W1] ^||
Z73: PR [W1] ^|
G74: PR [W45] '        Card Copiers
H74: (,0) U @IF(@ISERR(H30*$BZ$13),0,H30*$BZ$13)
I74: (,0) U [W9] @IF(@ISERR(I30*$BZ$13),0,I30*$BZ$13)
J74: (,0) U @IF(@ISERR(J30*$BZ$13),0,J30*$BZ$13)
K74: (,0) U [W9] @IF(@ISERR(K30*$BZ$13),0,K30*$BZ$13)
L74: (,0) U @IF(@ISERR(L30*$BZ$13),0,L30*$BZ$13)
M74: (,0) U @IF(@ISERR(M30*$BZ$13),0,M30*$BZ$13)
N74: PR [W1] ||
O74: (,0) U @IF(@ISERR(O30*$BZ$13),0,O30*$BZ$13)
P74: PR [W1] ||
Q74: (,0) U @IF(@ISERR(Q30*$BZ$13),0,Q30*$BZ$13)
R74: (,0) U [W9] @IF(@ISERR(R30*$BZ$13),0,R30*$BZ$13)
S74: (,0) U @IF(@ISERR(S30*$BZ$13),0,S30*$BZ$13)
T74: (,0) U [W9] @IF(@ISERR(T30*$BZ$13),0,T30*$BZ$13)
U74: (,0) U @IF(@ISERR(U30*$BZ$13),0,U30*$BZ$13)
V74: (,0) U @IF(@ISERR(V30*$BZ$13),0,V30*$BZ$13)
W74: PR [W1] ||
X74: (,0) U @IF(@ISERR(X30*$BZ$13),0,X30*$BZ$13)
Y74: PR [W1] ^||
Z74: PR [W1] ^|
G75: PR [W45] '        Court Costs
H75: (,0) U @IF(@ISERR(H31*$BZ$13),0,H31*$BZ$13)
I75: (,0) U [W9] @IF(@ISERR(I31*$BZ$13),0,I31*$BZ$13)
J75: (,0) U @IF(@ISERR(J31*$BZ$13),0,J31*$BZ$13)
K75: (,0) U [W9] @IF(@ISERR(K31*$BZ$13),0,K31*$BZ$13)
```

continued...

...from previous page

```
L75: (,0) U @IF(@ISERR(L31*$BZ$13),0,L31*$BZ$13)
M75: (,0) U @IF(@ISERR(M31*$BZ$13),0,M31*$BZ$13)
N75: PR [W1] ||
O75: (,0) U @IF(@ISERR(O31*$BZ$13),0,O31*$BZ$13)
P75: PR [W1] ||
Q75: (,0) U @IF(@ISERR(Q31*$BZ$13),0,Q31*$BZ$13)
R75: (,0) U [W9] @IF(@ISERR(R31*$BZ$13),0,R31*$BZ$13)
S75: (,0) U @IF(@ISERR(S31*$BZ$13),0,S31*$BZ$13)
T75: (,0) U [W9] @IF(@ISERR(T31*$BZ$13),0,T31*$BZ$13)
U75: (,0) U @IF(@ISERR(U31*$BZ$13),0,U31*$BZ$13)
V75: (,0) U @IF(@ISERR(V31*$BZ$13),0,V31*$BZ$13)
W75: PR [W1] ||
X75: (,0) U @IF(@ISERR(X31*$BZ$13),0,X31*$BZ$13)
Y75: PR [W1] ^||
Z75: PR [W1] ^|
H76: (,0) U @IF(@ISERR(H32*$BZ$13),0,H32*$BZ$13)
I76: (,0) U [W9] @IF(@ISERR(I32*$BZ$13),0,I32*$BZ$13)
J76: (,0) U @IF(@ISERR(J32*$BZ$13),0,J32*$BZ$13)
K76: (,0) U [W9] @IF(@ISERR(K32*$BZ$13),0,K32*$BZ$13)
L76: (,0) U @IF(@ISERR(L32*$BZ$13),0,L32*$BZ$13)
M76: (,0) U @IF(@ISERR(M32*$BZ$13),0,M32*$BZ$13)
N76: PR [W1] ||
O76: (,0) U @IF(@ISERR(O32*$BZ$13),0,O32*$BZ$13)
P76: PR [W1] ||
Q76: (,0) U @IF(@ISERR(Q32*$BZ$13),0,Q32*$BZ$13)
R76: (,0) U [W9] @IF(@ISERR(R32*$BZ$13),0,R32*$BZ$13)
S76: (,0) U @IF(@ISERR(S32*$BZ$13),0,S32*$BZ$13)
T76: (,0) U [W9] @IF(@ISERR(T32*$BZ$13),0,T32*$BZ$13)
U76: (,0) U @IF(@ISERR(U32*$BZ$13),0,U32*$BZ$13)
V76: (,0) U @IF(@ISERR(V32*$BZ$13),0,V32*$BZ$13)
W76: PR [W1] ||
X76: (,0) U @IF(@ISERR(X32*$BZ$13),0,X32*$BZ$13)
Y76: PR [W1] ^||
Z76: PR [W1] ^|
H77: (,0) U @IF(@ISERR(H33*$BZ$13),0,H33*$BZ$13)
I77: (,0) U [W9] @IF(@ISERR(I33*$BZ$13),0,I33*$BZ$13)
J77: (,0) U @IF(@ISERR(J33*$BZ$13),0,J33*$BZ$13)
K77: (,0) U [W9] @IF(@ISERR(K33*$BZ$13),0,K33*$BZ$13)
L77: (,0) U @IF(@ISERR(L33*$BZ$13),0,L33*$BZ$13)
```

continued...

...from previous page

```
M77: (,0) U @IF(@ISERR(M33*$BZ$13),0,M33*$BZ$13)
N77: PR [W1] ||
O77: (,0) U @IF(@ISERR(O33*$BZ$13),0,O33*$BZ$13)
P77: PR [W1] ||
Q77: (,0) U @IF(@ISERR(Q33*$BZ$13),0,Q33*$BZ$13)
R77: (,0) U [W9] @IF(@ISERR(R33*$BZ$13),0,R33*$BZ$13)
S77: (,0) U @IF(@ISERR(S33*$BZ$13),0,S33*$BZ$13)
T77: (,0) U [W9] @IF(@ISERR(T33*$BZ$13),0,T33*$BZ$13)
U77: (,0) U @IF(@ISERR(U33*$BZ$13),0,U33*$BZ$13)
V77: (,0) U @IF(@ISERR(V33*$BZ$13),0,V33*$BZ$13)
W77: PR [W1] ||
X77: (,0) U @IF(@ISERR(X33*$BZ$13),0,X33*$BZ$13)
Y77: PR [W1] ^||
Z77: PR [W1] ^|
G78: PR [W45] 'Other:
H78: (,0) U @IF(@ISERR(H34*$BZ$13),0,H34*$BZ$13)
I78: (,0) U [W9] @IF(@ISERR(I34*$BZ$13),0,I34*$BZ$13)
J78: (,0) U @IF(@ISERR(J34*$BZ$13),0,J34*$BZ$13)
K78: (,0) U [W9] @IF(@ISERR(K34*$BZ$13),0,K34*$BZ$13)
L78: (,0) U @IF(@ISERR(L34*$BZ$13),0,L34*$BZ$13)
M78: (,0) U @IF(@ISERR(M34*$BZ$13),0,M34*$BZ$13)
N78: PR [W1] ||
O78: (,0) U @IF(@ISERR(O34*$BZ$13),0,O34*$BZ$13)
P78: PR [W1] ||
Q78: (,0) U @IF(@ISERR(Q34*$BZ$13),0,Q34*$BZ$13)
R78: (,0) U [W9] @IF(@ISERR(R34*$BZ$13),0,R34*$BZ$13)
S78: (,0) U @IF(@ISERR(S34*$BZ$13),0,S34*$BZ$13)
T78: (,0) U [W9] @IF(@ISERR(T34*$BZ$13),0,T34*$BZ$13)
U78: (,0) U @IF(@ISERR(U34*$BZ$13),0,U34*$BZ$13)
V78: (,0) U @IF(@ISERR(V34*$BZ$13),0,V34*$BZ$13)
W78: PR [W1] ||
X78: (,0) U @IF(@ISERR(X34*$BZ$13),0,X34*$BZ$13)
Y78: PR [W1] ^||
Z78: PR [W1] ^|
G79: PR [W45] '    Printing
H79: (,0) U @IF(@ISERR(H35*$BZ$13),0,H35*$BZ$13)
I79: (,0) U [W9] @IF(@ISERR(I35*$BZ$13),0,I35*$BZ$13)
J79: (,0) U @IF(@ISERR(J35*$BZ$13),0,J35*$BZ$13)
K79: (,0) U [W9] @IF(@ISERR(K35*$BZ$13),0,K35*$BZ$13)
```

continued...

...from previous page

```
L79:  (,0)  U  @IF(@ISERR(L35*$BZ$13),0,L35*$BZ$13)
M79:  (,0)  U  @IF(@ISERR(M35*$BZ$13),0,M35*$BZ$13)
N79:  PR [W1]  ||
O79:  (,0)  U  @IF(@ISERR(O35*$BZ$13),0,O35*$BZ$13)
P79:  PR [W1]  ||
Q79:  (,0)  U  @IF(@ISERR(Q35*$BZ$13),0,Q35*$BZ$13)
R79:  (,0)  U  [W9] @IF(@ISERR(R35*$BZ$13),0,R35*$BZ$13)
S79:  (,0)  U  @IF(@ISERR(S35*$BZ$13),0,S35*$BZ$13)
T79:  (,0)  U  [W9] @IF(@ISERR(T35*$BZ$13),0,T35*$BZ$13)
U79:  (,0)  U  @IF(@ISERR(U35*$BZ$13),0,U35*$BZ$13)
V79:  (,0)  U  @IF(@ISERR(V35*$BZ$13),0,V35*$BZ$13)
W79:  PR [W1]  ||
X79:  (,0)  U  @IF(@ISERR(X35*$BZ$13),0,X35*$BZ$13)
Y79:  PR [W1]  ^||
Z79:  PR [W1]  ^|
G80:  PR [W45]  '    Office Supplies
H80:  (,0)  U  @IF(@ISERR(H36*$BZ$13),0,H36*$BZ$13)
I80:  (,0)  U  [W9] @IF(@ISERR(I36*$BZ$13),0,I36*$BZ$13)
J80:  (,0)  U  @IF(@ISERR(J36*$BZ$13),0,J36*$BZ$13)
K80:  (,0)  U  [W9] @IF(@ISERR(K36*$BZ$13),0,K36*$BZ$13)
L80:  (,0)  U  @IF(@ISERR(L36*$BZ$13),0,L36*$BZ$13)
M80:  (,0)  U  @IF(@ISERR(M36*$BZ$13),0,M36*$BZ$13)
N80:  PR [W1]  ||
O80:  (,0)  U  @IF(@ISERR(O36*$BZ$13),0,O36*$BZ$13)
P80:  PR [W1]  ||
Q80:  (,0)  U  @IF(@ISERR(Q36*$BZ$13),0,Q36*$BZ$13)
R80:  (,0)  U  [W9] @IF(@ISERR(R36*$BZ$13),0,R36*$BZ$13)
S80:  (,0)  U  @IF(@ISERR(S36*$BZ$13),0,S36*$BZ$13)
T80:  (,0)  U  [W9] @IF(@ISERR(T36*$BZ$13),0,T36*$BZ$13)
U80:  (,0)  U  @IF(@ISERR(U36*$BZ$13),0,U36*$BZ$13)
V80:  (,0)  U  @IF(@ISERR(V36*$BZ$13),0,V36*$BZ$13)
W80:  PR [W1]  ||
X80:  (,0)  U  @IF(@ISERR(X36*$BZ$13),0,X36*$BZ$13)
Y80:  PR [W1]  ^||
Z80:  PR [W1]  ^|
G81:  PR [W45]  '        Revenue Stamps
H81:  (,0)  U  @IF(@ISERR(H37*$BZ$13),0,H37*$BZ$13)
I81:  (,0)  U  [W9] @IF(@ISERR(I37*$BZ$13),0,I37*$BZ$13)
J81:  (,0)  U  @IF(@ISERR(J37*$BZ$13),0,J37*$BZ$13)
```

continued...

...from previous page

```
K81: (,0) U [W9] @IF(@ISERR(K37*$BZ$13),0,K37*$BZ$13)
L81: (,0) U @IF(@ISERR(L37*$BZ$13),0,L37*$BZ$13)
M81: (,0) U @IF(@ISERR(M37*$BZ$13),0,M37*$BZ$13)
N81: PR [W1] ||
O81: (,0) U @IF(@ISERR(O37*$BZ$13),0,O37*$BZ$13)
P81: PR [W1] ||
Q81: (,0) U @IF(@ISERR(Q37*$BZ$13),0,Q37*$BZ$13)
R81: (,0) U [W9] @IF(@ISERR(R37*$BZ$13),0,R37*$BZ$13)
S81: (,0) U @IF(@ISERR(S37*$BZ$13),0,S37*$BZ$13)
T81: (,0) U [W9] @IF(@ISERR(T37*$BZ$13),0,T37*$BZ$13)
U81: (,0) U @IF(@ISERR(U37*$BZ$13),0,U37*$BZ$13)
V81: (,0) U @IF(@ISERR(V37*$BZ$13),0,V37*$BZ$13)
W81: PR [W1] ||
X81: (,0) U @IF(@ISERR(X37*$BZ$13),0,X37*$BZ$13)
Y81: PR [W1] ^||
Z81: PR [W1] ^|
H82: (,0) U @IF(@ISERR(H38*$BZ$13),0,H38*$BZ$13)
I82: (,0) U [W9] @IF(@ISERR(I38*$BZ$13),0,I38*$BZ$13)
J82: (,0) U @IF(@ISERR(J38*$BZ$13),0,J38*$BZ$13)
K82: (,0) U [W9] @IF(@ISERR(K38*$BZ$13),0,K38*$BZ$13)
L82: (,0) U @IF(@ISERR(L38*$BZ$13),0,L38*$BZ$13)
M82: (,0) U @IF(@ISERR(M38*$BZ$13),0,M38*$BZ$13)
N82: PR [W1] ||
O82: (,0) U @IF(@ISERR(O38*$BZ$13),0,O38*$BZ$13)
P82: PR [W1] ||
Q82: (,0) U @IF(@ISERR(Q38*$BZ$13),0,Q38*$BZ$13)
R82: (,0) U [W9] @IF(@ISERR(R38*$BZ$13),0,R38*$BZ$13)
S82: (,0) U @IF(@ISERR(S38*$BZ$13),0,S38*$BZ$13)
T82: (,0) U [W9] @IF(@ISERR(T38*$BZ$13),0,T38*$BZ$13)
U82: (,0) U @IF(@ISERR(U38*$BZ$13),0,U38*$BZ$13)
V82: (,0) U @IF(@ISERR(V38*$BZ$13),0,V38*$BZ$13)
W82: PR [W1] ||
X82: (,0) U @IF(@ISERR(X38*$BZ$13),0,X38*$BZ$13)
Y82: PR [W1] ^||
Z82: PR [W1] ^|
H83: (,0) U @IF(@ISERR(H39*$BZ$13),0,H39*$BZ$13)
I83: (,0) U [W9] @IF(@ISERR(I39*$BZ$13),0,I39*$BZ$13)
J83: (,0) U @IF(@ISERR(J39*$BZ$13),0,J39*$BZ$13)
K83: (,0) U [W9] @IF(@ISERR(K39*$BZ$13),0,K39*$BZ$13)
```

continued...

...from previous page

```
L83: (,0) U @IF(@ISERR(L39*$BZ$13),0,L39*$BZ$13)
M83: (,0) U @IF(@ISERR(M39*$BZ$13),0,M39*$BZ$13)
N83: PR [W1] ||
O83: (,0) U @IF(@ISERR(O39*$BZ$13),0,O39*$BZ$13)
P83: PR [W1] ||
Q83: (,0) U @IF(@ISERR(Q39*$BZ$13),0,Q39*$BZ$13)
R83: (,0) U [W9] @IF(@ISERR(R39*$BZ$13),0,R39*$BZ$13)
S83: (,0) U @IF(@ISERR(S39*$BZ$13),0,S39*$BZ$13)
T83: (,0) U [W9] @IF(@ISERR(T39*$BZ$13),0,T39*$BZ$13)
U83: (,0) U @IF(@ISERR(U39*$BZ$13),0,U39*$BZ$13)
V83: (,0) U @IF(@ISERR(V39*$BZ$13),0,V39*$BZ$13)
W83: PR [W1] ||
X83: (,0) U @IF(@ISERR(X39*$BZ$13),0,X39*$BZ$13)
Y83: PR [W1] ^||
Z83: PR [W1] ^|
G84: PR [W45] 'Capitol Outlay
H84: (,0) U @IF(@ISERR(H40*$BZ$13),0,H40*$BZ$13)
I84: (,0) U [W9] @IF(@ISERR(I40*$BZ$13),0,I40*$BZ$13)
J84: (,0) U @IF(@ISERR(J40*$BZ$13),0,J40*$BZ$13)
K84: (,0) U [W9] @IF(@ISERR(K40*$BZ$13),0,K40*$BZ$13)
L84: (,0) U @IF(@ISERR(L40*$BZ$13),0,L40*$BZ$13)
M84: (,0) U @IF(@ISERR(M40*$BZ$13),0,M40*$BZ$13)
N84: PR [W1] ||
O84: (,0) U @IF(@ISERR(O40*$BZ$13),0,O40*$BZ$13)
P84: PR [W1] ||
Q84: (,0) U @IF(@ISERR(Q40*$BZ$13),0,Q40*$BZ$13)
R84: (,0) U [W9] @IF(@ISERR(R40*$BZ$13),0,R40*$BZ$13)
S84: (,0) U @IF(@ISERR(S40*$BZ$13),0,S40*$BZ$13)
T84: (,0) U [W9] @IF(@ISERR(T40*$BZ$13),0,T40*$BZ$13)
U84: (,0) U @IF(@ISERR(U40*$BZ$13),0,U40*$BZ$13)
V84: (,0) U @IF(@ISERR(V40*$BZ$13),0,V40*$BZ$13)
W84: PR [W1] ||
X84: (,0) U @IF(@ISERR(X40*$BZ$13),0,X40*$BZ$13)
Y84: PR [W1] ^||
Z84: PR [W1] ^|
H85: (,0) U @IF(@ISERR(H41*$BZ$13),0,H41*$BZ$13)
I85: (,0) U [W9] @IF(@ISERR(I41*$BZ$13),0,I41*$BZ$13)
J85: (,0) U @IF(@ISERR(J41*$BZ$13),0,J41*$BZ$13)
K85: (,0) U [W9] @IF(@ISERR(K41*$BZ$13),0,K41*$BZ$13)
```

continued...

...from previous page

```
L85: (,0)  U  @IF(@ISERR(L41*$BZ$13),0,L41*$BZ$13)
M85: (,0)  U  @IF(@ISERR(M41*$BZ$13),0,M41*$BZ$13)
N85: PR [W1] ||
O85: (,0)  U  @IF(@ISERR(O41*$BZ$13),0,O41*$BZ$13)
P85: PR [W1] ||
Q85: (,0)  U  @IF(@ISERR(Q41*$BZ$13),0,Q41*$BZ$13)
R85: (,0)  U  [W9] @IF(@ISERR(R41*$BZ$13),0,R41*$BZ$13)
S85: (,0)  U  @IF(@ISERR(S41*$BZ$13),0,S41*$BZ$13)
T85: (,0)  U  [W9] @IF(@ISERR(T41*$BZ$13),0,T41*$BZ$13)
U85: (,0)  U  @IF(@ISERR(U41*$BZ$13),0,U41*$BZ$13)
V85: (,0)  U  @IF(@ISERR(V41*$BZ$13),0,V41*$BZ$13)
W85: PR [W1] ||
X85: (,0)  U  @IF(@ISERR(X41*$BZ$13),0,X41*$BZ$13)
Y85: PR [W1] ^||
G86: PR [W45] 'TOTAL
H86: (,0)  U  @IF(@ISERR(H42*$BZ$13),0,H42*$BZ$13)
I86: (,0)  U  [W9] @IF(@ISERR(I42*$BZ$13),0,I42*$BZ$13)
J86: (,0)  U  @IF(@ISERR(J42*$BZ$13),0,J42*$BZ$13)
K86: (,0)  U  [W9] @IF(@ISERR(K42*$BZ$13),0,K42*$BZ$13)
L86: (,0)  U  @IF(@ISERR(L42*$BZ$13),0,L42*$BZ$13)
M86: (,0)  U  @IF(@ISERR(M42*$BZ$13),0,M42*$BZ$13)
N86: PR [W1] ||
O86: (,0)  U  @IF(@ISERR(O42*$BZ$13),0,O42*$BZ$13)
P86: PR [W1] ||
Q86: (,0)  U  @IF(@ISERR(Q42*$BZ$13),0,Q42*$BZ$13)
R86: (,0)  U  [W9] @IF(@ISERR(R42*$BZ$13),0,R42*$BZ$13)
S86: (,0)  U  @IF(@ISERR(S42*$BZ$13),0,S42*$BZ$13)
T86: (,0)  U  [W9] @IF(@ISERR(T42*$BZ$13),0,T42*$BZ$13)
U86: (,0)  U  @IF(@ISERR(U42*$BZ$13),0,U42*$BZ$13)
V86: (,0)  U  @IF(@ISERR(V42*$BZ$13),0,V42*$BZ$13)
W86: PR [W1] ||
X86: (,0)  U  @IF(@ISERR(X42*$BZ$13),0,X42*$BZ$13)
Y86: PR [W1] ^||
Z86: PR [W1] ^|
H87: U '========
I87: U [W9] '========
J87: U '========
K87: U [W9] '========
L87: U '========
```

continued...

...from previous page

```
M87: U '========
N87: PR [W1] ^|
O87: U '========
P87: PR [W1] ^|
Q87: U '========
R87: U [W9] '========
S87: U '========
T87: U [W9] '========
U87: U '========
V87: U '========
W87: PR [W1] ^|
X87: U '========
Y87: PR [W1] ^||
Z87: PR [W1] ^|
H88: (H) U @NA
I88: (H) U [W9] @NA
J88: (H) U @NA
K88: (H) U [W9] @NA
L88: (H) U @NA
M88: (H) U @NA
N88: PR [W1] ||
O88: (H) U @NA
P88: PR [W1] ||
Q88: (H) U @NA
R88: (H) U [W9] @NA
S88: (H) U @NA
T88: (H) U [W9] @NA
U88: (H) U @NA
V88: (H) U @NA
W88: PR [W1] ||
X88: (H) U 99999
Y88: PR [W1] ^||
Z88: PR [W1] ^|
G89: PR [W45] \=
H89: PR \=
I89: PR [W9] \=
J89: PR \=
K89: PR [W9] \=
L89: PR \=
```

continued...

...from previous page

```
M89: PR \=
N89: PR [W1] \=
O89: PR \=
P89: PR [W1] \=
Q89: PR \=
R89: PR [W9] \=
S89: PR \=
T89: PR [W9] \=
U89: PR \=
V89: PR \=
W89: PR [W1] \=
X89: PR \=
Y89: PR [W1] \=
Z89: PR [W1] \=
N90: (H) PR [W1] @NA
P90: (H) PR [W1] @NA
W90: (H) PR [W1] @NA
Y90: PR [W1] ^|
Z90: PR [W1] ^|
```

Cell Listing: Figure 7.5

```
AH65: PR [W45] 'SCHEDULE DR:  SUMMARY OF DEFLATED ACTUAL AND REQUEST
      BUDGET RATIOS
AR65: PR [W2] ^||
AH66: PR [W45] 'UNIT:  Department of Public Works
AR66: PR [W2] ^||
AH67: PR [W45] '\=
AI67: PR [W15] \=
AJ67: PR [W15] \=
AK67: PR [W13] \=
AL67: PR [W13] \=
AM67: PR [W13] \=
AN67: PR [W13] \=
AO67: PR [W13] \=
AP67: PR [W13] \=
AQ67: PR [W13] \=
AR67: PR [W2] |||
AH68: PR [W45] "Deflator Factor:
AI68: (P2) PR [W15] +BZ12*0.01
AR68: PR [W2] ^||
AK69: (G) PR [W13] ^1986-87
AM69: PR [W13] ^1987-88
AO69: PR [W13] ^1988-89
AQ69: PR [W13] ^1989-90
AR69: PR [W2] ^||
AI70: PR [W15] ^% Total Exp
AJ70: PR [W15] ^% Total Exp
AK70: PR [W13] ^% Change
AL70: PR [W13] ^% Total Exp
AM70: PR [W13] ^% Change
AN70: PR [W13] ^% Total Exp
AO70: PR [W13] ^% Change
AP70: PR [W13] ^% Total Exp
AQ70: PR [W13] ^% Change
AR70: PR [W2] ^||
AI71: PR [W15] ^1985-86
AJ71: PR [W15] ^1986-87
AK71: PR [W13] ^Previous
AL71: PR [W13] ^1987-88
AM71: PR [W13] ^From Previous
```

continued...

...from previous page

```
AN71: PR [W13] ^1988-89
AO71: PR [W13] ^From Previous
AP71: PR [W13] ^1989-90
AQ71: PR [W13] ^From Previous
AR71: PR [W2] ^||
AH72: PR [W45] 'Personal Services:
AI72: PR [W15] ^Actual
AJ72: PR [W15] ^Actual
AK72: PR [W13] ^Year
AL72: PR [W13] ^Budgeted
AM72: PR [W13] ^Year
AN72: PR [W13] ^Requested
AO72: PR [W13] ^Year
AP72: PR [W13] ^Requested
AQ72: PR [W13] ^Year
AR72: PR [W2] ^||
AK73: (P2) U [W13] @IF(@ISERR((AC73-AB73)/AB73),0,(AC73-AB73)/AB73)
AM73: (P2) U [W13] @IF(@ISERR((AD73-AC73)/AC73),0,(AD73-AC73)/AC73)
AO73: (P2) U [W13] @IF(@ISERR((AE73-AD73)/AD73),0,(AE73-AD73)/AD73)
AQ73: (P2) U [W13] @IF(@ISERR((AF73-AE73)/AE73),0,(AF73-AE73)/AE73)
AR73: PR [W2] ^||
AH74: PR [W45] +AH10
AI74: (P2) U [W15] (AB74/$AB$106)
AJ74: (P2) U [W15] (AC74/$AC$106)
AK74: (P2) U [W13] @IF(@ISERR((AC74-AB74)/AB74),0,(AC74-AB74)/AB74)
AL74: (P2) U [W13] (AD74/$AD$106)
AM74: (P2) U [W13] @IF(@ISERR((AD74-AC74)/AC74),0,(AD74-AC74)/AC74)
AN74: (P2) U [W13] (AE74/$AE$106)
AO74: (P2) U [W13] @IF(@ISERR((AE74-AD74)/AD74),0,(AE74-AD74)/AD74)
AP74: (P2) U [W13] (AF74/$AF$106)
AQ74: (P2) U [W13] @IF(@ISERR((AF74-AE74)/AE74),0,(AF74-AE74)/AE74)
AR74: PR [W2] ^||
AH75: PR [W45] +AH11
AI75: (P2) U [W15] (AB75/$AB$106)
AJ75: (P2) U [W15] (AC75/$AC$106)
AK75: (P2) U [W13] @IF(@ISERR((AC75-AB75)/AB75),0,(AC75-AB75)/AB75)
AL75: (P2) U [W13] (AD75/$AD$106)
AM75: (P2) U [W13] @IF(@ISERR((AD75-AC75)/AC75),0,(AD75-AC75)/AC75)
AN75: (P2) U [W13] (AE75/$AE$106)
```

continued...

...from previous page

```
AO75: (P2) U [W13] @IF(@ISERR((AE75-AD75)/AD75),0,(AE75-AD75)/AD75)
AP75: (P2) U [W13] (AF75/$AF$106)
AQ75: (P2) U [W13] @IF(@ISERR((AF75-AE75)/AE75),0,(AF75-AE75)/AE75)
AR75: PR [W2] ^||
AI76: (P2) U [W15] (AB76/$AB$106)
AR76: PR [W2] ^||
AH77: PR [W45] 'Supporting Services:
AI77: (P2) U [W15] (AB77/$AB$106)
AR77: PR [W2] ^||
AH78: PR [W45] +AH14
AI78: (P2) U [W15] (AB78/$AB$106)
AJ78: (P2) U [W15] (AC78/$AC$106)
AK78: (P2) U [W13] @IF(@ISERR((AC78-AB78)/AB78),0,(AC78-AB78)/AB78)
AL78: (P2) U [W13] (AD78/$AD$106)
AM78: (P2) U [W13] @IF(@ISERR((AD78-AC78)/AC78),0,(AD78-AC78)/AC78)
AN78: (P2) U [W13] (AE78/$AE$106)
AO78: (P2) U [W13] @IF(@ISERR((AE78-AD78)/AD78),0,(AE78-AD78)/AD78)
AP78: (P2) U [W13] (AF78/$AF$106)
AQ78: (P2) U [W13] @IF(@ISERR((AF78-AE78)/AE78),0,(AF78-AE78)/AE78)
AR78: PR [W2] ^||
AH79: PR [W45] +AH15
AI79: (P2) U [W15] (AB79/$AB$106)
AJ79: (P2) U [W15] (AC79/$AC$106)
AK79: (P2) U [W13] @IF(@ISERR((AC79-AB79)/AB79),0,(AC79-AB79)/AB79)
AL79: (P2) U [W13] (AD79/$AD$106)
AM79: (P2) U [W13] @IF(@ISERR((AD79-AC79)/AC79),0,(AD79-AC79)/AC79)
AN79: (P2) U [W13] (AE79/$AE$106)
AO79: (P2) U [W13] @IF(@ISERR((AE79-AD79)/AD79),0,(AE79-AD79)/AD79)
AP79: (P2) U [W13] (AF79/$AF$106)
AQ79: (P2) U [W13] @IF(@ISERR((AF79-AE79)/AE79),0,(AF79-AE79)/AE79)
AR79: PR [W2] ^||
AH80: PR [W45] +AH16
AI80: (P2) U [W15] (AB80/$AB$106)
AJ80: (P2) U [W15] (AC80/$AC$106)
AK80: (P2) U [W13] @IF(@ISERR((AC80-AB80)/AB80),0,(AC80-AB80)/AB80)
AL80: (P2) U [W13] (AD80/$AD$106)
AM80: (P2) U [W13] @IF(@ISERR((AD80-AC80)/AC80),0,(AD80-AC80)/AC80)
AN80: (P2) U [W13] (AE80/$AE$106)
AO80: (P2) U [W13] @IF(@ISERR((AE80-AD80)/AD80),0,(AE80-AD80)/AD80)
```

continued...

...from previous page

```
AP80: (P2) U [W13] (AF80/$AF$106)
AQ80: (P2) U [W13] @IF(@ISERR((AF80-AE80)/AE80),0,(AF80-AE80)/AE80)
AR80: PR [W2] ^||
AH81: PR [W45] +AH17
AI81: (P2) U [W15] (AB81/$AB$106)
AJ81: (P2) U [W15] (AC81/$AC$106)
AK81: (P2) U [W13] @IF(@ISERR((AC81-AB81)/AB81),0,(AC81-AB81)/AB81)
AL81: (P2) U [W13] (AD81/$AD$106)
AM81: (P2) U [W13] @IF(@ISERR((AD81-AC81)/AC81),0,(AD81-AC81)/AC81)
AN81: (P2) U [W13] (AE81/$AE$106)
AO81: (P2) U [W13] @IF(@ISERR((AE81-AD81)/AD81),0,(AE81-AD81)/AD81)
AP81: (P2) U [W13] (AF81/$AF$106)
AQ81: (P2) U [W13] @IF(@ISERR((AF81-AE81)/AE81),0,(AF81-AE81)/AE81)
AR81: PR [W2] ^||
AH82: PR [W45] +AH18
AI82: (P2) U [W15] (AB82/$AB$106)
AJ82: (P2) U [W15] (AC82/$AC$106)
AK82: (P2) U [W13] @IF(@ISERR((AC82-AB82)/AB82),0,(AC82-AB82)/AB82)
AL82: (P2) U [W13] (AD82/$AD$106)
AM82: (P2) U [W13] @IF(@ISERR((AD82-AC82)/AC82),0,(AD82-AC82)/AC82)
AN82: (P2) U [W13] (AE82/$AE$106)
AO82: (P2) U [W13] @IF(@ISERR((AE82-AD82)/AD82),0,(AE82-AD82)/AD82)
AP82: (P2) U [W13] (AF82/$AF$106)
AQ82: (P2) U [W13] @IF(@ISERR((AF82-AE82)/AE82),0,(AF82-AE82)/AE82)
AR82: PR [W2] ^||
AH83: PR [W45] +AH19
AI83: (P2) U [W15] (AB83/$AB$106)
AJ83: (P2) U [W15] (AC83/$AC$106)
AK83: (P2) U [W13] @IF(@ISERR((AC83-AB83)/AB83),0,(AC83-AB83)/AB83)
AL83: (P2) U [W13] (AD83/$AD$106)
AM83: (P2) U [W13] @IF(@ISERR((AD83-AC83)/AC83),0,(AD83-AC83)/AC83)
AN83: (P2) U [W13] (AE83/$AE$106)
AO83: (P2) U [W13] @IF(@ISERR((AE83-AD83)/AD83),0,(AE83-AD83)/AD83)
AP83: (P2) U [W13] (AF83/$AF$106)
AQ83: (P2) U [W13] @IF(@ISERR((AF83-AE83)/AE83),0,(AF83-AE83)/AE83)
AR83: PR [W2] ^||
AH84: PR [W45] +AH20
AI84: (P2) U [W15] (AB84/$AB$106)
AJ84: (P2) U [W15] (AC84/$AC$106)
```

continued...

...from previous page

```
AK84: (P2) U [W13] @IF(@ISERR((AC84-AB84)/AB84),0,(AC84-AB84)/AB84)
AL84: (P2) U [W13] (AD84/$AD$106)
AM84: (P2) U [W13] @IF(@ISERR((AD84-AC84)/AC84),0,(AD84-AC84)/AC84)
AN84: (P2) U [W13] (AE84/$AE$106)
AO84: (P2) U [W13] @IF(@ISERR((AE84-AD84)/AD84),0,(AE84-AD84)/AD84)
AP84: (P2) U [W13] (AF84/$AF$106)
AQ84: (P2) U [W13] @IF(@ISERR((AF84-AE84)/AE84),0,(AF84-AE84)/AE84)
AR84: PR [W2] ^||
AH85: PR [W45] +AH21
AI85: (P2) U [W15] (AB85/$AB$106)
AJ85: (P2) U [W15] (AC85/$AC$106)
AK85: (P2) U [W13] @IF(@ISERR((AC85-AB85)/AB85),0,(AC85-AB85)/AB85)
AL85: (P2) U [W13] (AD85/$AD$106)
AM85: (P2) U [W13] @IF(@ISERR((AD85-AC85)/AC85),0,(AD85-AC85)/AC85)
AN85: (P2) U [W13] (AE85/$AE$106)
AO85: (P2) U [W13] @IF(@ISERR((AE85-AD85)/AD85),0,(AE85-AD85)/AD85)
AP85: (P2) U [W13] (AF85/$AF$106)
AQ85: (P2) U [W13] @IF(@ISERR((AF85-AE85)/AE85),0,(AF85-AE85)/AE85)
AR85: PR [W2] ^||
AH86: PR [W45] +AH22
AI86: (P2) U [W15] (AB86/$AB$106)
AJ86: (P2) U [W15] (AC86/$AC$106)
AK86: (P2) U [W13] @IF(@ISERR((AC86-AB86)/AB86),0,(AC86-AB86)/AB86)
AL86: (P2) U [W13] (AD86/$AD$106)
AM86: (P2) U [W13] @IF(@ISERR((AD86-AC86)/AC86),0,(AD86-AC86)/AC86)
AN86: (P2) U [W13] (AE86/$AE$106)
AO86: (P2) U [W13] @IF(@ISERR((AE86-AD86)/AD86),0,(AE86-AD86)/AD86)
AP86: (P2) U [W13] (AF86/$AF$106)
AQ86: (P2) U [W13] @IF(@ISERR((AF86-AE86)/AE86),0,(AF86-AE86)/AE86)
AR86: PR [W2] ^||
AH87: PR [W45] +AH23
AI87: (P2) U [W15] (AB87/$AB$106)
AJ87: (P2) U [W15] (AC87/$AC$106)
AK87: (P2) U [W13] @IF(@ISERR((AC87-AB87)/AB87),0,(AC87-AB87)/AB87)
AL87: (P2) U [W13] (AD87/$AD$106)
AM87: (P2) U [W13] @IF(@ISERR((AD87-AC87)/AC87),0,(AD87-AC87)/AC87)
AN87: (P2) U [W13] (AE87/$AE$106)
AO87: (P2) U [W13] @IF(@ISERR((AE87-AD87)/AD87),0,(AE87-AD87)/AD87)
AP87: (P2) U [W13] (AF87/$AF$106)
```

continued...

...from previous page

```
AQ87: (P2) U [W13] @IF(@ISERR((AF87-AE87)/AE87),0,(AF87-AE87)/AE87)
AR87: PR [W2] ^||
AH88: PR [W45] +AH24
AI88: (P2) U [W15] (AB88/$AB$106)
AJ88: (P2) U [W15] (AC88/$AC$106)
AK88: (P2) U [W13] @IF(@ISERR((AC88-AB88)/AB88),0,(AC88-AB88)/AB88)
AL88: (P2) U [W13] (AD88/$AD$106)
AM88: (P2) U [W13] @IF(@ISERR((AD88-AC88)/AC88),0,(AD88-AC88)/AC88)
AN88: (P2) U [W13] (AE88/$AE$106)
AO88: (P2) U [W13] @IF(@ISERR((AE88-AD88)/AD88),0,(AE88-AD88)/AD88)
AP88: (P2) U [W13] (AF88/$AF$106)
AQ88: (P2) U [W13] @IF(@ISERR((AF88-AE88)/AE88),0,(AF88-AE88)/AE88)
AR88: PR [W2] ^||
AH89: PR [W45] +AH25
AI89: (P2) U [W15] (AB89/$AB$106)
AJ89: (P2) U [W15] (AC89/$AC$106)
AK89: (P2) U [W13] @IF(@ISERR((AC89-AB89)/AB89),0,(AC89-AB89)/AB89)
AL89: (P2) U [W13] (AD89/$AD$106)
AM89: (P2) U [W13] @IF(@ISERR((AD89-AC89)/AC89),0,(AD89-AC89)/AC89)
AN89: (P2) U [W13] (AE89/$AE$106)
AO89: (P2) U [W13] @IF(@ISERR((AE89-AD89)/AD89),0,(AE89-AD89)/AD89)
AP89: (P2) U [W13] (AF89/$AF$106)
AQ89: (P2) U [W13] @IF(@ISERR((AF89-AE89)/AE89),0,(AF89-AE89)/AE89)
AR89: PR [W2] ^||
AH90: PR [W45] +AH26
AI90: (P2) U [W15] (AB90/$AB$106)
AJ90: (P2) U [W15] (AC90/$AC$106)
AK90: (P2) U [W13] @IF(@ISERR((AC90-AB90)/AB90),0,(AC90-AB90)/AB90)
AL90: (P2) U [W13] (AD90/$AD$106)
AM90: (P2) U [W13] @IF(@ISERR((AD90-AC90)/AC90),0,(AD90-AC90)/AC90)
AN90: (P2) U [W13] (AE90/$AE$106)
AO90: (P2) U [W13] @IF(@ISERR((AE90-AD90)/AD90),0,(AE90-AD90)/AD90)
AP90: (P2) U [W13] (AF90/$AF$106)
AQ90: (P2) U [W13] @IF(@ISERR((AF90-AE90)/AE90),0,(AF90-AE90)/AE90)
AR90: PR [W2] ^||
AH91: PR [W45] +AH27
AI91: (P2) U [W15] (AB91/$AB$106)
AJ91: (P2) U [W15] (AC91/$AC$106)
AK91: (P2) U [W13] @IF(@ISERR((AC91-AB91)/AB91),0,(AC91-AB91)/AB91)
```

continued...

...from previous page

```
AL91: (P2) U [W13] (AD91/$AD$106)
AM91: (P2) U [W13] @IF(@ISERR((AD91-AC91)/AC91),0,(AD91-AC91)/AC91)
AN91: (P2) U [W13] (AE91/$AE$106)
AO91: (P2) U [W13] @IF(@ISERR((AE91-AD91)/AD91),0,(AE91-AD91)/AD91)
AP91: (P2) U [W13] (AF91/$AF$106)
AQ91: (P2) U [W13] @IF(@ISERR((AF91-AE91)/AE91),0,(AF91-AE91)/AE91)
AR91: PR [W2] ^||
AH92: PR [W45] +AH28
AI92: (P2) U [W15] (AB92/$AB$106)
AJ92: (P2) U [W15] (AC92/$AC$106)
AK92: (P2) U [W13] @IF(@ISERR((AC92-AB92)/AB92),0,(AC92-AB92)/AB92)
AL92: (P2) U [W13] (AD92/$AD$106)
AM92: (P2) U [W13] @IF(@ISERR((AD92-AC92)/AC92),0,(AD92-AC92)/AC92)
AN92: (P2) U [W13] (AE92/$AE$106)
AO92: (P2) U [W13] @IF(@ISERR((AE92-AD92)/AD92),0,(AE92-AD92)/AD92)
AP92: (P2) U [W13] (AF92/$AF$106)
AQ92: (P2) U [W13] @IF(@ISERR((AF92-AE92)/AE92),0,(AF92-AE92)/AE92)
AR92: PR [W2] ^||
AH93: PR [W45] +AH29
AI93: (P2) U [W15] (AB93/$AB$106)
AR93: PR [W2] ^||
AH94: PR [W45] +AH30
AI94: (P2) U [W15] (AB94/$AB$106)
AJ94: (P2) U [W15] (AC94/$AC$106)
AK94: (P2) U [W13] @IF(@ISERR((AC94-AB94)/AB94),0,(AC94-AB94)/AB94)
AL94: (P2) U [W13] (AD94/$AD$106)
AM94: (P2) U [W13] @IF(@ISERR((AD94-AC94)/AC94),0,(AD94-AC94)/AC94)
AN94: (P2) U [W13] (AE94/$AE$106)
AO94: (P2) U [W13] @IF(@ISERR((AE94-AD94)/AD94),0,(AE94-AD94)/AD94)
AP94: (P2) U [W13] (AF94/$AF$106)
AQ94: (P2) U [W13] @IF(@ISERR((AF94-AE94)/AE94),0,(AF94-AE94)/AE94)
AR94: PR [W2] ^||
AH95: PR [W45] +AH31
AI95: (P2) U [W15] (AB95/$AB$106)
AJ95: (P2) U [W15] (AC95/$AC$106)
AK95: (P2) U [W13] @IF(@ISERR((AC95-AB95)/AB95),0,(AC95-AB95)/AB95)
AL95: (P2) U [W13] (AD95/$AD$106)
AM95: (P2) U [W13] @IF(@ISERR((AD95-AC95)/AC95),0,(AD95-AC95)/AC95)
AN95: (P2) U [W13] (AE95/$AE$106)
```

continued...

...from previous page

```
AO95: (P2) U [W13] @IF(@ISERR((AE95-AD95)/AD95),0,(AE95-AD95)/AD95)
AP95: (P2) U [W13] (AF95/$AF$106)
AQ95: (P2) U [W13] @IF(@ISERR((AF95-AE95)/AE95),0,(AF95-AE95)/AE95)
AR95: PR [W2] ^||
AI96: (P2) U [W15] (AB96/$AB$106)
AR96: PR [W2] ^||
AI97: (P2) U [W15] (AB97/$AB$106)
AR97: PR [W2] ^||
AH98: PR [W45] +AH34
AI98: (P2) U [W15] (AB98/$AB$106)
AR98: PR [W2] ^||
AH99: PR [W45] +AH35
AI99: (P2) U [W15] (AB99/$AB$106)
AJ99: (P2) U [W15] (AC99/$AC$106)
AK99: (P2) U [W13] @IF(@ISERR((AC99-AB99)/AB99),0,(AC99-AB99)/AB99)
AL99: (P2) U [W13] (AD99/$AD$106)
AM99: (P2) U [W13] @IF(@ISERR((AD99-AC99)/AC99),0,(AD99-AC99)/AC99)
AN99: (P2) U [W13] (AE99/$AE$106)
AO99: (P2) U [W13] @IF(@ISERR((AE99-AD99)/AD99),0,(AE99-AD99)/AD99)
AP99: (P2) U [W13] (AF99/$AF$106)
AQ99: (P2) U [W13] @IF(@ISERR((AF99-AE99)/AE99),0,(AF99-AE99)/AE99)
AR99: PR [W2] ^||
AH100: PR [W45] +AH36
AI100: (P2) U [W15] (AB100/$AB$106)
AJ100: (P2) U [W15] (AC100/$AC$106)
AK100: (P2) U [W13] @IF(@ISERR((AC100-AB100)/AB100),0,(AC100-AB100)
      /AB100)
AL100: (P2) U [W13] (AD100/$AD$106)
AM100: (P2) U [W13] @IF(@ISERR((AD100-AC100)/AC100),0,(AD100-AC100)
      /AC100)
AN100: (P2) U [W13] (AE100/$AE$106)
AO100: (P2) U [W13] @IF(@ISERR((AE100-AD100)/AD100),0,(AE100-AD100)
      /AD100)
AP100: (P2) U [W13] (AF100/$AF$106)
AQ100: (P2) U [W13] @IF(@ISERR((AF100-AE100)/AE100),0,(AF100-AE100)
      /AE100)
AR100: PR [W2] ^||
AH101: PR [W45] +AH37
```

continued...

...from previous page

```
AI101: (P2) U [W15] (AB101/$AB$106)
AJ101: (P2) U [W15] (AC101/$AC$106)
AK101: (P2) U [W13] @IF(@ISERR((AC101-AB101)/AB101),0,(AC101-AB101)
       /AB101)
AL101: (P2) U [W13] (AD101/$AD$106)
AM101: (P2) U [W13] @IF(@ISERR((AD101-AC101)/AC101),0,(AD101-AC101)
       /AC101)
AN101: (P2) U [W13] (AE101/$AE$106)
AO101: (P2) U [W13] @IF(@ISERR((AE101-AD101)/AD101),0,(AE101-AD101)
       /AD101)
AP101: (P2) U [W13] (AF101/$AF$106)
AQ101: (P2) U [W13] @IF(@ISERR((AF101-AE101)/AE101),0,(AF101-AE101)
       /AE101)
AR101: PR [W2] ^||
AI102: (P2) U [W15] (AB102/$AB$106)
AR102: PR [W2] ^||
AI103: (P2) U [W15] (AB103/$AB$106)
AR103: PR [W2] ^||
AH104: PR [W45] +AH40
AI104: (P2) U [W15] (AB104/$AB$106)
AJ104: (P2) U [W15] (AC104/$AC$106)
AK104: (P2) U [W13] @IF(@ISERR((AC104-AB104)/AB104),0,(AC104-AB104)
       /AB104)
AL104: (P2) U [W13] (AD104/$AD$106)
AM104: (P2) U [W13] @IF(@ISERR((AD104-AC104)/AC104),0,(AD104-AC104)
       /AC104)
AN104: (P2) U [W13] (AE104/$AE$106)
AO104: (P2) U [W13] @IF(@ISERR((AE104-AD104)/AD104),0,(AE104-AD104)
       /AD104)
AP104: (P2) U [W13] (AF104/$AF$106)
AQ104: (P2) U [W13] @IF(@ISERR((AF104-AE104)/AE104),0,(AF104-AE104)
       /AE104)
AR104: PR [W2] |||
AI105: (P2) U [W15] (AB105/$AB$106)
AJ105: (P2) U [W15] "----------
AK105: (P2) U [W13] "----------
AL105: (P2) U [W13] "----------
AM105: (P2) U [W13] "----------
AN105: (P2) U [W13] "----------
```

continued...

...from previous page

```
AO105: (P2) U [W13] "----------
AP105: (P2) U [W13] "----------
AQ105: (P2) U [W13] "----------
AR105: PR [W2] ^||
AH106: PR [W45] +AH42
AI106: (P2) U [W15] (AB106/$AB$106)
AJ106: (P2) U [W15] (AC106/$AC$106)
AK106: (P2) U [W13] @IF(@ISERR((AC106-AB106)/AB106),0,(AC106-AB106)
       /AB106)
AL106: (P2) U [W13] (AD106/$AD$106)
AM106: (P2) U [W13] @IF(@ISERR((AD106-AC106)/AC106),0,(AD106-AC106)
       /AC106)
AN106: (P2) U [W13] (AE106/$AE$106)
AO106: (P2) U [W13] @IF(@ISERR((AE106-AD106)/AD106),0,(AE106-AD106)
       /AD106)
AP106: (P2) U [W13] (AF106/$AF$106)
AQ106: (P2) U [W13] @IF(@ISERR((AF106-AE106)/AE106),0,(AF106-AE106)
       /AE106)
AR106: PR [W2] ^||
AI107: U [W15] "=========
AJ107: U [W15] "=========
AK107: U [W13] "=========
AL107: U [W13] "=========
AM107: U [W13] "=========
AN107: U [W13] "=========
AO107: U [W13] "=========
AP107: U [W13] "=========
AQ107: U [W13] "=========
AR107: (,0) PR [W2] |||
AH108: PR [W45] \=
AI108: PR [W15] \=
AJ108: PR [W15] \=
AK108: PR [W13] \=
AL108: PR [W13] \=
AM108: PR [W13] \=
AN108: PR [W13] \=
AO108: PR [W13] \=
AP108: PR [W13] \=
AQ108: PR [W13] \=
```

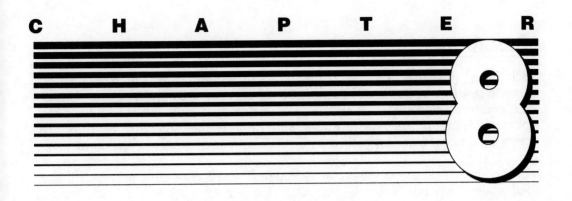

CHAPTER

8

SCHEDULE T

DESCRIPTION

Schedule T (Figure 8.1) includes expenditure projections based on a compounded growth rate factor calculated in terms of five-year averages of expenditure objects. Expenditure projections are arrayed alongside actual expenditures. Actual and projected expenditure differences and their percentage differentials are computed to compare expenditure objects within and across the biennium.

In the next section, you will create Schedule T and a data table on which it and Schedule F depend. You will create Schedule F in Chapter 9.

	AY	AZ	BA	BB	BC	BD	B
88 SCHEDULE T: BUDGET TREND PROJECTION MODEL [ANNUAL [FIVE-YEAR AVERAGE] COMPOUND GROWTH RATE WITH 1987-88 BASE YEAR]							
89 UNIT: Department of Public Works							
90							
91							
92				ANNUAL			
93				COMPOUND	PROJECTED	ACTUAL	DIFFERENCE % DIFFE
94				GROWTH RATE	REQUEST	REQUEST	REQUEST REQUE
95 Personal Services:				1983-88	1988-89	1988-89	1988-89 1988-
96 Man Years							
97 Salaries				4.16%	1,451,766	1,449,839	(1,927)
98 Benefits				0.00%	0	12,500	12,500
99						0	
100 Supporting Services:						0	
101 Travel				1.26%	64,809	64,960	151
102 Telephone Tolls and Rental				3.27%	16,269	15,754	(515)
103 Postage				5.63%	73,943	75,560	1,617
104 Rent - State Owned Buildings				4.75%	10,475	14,400	3,925 3
105 Rent - Privately Owned Buildings				5.40%	6,956	12,600	5,644 8
106 Building Improvements				40.64%	563	400	(163) -2
107 Utility Charges				25.88%	629	500	(129) -2
108 Rent of Data Processing Equipment				5.38%	48,479	46,000	(2,479) -
109 Rent of Office Equipment				2.58%	4,103	4,400	297
110 Maint. & Rep. of Office Equipment				0.00%	0	0	0
111 Maint. & Rep. of Ofc. Equip. - Contract				-0.12%	7,990	5,000	(2,990) -3
112 Maint. & Rep. of Automobile Vehicles				0.00%	0	0	0
113 Maint. & Rep. of Other Equipment				0.00%	0	0	0
114 Data Processing Contractual Service				192.19%	245,439	89,000	(156,439) -6
115 Insurance, Subscriptions, Brinks				6.16%	637	600	(37) -
116 Miscellaneous Services:						0	
117 Card Copiers				0.00%	0	0	0
118 Court Costs				0.00%	1,578	0	(1,578) -10
119						0	
120						0	
121 Other:						0	
122 Printing				200.29%	282,275	96,700	(185,575) -6
123 Office Supplies				14.75%	41,311	30,000	(11,311) -2
124 Revenue Stamps				0.00%	0	0	0
125						0	
126						0	
127 Capital Outlay				54.37%	53,295	56,523	3,228
128							
129 TOTAL				6.37%	1,987,217	1,974,736	(12,481) -0
130							
131							

Figure 8.1   Schedule T

BF	BG	BH	BI	BJ	BK	BL	BM		BN	BO	BP	BQ

PROJECTED REQUEST 1989-90	ACTUAL REQUEST 1989-90	DIFFERENCE REQUEST 1989-90	% DIFFERENCE REQUEST 1989-90					
1,512,142	1,553,500	41,358	2.74%					
0	17,500	17,500	0.00%					
		0						
		0						
65,628	74,500	8,872	13.52%					
16,801	15,754	(1,047)	-6.23%					
78,107	75,607	(2,500)	-3.20%					
10,972	14,400	3,428	31.25%					
7,332	13,600	6,268	85.49%					
791	400	(391)	-49.45%					
792	500	(292)	-36.90%					
51,092	46,000	(5,092)	-9.97%					
4,209	4,400	191	4.54%					
0	0	0	0.00%					
7,980	5,000	(2,980)	-37.34%					
0	0	0	0.00%					
0	0	0	0.00%					
717,145	94,000	(623,145)	-86.89%					
676	600	(76)	-11.27%					
		0						
0	0	0	0.00%					
1,578	0	(1,578)	-100.00%					
		0						
		0						
		0						
847,849	96,745	(750,904)	-88.59%					
47,407	30,000	(17,407)	-36.72%					
0	0	0	0.00%					
		0						
		0						
82,273	34,523	(47,750)	-58.04%					
2,113,843	2,077,029	(36,814)	-1.74%					

151

CONSTRUCTING SCHEDULE T

Before you create Schedule T, enter the data necessary to construct the Schedules T & F Data Table (see Figure 8.2). First, enter the table borders and the label, numerical, divider, and underscore data found in the range AX1..BC42. Next, enter the labels in the range BD6..BF7.

	AY	AZ	BA	BB	BC	BD	BE
1	SCHEDULES T & F DATA TABLE: SUMMARY OF ACTUAL EXPENDITURES [1981-87]						
2	UNIT: DEPARTMENT OF PUBLIC WORKS						
3							
4							
5							
6		1981-82	1982-83	1983-84	1984-85	1985-86	1986-87
7	Personal Services:	Actual	Actual	Actual	Actual	Actual	Actual
8	Man Years	85	88	90	90	98	1
9	Salaries	1,034,583	1,140,400	1,240,357	1,345,250	1,352,400	1,380,0
10	Benefits	0	0	0	0	0	
11							
12	Supporting Services:						
13	Travel	58,425	60,537	63,540	67,300	70,000	70,0
14	Telephone Tolls and Rental	12,600	13,475	12,800	13,500	14,000	14,6
15	Postage	55,093	53,550	53,701	55,890	60,000	69,0
16	Rent - State Owned Buildings	7,548	7,980	8,300	9,500	10,000	10,0
17	Rent - Privately Owned Buildings	4,986	5,100	5,400	6,000	6,600	6,6
18	Building Improvements	455	455	500	300	100	1
19	Utility Charges	175	189	200	225	250	2
20	Rent of Data Processing Equipment	35,435	35,500	36,395	37,880	40,100	45,2
21	Rent of Office Equipment	3,480	3,545	3,900	3,750	4,000	4,1
22	Maint. & Rep. of Office Equipment	325	350	350	350	0	
23	Maint. & Rep. of Ofc. Equip. - Contract	7,999	8,100	8,200	7,500	8,000	8,1
24	Maint. & Rep. of Automobile Vehicles	2,512	2,540	4,000	2,550	0	
25	Maint. & Rep. of Other Equipment	0	0	0	0	0	
26	Data Processing Contractual Service	7,039	7,350	7,500	7,600	80,000	82,0
27	Insurance, Subscriptions, Brinks	450	450	475	475	500	5
28	Miscellaneous Services:						
29	Card Copiers	0	0	0	0	0	
30	Court Costs	4,500	3,000	267	0	0	
31							
32							
33	Other:						
34	Printing	6,845	7,000	7,550	8,250	89,000	92,0
35	Office Supplies	19,005	19,200	19,467	20,500	24,000	24,0
36	Revenue Stamps	0	0	0	0	0	
37						0	
38							
39	Capital Outlay	5,962	5,980	6,255	6,503	7,306	12,0
40							
41	TOTAL	1,267,417	1,374,701	1,479,157	1,593,323	1,766,256	1,818,6
42							
43							
44							

Figure 8.2   Schedules T & F Data Table

BF	BG	BH	BI	BJ	BK	BL	BM	BN	BO	BP	BQ
								||		\=	{MENUBRAN
								||			{BRANCH F
								||			
								||		MENU=	A_SCHs
								||			GO TO SCH
1987-88								||			{MENUCALL
Actual								||			
101								||		FINISH=	{QUIT}
1,393,800								||			
0								||			
								||		SCHAM=	A_SCH
								||			GO TO SCH
64,000								||			{SCHAMA}
15,754								||			
70,000								||		SCHMA=	{GOTO}SCH
10,000								||			{BRANCH \
6,600								||			
400								||		SCHADM=	{GOTO}SCH
500								||			{BRANCH \
48,000								||			
4,000								||		B_SCHs	PC
0								||			GO TO SCH
8,000								||			{PCSCHBM}
0								||			
0								||		PCSCHBM=	
84,000								||			
600								||			
								||		MISCHBM=	
0								||			
1,578								||		WCSCHBM=	
								||			
								||			
94,000								||		NCSCHBM=	
36,000								||			
0								||		OCSCHBM=	
								||			
34,523								||		FFSCHBM=	
1,868,177								||			

Move to cell BD8, and enter +AB9 (1985-86 Actual Man Hours cell reference to Schedule A). Copy the entry in cell BD8 to the range BD8..BF42, erase any zeros that appear in rows not dedicated to expenditure objects, and edit the dividers and underscores in the ranges BD40..BF40 and BD42..BF42, respectively, so they are aligned to the right.

Once the data table is finished, enter the border and label entries for schedule T as shown in Figure 8.1. Split the screen horizontally, as depicted in Figure 8.3, with the Schedules T and F Data Table in the top window and Schedule T in the bottom window. Then, enter the following formula in cell BA97:

```
@IF(@ISERR((BB9-BA9)/BA9+(BC9-BB9)/BB9+(BD9-BC9)/BC9+(BE9-BD9)
/BD 9+(BF9-BE9)/BE9)/5),O,((BB9-BA9)/BA9+(BC9-BB9)/BB 9+(BD9-B
C9)/BC9+(BE9-BD9)/BD9+(BF9-BE9)/BE9)/5)
```

In addition to suppressing ERR messages, the above formula causes the data in cell BB9 (1984-85 salary expenditures data located in the Schedules T & F Data Table) to be subtracted from the data in cell BB9 (1983-84 salary expenditures data, also located in the data table) and the difference to be divided by the data in the former cell. The quotient is then added to quotients (entered and calculated the same way) through the budget year 1987-88, and the total of all quotients is divided by 5. The resulting percentage (4.16%) is the annual compound growth rate (five-year average) for salary expenditures between 1983 and 1985.

Copy the formula to the range BA98..BA129, and erase any resultant ERR messages.

To compute the projected expenditure requests for the 1988-89 budget year, enter the following into cell BB97:

```
(BA97*BF9)+BF9
```

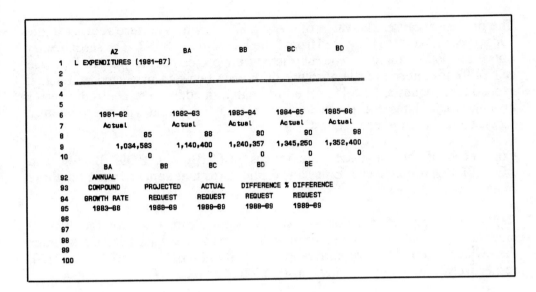

Figure 8.3   *Schedule T and Schedules T & F Data Table: Horizontally Split Screen*

This step multiplies the data in cell BF9 (actual salary expenditures for 1987-88 through the current budget year) by the formula in cell BA97 (the annual compound growth rate for salary expenditures). The resulting product is added to BF9 to create the 1988-89 projected request for salary expenditures.

Copy the contents of cell BB97 to range BB98..BB129, and erase any ERR messages.

Next, make the following entries:

1. Enter the value +AE10 in cell BC97.

2. Enter the formula +BC97-BB97 in cell BD97.

3. Enter the formula

    @IF(@ISERR((BC97-BB97)/BB97),0,(BC97-BB97)/BB97

    in cell BE97.

The first entry causes the value of the actual salary expenditure request in the budget year 1988-89 to be posted from Schedule A to cell BC97. The second entry causes the posted amount to be subtracted from projected salary expenditures in cell BB97 to determine the absolute difference between projected and actual expenditure requests, 1988-89. The third entry, in addition to controlling error messages, calculates the percentage change in the actual salary expenditure request and the projected request.

Copy each of the entries to the ranges BC97..BC129, BD97..BD129, and BE97..BE129, respectively. Erase any errant zeros that appear within the three ranges.

Replicate the preceding steps to construct similar categories for the 1989-90 biennium. Once all remaining formula-dependent entries have been made, enter the divider and underscore entries in ranges BA128..BI128 and BA130..BI130, respectively. This completes the construction of Schedule T.

Cell Listing: Figure 8.1

```
AX88: PR [W2] \|
AY88: PR [W45] ^SCHEDULE T:  BUDGET TREND PROJECTION MODEL(ANNUAL
      (FIVE-YEAR AVERAGE) COMPOUND GROWTH RATE WITH 1987-88 BASE
      YEAR)
AX89: PR [W2] \|
AY89: PR [W45] 'UNIT:  Department of Public Works
AX90: PR [W2] \|
AY90: PR [W45] \=
AZ90: PR [W20] \=
·BA90: PR [W15] \=
BB90: PR [W13] \=
BC90: PR [W12] \=
BD90: PR [W12] \=
BE90: PR [W12] \=
BF90: PR [W13] \=
BG90: PR [W12] \=
BH90: PR [W12] \=
BI90: PR [W12] \=
BJ90: PR [W12] \=
BK90: PR [W12] \=
BL90: PR [W12] \=
```

continued...

...from previous page

```
BM90: PR [W12] \=
AX91: PR [W2] \|
AX92: PR [W2] \|
BA92: PR [W15] ^ANNUAL
AX93: PR [W2] \|
BA93: PR [W15] ^COMPOUND
BB93: PR [W13] ^PROJECTED
BC93: PR [W12] ^ACTUAL
BD93: PR [W12] ^DIFFERENCE
BE93: PR [W12] ^% DIFFERENCE
BF93: PR [W13] ^PROJECTED
BG93: PR [W12] ^ACTUAL
BH93: PR [W12] ^DIFFERENCE
BI93: PR [W12] ^% DIFFERENCE
AX94: PR [W2] \|
BA94: PR [W15] ^GROWTH RATE
BB94: PR [W13] ^REQUEST
BC94: PR [W12] ^REQUEST
BD94: PR [W12] ^REQUEST
BE94: PR [W12] ^REQUEST
BF94: PR [W13] ^REQUEST
BG94: PR [W12] ^REQUEST
BH94: PR [W12] ^REQUEST
BI94: PR [W12] ^REQUEST
AX95: PR [W2] \|
AY95: PR [W45] 'Personal Services:
BA95: PR [W15] ^1983-88
BB95: PR [W13] ^1988-89
BC95: PR [W12] ^1988-89
BD95: PR [W12] ^1988-89
BE95: PR [W12] ^1988-89
BF95: PR [W13] ^1989-90
BG95: PR [W12] ^1989-90
BH95: PR [W12] ^1989-90
BI95: PR [W12] ^1989-90
AX96: PR [W2] \|
AY96: PR [W45] '    Man Years
BE96: (P2) PR [W12] ^
AX97: PR [W2] \|
```

continued...

...from previous page

```
AY97: PR [W45] '     Salaries
BA97: (P2) PR [W15] @IF(@ISERR((BB9-BA9)/BA9+(BC9-BB9)/BB9+(BD9-BC9)
                    9 +(BE9-BD9)/BD9+(BF9-BE9)/BE9/5),0,((BB9-BA9)/B
                    (BC9-BB9)/BB9+(BD9-BC9)/BC9+(BE9-BD9)/BD9+(BF9-B
                    /BE9)/5)
BB97: (,0) PR [W13] (BA97*BF9)+BF9
BC97: PR [W12] +AE10
BD97: PR [W12] +BC97-BB97
BE97: (P2) PR [W12] @IF(@ISERR((BC97-BB97)/BB97),0,(BC97-BB97)/BB97)
BF97: PR [W13] (BA97*BB97)+BB97
BG97: PR [W12] +AF10
BH97: PR [W12] +BG97-BF97
BI97: (P2) PR [W12] @IF(@ISERR((BG97-BF97)/BF97),0,(BG97-BF97)/BF97)
AX98: PR [W2] \|
AY98: PR [W45] '     Benefits
BA98: (P2) PR [W15] @IF(@ISERR((BB10-BA10)/BA10+(BC10-BB10)/BB10+(BD
                    BC10)/BC10+(BE10-BD10)/BD10+(BF10-BE10)/BE10 /5)
                    ((BB10-BA10)/BA10+(BC10-BB10)/BB10+(BD10-BC10)/B
                    +(BE10-BD10)/BD10+(BF10-BE10)/BE10)/5)
BB98: (,0) PR [W13] (BA98*BF10)+BF10
BC98: PR [W12] +AE11
BD98: PR [W12] +BC98-BB98
BE98: (P2) PR [W12] @IF(@ISERR((BC98-BB98)/BB98),0,(BC98-BB98)/BB98)
BF98: PR [W13] (BA98*BB98)+BB98
BG98: PR [W12] +AF11
BH98: PR [W12] +BG98-BF98
BI98: (P2) PR [W12] @IF(@ISERR((BG98-BF98)/BF98),0,(BG98-BF98)/BF98)
AX99: PR [W2] \|
BC99: PR [W12] +AE12
BG99: PR [W12] +AF12
AX100: PR [W2] \|
AY100: PR [W45] 'Supporting Services:
BC100: PR [W12] +AE13
BG100: PR [W12] +AF13
AX101: PR [W2] \|
AY101: PR [W45] '    Travel
BA101: (P2) PR [W15] @IF(@ISERR((BB13-BA13)/BA13+(BC13-BB13)/BB13+(BD
                    -BC13)/BC13+(BE13-BD13)/BD13+(BF13-BE113)/BE13/5
                    0,((BB13-BA13)/BA13+(BC13-BB13)/BB13+(BD13-BC13)
                    C13+(BE13-BD13)/BD13+(BF13-BE13)/BE13)/5)
```

continued...

...from previous page

```
BB101: (,0) PR [W13] (BA101*BF13)+BF13
BC101: PR [W12] +AE14
BD101: PR [W12] +BC101-BB101
BE101: (P2) PR [W12] @IF(@ISERR((BC101-BB101)/BB101),0,(BC101-BB101)/BB
              101)
BF101: PR [W13] (BA101*BB101)+BB101
BG101: PR [W12] +AF14
BH101: PR [W12] +BG101-BF101
BI101: (P2) PR [W12] @IF(@ISERR((BG101-BF101)/BF101),0,(BG101-BF101)/BF
              101)
AX102: PR [W2] \|
AY102: PR [W45] '    Telephone Tolls and Rental
BA102: (P2) PR [W15] @IF(@ISERR((BB14-BA14)/BA14+(BC14-BB14)/BB14+(BD14
              -BC14)/BC14+(BE14-BD14)/BD14+(BF14-BE14)/BE14/5),0
              ,((BB14-BA14)/BA14+(BC14-BB14)/BB14+(BD14-BC14)/BC
              14+(BE14-BD14)/BD14+(BF14-BE14)/BE14)/5)
BB102: (,0) PR [W13] (BA102*BF14)+BF14
BC102: PR [W12] +AE15
BD102: PR [W12] +BC102-BB102
BE102: (P2) PR [W12] @IF(@ISERR((BC102-BB102)/BB102),0,(BC102-BB102)/BB
              102)
BF102: PR [W13] (BA102*BB102)+BB102
BG102: PR [W12] +AF15
BH102: PR [W12] +BG102-BF102
BI102: (P2) PR [W12] @IF(@ISERR((BG102-BF102)/BF102),0,(BG102-BF102)/BF
              102)
AX103: PR [W2] \|
AY103: PR [W45] '    Postage
BA103: (P2) PR [W15] @IF(@ISERR((BB15-BA15)/BA15+(BC15-BB15)/BB15+(BD15
              -BC15)/BC15+(BE15-BD15)/BD15+(BF15-BE15)/BE15/5),0
              ,((BB15-BA15)/BA15+(BC15-BB15)/BB15+(BD15-BC15)/BC
              15+(BE15-BD15)/BD15+(BF15-BE15)/BE15)/5)
BB103: (,0) PR [W13] (BA103*BF15)+BF15
BC103: PR [W12] +AE16
BD103: PR [W12] +BC103-BB103
BE103: (P2) PR [W12] @IF(@ISERR((BC103-BB103)/BB103),0,(BC103-BB103)/BB
              103)
BF103: PR [W13] (BA103*BB103)+BB103
BG103: PR [W12] +AF16
```

continued...

...from previous page

```
BH103: PR [W12] +BG103-BF103
BI103: (P2) PR [W12] @IF(@ISERR((BG103-BF103)/BF103),0,(BG103-BF103)
                  103)
AX104: PR [W2] \|
AY104: PR [W45] '    Rent - State Owned Buildings
BA104: (P2) PR [W15] @IF(@ISERR((BB16-BA16)/BA16+(BC16-BB16)/BB16+(B
                  -BC16)/BC16+(BE16-BD16)/BD16+(BF16-BE16)/BE16/5
                  ,((BB16-BA16)/BA16+(BC16-BB16)/BB16+(BD16-BC16)
                  16+(BE16-BD16)/BD16+(BF16-BE16)/BE16)/5)
BB104: (,0) PR [W13] (BA104*BF16)+BF16
BC104: PR [W12] +AE17
BD104: PR [W12] +BC104-BB104
BE104: (P2) PR [W12] @IF(@ISERR((BC104-BB104)/BB104),0,(BC104-BB104)
                  104)
BF104: PR [W13] (BA104*BB104)+BB104
BG104: PR [W12] +AF17
BH104: PR [W12] +BG104-BF104
BI104: (P2) PR [W12] @IF(@ISERR((BG104-BF104)/BF104),0,(BG104-BF104)
                  104)
AX105: PR [W2] \|
AY105: PR [W45] '    Rent - Privately Owned Buildings
BA105: (P2) PR [W15] @IF(@ISERR((BB17-BA17)/BA17+(BC17-BB17)/BB17+(B
                  -BC17)/BC17+(BE17-BD17)/BD17+(BF17-BE17)/BE17/5
                  ,((BB17-BA17)/BA17+(BC17-BB17)/BB17+(BD17-BC17)
                  17+(BE17-BD17)/BD17+(BF17-BE17)/BE17)/5)
BB105: (,0) PR [W13] (BA105*BF17)+BF17
BC105: PR [W12] +AE18
BD105: PR [W12] +BC105-BB105
BE105: (P2) PR [W12] @IF(@ISERR((BC105-BB105)/BB105),0,(BC105-BB105)
                  105)
BF105: PR [W13] (BA105*BB105)+BB105
BG105: PR [W12] +AF18
BH105: PR [W12] +BG105-BF105
BI105: (P2) PR [W12] @IF(@ISERR((BG105-BF105)/BF105),0,(BG105-BF105)
                  105)
AX106: PR [W2] \|
AY106: PR [W45] '    Building Improvements
```

continued...

...from previous page

```
BA106: (P2) PR [W15] @IF(@ISERR((BB18-BA18)/BA18+(BC18-BB18)/BB18+(BD18
                      -BC18)/BC18+(B     E18-BD18)/BD18+(BF18-BE18)/BE18/
                      5),0,((BB18-BA18)/BA18+(BC18-BB18)/BB18+(BD18-BC18
                      )/BC18+(BE18-BD18)/BD18+(BF18-BE18)/BE18)/5)
BB106: (,0) PR [W13] (BA106*BF18)+BF18
BC106: PR [W12] +AE19
BD106: PR [W12] +BC106-BB106
BE106: (P2) PR [W12] @IF(@ISERR((BC106-BB106)/BB106),0,(BC106-BB106)/BB
                      106)
BF106: PR [W13] (BA106*BB106)+BB106
BG106: PR [W12] +AF19
BH106: PR [W12] +BG106-BF106
BI106: (P2) PR [W12] @IF(@ISERR((BG106-BF106)/BF106),0,(BG106-BF106)/BF
                      106)
AX107: PR [W2] \|
AY107: PR [W45] '    Utility Charges
BA107: (P2) PR [W15] @IF(@ISERR((BB19-BA19)/BA19+(BC19-BB19)/BB19+(BD19
                      -BC19)/BC19+(B     E19-BD19)/BD19+(BF19-BE19)/BE19/
                      5),0,((BB19-BA19)/BA19+(BC19-BB19)/BB19+(BD19-BC19
                      )/BC19+(BE19-BD19)/BD19+(BF19-BE19)/BE19)/5)
BB107: (,0) PR [W13] (BA107*BF19)+BF19
BC107: PR [W12] +AE20
BD107: PR [W12] +BC107-BB107
BE107: (P2) PR [W12] @IF(@ISERR((BC107-BB107)/BB107),0,(BC107-BB107)/BB
                      107)
BF107: PR [W13] (BA107*BB107)+BB107
BG107: PR [W12] +AF20
BH107: PR [W12] +BG107-BF107
BI107: (P2) PR [W12] @IF(@ISERR((BG107-BF107)/BF107),0,(BG107-BF107)/BF
                      107)
AX108: PR [W2] \|
AY108: PR [W45] '   Rent of Data Processing Equipment
BA108: (P2) PR [W15] @IF(@ISERR((BB20-BA20)/BA20+(BC20-BB20)/BB20+(BD20
                      -BC20)/BC20+(BE20-BD20)/BD20+(BF20-BE20)/BE20/5),0
                      ,((BB20-BA20)/BA20+(BC20-BB20)/BB20+(BD20-BC20)/BC
                      20+(BE20-BD20)/BD20+(BF20-BE    20)/BE20)/5)
BB108: (,0) PR [W13] (BA108*BF20)+BF20
BC108: PR [W12] +AE21
```

continued...

...from previous page

```
BD108: PR [W12] +BC108-BB108
BE108: (P2) PR [W12] @IF(@ISERR((BC108-BB108)/BB108),0,(BC108-BB108)
                    108)
BF108: PR [W13] (BA108*BB108)+BB108
BG108: PR [W12] +AF21
BH108: PR [W12] +BG108-BF108
BI108: (P2) PR [W12] @IF(@ISERR((BG108-BF108)/BF108),0,(BG108-BF108)
                    108)
AX109: PR [W2] \|
AY109: PR [W45] '    Rent of Office Equipment
BA109: (P2) PR [W15] @IF(@ISERR((BB21-BA21)/BA21+(BC21-BB21)/BB21+(B
                    -BC21)/BC21+(BE21-BD21)/BD21+(BF21-BE21)/BE21/5
                    ,((BB21-BA21)/BA21+(BC21-BB21)/BB21+(BD21-BC21)
                    21+(BE21-BD21)/BD21+(BF21-BE21)/BE21)/5)
BB109: (,0) PR [W13] (BA109*BF21)+BF21
BC109: PR [W12] +AE22
BD109: PR [W12] +BC109-BB109
BE109: (P2) PR [W12] @IF(@ISERR((BC109-BB109)/BB109),0,(BC109-BB109)
                    109)
BF109: PR [W13] (BA109*BB109)+BB109
BG109: PR [W12] +AF22
BH109: PR [W12] +BG109-BF109
BI109: (P2) PR [W12] @IF(@ISERR((BG109-BF109)/BF109),0,(BG109-BF109)
                    109)
AX110: PR [W2] \|
AY110: PR [W45] '    Maint. & Rep. of Office Equipment
BA110: (P2) PR [W15] @IF(@ISERR((BB22-BA22)/BA22+(BC22-BB22)/BB22+(BI
                    -BC22)/BC22+(BE22-BD22)/BD22+(BF22-BE22)/BE22/5
                    ,((BB22-BA  22)/BA22+(BC22-BB22)/BB22+(BD22-BC2
                    BC22+(BE22-BD22)/BD22+(BF22-BE22)/BE22)/5)
BB110: (,0) PR [W13] (BA110*BF22)+BF22
BC110: PR [W12] +AE23
BD110: PR [W12] +BC110-BB110
BE110: (P2) PR [W12] @IF(@ISERR((BC110-BB110)/BB110),0,(BC110-BB110)
                    110)
BF110: PR [W13] (BA110*BB110)+BB110
BG110: PR [W12] +AF23
BH110: PR [W12] +BG110-BF110
BI110: (P2) PR [W12] @IF(@ISERR((BG110-BF110)/BF110),0,(BG110-BF110)
                    110)
```

continued...

...from previous page

```
AX111: PR [W2] \|
AY111: PR [W45] '   Maint. & Rep. of Ofc. Equip. - Contract
BA111: (P2) PR [W15] @IF(@ISERR((BB23-BA23)/BA23+(BC23-BB23)/BB23+(BD23
                -BC23)/BC23+(B      E23-BD23)/BD23+(BF23-BE23)/BE23/
                5),0,((BB23-BA23)/BA23+(BC23-BB23)/BB23+(BD23-BC23
                )/BC23+(BE23-BD23)/BD23+(BF23-BE23)/BE23)/5)
BB111: (,0) PR [W13] (BA111*BF23)+BF23
BC111: PR [W12] +AE24
BD111: PR [W12] +BC111-BB111
BE111: (P2) PR [W12] @IF(@ISERR((BC111-BB111)/BB111),0,(BC111-BB111)/BB
                111)
BF111: PR [W13] (BA111*BB111)+BB111
BG111: PR [W12] +AF24
BH111: PR [W12] +BG111-BF111
BI111: (P2) PR [W12] @IF(@ISERR((BG111-BF111)/BF111),0,(BG111-BF111)/BF
                111)
AX112: PR [W2] \|
AY112: PR [W45] '   Maint. & Rep. of Automobile Vehicles
BA112: (P2) PR [W15] @IF(@ISERR((BB24-BA24)/BA24+(BC24-BB24)/BB24+(BD24
                -BC24)/BC24+(BE24-BD24)/BD24+(BF24-BE24)/BE24/5),0
                ,((BB24-BA24)/BA24+(BC24-BB24)/BB24+(BD24-BC24)/BC
                24+(BE24-BD24)/BD24+(BF24-BE24)/BE24)/5)
BB112: (,0) PR [W13] (BA112*BF24)+BF24
BC112: PR [W12] +AE25
BD112: PR [W12] +BC112-BB112
BE112: (P2) PR [W12] @IF(@ISERR((BC112-BB112)/BB112),0,(BC112-BB112)/BB
                112)
BF112: PR [W13] (BA112*BB112)+BB112
BG112: PR [W12] +AF25
BH112: PR [W12] +BG112-BF112
BI112: (P2) PR [W12] @IF(@ISERR((BG112-BF112)/BF112),0,(BG112-BF112)/BF
                112)
AX113: PR [W2] \|
AY113: PR [W45] '   Maint. & Rep. of Other Equipment
BA113: (P2) PR [W15] @IF(@ISERR((BB25-BA25)/BA25+(BC25-BB25)/BB25+(BD25
                -BC 25)/BC25+(BE25-BD25)/BD25+(BF25-BE25)/BE25/5),
                0,((BB25-BA25)/BA25+(BC25-BB25)/BB25+(BD25-BC25)/B
                C25+(BE25-BD25)/BD25+(BF25-BE25)/BE25)/5)
BB113: (,0) PR [W13] (BA113*BF25)+BF25
```

continued...

...from previous page

```
BC113: PR [W12] +AE26
BD113: PR [W12] +BC113-BB113
BE113: (P2) PR [W12] @IF(@ISERR((BC113-BB113)/BB113),0,(BC113-BB113)/
                        113)
BF113: PR [W13] (BA113*BB113)+BB113
BG113: PR [W12] +AF26
BH113: PR [W12] +BG113-BF113
BI113: (P2) PR [W12] @IF(@ISERR((BG113-BF113)/BF113),0,(BG113-BF113)/
                        113)
AX114: PR [W2] \|
AY114: PR [W45] '   Data Processing Contractual Service
BA114: (P2) PR [W15] @IF(@ISERR((BB26-BA26)/BA26+(BC26-BB26)/BB26+(BD2
                        -BC2 6)/BC26+(BE26-BD26)/BD26+(BF26-BE26)/BE26/5)
                        0,((BB26-BA26)/BA26+( BC26-BB26)/BB26+(BD26-BC26)
                        /BC26+(BE26-BD26)/BD26+(BF26-BE26)/BE26)/5)
BB114: (,0) PR [W13] (BA114*BF26)+BF26
BC114: PR [W12] +AE27
BD114: PR [W12] +BC114-BB114
BE114: (P2) PR [W12] @IF(@ISERR((BC114-BB114)/BB114),0,(BC114-BB114)/B
                        114)
BF114: PR [W13] (BA114*BB114)+BB114
BG114: PR [W12] +AF27
BH114: PR [W12] +BG114-BF114
BI114: (P2) PR [W12] @IF(@ISERR((BG114-BF114)/BF114),0,(BG114-BF114)/B
                        114)
AX115: PR [W2] \|
AY115: PR [W45] '   Insurance, Subscriptions, Brinks
BA115: (P2) PR [W15] @IF(@ISERR((BB27-BA27)/BA27+(BC27-BB27)/BB27+(BD2
                        -BC27)/BC27+(BE27-BD27)/BD27+(BF27-BE27)/BE27/5),(
                        ,((BB27-BA27)/BA27+(B C27-BB27)/BB27+(BD27-BC27)/
                        C27+(BE27-BD27)/BD27+(BF27-BE27)/BE27)/5)
BB115: (,0) PR [W13] (BA115*BF27)+BF27
BC115: PR [W12] +AE28
BD115: PR [W12] +BC115-BB115
BE115: (P2) PR [W12] @IF(@ISERR((BC115-BB115)/BB115),0,(BC115-BB115)/BB
                        115)
BF115: PR [W13] (BA115*BB115)+BB115
BG115: PR [W12] +AF28
BH115: PR [W12] +BG115-BF115
```

continued...

...from previous page

```
BI115: (P2) PR [W12] @IF(@ISERR((BG115-BF115)/BF115),0,(BG115-BF115)/BF
                    115)
AX116: PR [W2] \|
AY116: PR [W45] '    Miscellaneous Services:
BC116: PR [W12] +AE29
BG116: PR [W12] +AF29
AX117: PR [W2] \|
AY117: PR [W45] '        Card Copiers
BA117: (P2) PR [W15] @IF(@ISERR((BB29-BA29)/BA29+(BC29-BB29)/BB29+(BD29
                    -BC 29)/BC29+(BE29-BD29)/BD29+(BF29-BE29)/BE29/5),
                    0,((BB 29-BA29)/BA29+(BC29-BB29)/BB29+(BD29-BC29)/
                    BC29+(BE29-BD29)/BD29+(BF29-BE29)/BE29)/5)
BB117: (,0) PR [W13] (BA117*BF29)+BF29
BC117: PR [W12] +AE30
BD117: PR [W12] +BC117-BB117
BE117: (P2) PR [W12] @IF(@ISERR((BC117-BB117)/BB117),0,(BC117-BB117)/BB
                    117)
BF117: PR [W13] (BA117*BB117)+BB117
BG117: PR [W12] +AF30
BH117: PR [W12] +BG117-BF117
BI117: (P2) PR [W12] @IF(@ISERR((BG117-BF117)/BF117),0,(BG117-BF117)/BF
                    117)
AX118: PR [W2] \|
AY118: PR [W45] '        Court Costs
BA118: (P2) PR [W15] @IF(@ISERR((BB30-BA30)/BA30+(BC30-BB30)/BB30+(BD30
                    -BC30)/BC30+(BE30-BD30)/BD30+(BF30-BE30)/BE30/5),0
                    ,((BB30-BA30)/BA30+(BC30-BB30)/BB30+(BD30-BC30)/BC
                    30+(BE30-BD30)/BD30+(BF30-BE30)/BE30)/5)
BB118: (,0) PR [W13] (BA118*BF30)+BF30
BC118: PR [W12] +AE31
BD118: PR [W12] +BC118-BB118
BE118: (P2) PR [W12] @IF(@ISERR((BC118-BB118)/BB118),0,(BC118-BB118)/BB
                    118)
BF118: PR [W13] (BA118*BB118)+BB118
BG118: PR [W12] +AF31
BH118: PR [W12] +BG118-BF118
BI118: (P2) PR [W12] @IF(@ISERR((BG118-BF118)/BF118),0,(BG118-BF118)/BF
                    118)
AX119: PR [W2] \|
```

continued...

...from previous page

```
BC119: PR [W12] +AE32
BG119: PR [W12] +AF32
AX120: PR [W2] \|
BC120: PR [W12] +AE33
BG120: PR [W12] +AF33
AX121: PR [W2] \|
AY121: PR [W45] 'Other:
BC121: PR [W12] +AE34
BG121: PR [W12] +AF34
AX122: PR [W2] \|
AY122: PR [W45] '    Printing
BA122: (P2) PR [W15] @IF(@ISERR((BB34-BA34)/BA34+(BC34-BB34)/BB34+(BD34
                -BC34)/BC34+(BE34-BD34)/BD34+(BF34-BE34)/BE34 5),0
                ,((BB34-BA34)/BA34+(BC34-BB34)/BB34+(BD34-BC34)/BC
                34+(BE34-BD34)/BD34+(BF34-BE34)/BE34)/5)
BB122: (,0) PR [W13] (BA122*BF34)+BF34
BC122: PR [W12] +AE35
BD122: PR [W12] +BC122-BB122
BE122: (P2) PR [W12] @IF(@ISERR((BC122-BB122)/BB122),0,(BC122-BB122)/BB
                122)
BF122: PR [W13] (BA122*BB122)+BB122
BG122: PR [W12] +AF35
BH122: PR [W12] +BG122-BF122
BI122: (P2) PR [W12] @IF(@ISERR((BG122-BF122)/BF122),0,(BG122-BF122)/BF
                122)
AX123: PR [W2] \|
AY123: PR [W45] '    Office Supplies
BA123: (P2) PR [W15] @IF(@ISERR((BB35-BA35)/BA35+(BC35-BB35)/BB35+(BD35
                -BC35)/BC35+(B      E35-BD35)/BD35+(BF35-BE35)/BE35/
                5),0,((BB35-BA35)/BA35+(BC35-BB35)/BB35+(BD35-BC35
                )/BC35+(BE35-BD35)/BD35+(BF35-BE35)/BE35)/5)
BB123: (,0) PR [W13] (BA123*BF35)+BF35
BC123: PR [W12] +AE36
BD123: PR [W12] +BC123-BB123
BE123: (P2) PR [W12] @IF(@ISERR((BC123-BB123)/BB123),0,(BC123-BB123)/BB
                123)
BF123: PR [W13] (BA123*BB123)+BB123
BG123: PR [W12] +AF36
BH123: PR [W12] +BG123-BF123
```

continued...

...from previous page

```
BI123: (P2) PR [W12] @IF(@ISERR((BG123-BF123)/BF123),0,(BG123-BF123)/BF
                   123)
AX124: PR [W2] \|
AY124: PR [W45] '    Revenue Stamps
BA124: (P2) PR [W15] @IF(@ISERR((BB36-BA36)/BA36+(BC36-BB36)/BB36+(BD36
                   -BC36)/BC36+(BE36-BD36)/BD36+(BF36-BE36)/BE36/5),0
                   ,((BB36-BA36)/BA36+(BC36-BB36)/BB36+(BD36-BC36)/BC
                   36+(BE36-BD36)/BD36+(BF36-BE36)/BE36)/5)
BB124: (,0) PR [W13] (BA124*BF36)+BF36
BC124: PR [W12] +AE37
BD124: PR [W12] +BC124-BB124
BE124: (P2) PR [W12] @IF(@ISERR((BC124-BB124)/BB124),0,(BC124-BB124)/BB
                   124)
BF124: PR [W13] (BA124*BB124)+BB124
BG124: PR [W12] +AF37
BH124: PR [W12] +BG124-BF124
BI124: (P2) PR [W12] @IF(@ISERR((BG124-BF124)/BF124),0,(BG124-BF124)/BF
                   124)
AX125: PR [W2] \|
BC125: PR [W12] +AE38
BG125: PR [W12] +AF38
AX126: PR [W2] \|
BC126: PR [W12] +AE39
BG126: PR [W12] +AF39
AX127: PR [W2] \|
AY127: PR [W45] 'Capital Outlay
BA127: (P2) PR [W15] @IF(@ISERR((BB39-BA39)/BA39+(BC39-BB39)/BB39+(BD39
                   -BC39)/BC39+(BE39-BD39)/BD39+(BF39-BE39)/BE39/5),0
                   ,((BB39-BA39)/BA39+(BC39-BB39)/BB39+(BD39-BC39)/BC
                   39+(BE39-BD39)/BD39+(BF39-BE39)/BE39)/5)
BB127: (,0) PR [W13] (BA127*BF39)+BF39
BC127: PR [W12] +AE40
BD127: PR [W12] +BC127-BB127
BE127: (P2) PR [W12] @IF(@ISERR((BC127-BB127)/BB127),0,(BC127-BB127)/BB
                   127)
BF127: PR [W13] (BA127*BB127)+BB127
BG127: PR [W12] +AF40
BH127: PR [W12] +BG127-BF127
```

continued...

...from previous page

```
BI127: (P2) PR [W12] @IF(@ISERR((BG127-BF127)/BF127),0,(BG127-BF127)/
                      127)
AX128: PR [W2] \|
BA128: (P2) PR [W15] "----------
BB128: (P2) PR [W13] "----------
BC128: PR [W12] +AE41
BD128: (P2) PR [W12] "----------
BE128: (P2) PR [W12] "----------
BF128: (P2) PR [W13] "----------
BG128: PR [W12] +AF41
BH128: (P2) PR [W12] "----------
BI128: (P2) PR [W12] "----------
AX129: PR [W2] \|
AY129: PR [W45] 'TOTAL
BA129: (P2) PR [W15] @IF(@ISERR((BB41-BA41)/BA41+(BC41-BB41)/BB41+(BD
                      -BC41)/BC41+(BE41-BD41)/BD41+(BF41-BE41)/BE41/5)
                      ,((BB41-BA41)/BA41+(BC41-BB41)/BB41+(BD41-BC41)/
                      41+(BE41-BD41)/BD41+(BF41-BE41)/BE41)/5)
BB129: (,0) PR [W13] (BA129*BF41)+BF41
BC129: PR [W12] +AE42
BD129: PR [W12] +BC129-BB129
BE129: (P2) PR [W12] @IF(@ISERR((BC129-BB129)/BB129),0,(BC129-BB129)/
                      129)
BF129: PR [W13] (BA129*BB129)+BB129
BG129: PR [W12] +AF42
BH129: PR [W12] +BG129-BF129
BI129: (P2) PR [W12] @IF(@ISERR((BG129-BF129)/BF129),0,(BG129-BF129)/
                      129)
AX130: PR [W2] \|
BA130: PR [W15] "=========
BB130: PR [W13] "=========
BC130: PR [W12] "=========
BD130: PR [W12] "=========
BE130: PR [W12] "=========
BF130: PR [W13] "=========
BG130: PR [W12] "=========
BH130: PR [W12] "=========
BI130: PR [W12] "=========
AX131: PR [W2] \|
```

continued...

...from previous page

```
AY131: PR [W45] \=
AZ131: PR [W20] \=
BA131: PR [W15] \=
BB131: PR [W13] \=
BC131: PR [W12] \=
BD131: PR [W12] \=
BE131: PR [W12] \=
BF131: PR [W13] \=
BG131: PR [W12] \=
BH131: PR [W12] \=
BI131: PR [W12] \=
BJ131: PR [W12] \=
BK131: PR [W12] \=
BL131: PR [W12] \=
BM131: PR [W12] \=
```

Cell Listing: Figure 8.2

```
AX1: PR [W2] \|
AY1: PR [W45] 'SCHEDULES T & F DATA TABLE:  SUMMARY OF ACTUAL
              EXPENDITURES (1981-1987)
AX2: PR [W2] \|
AY2: PR [W45] 'UNIT:  DEPARTMENT OF PUBLIC WORKS
AX3: PR [W2] \|
AY3: PR [W45] \=
AZ3: PR [W20] \=
BA3: PR [W15] \=
BB3: PR [W13] \=
BC3: PR [W12] \=
BD3: PR [W12] \=
BE3: PR [W12] \=
BF3: PR [W13] \=
BG3: PR [W12] \=
BH3: PR [W12] \=
BI3: PR [W12] \=
```

continued...

...from previous page

```
BJ3: PR [W12] \=
BK3: PR [W12] \=
BL3: PR [W12] \=
BM3: PR [W12] \=
AX4: PR [W2]  |||
AX5: PR [W2]  \|
AZ5: (H) U [W20] ^81
BA5: (H) U [W15] ^82
BB5: (H) U [W13] ^83
BC5: (H) U [W12] ^84
BD5: (H) U [W12] ^85
BE5: (H) U [W12] ^86
BF5: (H) U [W13] ^87
BG5: (H) U [W12] ^88
BH5: (H) U [W12] ^89
AX6: PR [W2]  \|
AZ6: PR [W20] ^1981-82
BA6: PR [W15] ^1982-83
BB6: PR [W13] ^1983-84
BC6: PR [W12] ^1984-85
BD6: PR [W12] ^1985-86
BE6: PR [W12] ^1986-87
BF6: PR [W13] ^1987-88
AX7: PR [W2]  \|
AY7: PR [W45] 'Personal Services:
AZ7: PR [W20] ^Actual
BA7: PR [W15] ^Actual
BB7: PR [W13] ^Actual
BC7: PR [W12] ^Actual
BD7: PR [W12] ^Actual
BE7: PR [W12] ^Actual
BF7: PR [W13] ^Actual
AX8: PR [W2]  \|
AY8: PR [W45] '    Man Years
AZ8: PR [W20] 85
BA8: PR [W15] 88
BB8: PR [W13] 90
BC8: PR [W12] 90
BD8: PR [W12] +AB9
```

continued...

...from previous page

```
BE8:  PR [W12] +AC9
BF8:  PR [W13] +AD9
AX9:  PR [W2] \|
AY9:  PR [W45] '     Salaries
AZ9:  PR [W20] 1034583
BA9:  PR [W15] 1140400
BB9:  PR [W13] 1240357
BC9:  PR [W12] 1345250
BD9:  PR [W12] +AB10
BE9:  PR [W12] +AC10
BF9:  PR [W13] +AD10
AX10: PR [W2] \|
AY10: PR [W45] '      Benefits
AZ10: PR [W20] 0
BA10: PR [W15] 0
BB10: PR [W13] 0
BC10: PR [W12] 0
BD10: PR [W12] +AB11
BE10: PR [W12] +AC11
BF10: PR [W13] +AD11
AX11: PR [W2] \|
AX12: PR [W2] \|
AY12: PR [W45] 'Supporting Services:
AX13: PR [W2] \|
AY13: PR [W45] '    Travel
AZ13: PR [W20] 58425
BA13: PR [W15] 60537
BB13: PR [W13] 63540
BC13: PR [W12] 67300
BD13: PR [W12] +AB14
BE13: PR [W12] +AC14
BF13: PR [W13] +AD14
AX14: PR [W2] \|
AY14: PR [W45] '    Telephone Tolls and Rental
AZ14: PR [W20] 12600
BA14: PR [W15] 13475
BB14: PR [W13] 12800
BC14: PR [W12] 13500
BD14: PR [W12] +AB15
```

continued...

...from previous page

```
BE14: PR [W12] +AC15
BF14: PR [W13] +AD15
AX15: PR [W2] \|
AY15: PR [W45] '    Postage
AZ15: PR [W20] 55093
BA15: PR [W15] 53550
BB15: PR [W13] 53701
BC15: PR [W12] 55890
BD15: PR [W12] +AB16
BE15: PR [W12] +AC16
BF15: PR [W13] +AD16
AX16: PR [W2] \|
AY16: PR [W45] '    Rent - State Owned Buildings
AZ16: PR [W20] 7548
BA16: PR [W15] 7980
BB16: PR [W13] 8300
BC16: PR [W12] 9500
BD16: PR [W12] +AB17
BE16: PR [W12] +AC17
BF16: PR [W13] +AD17
AX17: PR [W2] \|
AY17: PR [W45] '    Rent - Privately Owned Buildings
AZ17: PR [W20] 4986
BA17: PR [W15] 5100
BB17: PR [W13] 5400
BC17: PR [W12] 6000
BD17: PR [W12] +AB18
BE17: PR [W12] +AC18
BF17: PR [W13] +AD18
AX18: PR [W2] \|
AY18: PR [W45] '    Building Improvements
AZ18: PR [W20] 455
BA18: PR [W15] 455
BB18: PR [W13] 500
BC18: PR [W12] 300
BD18: PR [W12] +AB19
BE18: PR [W12] +AC19
BF18: PR [W13] +AD19
AX19: PR [W2] \|
```

continued...

...from previous page

```
AY19: PR [W45] '    Utility Charges
AZ19: PR [W20] 175
BA19: PR [W15] 189
BB19: PR [W13] 200
BC19: PR [W12] 225
BD19: PR [W12] +AB20
BE19: PR [W12] +AC20
BF19: PR [W13] +AD20
AX20: PR [W2] \|
AY20: PR [W45] '    Rent of Data Processing Equipment
AZ20: PR [W20] 35435
BA20: PR [W15] 35500
BB20: PR [W13] 36395
BC20: PR [W12] 37880
BD20: PR [W12] +AB21
BE20: PR [W12] +AC21
BF20: PR [W13] +AD21
AX21: PR [W2] \|
AY21: PR [W45] '    Rent of Office Equipment
AZ21: PR [W20] 3480
BA21: PR [W15] 3545
BB21: PR [W13] 3900
BC21: PR [W12] 3750
BD21: PR [W12] +AB22
BE21: PR [W12] +AC22
BF21: PR [W13] +AD22
AX22: PR [W2] \|
AY22: PR [W45] '    Maint. & Rep. of Office Equipment
AZ22: PR [W20] 325
BA22: PR [W15] 350
BB22: PR [W13] 350
BC22: PR [W12] 350
BD22: PR [W12] +AB23
BE22: PR [W12] +AC23
BF22: PR [W13] +AD23
AX23: PR [W2] \|
AY23: PR [W45] '    Maint. & Rep. of Ofc. Equip. - Contract
AZ23: PR [W20] 7999
BA23: PR [W15] 8100
```

continued...

...from previous page

```
BB23: PR [W13] 8200
BC23: PR [W12] 7500
BD23: PR [W12] +AB24
BE23: PR [W12] +AC24
BF23: PR [W13] +AD24
AX24: PR [W2] \|
AY24: PR [W45] '   Maint. & Rep. of Automobile Vehicles
AZ24: PR [W20] 2512
BA24: PR [W15] 2540
BB24: PR [W13] 4000
BC24: PR [W12] 2550
BD24: PR [W12] +AB25
BE24: PR [W12] +AC25
BF24: PR [W13] +AD25
AX25: PR [W2] \|
AY25: PR [W45] '   Maint. & Rep. of Other Equipment
AZ25: PR [W20] 0
BA25: PR [W15] 0
BB25: PR [W13] 0
BC25: PR [W12] 0
BD25: PR [W12] +AB26
BE25: PR [W12] +AC26
BF25: PR [W13] +AD26
AX26: PR [W2] \|
AY26: PR [W45] '   Data Processing Contractual Service
AZ26: PR [W20] 7039
BA26: PR [W15] 7350
BB26: PR [W13] 7500
BC26: PR [W12] 7600
BD26: PR [W12] +AB27
BE26: PR [W12] +AC27
BF26: PR [W13] +AD27
AX27: PR [W2] \|
AY27: PR [W45] '   Insurance, Subscriptions, Brinks
AZ27: PR [W20] 450
BA27: PR [W15] 450
BB27: PR [W13] 475
BC27: PR [W12] 475
BD27: PR [W12] +AB28
```

continued...

...from previous page

```
BE27:  PR [W12] +AC28
BF27:  PR [W13] +AD28
AX28:  PR [W2]  |||
AY28:  PR [W45] '    Miscellaneous Services:
AX29:  PR [W2]  \|
AY29:  PR [W45] '        Card Copiers
AZ29:  PR [W20] 0
BA29:  PR [W15] 0
BB29:  PR [W13] 0
BC29:  PR [W12] 0
BD29:  PR [W12] +AB30
BE29:  PR [W12] +AC30
BF29:  PR [W13] +AD30
AX30:  PR [W2]  \|
AY30:  PR [W45] '        Court Costs
AZ30:  PR [W20] 4500
BA30:  PR [W15] 3000
BB30:  PR [W13] 267
BC30:  PR [W12] 0
BD30:  PR [W12] +AB31
BE30:  PR [W12] +AC31
BF30:  PR [W13] 1578
AX31:  PR [W2]  \|
AX32:  PR [W2]  \|
AX33:  PR [W2]  \|
AY33:  PR [W45] 'Other:
AX34:  PR [W2]  \|
AY34:  PR [W45] '   Printing
AZ34:  PR [W20] 6845
BA34:  PR [W15] 7000
BB34:  PR [W13] 7550
BC34:  PR [W12] 8250
BD34:  PR [W12] +AB35
BE34:  PR [W12] +AC35
BF34:  PR [W13] +AD35
AX35:  PR [W2]  \|
AY35:  PR [W45] '   Office Supplies
AZ35:  PR [W20] 19005
BA35:  PR [W15] 19200
```

continued...

...from previous page

```
BB35: PR [W13] 19467
BC35: PR [W12] 20500
BD35: PR [W12] +AB36
BE35: PR [W12] +AC36
BF35: PR [W13] +AD36
AX36: PR [W2] \|
AY36: PR [W45] '    Revenue Stamps
AZ36: PR [W20] 0
BA36: PR [W15] 0
BB36: PR [W13] 0
BC36: PR [W12] 0
BD36: PR [W12] +AB37
BE36: PR [W12] +AC37
BF36: PR [W13] +AD37
AX37: PR [W2] \|
BD37: PR [W12] +AB38
BE37: PR [W12] +AC38
AX38: PR [W2] \|
AX39: PR [W2] \|
AY39: PR [W45] 'Capital Outlay
AZ39: PR [W20] 5962
BA39: PR [W15] 5980
BB39: PR [W13] 6255
BC39: PR [W12] 6503
BD39: PR [W12] +AB40
BE39: PR [W12] +AC40
BF39: PR [W13] +AD40
AX40: PR [W2] \|
AZ40: (P2) PR [W20] "----------
BA40: (P2) PR [W15] "----------
BB40: (P2) PR [W13] "----------
BC40: (P2) PR [W12] "----------
BD40: (P2) PR [W12] "----------
BE40: (P2) PR [W12] "----------
BF40: (P2) PR [W13] "----------
AX41: PR [W2] \|
AY41: PR [W45] 'TOTAL
AZ41: PR [W20] @SUM(AZ9..AZ39)
BA41: PR [W15] @SUM(BA9..BA39)
```

continued...

...from previous page

```
BB41: PR [W13] @SUM(BB9..BB39)
BC41: PR [W12] @SUM(BC9..BC39)
BD41: PR [W12] +SCHAT
BE41: PR [W12] +AC42
BF41: PR [W13] +AD42
AX42: PR [W2] \|
AZ42: PR [W20] "=========
BA42: PR [W15] "=========
BB42: PR [W13] "=========
BC42: PR [W12] "=========
BD42: PR [W12] "=========
BE42: PR [W12] "=========
BF42: PR [W13] "=========
AX43: PR [W2] \|
AX44: PR [W2] \|
AY44: PR [W45] '\=
AZ44: PR [W20] \=
BA44: PR [W15] \=
BB44: PR [W13] \=
BC44: PR [W12] \=
BD44: PR [W12] \=
BE44: PR [W12] \=
BF44: PR [W13] \=
BG44: PR [W12] \=
BH44: PR [W12] \=
BI44: PR [W12] \=
BJ44: PR [W12] \=
BK44: PR [W12] \=
BL44: PR [W12] \=
BM44: PR [W12] \=
```

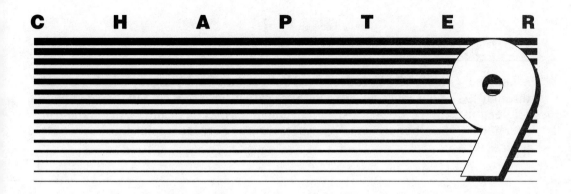

CHAPTER 9

SCHEDULE F

DESCRIPTION

Schedule F (Figure 9.1) includes actual budget data from budget periods 1980-81 through 1987-88. Only select expenditure categories are included in Schedule F for demonstration purposes. Any or all line items may be included, depending on user needs. The schedule also displays forecast and error data through the budget period 1988-89.

	AY	AZ	BA	BB	BC	BD	BE
302	SCHEDULE F: BUDGET FORECAST (EXPONENTIAL SMOOTHING) MODEL ($000)						
303	UNIT: DEPARTMENT OF PUBLIC WORKS						
304							
305							
306	Weight=	1.6					
307							
308		1981-82	1982-83	1983-84	1984-85	1985-86	1986-
309	Man Years Actual	85.0	88.0	90.0	90.0	98.0	100
310	Man Years Forecast	85.0	85.0	89.7	90.2	89.9	102.
311	Man Years Error Factor	0.0	3.0	0.3	-0.2	8.1	-2
312	Salaries Actual	1034.6	1140.4	1240.4	1345.3	1352.4	1380
313	Salaries Forecast	1034.6	1034.6	1200.4	1263.0	1391.9	1330
314	Salaries Error Factor	0.0	105.8	40.0	82.2	-39.5	50
315	Travel Actual	58.4	60.5	63.5	67.3	70.0	70
316	Travel Forecast	58.4	58.4	61.7	64.6	68.9	70
317	Travel Error Factor	0.0	2.1	1.8	2.7	1.1	-0
318	Telephone Tolls and Rental Actual	12.6	13.5	12.8	13.5	14.0	14
319	Telephone Tolls and Rental Forecast	12.6	12.6	14.0	14.3	13.5	13
320	Telephone Tolls and Rental Error Factor	0.0	0.9	0.2	-0.5	-0.3	1
321	Postage Actual	55.1	53.6	53.7	55.9	60.0	89
322	Postage Forecast	55.1	55.1	52.7	50.5	55.5	70
323	Postage Error Factor	0.0	-1.5	-1.4	3.2	9.5	13
324	Capital Outlay Actual	6.0	6.0	6.3	6.5	7.3	12
325	Capital Outlay Forecast	6.0	6.0	6.0	6.4	7.3	8
326	Capital Outlay Error Factor	0.0	0.0	0.3	0.5	0.9	4
327	Total Actual	1267.4	1374.7	1476.2	1593.3	1818	
328	Total Forecast	1267.4	1267.4	1435.5	1503.9	1644.0	1835
329	Total Error Factor	0.0	107.3	43.6	89.4	122.2	-17
330							
331							
332							
333							
334							

Figure 9.1   Schedule F

BF	BG	BH	BI	BJ	BK	BL	BM		BN	BO	BP	BQ
								‖				
								‖				
								‖				
								‖				
1987-88	1988-89							‖				
101.0								‖				
98.5	102.4							‖				
2.5								‖				
1393.8								‖				
1408.3	1385.6							‖				
−14.5								‖				
64.0								‖				
69.6	60.8							‖				
−5.6								‖				
15.8								‖				
14.8	19.0							‖				
2.7								‖				
70.0								‖				
91.5	90.9							‖				
−0.4								‖				
34.5								‖				
16.2	56.8							‖				
25.9								‖				
1868.2								‖				
1809.0	1801.7							‖				
59.2								‖				

The forecasts are calculated by using a technique called exponential smoothing, which assigns weights to the data. The more recent the data, the greater the weights that are assigned. The error data represent the difference between actual and forecast data. If the error value has a positive sign, the current forecast is too low; the next forecast would be the sum of the current forecast plus a fraction of the error. If the error has a negative value, the current forecast is too high; the next forecast would be the current forecast minus a fraction of the error.

The model in Schedule F depends on two equations that are updated in succeeding budget periods:

Error = Actual Expenditure Data - Current Forecast

Next Forecast = Current Forecast + Weight * Error

The weight factors range from 0 to 1.0 in 0.1 increments. The higher the trend, the more regular the pattern of change in the data.

Choosing the best weight to apply can be performed subjectively by assigning varying weights and then selecting the one that appears to result in the most realistic forecast. A more objective technique is to calculate the mean-squared errors (MSE) of different smoothing weights and choose the weight associated with the lowest MSE. (For a review of the forecasting technique used in this chapter, see Everette S. Gardner, Jr., "Forecasting: Short-Range Forecasting," *Lotus*, 3:2 [February, 1987], pp. 54-58). Figure 9.2 shows Schedule F Data Table 1, which is used for objectively determining how well individual weights perform.

The calculation of weights and their application to the data in Schedule F are macro-driven. In the following section, Schedule F will first be constructed, followed by the macros that automate the application of alternate weights. Next, the Schedule F Data Table 1, which includes the MSE Model for generating alternative smoothing weights, will be constructed, followed finally by the macros that drive it.

CONSTRUCTING SCHEDULE F

Begin creating Schedule F by entering the schedule borders and labels appearing in ranges AY302..AY329, the numerical value in cell AZ306, and the labels appearing in AZ308..BG308. (The numerical value in cell AZ306 will be changed to a formula later to automate the entry of alternate weights.) Then, divide the screen horizontally as shown in Figure 9.3 to display the Schedules T & F Data Table in the top window and the Schedule F in the bottom window.

(See next page)

	AY	AZ	BA	BB	BC	BD	
335	SCHEDULE F DATA TABLE 1: MEAN-SQUARED ERROR MODEL FOR GENERATING DIFFERENT SMOOTHING WEIGHTS						
336	UNIT: DEPARTMENT OF PUBLIC WORKS						
337	===						
338							
339		Man Years MSE=	12.50				
340		Salaries MSE=	3403.59				
341		Travel MSE=	6.95				
342		Telephone MSE=	1.34				
343		Postage MSE=	40.94				
344		Capital Outlays MSE=	99.54				
345		Total MSE=	5734.36				
346							
347							
348		Weight	MSE				
349			5734.36				
350		0.0	153731.21				
351		0.1	105038.14				
352		0.2	73252.39				
353		0.3	52315.45				
354		0.4	38940.86				
355		0.5	28655.57				
356		0.6	22292.98				
357		0.7	17660.87				
358		0.8	14327.95				
359		0.9	11889.84				
360		1.0	10079.77				
361							
362							
363							
364							
365							
366							
367							
368							
369							
370							
371							
372							
373							
374							
375							
376							
377							
378							
379							
380							
381							
382							

Figure 9.2   Schedule F Data Table 1

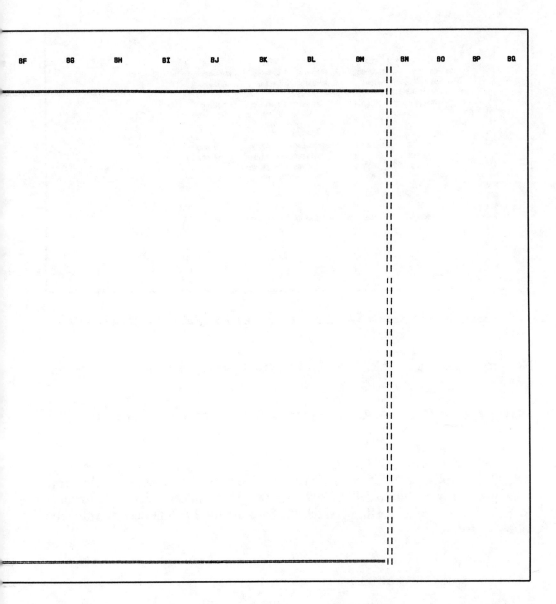

8F	8G	8H	8I	8J	8K	8L	8M	8N	8O	8P	8Q

	AZ	BA	BB	BC	BD
	AZ	BA	BB	BC	BD
6	1981–82	1982–83	1983–84	1984–85	1985–86
7	Actual	Actual	Actual	Actual	Actual
8	85	88	90	90	98
9	1,034,583	1,140,400	1,240,357	1,345,250	1,352,400
10	0	0	0	0	0
11					
12					
13	58,425	60,537	63,540	67,300	70,000
14	12,600	13,475	12,800	13,500	14,000
15	55,093	53,550	53,701	55,890	60,000
	AZ	BA	BB	BC	BD
305					
306	1.6				
307					
308	1981–82	1982–83	1983–84	1984–85	1985–86
309					
310					
311					
312					
313					

Figure 9.3   *Schedule F and Schedules T & F Data Table: Horizontally Split Screen*

Next, format the range AZ309..BG329 for fixed format with one decimal place:

/Range Format Fixed 1 **<Return>** **<AZ309..BG329>** **<Return>**

Enter cell reference +AZ8 in cell AZ309, and then copy the entry to the range AZ309..BF8. Next, enter in cell AZ310 the value of the first forecast as the same value previously posted to cell AZ309 (+AZ8). Enter in cell AZ311 the formula AZ8-AZ310. In cell BA310, in which the forecast for 1982-83 occurs, enter the following formula:

+AZ310+$AZ$306*AZ311

The first entry and the accompanying copy command allow the man-years entries appearing in the Schedules T & F Data Table to be posted to the man-years data row in Schedule F. The second entry sets the 1981-82 man-years forecast equal to the first man-years entry. The first formula entry calculates the error factor for 1981-82. The second formula in cell BA310 specifies that the man-years forecast for budget year 1982-83 is equal to the forecast for 1981-82 plus the smoothing weight multiplied by the error factor for the 1981-82 man-years forecast.

Copy the forecast updating formula in cell BA310 to range BB310..BG310. Copy the error-calculating formula in cell AZ311 to the range BA311..BF311.

The remaining entries in Schedule F are made by replicating the entry techniques used to construct the man-years actual, forecast, and error factor entries, but with one difference: the expenditure object entries, unlike the man-years entries, are entered in thousands of dollars. For example, enter the cell entries in the range AZ312..BA314 as follows:

Cell	Formula
AZ312:	+AZ9/1000
BA312:	+BA9/1000
AZ313:	+AZ9/1000
BA313:	+AZ313+AZ306$*AZ314
AZ314:	+AZ9/1000-AZ313
BA314:	+BA9/1000-BA313

Once the above formulas have been entered in the actual, forecast, and error factor cells of salary object expenditures for budget years 1981-82 and 1982-83, the remaining portions of the three salary object entries in the range BA312..BA314 should be copied to the ranges BB312..BF312, BB313..BG313, and BB314..BF314, respectively. Next, make the remaining entries in Schedule F by replicating the techniques used to enter data into range AZ312..BA314.

SCHEDULE F MACRO

Lotus 1-2-3's macro capability is an invaluable feature that allows for the automatic manipulation and customization of worksheet applications. Lotus 1-2-3's Advanced Macro Commands are used in this application as a high-level programming language both to automate and customize a variety of spreadsheet features. In this particular section, a macro is developed that automates the application of alternate weights to the data in Spreadsheet F for forecasting purposes.

The macro is named \w and consists of the following lines. (Note: Although cell BZ73 is displayed as two lines due to page width limitations, please enter it and all other multiline cells on one line in the worksheet application. Also, please note that there is a space between "BEEP" and "0" in the second line of BZ73. Whenever such spaces occur between first character entries on the second and subsequent lines of multiline cell displays, the spaces(s) will be so indicated.)

<u>Cell</u>   <u>Macro Entry</u>

```
BX143:  Smoothing Weight=
BY143:  \w=
BZ143:  {WINDOWSOFF}{BEEP 0}{BEEP 3}{BEEP 0}{BEEP 3}{BEEP 0}{BEE
        P 3 }{BEEP 0}{INDICATE ENTER}~
BZ144:  {GETNUMBER "Enter Smoothing Weight Factor (limit entry T
        o 1 decimal place): ",BZ140}
BZ145:  {INDICATE WAIT}
BZ146:  {PANELOFF}
BZ147:  {CALC}
BZ148:  {WINDOWSON}
BZ149:  {GOTO}AY302~
BZ150:  {INDICATE}{ESC}
BZ151:  {BEEP 0}{BEEP 3}{BEEP 0}{BEEP 3}{BEEP 0}{BEEP3}{BEEP 0}
```

After entering each of the above cells, name the macro \w by placing the cursor in cell BY73 and entering the following:

/Range Name Create \w <Return> <Return>

Cells BX143 and BY143 are references to the smoothing weight and to the overall macro, respectively. Because each line of a macro must be entered as a label, the slash (/) in BY143 must be immediately preceded by a single right apostrophe (').

When the \w macro is activated by pressing the Alt/W key combination, cell BZ1433 suppresses the redrawing of the display screen, {WINDOWSOFF}, during the execution of the macro, sounds alternate tones of the computer bell to attract your attention, and prompts you, {INDICATE ENTER}, in the status mode indicator box (upper right corner of the screen) to enter information (to be requested of the user in the next step) on the command line of the control panel. Step BZ144 prompts you on the command line to enter a weight factor and then automatically posts the weight to cell BZ140 to the right of the Smoothing Weight = reference entered in step BX143.

Move the cursor to cell AZ306 in Schedule F, and enter the cell reference + BZ140. For forecasting purposes, this entry facilitates the inseriatim posting of the weight that initially is to be entered on the command line in response to the prompt, "Enter Smoothing Weight Factor (limit entry to 1 decimal place)." This entry is posted to cell BZ140 and then to cell AZ306 and, subsequently, is posted to each of the forecast formulas that appear in the range BA310..BG328. **Note:** Disregard any error terms that appear on Schedule F after the entry of + BZ140 in cell AZ306. These will disappear the first time the macro is run.

Cell BZ145, {INDICATE WAIT}, changes the status mode indicator to "WAIT" so you will know that 1-2-3 is executing the macro. Cell BZ146, {PANELOFF}, suppresses the redrawing of the control panel during macro execution. The {CALC} command in cell BZ147 recalculates the worksheet application, incorporating the weight factor entered each time the macro is activated.

The {WINDOWSON} command in BZ148 reactivates the redrawing of the display screen, and the {GOTO}AY302 entry in cell BZ149 positions Schedule F on the screen after Schedule F has been recalculated with the most recently entered weight factor. Cell BZ150, {INDICATE}{ESC}, causes the "WAIT" message appearing in the status mode indicator to change to "READY," and cell BZ151 sounds a bell to alert you that the calculation of the macro has been completed.

CONSTRUCTING SCHEDULE F DATA TABLE 1

Begin the construction of the data table by entering the spreadsheet borders.
Next, enter the labels in range AY335..AZ345 and in cells AZ348 and BA348.

Enter the following formulas in the cells located in the range BA339..BA345:

1. In cell BA339 enter

`@VAR($AZ$311..$BF$311)+@AVG($AZ$311..$BF $311)^2`

2. In cell BA340 enter

`@VAR($AZ$314..$BF$314)+@AVG($AZ$314..$BF $314)^2`

3. In cell BA341 enter

`@VAR($AZ$317..$BF$317)+@AVG($AZ$317..$BF $317)^2`

4. In cell BA342 enter

`$320)+@AVG($AZ$320..$BF $320)^2`

5. In cell BA343 enter

`@VAR($AZ$323..$BF$323)+@AVG($AZ$323..$BF $9323)^2`

6. In cell BA344 enter

`@VAR($AZ$326..$BF$326)+@AVG($AZ$326..$BF $326)^2`

7. In cell BA345 enter

`@VAR($AZ$329..$BF$329)+@AVG($AZ$329..$BF $329)^2`

Each of these entries adds the variance of the error factors for each of the expenditure objects in Schedule F to the square of their average for budget years 1981-82 through 1987-88.

Next, enter as values the weights in the range AZ320..AZ350, and give the range a fixed format with one decimal place. Give the range BA349..BA370 a fixed format with two decimal places.

Before moving to the next section to construct the macro that automates the calculation of the most appropriate weight for exponential smoothing purposes, give cell BA349 the name EXPNAME. The function of this particular entry will become clear in the next section.

SCHEDULE F DATA TABLE 1 MACRO

The macro for automating the calculation of the most appropriate weight to apply to exponential smoothing is named \e. Enter each of its lines as follows, and name the macro \e:

Cell	Macro Entry

```
BY76:  \e=
BZ76:  {WINDOWSOFF}{BEEP 0}{BEEP 3}{BEEP 0}{BEEP3}{BEEP0}{BEEP
       3}{BEEP 0}{INDICATE ENTER}~
BZ77:  {GETLABEL "Enter line-item to smooth (MY, Sal, Tvl, Tel,
       Post, Capout, Tot) ",EXPNAME}
BZ78:  {IF@LEFT(EXPNAME,2)<>"MY"#AND#@LEFT(EXPNAME,3)<>"SAL" AN
       D#@LEFT(EXPNAME,3)<>"TVL"#AND#@LEFT(EXPNAME,3)<> TEL"#AND
       #@LEFT(EXPNAME,4)<>"POST"#AND#@LEFT(EXPNAME,6)<>"CAPOUT"#
       AND#@LEFT(EXPNAME,3)<>"TOT"}{BRANCH ERRORBRANCH2}
BZ79:  {IF EXPNAME="MY"}/cBA339~BA349~
BZ80:  {IF EXPNAME="SAL"}/cBA340~BA349~
BZ81:  {IF EXPNAME="TVL"}/cBA341~BA349~
BZ82:  {IF EXPNAME="TEL"}/cBA342~BA349~
BZ83:  {IF EXPNAME="POST"}/cBA343~BA349~
BZ84:  {IF EXPNAME="CAPOUT"}/cBA344~BA349~
BZ85:  {IF EXPNAME="TOT"}/cBA345~BA349~
BZ86:  {INDICATE WAIT}
```

continued...

...from previous page

```
BZ87:  {PANELOFF}
BZ88:  {CALC}
BZ89:  /dt1AZ349.BA360~AZ306~
BZ90:  {WINDOWSON}
BZ91:  {GOTO}AZ349~
BZ92:  {INDICATE}{ESC}
BZ93:  {BEEP 0}{BEEP 3}{BEEP 0}{BEEP 3}{BEEP 0}{BEEP 3}{BEEP 0}
BZ94:  {UP}
BZ95:  {QUIT}
BZ96:  {BEEP 0}{BEEP 3}{BEEP 0}{BEEP 3}{BEEP 0}{BEEP 3}{BEEP 0}
BZ97:  Not a valid line-item entry.  Press Return to continue.{
       ?}{ESC}
BZ98:  {BRANCH \e}
```

Cell BY76 is the macro reference. As with macro \w, the reverse slash should be preceded by a single right apostrophe so 1-2-3 will not treat the entry as the command to activate its menu system.

Cell BZ76 disengages the redrawing of the screen during the macro's execution, sounds the bell, and changes the entry in the status mode indicator box from "READY" to "ENTER." BZ77 prompts the user to enter on the command line an abbreviation of the line-item category for which the appropriate smoothing weight should be calculated. For example, entering "MY" on the command line causes the macro to enter "MY" in the cell named EXPNAME, which, you will recall from the last entry in the previous section, is BA349.

Thus begins the process for calculating the most appropriate smoothing weight for forecasting Man Years. For example, entering "Sal" on the command line begins calculation of the most appropriate smoothing weight for forecasting Salary Expenditures, etc.

Cell BZ78 marks the beginning of a loop that instructs the macro to move to the cell named ERRORBRANCH2 (BZ96) in case the user erroneously enters a line-item abbreviation that is not solicited in the command line prompt. Give cell BZ96 the name ERRORBRANCH2. When the macro arrives at BZ96, the bell sounds to alert you of the entry error. BZ97, the second entry in the loop, instructs you on the command line that an invalid entry has been made and prompts you to enter RETURN to continue. The BZ98 entry initiates the final step of the loop and returns the cursor to BZ76, where the macro again begins the process of deflator calculation.

The entries in the range BZ79..BZ85 cause the macro to check the value posted to the cell named EXPNAME and to copy into that cell location the numerical value of the cell from within the range BA339..BA345 (located in the Schedule F Data Table 1) that corresponds with the line item most recently entered on the command line (MY, SAL, TVL, etc.). Give cell BA349 the name EXPNAME.

BZ86 changes the status mode indicator entry from "ENTER" to "WAIT" so you will know that the macro is calculating the most appropriate weight for exponential smoothing purposes. BZ87 deactivates the command line panel while the calculation is taking place, and BZ88 recalculates the worksheet. The formula in cell BZ89 calculates the data table area in the range AZ349..AZ306.

The three steps of the macro — BZ90, BZ91, and BZ92 — reactivate the screen, move the cursor into cell AZ349 to display Schedule F Data Table 1 on the screen, and change the status mode indicator entry from "WAIT" to "READY."

Cell Listing: Figure 9.2

```
AY335: PR [W45] 'SCHEDULE F DATA TABLE 1:  MODEL FOR GENERATING
       DIFFERENT SMOOTHING WEIGHTS
AY336: PR [W45] 'UNIT:  DEPARTMENT OF PUBLIC WORKS
AY337: PR [W45] \=
AZ337: PR [W20] \=
BA337: PR [W15] \=
BB337: PR [W13] \=
BC337: PR [W12] \=
BD337: PR [W12] \=
BE337: PR [W12] \=
BF337: PR [W13] \=
BG337: PR [W12] \=
BH337: PR [W12] \=
BI337: PR [W12] \=
BJ337: PR [W12] \=
BK337: PR [W12] \=
BL337: PR [W12] \=
BM337: PR [W12] \=
AZ339: PR [W20] 'Man Years MSE=
BA339: (F2) U [W15] @VAR($AZ$311..$BF$311)+@AVG($AZ$311..$BF$311)^2
AZ340: PR [W20] 'Salaries MSE=
```

continued...

...from previous page

```
BA340: (F2) U [W15] @VAR($AZ$314..$BF$314)+@AVG($AZ$314..$BF$314)^2
AZ341: PR [W20] 'Travel MSE=
BA341: (F2) U [W15] @VAR($AZ$317..$BF$317)+@AVG($AZ$317..$BF$317)^2
AZ342: PR [W20] 'Telephone MSE=
BA342: (F2) U [W15] @VAR($AZ$320..$BF$320)+@AVG($AZ$320..$BF$320)^2
AZ343: PR [W20] 'Postage MSE=
BA343: (F2) U [W15] @VAR($AZ$323..$BF$323)+@AVG($AZ$323..$BF$323)^2
AZ344: PR [W20] 'Capital Outlays MSE=
BA344: (F2) U [W15] @VAR($AZ$326..$BF$326)+@AVG($AZ$326..$BF$326)^2
AZ345: PR [W20] 'Total MSE=
BA345: (F2) U [W15] @VAR($AZ$329..$BF$329)+@AVG($AZ$329..$BF$329)^2
AZ348: PR [W20] "Weight
BA348: PR [W15] "MSE
BA349: (F2) U [W15] @VAR($AZ$329..$BF$329)+@AVG($AZ$329..$BF$329)^2
AZ350: (F1) U [W20] 0
BA350: (F2) U [W15] 153731.20565
AZ351: (F1) U [W20] 0.1
BA351: (F2) U [W15] 105038.143387
AZ352: (F1) U [W20] 0.2
BA352: (F2) U [W15] 73252.392965
AZ353: (F1) U [W20] 0.3
BA353: (F2) U [W15] 52315.445018
AZ354: (F1) U [W20] 0.4
BA354: (F2) U [W15] 38340.857807
AZ355: (F1) U [W20] 0.5
BA355: (F2) U [W15] 28855.570902
AZ356: (F1) U [W20] 0.6
BA356: (F2) U [W15] 22292.978447
AZ357: (F1) U [W20] 0.7
BA357: (F2) U [W15] 17660.868552
AZ358: (F1) U [W20] 0.8
BA358: (F2) U [W15] 14327.948076
AZ359: (F1) U [W20] 0.9
BA359: (F2) U [W15] 11888.8411805
AZ360: (F1) U [W20] 1
BA360: (F2) U [W15] 10079.7722957
AZ361: (F1) U [W20] 1.1
BA361: (F2) U [W15] 8726.2161271
AZ362: (F1) U [W20] 1.2
```

continued...

...from previous page

```
BA362: (F2) U [W15] 7710.2157728
AZ363: (F1) U [W20] 1.3
BA363: (F2) U [W15] 6949.4315706
AZ364: (F1) U [W20] 1.4
BA364: (F2) U [W15] 6382.8846181
AZ365: (F1) U [W20] 1.5
BA365: (F2) U [W15] 5960.3966848
AZ366: (F1) U [W20] 1.6
BA366: (F2) U [W15] 5634.4991325
AZ367: (F1) U [W20] 1.7
BA367: (F2) U [W15] 5355.6841483
AZ368: (F1) U [W20] 1.8
BA368: (F2) U [W15] 5074.8987471
AZ369: (F1) U [W20] 1.9
BA369: (F2) U [W15] 4761.7322841
AZ370: (F1) U [W20] 2
BA370: (F2) U [W15] 4453.4183106
```

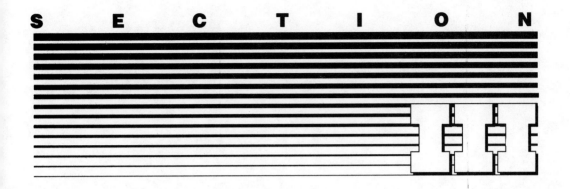

WORKSHEET APPLICATION
HOUSEKEEPING FUNCTIONS

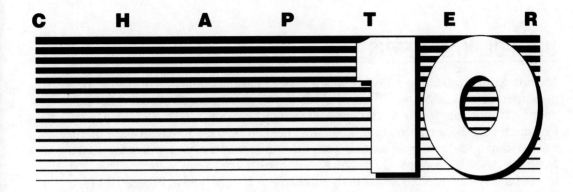

GETTING AROUND THE
WORKSHEET APPLICATION

USER-DEFINED MENUS

Moving from schedule to schedule in a worksheet application as large as the one presented in this book would be difficult if you had to recall spreadsheet cell coordinates or range names and invoke them by pressing 1-2-3's F5 (Goto) key. Fortunately, 1-2-3's macro command language can be used to construct a menu system that greatly simplifies this task. In this chapter, you will use 1-2-3's MENUBRANCH command structure to construct the menu system. The first level of the system used to locate budget schedules is displayed in Figure 10.1 (see p. 203) as it appears on 1-2-3's command line.

In this chapter you will create a portion of the menu system that applies only to displaying budget schedules and a menu-drive enhancement of 1-2-3's horizontal and vertical window-splitting command function. Expansion of the main menu to include options for splitting the screen, graphics, and display of data tables upon which graphing functions depend will be explored in Chapters 11 and 12. Optional entries for automating the display of data tables are listed in Appendix A.

The worksheet's menu system consists of the following cell/macro entries for locating budget schedules. (Note that adjacent menu text can overlap, so column widths do not need to be unnecessarily extended.)

<u>Cell</u>   <u>Macro Entry</u>

```
BP1:  \m=
BQ1:  {MENUBRANCH MENU}
BQ2:  {BRANCH FINISH}
BP4:  MENU=
BQ4:  A_SCHs
BR4:  B_SCHs
BS4:  C_SCH
BT4:  Rs/T/F_SCHs
BQ5:  GO TO SCHEDULE As
BR5:  GO TO SCHEDULE Bs
BS5:  GO TO SCHEDULE Cs
BT5:  GO TO SCHEDULES Rs T & F
BQ6:  {MENUCALL SCHAM}{MENUBRANCH MENU}
BR6:  {MENUCALL B_SCHs}{MENUBRANCH MENU}
BS6:  {MENUCALL SCHCM}{MENUBRANCH MENU}
```

continued...

...from previous page

```
BT6:  {MENUCALL SCHRM}{MENUBRANCH MENU}
BP8:  FINISH=
BQ8:  {QUIT}
BP11: SCHAM=
BQ11: A_SCH
BR11: DA_SCH
BQ12: GO TO SCHEDULE A
BR12: GO TO SCHEDULE DA (DEFLATED SCHEDULE A)
BQ13: {SCHAMA}
BR13: {SCHADM}
BP15: SCHMA=
BQ15: {GOTO}SCHA~
BQ16: {BRANCH \m}
BP18: SCHADM=
BQ18: {GOTO}SCHDA~
BQ19: {BRANCH \m}
BP21: B_SCHs
BQ21: PC
BR21: MI
BS21: WC
BT21: NCS
BU21: OC
BV21: FF
BQ22: GO TO SCHEDULE PC
BR22: GO TO SCHEDULE MI
BS22: GO TO SCHEDULE WC
BT22: GO TO SCHEDULE NCS
BU22: GO TO SCHEDULE OC
BV22: GO TO SCHEDULE FF
BQ23: {PCSCHBM}
BR23: {MISCHBM}
BS23: {WCSCHBM}
BT23: {NCSCHBM}
BU23: {OCSCHBM}
BV23: {FFSCHBM}
BQ25: PCSCHBM=
BR25: {GOTO}PCSCHB~
BR26: {BRANCH \m}
BQ28: MISCHBM=
```

continued...

...from previous page

```
BR28:  {GOTO}MISCHB~
BR29:  {BRANCH \m}
BQ31:  WCSCHBM=
BR31:  {GOTO}WCSCHB~
BR32:  {BRANCH \m}
BQ34:  NCSCHBM=
BR34:  {GOTO}NCSCHB~
BR35:  {BRANCH \m}
BQ37:  OCSCHBM=
BR37:  {GOTO}OCSCHB~
BR38:  {BRANCH \m}
BR40:  {GOTO}FFSCHB~
BR41:  {BRANCH \m}
BP44:  SCHCM=
BQ44:  C_SCH
BR44:  DC_SCH
BQ45:  GO TO SCHEDULE C
BR45:  GO TO DEFLATED SCHEDULE C
BQ46:  {SCHCMC}
BR46:  {SCHDCM}
BQ48:  SCHCMC=
BR48:  {GOTO}SCHC~
BR:    {BRANCH \m}
BQ51:  SCHDCM=
BR51:  {GOTO}SCHDC~
BR52:  {BRANCH \m}
BP55:  SCHRM=
BQ55:  R_SCH
BR55:  DR_SCH
BS55:  T_SCH
BT55:  F_SCH
BQ56:  GO TO SCHEDULE R
BR56:  GO TO SCHEDULE DR (DEFLATED SCHEDULE R)
BS56:  GO TO SCHEDULE T
BT56:  GO TO SCHEDULE F
BQ57:  {SCHRMR}
BR57:  {SCHRMD}
BS57:  {SCHTMT}
BT57:  {SCHFMF}
```

continued...

...from previous page

```
BQ59:  SCHRMR=
BR59:  {GOTO}SCHR~
BR60:  {BRANCH \m}
BQ61:  SCHRMD=
BR62:  {GOTO}SCHDR~
BR63:  {BRANCH \m}
BQ65:  SCHTMT=
BR65:  {GOTO}SCHT~
BR66:  {BRANCH \m}
BQ68:  SCHFMF=
BR68:  {GOTO}SCHF~
BR69:  {BRANCH \m}
```

Your first step in constructing the system is to name the macro that drives it. Move the cursor to BQ1, and name the macro \m. Entry BP1 is the macro cell reference. When you use the Alt/M key combination, the cursor moves to the cell named \m (BQ1) and invokes the menu. Give range BQ1..BQ1 the name \m at this time. The entry {MENUBRANCH MENU} in cell BQ1 causes the cursor to move to the cell named MENU (BQ4). Move the cursor to cell BQ4, and give the name MENU to the range BQ4..BQ4 before proceeding further. The MENU= label entry in BP4 is the main menu reference cell.

The {BRANCH FINISH} command in BQ2 causes 1-2-3 to stop executing the macro if you press the Esc key instead of selecting an item on the menu. When the Esc key is pressed, the macro executes cell BQ2 and proceeds to cell BQ8. There, the macro encounters the {QUIT} command, which halts the macro's execution. The label in cell BP8 is the cell reference for the cell named FINISH (BQ8). Move the cursor to cell BQ8 and name it FINISH at this time.

The main menu (see Figure 10.1) includes four menu choices for moving around the worksheet. These choices include the first row of entries in the macro range BQ4..BT4. Each of these entries (A_Schs, B_Schs, C_Schs, and Rs/T/F_Schs) is an item you would choose to display Schedules A, B, C, Rs, T, and F, respectively. For example, to display Schedule A, you would begin by toggling to A_Sch and pressing the Enter key or the "A" key. Enter each entry in the above range according to its cell reference.

```
AA1: [W45] ^SCHEDULE A:  SUMMARY OF ACTUAL AND REQUESTED EXPENDITURES        MENU
A_SCHs  B_SCHs  C_SCH  Rs/T/F_SCHs
GO TO SCHEDULE As
                      AA                              AB         AC
1   SCHEDULE A:  SUMMARY OF ACTUAL AND REQUESTED EXPENDITURES
2   UNIT:  Department of Public Works
3   ═══════════════════════════════════════════════════════════════
4
5
6
7                                            1985-86    1986-87
8   Personal Services:                       Actual     Actual
9     Man Years                                  98        100
10    Salaries                              1,352,400  1,380,000
11    Benefits                                      0          0
12
13  Supporting Services:
14    Travel                                   70,000     70,000
15    Telephone Tolls and Rental               14,000     14,657
16    Postage                                  60,000     69,000
17    Rent - State Owned Buildings             10,000     10,000
18    Rent - Privately Owned Buildings          6,600      6,600
19    Building Improvements                       100        100
20    Utility Charges                             250        250
```

Figure 10.1   Main Menu Options for Locating Budget Schedules

The entries in the second row of the macro (range BQ5..BT5) are descriptions of the functions of each of the main menu items. The third row of the macro (range BQ6..BT6) consists of commands that invoke submenus. For example, the {MENUCALL} entries BQ6, BR6, BS6, and BT6 each move the cursor to the cell locations named SCHAM (BQ11), B_SCHs (BP21), SCHCM (BQ44), and SCHRM (BQ55), respectively. Go to each of these locations and name each cell accordingly. The entries in cells BP11, BP21, BP44, and BP55 are cell references for the entries just mentioned. The {MENUBRANCH MENU} specifications to the right of the {MENUCALL} entries return macro control to the main menu, which will be redisplayed after its menu items have been selected.

The cell reference SCHAM= refers to a submenu that allows you to choose between displaying Schedule A or Schedule DA. For example, if you display Schedule A (either by toggling A_SCH or by pressing the "A" key), the main menu will disappear from 1-2-3's command line. In its place is the submenu that displays the choices, A_SCH (BQ11) and DA_SCH (BR11). Toggling either of these options displays designated schedules in cell BQ12, GO TO SCHEDULE A, or cell BR11, GO TO SCHEDULE DA (DEFLATED SCHEDULE A).

The {SCHAMA} and {SCHADM} entries in cells BQ13 and BR13, respectively, direct the cursor to the cells bearing those names (BQ15 and BQ18). Give cells BQ15 and BQ18 the names SCHMA and SCHADM, respectively. When the cursor arrives at the selected cell, the macro command found there, {GOTO}SCHA or {GOTO}SCHDA, is activated. The command {GOTO}SCHA directs the cursor to the range named SCHA, which automatically displays the area within that range. Range SCHA is the name of the area in which Schedule A is displayed (range AA1..AF44), and SCHDA is the name of the area occupied by Schedule DA (range AA65..AF108). Create and assign these range names.

The {BRANCH \m} commands in cells BQ16 and BQ19 cause the macro to branch to the main menu that reappears after the designated schedules are displayed. The entries SCHMA= and SCHADM= are simply cell reference labels referring to locations BQ15 and BQ18.

The submenus for automating the display of the six Schedules B, Schedules C and DC, Schedules R and DR, and Schedules T and F are located in the cell ranges BP21..BV21, BQ44..BR44, and BQ55..BT55, respectively. The techniques for creating these submenus are the same as those applied to the Schedule A and DA submenus. Using the previous listing of cell/macro entries as a guide, create the remaining submenus. Create the following cell/range names as you construct the submenus:

Cell	**Range Name**
BR25	PCSCHBM
BR28	MISCHBM
BR31	WCSCHBM
BR34	NCSCHBM
BR37	OCSCHBM
BR40	FFSCHBM
A82..E136	PCSCHB
A139..E193	MISCHB
A196..E250	WCSCHB
A253..E307	NCSCHB
A311..F364	OCSCHB
A367..E419	FFSCHB
BR48	SCHCMC
BR51	SCHDCM

continued...

<u>Cell</u>	<u>Range Name</u>
G1..X43	SCHC
G45..X87	SCHDC
BR59	SCHRMR
BR61	SCHRMD
BR63	SCHTMT
BR65	SCHFMF
AH1..AQ43	SCHR
AH65..AQ107	SCHDR
AY88..BI130	SCHT
AY302..BM333	SCHF

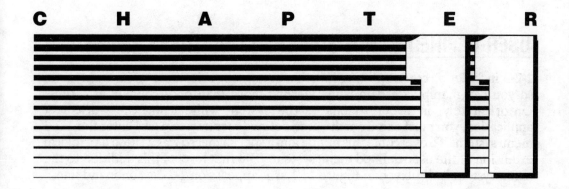

AUTOMATIC
WINDOW-SPLITTING UTILITY

USER-DEFINED MENUS FOR SPLITTING THE SCREEN

1-2-3 includes a screen-splitting function among the selections on its main menu so you can manipulate data while viewing more than one schedule at a time. Unfortunately, in order to enable the system while using the worksheet application, you must exit from the user-defined menu system and enter the 1-2-3 menu system. To overcome this limitation, a special macro was written as a logical extension of the user-defined menu system. The first level of this addition to the menu system is displayed in Figure 11.1 as it appears on 1-2-3's command line.

```
AA1: [W45] ^SCHEDULE A:  SUMMARY OF ACTUAL AND REQUESTED EXPENDITURES      MENU
A_SCHs  B_SCHs  C_SCH  Rs/T/F_SCHs  WINDOWS
GO TO SCHEDULE As
                        AA                    AB        AC
1    SCHEDULE A:  SUMMARY OF ACTUAL AND REQUESTED EXPENDITURES
2    UNIT:  Department of Public Works
3    ===========================================================================
4
5
6
7                                            1985-86    1986-87
8    Personal Services:                      Actual     Actual
9       Man Years                                98        100
10      Salaries                           1,352,400  1,380,000
11      Benefits                                   0          0
12
13   Supporting Services:
14      Travel                                70,000     70,000
15      Telephone Tolls and Rental            14,000     14,657
16      Postage                               60,000     69,000
17      Rent - State Owned Buildings          10,000     10,000
18      Rent - Privately Owned Buildings       6,600      6,600
19      Building Improvements                    100        100
20      Utility Charges                          250        250
```

Figure 11.1   *Main Menu Option for Splitting the Screen*

Add the macro to the worksheet's menu system by moving the cursor to cell BU4 and making the following entries:

Cell   Macro Entry

```
BU4:  WINDOWS
BU5:  GO TO WINDOWS SUBMENU
BU6:  {MENUCALL WINDOWS}{MENUBRANCH MENUS}
BP71: WINDOWS=
BQ71: H_TWO_WINDOWS
BR71: V_TWO_WINDOWS
BS71: ONE_WINDOW
BQ72: SPLIT SCREEN HORIZONTALLY
BR72: SPLIT SCREEN VERTICALLY
BS72: RETURN TO FULL SCREEN
BQ73: {WINDOWSHM}
BR73: {WINDOWSVM}
BS73: /wwc
BQ75: WINDOWSHM=
BS75: {GOTO}SCHA~
BS:   {DOWN 10}~
BS77: /wwh
BQ79: WINDOWSVM=
BS79: {GOTO}SCHA~
BS80: {RIGHT 1}~
BS81: /wwv
BP71: WINDOWS=
BQ71: H_TWO_WINDOWS
BR71: V_TWO_WINDOWS
BS71: ONE_WINDOW
BQ72: SPLIT SCREEN HORIZONTALLY
BR72: SPLIT SCREEN VERTICALLY
BS72: RETURN TO FULL SCREEN
BQ73: {WINDOWSHM}
BR73: {WINDOWSVM}
BS73: /wwc
BQ75: WINDOWSHM=
BS75: {GOTO}SCHA~
BS76: {DOWN 10}~
BS77: /wwh
```

continued...

...from previous page

```
BQ79: WINDOWSVM=
BS79: {GOTO}SCHA~
BS80: {RIGHT 1}~
BS81: /wwv
```

The cell entries in the first two lines of the windows portion of the menu system, WINDOWS and GO TO WINDOWS SUBMENU (cells BU4 and BU5), are labels. WINDOWS is the selection label and GO TO WINDOWS SUBMENU is the description of the function to be performed. The BU6 cell entry in the third row, {MENUCALL WINDOWS}{MENUBRANCH MENUS}, is a command that directs the macro to the range named WINDOWS. Move the cursor to BQ71 and give the range BQ71..BQ71 the name WINDOWS.

The WINDOWS= entry in BP71 is the cell reference for the remainder of the windows submenu macro. The submenu consists of the three submenu selection options, H_TWO_WINDOWS, V_TWO_WINDOWS, and ONE_WINDOW (cells BQ71, BR71, and BS71, respectively). The entries in BQ72, BR72, and BS72 describe the functions performed by the options: SPLIT SCREEN HORIZONTALLY, SPLIT SCREEN VERTICALLY, and RETURN TO FULL SCREEN. The entries {WINDOWSHM} and {WINDOWSVM} in cells BQ73 and BR73, respectively, direct the macro to the cell locations that have been assigned those range names. Move the cursor to ranges BS75..BS75 and BS79..BS79, and name them {WINDOWSHM} and {WINDOWSVM}, respectively. The WINDOWSSHM= and WINDOWSVM= entries in BQ75 and BQ79 are cell references for the macro commands located in the named range locations.

The two {GOTO}SCHA~ commands in BS75 and BS79 display Schedule A on the screen. This feature is helpful because most occasions that require a divided screen involve visually coordinating data manipulation between Schedule A and other schedules on which Schedule A depends. The {DOWN 10}~ and {RIGHT 1}~ commands in BS76 and BS80, respectively, move the cursor to the middle of the screen so that the screen is divided in approximately equal halves, both horizontally and vertically.

The commands that divide the screen horizontally and vertically are in cells BS77 and BS81, respectively. The entry in BS73 returns the display to a full screen when the entry ONE_WINDOW (cell BS71) is toggled or the "O" key is pressed.

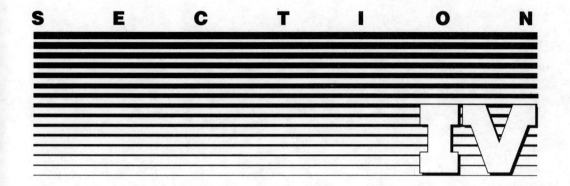

S E C T I O N

IV

WORKSHEET APPLICATION GRAPHICS

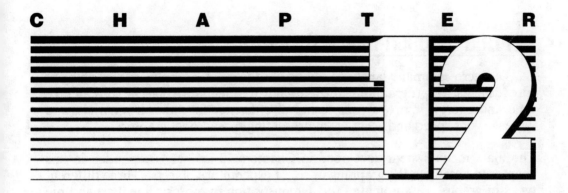

MAIN GRAPHICS DATA MENUS
AND SCHEDULE A GRAPHICS

SETTING UP USER-DEFINED MENUS

1-2-3's macro command language can be used to greatly simplify the graphing of spreadsheets. By programming the graphing of expenditure objects, you can save time and energy, improve your technical efficiency for "what-if" analysis, and increase your speed and accuracy in presenting spreadsheet graphics.

The main menu system developed in Chapters 10 and 11 is expanded in this chapter to automate the graphing of select expenditure objects. Three different types of graphs are automated for demonstration purposes: line, bar, and pie charts. Expenditure objects may be graphed in both current and real dollars. Numerous types of overlays are illustrated and may be applied to actual, trend, and forecast data. The main menu, expanded to include the graphics option, is displayed in Figure 12.1 as it appears on 1-2-3's command line.

```
AA1: [W45] ^SCHEDULE A:  SUMMARY OF ACTUAL AND REQUESTED EXPENDITURES        MENU
A_SCHs  B_SCHs  C_SCH  Rs/T/F_SCHs  WINDOWS  GRAPH
GO TO SCHEDULE As
                        AA                      AB          AC
1    SCHEDULE A:  SUMMARY OF ACTUAL AND REQUESTED EXPENDITURES
2    UNIT:  Department of Public Works
3    =============================================================
4
5
6
7                                               1985-86     1986-87
8    Personal Services:                          Actual      Actual
9       Man Years                                    98         100
10      Salaries                               1,352,400   1,380,000
11      Benefits                                       0           0
12
13   Supporting Services:
14      Travel                                    70,000      70,000
15      Telephone Tolls and Rental                14,000      14,657
16      Postage                                   60,000      69,000
17      Rent - State Owned Buildings              10,000      10,000
18      Rent - Privately Owned Buildings           6,800       6,800
19      Building Improvements                        100         100
20      Utility Charges                              250         250
```

Figure 12.1   *Main Menu Option for Graphics*

The main menu consists of the following cell/macro entries:

<u>**Cell**</u>   <u>**Macro Entry**</u>

```
BW4: GRAPH
BW5: GRAPH SCHEDULES
BW6: {MENUCALL GRAPH}{MENUBRANCH MENU}
```

Cells BW4 and BW5 consist of the menu option and option description entries. The {MENUCALL GRAPH} portion of the BW6 entry directs the flow of the macro to the cell named GRAPH. Move to cell BR268 at this time and give the range BR268..BR268 the name GRAPH. This is the location of the second level of the graph menu system or the first level of the graph submenu system. The {MENUBRANCH MENU} command in BW6 causes the flow of the macro to return to the main menu once execution of submenu functions is finished.

MAIN GRAPHICS SUBMENU

The first level of the graph submenu system (see Figure 12.2) includes eight schedule options: Schedules A, C, R, DA, DC, DR, T, and F. Each of these schedules is dependent on data tables for graphing purposes, as will be explained during the construction of the submenu system. The cell/macros for this first level of the submenu system consist of the following entries:

<u>**Cell**</u>   <u>**Macro Entry**</u>

```
BQ268: 'GRAPH=
BR268: ^1A_SCH
BS268: '2C_SCH
BT268: '3R_SCH
BU268: ^4DA_SCH
BV268: ^5DC_SCH
BW268: ^6DR_SCH
BX268: ^7T_SCH
BY268: ^8F_SCH
BR269: ^GRAPH SCHEDULE A
BS269: ^GRAPH SCHEDULE C
BT269: ^GRAPH SCHEDULE R
BU269: ^GRAPH SCHEDULE DA (DEFLATED SCHEDULE A)
```

continued...

...from previous page

```
BV269: ^GRAPH SCHEDULE DC (DEFLATED SCHEDULE C}
BW269: ^GRAPH SCHEDULE DR (DEFLATED SCHEDULE R)
BX269: ^GRAPH SCHEDULE T
BY269: ^GRAPH SCHEDULE F
BR270: ^{MENUCALL AGRAPH}
BS270: ^{MENUCALL CGRAPH}
BT270: ^{MENUCALL RGRAPH}
BU270: ^{MENUCALL DAGRAPH}
BV270: ^{MENUCALL DCGRAPH}
BW270: ^{MENUCALL DRGRAPH}
BX270: ^{MENUCALL TGRAPH}
BY270: ^{MENUCALL FGRAPH}
```

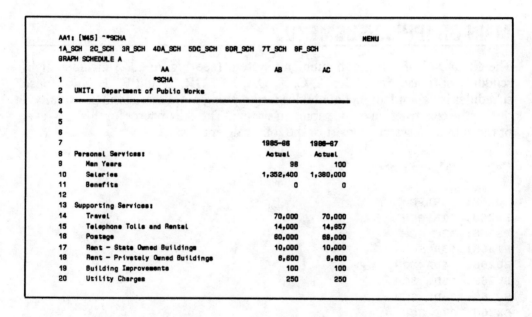

Figure 12.2   Submenu Budget Schedule Graphing Options

Use the same techniques for constructing the first three rows of the main submenu as you did in Chapter 10 to construct the main submenu for getting around the worksheet application. Make those entries now. The entries for the third row of the submenu (row 270) include cell name references following each of the MENUCALL commands. Move the cursor to cell BS273 and give the range BS273..BS273 the name AGRAPH. This directs the macro to the second level of the graphics submenu system, which is the main submenu for graphing Schedule A data. (Note: In this chapter, it will be assumed that the techniques for menu/submenu construction that were used in Chapters 10 and 11 require no further instruction. Therefore, only those macro techniques that have not been explained previously will be fully elaborated in this chapter.)

SECONDARY GRAPHICS
SUBMENUS: SCHEDULE A MAIN SUBMENU

The {MENU CALL AGRAPH} in cell BS270 refers to the third level of the graphics submenu system. Move to cell BS273 and create the range name AGRAPH for the range BT273..BT273; this is the name of the third level. To construct the Schedule A main submenu (see Figure 12.3), make the following entries:

<u>Cell</u>   <u>Macro Entry</u>

```
BR273:  AGRAPH=
BS273:  LINE_GRAPHA
BT273:  BAR_GRAPHA
BU273:  PIE_GRAPHA
BS274:  DO LINE GRAPHS OF SCHEDULE A
BT274:  DO BAR GRAPHS OF SCHEDULE A
BU274:  DO PIE GRAPHS OF SCHEDULE A
BS275:  {MENUCALL ALINE}
BT275:  {MENUCALL ABAR}
BU275:  {MENUCALL APIE}
```

```
AA1: [W45] ^*SCHA                                                    MENU
LINE_GRAPHA  BAR_GRAPHA  PIE_GRAPHA
DO LINE GRAPHS OF SCHEDULE A
                        AA                      AB          AC
1                             *SCHA
2      UNIT:  Department of Public Works
3      ================================================================
4
5
6
7                                             1985-86     1986-87
8      Personal Services:                     Actual      Actual
9          Man Years                              98         100
10         Salaries                        1,352,400   1,380,000
11         Benefits                                0           0
12
13     Supporting Services:
14         Travel                             70,000      70,000
15         Telephone Tolls and Rental         14,000      14,657
16         Postage                            60,000      69,000
17         Rent - State Owned Buildings       10,000      10,000
18         Rent - Privately Owned Buildings    6,600       6,600
19         Building Improvements                 100         100
20         Utility Charges                       250         250
```

Figure 12.3   Graphics Submenu Options for Schedule A

The main menu of the Schedule A graphics submenu provides you with three options. You can choose to draw line, bar, or pie charts. The following sections provide instructions for constructing each of the three graph types.

SECONDARY GRAPHICS
SUBMENUS: SCHEDULE A LINE CHART

The {MENU CALL ALINE} in cell BS270 refers to the third level of the submenu system. Move to cell BT278, and create the range name ALINE for the range BT278..BT278. This submenu includes options for generating individual line graphs of seven Schedule A line-items: Total Expenditures, Man Years, Salaries, Travel, Telephone, Postage, and Capital Outlays (see Figure 12.4).

```
AA1: [W45] ^*SCHA                                    MENU
1TOTA  2MAN_YRSA  3SALA  4TRAVA  5TELA  6POSTA  7CAPL_OUTLA
TOTAL EXPENDITURES
                          AA              AB        AC
1               *SCHA
2    UNIT:  Department of Public Works
3    ================================================
4
5
6
7                                       1985-86   1986-87
8    Personal Services:                 Actual    Actual
9        Man Years                          98       100
10       Salaries                    1,352,400  1,380,000
11       Benefits                            0         0
12
13   Supporting Services:
14       Travel                         70,000    70,000
15       Telephone Tolls and Rental     14,000    14,657
16       Postage                        60,000    69,000
17       Rent - State Owned Buildings   10,000    10,000
18       Rent - Privately Owned Buildings 6,800    6,800
19       Building Improvements             100       100
20       Utility Charges                   250       250
```

Figure 12.4 *Schedule A Submenu Options for Graphing Individual Objects of Expenditure*

Make the following third-level submenu entries:

Cell **Macro Entry**

```
BS278: ALINE=
BT278: 1TOTA
BU278: 2MAN_YRSA
BV278: 3SALA
BW278: 4TRAVA
BX278: 5TELA
BY278: 6POSTA
BZ278: 7CAPL_OUTLA
BT279: TOTAL EXPENDITURES
BU279: MAN YEARS
BV279: SALARY EXPENDITURES
BW279: TRAVEL EXPENDITURES
BX279: TELEPHONE EXPENDITURES
```

continued...

...from previous page

```
BY279: POSTAGE EXPENDITURES
BZ279: CAPITAL OUTLAY EXPS
BT280: {INDICATE WAIT}{CALC}{PANELOFF}{WINDOWSOFF}
BU280: {INDICATE WAIT}{CALC}{PANELOFF}{WINDOWSOFF}
BV280: {INDICATE WAIT}{CALC}{PANELOFF}{WINDOWSOFF}
BW280: {INDICATE WAIT}{CALC}{PANELOFF}{WINDOWSOFF}
BX280: {INDICATE WAIT}{CALC}{PANELOFF}{WINDOWSOFF}
BY280: {INDICATE WAIT}{CALC}{PANELOFF}{WINDOWSOFF}
BZ280: {INDICATE WAIT}{CALC}{PANELOFF}{WINDOWSOFF}
BT281: /grg
BU281: /grg
BV281: /grg
BW281: /grg
BX281: /grg
BY281: /grg
BZ281: /grg
BT282: tl
BU282: tl
BV282: tl
BW282: tl
BX282: tl
BY282: tl
BZ282: tl
BT283: aAB42.AF42~
BU283: aAB9.AF9~
BV283: aAB10.AF10~
BW283: aAB14.AF14~
BX283: aAB15.AF15~
BY283: aAB16.AF16~
BZ283: aAB40.AF40~
BT284: xAB7.AF7~
BU284: xAB7.AF7~
BV284: xAB7.AF7~
BW284: xAB7.AF7~
BX284: xAB7.AF7~
BY284: xAB7.AF7~
BZ284: xAB7.AF7~
BT285: o
BU285: o
```

continued...

...from previous page

```
BV285: o
BW285: o
BX285: o
BY285: o
BZ285: o
BT286: cfab
BU286: cfab
BV286: cfab
BW286: cfab
BX286: cfab
BY286: cfab
BZ286: cfab
BT287: q
BU287: q
BV287: q
BW287: q
BX287: q
BY287: q
BZ287: q
BT288: tfDepartment of Public Works~
BU288: tfDepartment of Public Works~
BV288: tfDepartment of Public Works~
BW288: tfDepartment of Public Works~
BX288: tfDepartment of Public Works~
BY288: tfDepartment of Public Works~
BZ288: tfDepartment of Public Works~
BT289: tsTotal Expenditures~
BU289: tsMan Years~
BV289: tsSalary Expenditures~
BW289: tsTravel Expenditures~
BX289: tsTelephone Expenditures~
BY289: tsPostage Expenditures~
BZ289: tsCapital Outlay Expenditures~
BT290: q
BU290: q
BV290: q
BW290: q
BX290: q
BY290: q
```

continued...

...from previous page

```
BZ290:  q
BT291:  v
BU291:  v
BV291:  v
BW291:  v
BX291:  v
BY291:  v
BZ291:  v
BT292:  q
BU292:  q
BV292:  q
BW292:  q
BX292:  q
BY292:  q
BZ292:  q
BT293:  {INDICATE}{BRANCH \m}
BU293:  {INDICATE}{BRANCH \m}
BV293:  {INDICATE}{BRANCH \m}
BW293:  {INDICATE}{BRANCH \m}
BX293:  {INDICATE}{BRANCH \m}
BY293:  {INDICATE}{BRANCH \m}
BZ293:  {INDICATE}{BRANCH \m}
```

The {INDICATE WAIT}, {CALC}, {PANELOFF}, and {WINDOWSOFF} entries in row 280 and the {INDICATE} entries in row 293 prompt you to wait, recalculate the worksheet, and freeze 1-2-3's command line and screen while all remaining calculations required for drawing graphs are going on. Recalculating the worksheet ensures that any changes that may have been made in the worksheet application and that have not yet been calculated will be incorporated with the line graphs to be drawn. The / in the /grg commands in row 281 activates the 1-2-3 menu system. The grg command activates 1-2-3's graph option and resets/clears any graph settings that may have been entered previously. The tl commands in row 282 specify the type of graph to be constructed as a line graph. The x commands in row 283 set the first data ranges of the graphs to those listed in columns BT, BU, BV, BW, BX, BY, and BZ. These ranges also correspond, respectively, with the data for the Schedule A line items previously designated to be graphed, which coincide, in turn, with the budget periods 1985-86 through 1989-90. The x commands in row 284 set the ranges for the data to be used in graphing the x-axis of the individual graphs. These data are the budget years specified above.

The o commands in row 285 summon a 1-2-3 submenu containing formatting options, including the cfab entries in row 286. The c entry causes the graph to appear in color. If you have a monochrome monitor or do not plan to graph in color, enter a b instead of a c in each of the option locations. The f command provides the option to draw lines or symbols in the graph; the a command selects the formats, lines, or symbols for the a range; and the b command draws symbols at data points and draws lines between data points. The q command returns you to the options submenu.

The t and f command combination specifies the first graph title line, which, in this case, is Department of Public Works. The tilde (~) symbol executes tf. (The t and s command combination similarly specifies individual graph titles, the second one to appear on the Schedule A line graphs.) These titles correspond to the line-item entries arrayed in row 289. The q, v, and q commands in rows 290-292 and the {BRANCH \m} commands in row 293 return the cursor to the previously invoked 1-2-3 submenu, activate the display of the graph, disengage the macro from the 1-2-3 menu system (after the graph is viewed), and return macro control to the worksheet application's main menu.

Creating graphs using Schedule A's line graph submenu is very easy. First, enter \m (Alt/M) to summon the main menu, and then choose the graph menu option by entering G or by moving the cursor to the GRAPH option and toggling with the Enter key. Second, when the line graph submenu appears, toggle or enter the first character of the menu option of the type of graph you want to draw (e.g., line, bar, or pie), and a listing of line items appears. Third, when the listing of schedule options appears, simply toggle or enter the one you want to graph, and it automatically is graphed with all scale, legend, title, etc. requirements intact. For example, when you get to step three, to graph Schedule A salary expenditures, toggle 3SALA, or enter 3 and press Return. Figure 12.5 shows the resulting line graph of Schedule A salary expenditures. Returning to the main menu is easy; simply press ESC.

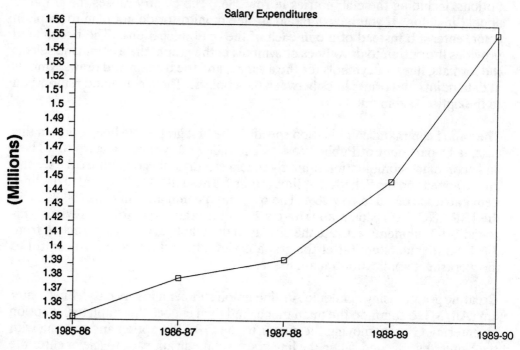

Figure 12.5   *Sample Line Graph of Schedule A: Salary Expenditures*

SECONDARY GRAPHICS
SUBMENUS: SCHEDULE A BAR CHART

The fourth level of the submenu graphics system is very similar to the third tier except that the graphing is done with bar graphs rather than line graphs. The entries necessary for constructing the submenu are identical with a few exceptions.

Move the cursor to cell BS295 and enter ABAR=, the Schedule A bar graphing macro reference label. Next, interface the fourth level with Schedule A's main graphic submenu by giving the range BT295..BT295 the name ABAR (the macro command reference = {MENUCALL ABAR} command in BT275). Using 1-2-3's Copy command, duplicate the first four rows of the Schedule A line graphing submenu with the upper left entry of the submenu located in cell BT295. Enter tb in each column of the next row (299) of the submenu, and enter cfan in each column of row 303. All remaining entries of the submenu are identical to those entered in the line graph system. Copy those entries into the bar graph submenu now. The tb entry causes the graphing to be done in the bar graph mode. The cfan entry is the same as the cfab line graph entry except that the n entry causes the symbols at data points and lines between data points, which were relevant for line-graphing purposes, not to be invoked. Check the accuracy of your entries by graphing the Schedule A bar graph expenditure objects before proceeding to the next section.

Continuing with the graphing example used in the previous section, note Figure 12.6, which shows the results of drawing a Schedule A salary expenditures bar graph.

(See next page)

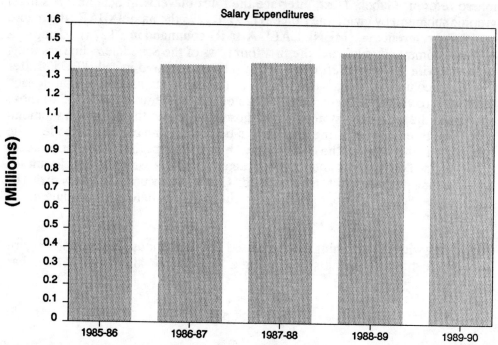

Figure 12.6   Sample Bar Graph of Schedule A: Salary Expenditures

SECONDARY GRAPHICS
SUBMENUS: SCHEDULE A PIE CHART

As noted in the MAIN GRAPHICS SUBMENU section, the worksheet schedules depend on data tables to automatically graph expenditure data because 1-2-3 requires that data be arrayed consecutively in a prescribed sequence in order to be graphed.

Schedule A's data table is displayed in Figure 12.7. The table is dependent on Schedule A for its data. The only feature in this data table that varies from the techniques used in constructing previous tables consists of the entries in column AV. As mentioned in the previous section, these values are for assigning the shadings of the pie chart wedges. Figure 12.7 shows these values to be 102, 1, 3, 7, 6, and 8. The 102 value explodes the wedge assigned to the salaries expenditure object. The expenditure objects featured in the table and the wedge value assignments or wedge(s) to be exploded may be changed to suit the purposes at hand. Use the following list of cells to construct the Schedule A Data Table before proceeding to the next section.

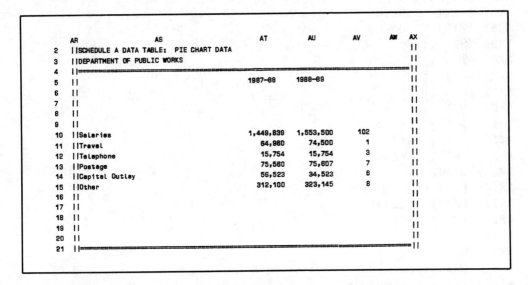

	AR	AS	AT	AU	AV	AW	AX
2	||SCHEDULE A DATA TABLE: PIE CHART DATA						||
3	||DEPARTMENT OF PUBLIC WORKS						||
4	||==						||
5	||		1987-88	1988-89			||
6	||						||
7	||						||
8	||						||
9	||						||
10	||Salaries		1,449,839	1,553,500	102		||
11	||Travel		64,960	74,500	1		||
12	||Telephone		15,754	15,754	3		||
13	||Postage		75,560	75,607	7		||
14	||Capital Outlay		56,523	34,523	6		||
15	||Other		312,100	323,145	8		||
16	||						||
17	||						||
18	||						||
19	||						||
20	||						||
21	||==						||

Figure 12.7   *Schedule A Data Table: Pie Chart Data*

Cell Listing: Figure 12.7

```
AS2:  [W40] 'SCHEDULE A DATA TABLE:  PIE CHART DATA
AX2:  [W2] \|
AS3:  [W40] 'DEPARTMENT OF PUBLIC WORKS
AX3:  [W2] \|
AS4:  [W40] \=
AT4:  [W12] \=
AU4:  [W12] \=
AV4:  \=
AW4:  \=
AX4:  [W2] \|
AT5:  [W12] ^1987-88
AU5:  [W12] ^1988-89
AX5:  [W2] \|
AX6:  [W2] \|
AX7:  [W2] \|
AX8:  [W2] \|
AX9:  [W2] \|
AS10: [W40] 'Salaries
AT10: [W12] +AE10
AU10: [W12] (AF10)
AV10: U 102
AX10: [W2] \|
AS11: [W40] 'Travel
AT11: [W12] +AE14
AU11: [W12] (AF14)
AV11: U 1
AX11: [W2] \|
AS12: [W40] 'Telephone
AT12: [W12] +AE15
AU12: [W12] (AF15)
AV12: U 3
AX12: [W2] \|
AS13: [W40] 'Postage
AT13: [W12] +AE16
AU13: [W12] (AF16)
AV13: U 7
AX13: [W2] \|
AS14: [W40] 'Capital Outlay
AT14: [W12] +AE40
```

continued...

...from previous page

```
AU14:  [W12]  +AF40
AV14:  U 6
AX14:  [W2]  \|
AS15:  [W40]  'Other
AT15:  [W12]  +AE42-@SUM(AT10..AT14)
AU15:  [W12]  +AF42-@SUM(AU10..AU14)
AV15:  U 8
AX15:  [W2]  \|
AX16:  [W2]  \|
AT17:  [W12]  ^
AX17:  [W2]  \|
AX18:  [W2]  \|
AX19:  [W2]  \|
AX20:  [W2]  \|
AS21:  [W40]  \=
AT21:  [W12]  \=
AU21:  [W12]  \=
AV21:  \=
AW21:  \=
AX21:  [W2]  \|
```

The next level of the submenu system consists of a submenu that automates the graphing of Schedule A pie charts (see Figure 12.8).

```
AA1: [W45] ^*SCHA                                                    MENU
1A_SCH_1988-89  2A_SCH_1989-90
SCHEDULE A, 1988-89:  SALARIES, TRAVEL, TELEPHONE, CAPITAL OUTLAYS, OTHER
                   AA                        AB          AC
    1                      ^*SCHA
    2    UNIT:  Department of Public Works
    3    ================================================================
    4
    5
    6
    7                                      1985-86     1986-87
    8    Personal Services:               Actual      Actual
    9       Man Years                          98         100
   10       Salaries                    1,352,400   1,380,000
   11       Benefits                            0           0
   12
   13    Supporting Services:
   14       Travel                         70,000      70,000
   15       Telephone Tolls and Rental     14,000      14,657
   16       Postage                        60,000      69,000
   17       Rent - State Owned Buildings   10,000      10,000
   18       Rent - Privately Owned Buildings 6,600      6,600
   19       Building Improvements             100         100
   20       Utility Charges                   250         250
```

Figure 12.8   Submenu Options for Graphing Schedule A Pie Charts

The cells and entries of the submenu are as follows:

<u>Cell</u>   <u>Macro Entry</u>

BS312: APIE=
BT312: 1A_SCH_1988-89
BU312: 2A_SCH_1989-90
BT313: SCHEDULE A, 1988-89: SALARIES, TRAVEL, TELEPHONE, CAPIT
       AL OUTLAYS, OTHER
BU313: SCHEDULE A, 1989-90: SALARIES, TRAVEL, TELEPHONE, CAPIT
       AL OUTLAYS, OTHER
BT314: {INDICATE WAIT}{CALC}{PANELOFF}{WINDOWSOFF}
BU314: {INDICATE WAIT}{CALC}{PANELOFF}{WINDOWSOFF}
BT315: /grg
BU315: /grg
BT316: tp
BU316: tp
BT317: aAT10.AT15~

continued...

...from previous page

```
BU317: aAU10.AU15~
BT318: xAS10.AS15~
BU318: xAS10.AS15~
BT319: bAV10.AV15~
BU319: bAV10.AV15~
BT320: oc
BU320: oc
BT321: tfDepartment of Public Works~
BU321: tfDepartment of Public Works~
BT322: tsRelATive Expenditure Request Share, 1988-89~
BU322: tsRelATive Expenditure Request Share, 1989-90~
BT323: q
BU323: q
BT324: v
BU324: v
BT325: q
BU325: q
BT326: {INDICATE}{BRANCH \m}
BU326: {INDICATE}{BRANCH \m}
```

The MENUCALL APIE in cell BU275 causes the Schedule A graphics submenu to activate the range named APIE (BT312..BT312); this is the starting point of the Schedule A pie graphics submenu. Move the cursor to BT312 and name the range before proceeding further. Cells BT312 and BU312 activate the drawing of pie charts for six expenditure categories for each budget year of the biennium. BT313 and BU313 describe the categories to be graphed, and cells BT316 and BU316 specify the type of graphs as "pie." (Note: Only those macro entries that mark a departure in function or technique from those created in macros presented in previous sections will be discussed in detail.)

The a commands in BT317 and BU317 specify the data ranges to be graphed in each of the biennial periods. These data ranges include expenditure object data located in a specially designed data table you will create in the next section. The x commands in cells BT318 and BU318 set the individual names of the expenditure objects to be graphed in each year of the biennium. These names include Salaries, Travel, Telephone, Postage, Capital Outlays, and a residual expenditure category — Other.

The b commands in cells BT319 and BU319 specify the values for shading the wedges of the pie graph. The o through c clusters in cells BT320 and BU320 assign the color option to the pie graphs. The remaining commands are self-explanatory; you should enter them before proceeding to the next section.

To draw a pie graph of the six expenditure objects for the first biennial period, select the PIE_GRAPHA option from the submenu and then the 1A_SCH_1988-89 option. To graph the same expenditure objects for the second biennial period, select the 2A_SCH_1989-80 option. The pie chart for the first biennial period is displayed in Figure 12.9.

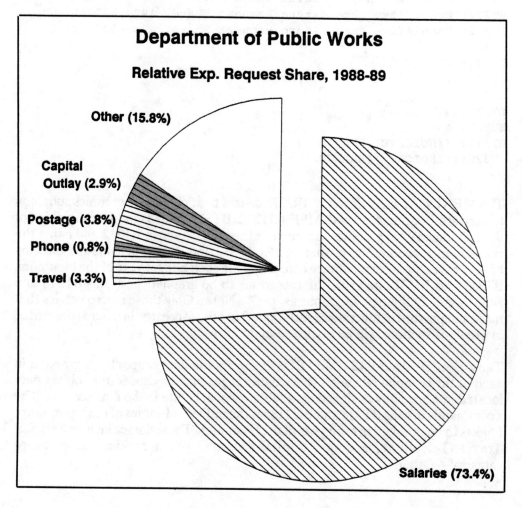

Figure 12.9   *Sample Pie Chart of Schedule A: Individual Objects of Expenditure—First Biennium Data*

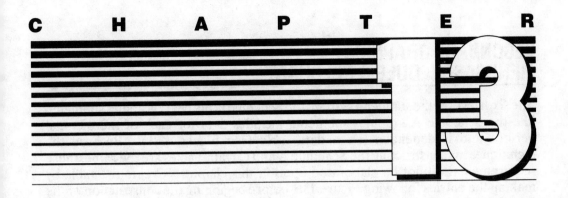

SCHEDULE C GRAPHICS

SECONDARY GRAPHICS
MENUS: SCHEDULE C PIE CHART

The sixth level of the submenu system, the Schedule C pie chart graphics submenu, like the Schedule A graphics submenu, includes data for each of the biennial periods and is dependent on a data table (see Figure 13.1). Because the techniques for constructing the Schedule A and C Data Tables are the same, those requirements will not be elaborated upon in this chapter. Create the table by making the entries following Figure 13.1 before beginning the construction of the Schedule C pie chart graphics submenu.

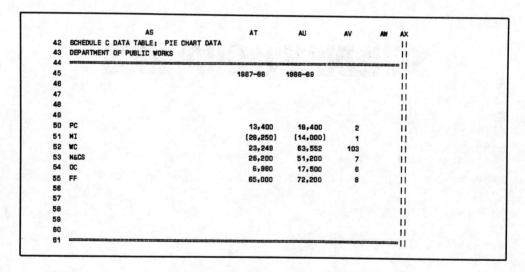

	AS	AT	AU	AV	AW	AX
42	SCHEDULE C DATA TABLE: PIE CHART DATA					‖
43	DEPARTMENT OF PUBLIC WORKS					‖
44						‖
45		1987-88	1988-89			‖
46						‖
47						‖
48						‖
49						‖
50	PC	13,400	18,400	2		‖
51	MI	(26,250)	(14,000)	1		‖
52	WC	23,249	63,552	103		‖
53	N&CS	26,200	51,200	7		‖
54	OC	6,960	17,500	6		‖
55	FF	65,000	72,200	8		‖
56						‖
57						‖
58						‖
59						‖
60						‖
61						‖

Figure 13.1   Schedule C Data Table: Pie Chart Data

Cell Listing: Figure 13.1

```
AS42: [W40] ^SCHEDULE C DATA TABLE:  PIE CHART DATA
AX42: [W2] \|
AS43: [W40] ^DEPARTMENT OF PUBLIC WORKS
AX43: [W2] \|
AS44: [W40] \=
AT44: [W12] \=
AU44: [W12] \=
AV44: \=
AW44: \=
AX44: [W2] \|
AT45: [W12] ^1987-88
AU45: [W12] ^1988-89
AX45: [W2] \|
AX46: [W2] \|
AX47: [W2] \|
AX48: [W2] \|
AX49: [W2] \|
AS50: [40] 'PC
AT50: [W12] +H42
AU50: [W12] +Q42
AV50: U 2
AX50: [W2] \|
AS51: [W40] 'MI
AT51: [W12] +I42
AU51: [W12] +R42
AV51: U 1
AX51: [W2] \|
AS52: [W40] 'WC
AT52: [W12] +J42
AU52: [W12] +S42
AV52: U 103
AX52: [W2] \|
AS53: [W40] 'N&CS
AT53: [W12] +K42
AU53: [W12] +T42
AV53: U 7
AX53: [W2] \|
AS54: [W40] 'OC
AT54: [W12] +L42
```

continued...

...from previous page

```
AU54:  [W12]  +U42
AV54:  U 6
AX54:  [W2]  \|
AS55:  [W40]  'FF
AT55:  [W12]  +M42
AU55:  [W12]  +V42
AV55:  U 8
AX55:  [W2]  \|
AX56:  [W2]  \|
AT57:  [W12]  ^
AX57:  [W2]  \|
AX58:  [W2]  \|
AX59:  [W2]  \|
AX60:  [W2]  \|
AS61:  [W40]  \=
AT61:  [W12]  \=
AU61:  [W12]  \=
AV61:  \=
AW61:  \=
AX61:  [W2]  \|
```

The BS268 cell entry, {MENUCALL CGRAPH}, appearing in the main graphics submenu created in Chapter 12 is the range name reference cell for the Schedule C graphics submenu. Your first step in constructing the submenu is to move the cursor to cell BS329 and give the range BS329..BS329 the name CGRAPH. Next, create the Schedule C pie chart graphics submenu (see Figure 13.2), which automates the graphing of Schedule C pie charts.

```
G1: [W45] 'SCHEDULE C:  MATRIX OF BUDGET CHANGE REQUESTS                    MENU
1_SCH_C_1988-89 PIE GRAPH  2_SCH_C_1989-90 PIE GRAPH
SCHEDULE C, 1989-90 PIE GRAPH:  PC, MI, WC, N&CS, OC, FF
                          G                    H       I       J
     1   SCHEDULE C:  MATRIX OF BUDGET CHANGE REQUESTS
     2   UNIT:  Department of Public Works
     3   ═══════════════════════════════════════════════════════
     4
     5                                                       1988-
     6   Change Categories                  PC      MI       WLC
     7   ──────────────────────────────────────────────────────
     8   Personal Services:
     9     Man Years
    10     Salaries                                [41,250] 19,789
    11     Benefits
    12
    13   Supporting Services:
    14     Travel
    15     Telephone Tolls and Rental
    16     Postage                        4,000            1,560
    17     Rent - State Owned Buildings   4,400
    18     Rent - Privately Owned Buildings
    19     Building Improvements
    20     Utility Charges
```

Figure 13.2   Submenu Options for Graphing Schedule C Pie Charts

The cells and entries of the Schedule C pie chart graphics submenu are as follows:

Cell   Macro Entry

```
R329:  CGRAPH=
BS329: 1_SCH_C_1988-89 PIE GRAPH
BT329: 2_SCH_C_1989-90 PIE GRAPH
BS330: SCHEDULE C, 1988-89 PIE GRAPH:   PC, MI, WC, N&CS, OC, FF
BT330: SCHEDULE C, 1989-90 PIE GRAPH:   PC, MI, WC, N&CS, OC, FF
BS331: {INDICATE WAIT}{CALC}{PANELOFF}{WINDOWSOFF}
BT331: {INDICATE WAIT}{CALC}{PANELOFF}{WINDOWSOFF}
BS332: /grg
BT332: /grg
BS333: tp
BT333: tp
BS334: aAT53.AT57~
BT334: aAU53.AU58~
BS335: xAS53.AS57~
```

continued...

...from previous page

```
BT335: xAS53.AS57~
BS336: bAV53.AV57~
BT336: bAV53.AV57~
BS337: oc
BT337: oc
BS338: tfDepartment of Public Works~
BT338: tfDepartment of Public Works~
BS339: ts1988-89 Expenditures Increase~
BT339: ts1989-90 Expenditures Increase~
BS340: q
BT340: q
BS341: v
BT341: v
BS342: q
BT342: q
BS343: {INDICATE}{BRANCH \m}
BT343: {INDICATE}{BRANCH \m}
```

As rows 329 and 330 suggest, the Schedule C graphics submenu allows you to draw pie charts for each of the biennial budget request years incorporating six price change categories: Price Changes (PC), Methods Improvements (MI), Other Continuing (OC), Workload Changes (WC), New and Changed Services (N&CS), and Full Financing (FF). The results of drawing a pie chart for the first biennial period are displayed in Figure 13.3.

After testing to be sure that the Schedule C graphics submenu and its supporting data table function properly, proceed to the next section and create Schedule R.

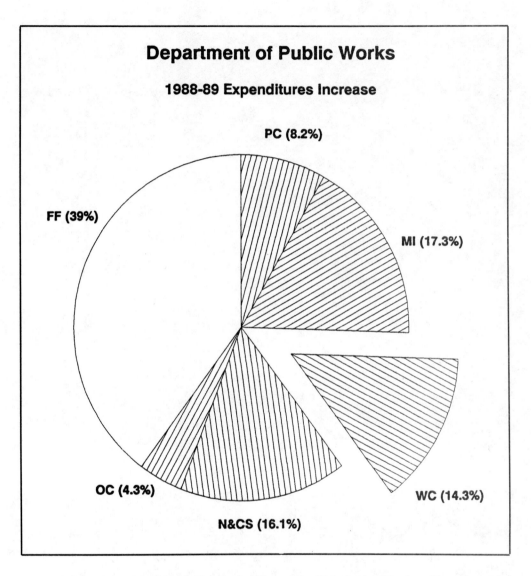

Department of Public Works

1988-89 Expenditures Increase

PC (8.2%)

FF (39%)

MI (17.3%)

OC (4.3%)

WC (14.3%)

N&CS (16.1%)

Figure 13.3   *Sample Pie Chart of Schedule C: Individual Budget Change*
          Request Categories

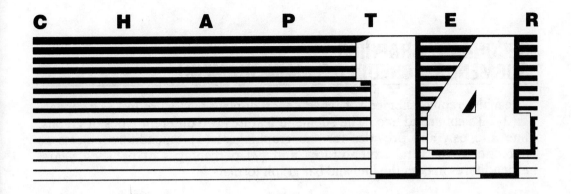

SCHEDULE R GRAPHICS

SECONDARY GRAPHICS
SUBMENUS: SCHEDULE R MAIN SUBMENU

The main graphics submenu of Schedule R is displayed in Figure 14.1 as it appears on 1-2-3's command line. The submenu features two different types of graphs, line and bar, and provides for the graphing of (1) expenditure objects as percentages of total expenditures and (2) percentages of between years' expenditures in both the line and bar graph formats.

```
AH1: [W45] 'SCHEDULE R:  SUMMARY OF ACTUAL AND REQUESTED BUDGET RATIOS      MENU
1LINE_GRAPHR  2BAR_GRAPHR  3LINE_GRAPH  4BAR_GRAPH
DO LINE GRAPHS OF SCHEDULE R % OF TOTAL EXPENDITURES
                       AH                       AI
1    SCHEDULE R:  SUMMARY OF ACTUAL AND REQUESTED BUDGET RATIOS
2    UNIT:  Department of Public Works
3    ==================================================
4
5
6                                      % Total Exp
7                                       1985-86
8    Personal Services:                 Actual
9        Man Years
10       Salaries                           76.57%
11       Benefits                            0.00%
12
13   Supporting Services:
14       Travel                              3.98%
15       Telephone Tolls and Rental          0.79%
16       Postage                             3.40%
17       Rent - State Owned Buildings        0.57%
18       Rent - Privately Owned Buildings    0.37%
19       Building Improvements               0.01%
20       Utility Charges                     0.01%
```

Figure 14.1   # 1 Line Graphics Option for Schedule R

Move the cursor to cell BS346 and give the range BS346..BS346 the name RGRAPH, which is the name of the Schedule R graphics submenu as specified by the MENUCALL RGRAPH command in cell BT270 of the main graphics menu. Then, to construct the Schedule R main graphics menu, make the following entries:

<u>Cell</u>	<u>Macro Entry</u>

BR346: RGRAPH=
BS346: 1LINE_GRAPHR
BT346: 2BAR_GRAPHR
BU346: 3LINE_GRAPH
BV346: 4BAR_GRAPH
BS347: DO LINE GRAPHS OF SCHEDULE R % OF TOTAL EXPENDITURES
BT347: DO BAR GRAPHS OF SCHEDULE R % OF TOTAL EXPENDITURES
BU347: DO LINE GRAPHS OF SCHEDULE R ANNUAL % EXPENDITURE CHANGES
BV347: DO BAR GRAPHS OF SCHEDULE R ANNUAL % EXPENDITURE CHANGES
BS348: {MENUCALL RLINE1}
BT348: {MENUCALL RBAR1}
BU348: {MENUCALL RLINE2}
BV348: {MENUCALL RBAR2}

SECONDARY GRAPHICS SUBMENUS: SCHEDULE R #1 LINE CHART

Before creating the Schedule R #1 line chart graphics submenu, enter the following list of cells to construct a data table upon which the submenu relies. The data table's name should be Schedule R Data Table: Annual % of Total Expenditure Factors (see Figure 14.2).

	AH	AI	AJ
109	SCHEDULE R DATA TABLE: ANNUAL % OF TOTAL EXPENDITURE FACTORS		
110	UNIT: DEPARTMENT OF PUBLIC WORKS		
111	═══════════════════════════════════════		
112			
113			
114		1985-86	1986-87
115			
116			
117	Salaries	76.57%	75.88%
118	Travel	3.96%	3.85%
119	Telephone	0.79%	0.81%
120	Postage	3.40%	3.79%
121	Capital Outlay	0.41%	0.67%
122	Other	14.86%	15.00%
123			
124			
125			
126			
127			
128	AH	AI	
129			
130			
131	═══════════════════════════════════════		

Figure 14.2   *Schedule R Data Table: Annual % of Total Expenditure Factors*

AK	AL	AM	AN	AO	AP	AQ	AR
1987-88	1988-89	1989-90					
74.81%	73.42%	74.79%					
3.43%	3.29%	3.59%					
0.84%	0.80%	0.76%					
3.75%	3.83%	3.64%					
1.85%	2.86%	1.66%					
15.53%	15.80%	15.56%					

Cell Listing: Figure 14.2

```
AH109: [W45] 'SCHEDULE R DATA TABLE: ANNUAL % OF TOTAL EXPENDITURES
            FACTORS
AR109: [W2] |||
10: [W45] 'UNIT:  DEPARTMENT OF PUBLIC WORKS
AR110: [W2] |||
AH111: [W45] \=
AI111: [W15] \=
AJ111: [W15] \=
AK111: [W13] \=
AL111: [W13] \=
AM111: [W13] \=
AN111: [W13] \=
AO111: [W13] \=
AP111: [W13] \=
AQ111: [W13] \=
AR111: [W2] |||
AR112: [W2] |||
AR113: [W2] |||
AI114: [W15] ^1985-86
AJ114: [W15] ^1986-87
AK114: [W13] ^1987-88
AL114: [W13] ^1988-89
AM114: [W13] ^1989-90
AR114: [W2] |||
AR115: [W2] |||
AR116: [W2] |||
AH117: [W45] 'Salaries
AI117: (P2) U [W15] (AI10)
AJ117: (P2) U [W15] (AJ10)
AK117: (P2) U [W13] (AL10)
AL117: (P2) U [W13] (AN10)
AM117: (P2) U [W13] (AP10)
AR117: [W2] |||
AH118: [W45] 'Travel
AI118: (P2) U [W15] (AI14)
AJ118: (P2) U [W15] (AJ14)
AK118: (P2) U [W13] (AL14)
AL118: (P2) U [W13] (AN14)
AM118: (P2) U [W13] (AP14)
```

continued...

...from previous page

```
AR118: [W2] |||
AH119: [W45] 'Telephone
AI119: (P2) U [W15] (AI15)
AJ119: (P2) U [W15] (AJ15)
AK119: (P2) U [W13] (AL15)
AL119: (P2) U [W13] (AN15)
AM119: (P2) U [W13] (AP15)
AR119: [W2] |||
AH120: [W45] 'Postage
AI120: (P2) U [W15] (AI16)
AJ120: (P2) U [W15] (AJ16)
AK120: (P2) U [W13] (AL16)
AL120: (P2) U [W13] (AN16)
AM120: (P2) U [W13] (AP16)
AR120: [W2] |||
AH121: [W45] 'Capital Outlay
AI121: (P2) U [W15] (AI40)
AJ121: (P2) U [W15] (AJ40)
AK121: (P2) U [W13] (AL40)
AL121: (P2) U [W13] (AN40)
AM121: (P2) U [W13] (AP40)
AR121: [W2] |||
AH122: [W45] 'Other
AI122: (P2) U [W15] 1-@SUM(AI117..AI121)
AJ122: (P2) U [W15] 1-@SUM(AJ117..AJ121)
AK122: (P2) U [W13] 1-@SUM(AK117..AK121)
AL122: (P2) U [W13] 1-@SUM(AL117..AL121)
AM122: (P2) U [W13] 1-@SUM(AM117..AM121)
AR122: [W2] |||
AR123: [W2] |||
AR125: [W2] |||
AR126: [W2] |||
AR127: [W2] |||
AR128: [W2] |||
AR129: [W2] |||
AR130: [W2] |||
AH131: [W45] \=
AI131: [W15] \=
AJ131: [W15] \=
```

continued...

...from previous page

```
AK131:  [W13]  \=
AL131:  [W13]  \=
AM131:  [W13]  \=
AN131:  [W13]  \=
AO131:  [W13]  \=
AP131:  [W13]  \=
AQ131:  [W13]  \=
AR131:  [W2]   |||
```

When the 1LINE_GRAPHR option is selected, the MENUCALL RLINE1 entry
in cell BS348 causes Schedule R's main graphics submenu to shift to Schedule R's
#1 line chart graphics submenu. Move the cursor to cell BT351 at this time, and
give the range BT351..BT351 the name RLINE1. Construct the submenu (see
Figure 14.3) by making the cell entries that follow the figure.

```
AH1: [W45] 'SCHEDULE R:  SUMMARY OF ACTUAL AND REQUESTED BUDGET RATIOS      MENU
1SALR  2TRAVR  3TELR  4POSTR  5CAP_OUTLAYR  6OTHERR
SALARY % OF TOTAL EXPENDITURES
                          AH                        AI
1    SCHEDULE R:  SUMMARY OF ACTUAL AND REQUESTED BUDGET RATIOS
2    UNIT:  Department of Public Works
3    ===========================================================
4
5
6                                           % Total Exp
7                                           1985-86
8    Personal Services:                     Actual
9       Man Years
10      Salaries                            78.57%
11      Benefits                            0.00%
12
13   Supporting Services:
14      Travel                              3.96%
15      Telephone Tolls and Rental          0.79%
16      Postage                             3.40%
17      Rent - State Owned Buildings        0.57%
18      Rent - Privately Owned Buildings    0.37%
19      Building Improvements               0.01%
20      Utility Charges                     0.01%
```

Figure 14.3   *Schedule R Submenu Options for Graphing Individual Objects of
                Expenditure*

Cell   **Macro Entry**

```
BS351: RLINE1=
BT351: 1SALR
BU351: 2TRAVR
BV351: 3TELR
BW351: 4POSTR
BX351: 5CAP_OUTLAYR
BY351: 6OTHERR
BT352: SALARY % OF TOTAL EXPENDITURES
BU352: TRAVEL % OF TOTAL EXPENDITURES
BV352: TELEPHONE % OF TOTAL EXPENDITURES
BW352: POSTAGE % OF TOTAL EXPENDITURES
BX352: CAPITAL % OF CAPITAL OUTLAY EXPS
BY352: OTHER % OF TOTAL EXPENDITURES
BT353: {INDICATE WAIT}{CALC}{PANELOFF}{WINDOWSOFF}
BU353: {INDICATE WAIT}{CALC}{PANELOFF}{WINDOWSOFF}
BV353: {INDICATE WAIT}{CALC}{PANELOFF}{WINDOWSOFF}
BW353: {INDICATE WAIT}{CALC}{PANELOFF}{WINDOWSOFF}
BX353: {INDICATE WAIT}{CALC}{PANELOFF}{WINDOWSOFF}
BY353: {INDICATE WAIT}{CALC}{PANELOFF}{WINDOWSOFF}
BT354: /grg
BU354: /grg
BV354: /grg
BW354: /grg
BX354: /grg
BY354: /grg
BT355: tl
BU355: tl
BV355: tl
BW355: tl
BX355: tl
BY355: tl
BT356: aAI117.AM117~
BU356: aAI118.AM118~
BV356: aAI119.AM119~
BW356: aAI120.AM120~
BX356: aAI121.AM121~
BY356: aAI122.AM122~
BT357: xAI114.AM114~
BU357: xAI114.AM114~
```

continued...

...from previous page

```
BV357: xAI114.AM114~
BW357: xAI114.AM114~
BX357: xAI114.AM114~
BY357: xAI114.AM114~
BT358: o
BU358: o
BV358: o
BW358: o
BX358: o
BY358: o
BT359: cfab
BU359: cfab
BV359: cfab
BW359: cfab
BX359: cfab
BY359: cfab
BT360: qsyfp0~q
BU360: qsyfp0~q
BV360: qsyfp0~q
BW360: qsyfp0~q
BX360: qsyfp0~q
BY360: qsyfp0~q
BT361: tfDepartment of Public Works~
BU361: tfDepartment of Public Works~
BV361: tfDepartment of Public Works~
BW361: tfDepartment of Public Works~
BX361: tfDepartment of Public Works~
BY361: tfDepartment of Public Works~
BT362: tsSalary %  of Total Expenditures~
BU362: tsTravel % of Total Expenditures~
BV362: tsTelephone % of Total Expenditures~
BW362: tsPostage % of Total Expenditures~
BX362: tsCapital Outlay % of Total Expenditures~
BY362: tsOther % of Total Expenditures~
BT363: q
BU363: q
BV363: q
BW363: q
BX363: q
```

continued...

...from previous page

```
BY363:  q
BT364:  v
BU364:  v
BV364:  v
BW364:  v
BX364:  v
BY364:  v
BT365:  q
BU365:  q
BV365:  q
BW365:  q
BX365:  q
BY365:  q
BT366:  {INDICATE}{BRANCH \m}
BU366:  {INDICATE}{BRANCH \m}
BV366:  {INDICATE}{BRANCH \m}
BW366:  {INDICATE}{BRANCH \m}
BX366:  {INDICATE}{BRANCH \m}
BY366:  {INDICATE}{BRANCH \m}
```

The range designations in the first and X data ranges of the submenu (rows 356 and 357) refer to data located in the Schedule R Data Table: Annual % of Total Expenditures Factors. The data in this table consist of select expenditure postings from Schedule R.

The only other entries in Schedule R's #1 line graphics submenu that differ from previously constructed macros and require clarification are those appearing in row 360. The q command causes the macro to abandon the previously called submenu. S calls 1-2-3's scaling option submenu; y selects the graph's y-axis for scaling; f specifies the format for scale numbers; p selects the percentage format; 0 sets the number of decimal places to zero; and q causes the macro to abandon the scaling option submenu.

Figure 14.4 displays the output of the submenu when the 1SALR (salary expenditures) option is selected.

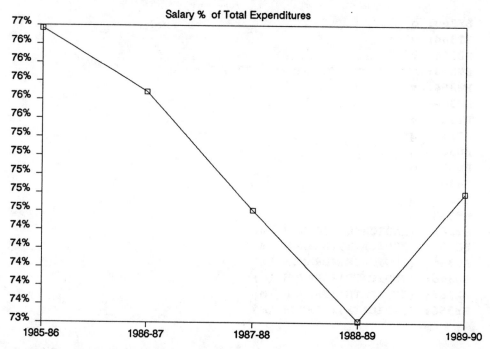

Figure 14.4   *Sample # 1 Line Graph of Schedule R: Salary % of Total Expenditures*

SECONDARY GRAPHICS
SUBMENUS: SCHEDULE R #1 BAR CHART

The Schedule R #1 bar chart graphics submenu (see Figure 14.5) graphs the same data as the Schedule R #1 line chart graphics submenu except that the data are presented in a bar rather than a line chart format, so you don't need to create a separate data table to graph Schedule R bar charts. Note that while the two categories of the Schedule R line charts are listed as #1 and #2 and the two categories of the Schedule R bar charts are listed as #1 and #2, the submenu options for the Schedule R line and bar charts are numbered in another way (i.e., from left to right in the order in which they appear as options).

```
AH1: [W45] 'SCHEDULE R:  SUMMARY OF ACTUAL AND REQUESTED BUDGET RATIOS      MENU
1LINE_GRAPHR  2BAR_GRAPHR  3LINE_GRAPH  4BAR_GRAPH
DO LINE GRAPHS OF SCHEDULE R % OF TOTAL EXPENDITURES
                          AH                    AI
1   SCHEDULE R:  SUMMARY OF ACTUAL AND REQUESTED BUDGET RATIOS
2   UNIT:  Department of Public Works
3   ==================================================
4
5
6                                        % Total Exp
7                                         1985-86
8   Personal Services:                     Actual
9       Man Years
10      Salaries                          78.57%
11      Benefits                           0.00%
12
13  Supporting Services:
14      Travel                             3.96%
15      Telephone Tolls and Rental         0.79%
16      Postage                            3.40%
17      Rent - State Owned Buildings       0.57%
18      Rent - Privately Owned Buildings   0.37%
19      Building Improvements              0.01%
20      Utility Charges                    0.01%
```

Figure 14.5   # 1 Bar Graphics Submenu Option for Schedule R

Before making the entries to create the Schedule R #1 bar chart graphics submenu, move the cursor to cell BT368 and give the range BT368..BT368 the name RBAR1, which will interface the Schedule R bar chart graphics submenu with the {MENUCALL RBAR1} command in Schedule R's main graphics menu.

Next, make the following entries to create the Schedule R #1 bar chart graphics submenu:

Cell   **Macro Entry**

BS368: RBAR1=
BT368: 1SALR
BU368: 2TRAVR
BV368: 3TELR
BW368: 4POSTR
BX368: 5CAP_OUTLAYR
BY368: 6OTHERR
BT369: SALARY % OF TOTAL EXPENDITURES

continued...

...from previous page

```
BU369: TRAVEL % OF TOTAL EXPENDITURES
BV369: TELEPHONE % OF TOTAL EXPENDITURES
BW369: POSTAGE % OF TOTAL EXPENDITURES
BX369: CAPITAL % OF CAPITAL OUTLAY EXPS
BY369: OTHER % OF TOTAL EXPENDITURES
BT370: {INDICATE WAIT}{CALC}{PANELOFF}{WINDOWSOFF}
BU370: {INDICATE WAIT}{CALC}{PANELOFF}{WINDOWSOFF}
BV370: {INDICATE WAIT}{CALC}{PANELOFF}{WINDOWSOFF}
BW370: {INDICATE WAIT}{CALC}{PANELOFF}{WINDOWSOFF}
BX370: {INDICATE WAIT}{CALC}{PANELOFF}{WINDOWSOFF}
BY370: {INDICATE WAIT}{CALC}{PANELOFF}{WINDOWSOFF}
BT371: /grg
BU371: /grg
BV371: /grg
BW371: /grg
BX371: /grg
BY371: /grg
BT372: tb
BU372: tb
BV372: tb
BW372: tb
BX372: tb
BY372: tb
BT373: aAI117.AM117~
BU373: aAI118.AM118~
BV373: aAI119.AM119~
BW373: aAI120.AM120~
BX373: aAI121.AM121~
BY373: aAI122.AM122~
BT374: xAI114.AM114~
BU374: xAI114.AM114~
BV374: xAI114.AM114~
BW374: xAI114.AM114~
BX374: xAI114.AM114~
BY374: xAI114.AM114~
BT375: o
BU375: o
BV375: o
BW375: o
```

continued...

...from previous page

```
BX375: o
BY375: o
BT376: cfan
BU376: cfan
BV376: cfan
BW376: cfan
BX376: cfan
BY376: cfan
BT377: qsyfp0~q
BU377: qsyfp0~q
BV377: qsyfp0~q
BW377: qsyfp0~q
BX377: qsyfp0~q
BY377: qsyfp0~q
BT378: tfDepartment of Public Works~
BU378: tfDepartment of Public Works~
BV378: tfDepartment of Public Works~
BW378: tfDepartment of Public Works~
BX378: tfDepartment of Public Works~
BY378: tfDepartment of Public Works~
BT379: tsSalary % of Total Expenditures~
BU379: tsTravel % of Total Expenditures~
BV379: tsTelephone % of Total Expenditures~
BW379: tsPostage % of Total Expenditures~
BX379: tsCapital Outlay % of Total Expenditures~
BY379: tsOther % of Total Expenditures~
BT380: q
BU380: q
BV380: q
BW380: q
BX380: q
BY380: q
BT381: v
BU381: v
BV381: v
BW381: v
BX381: v
BY381: v
```

continued...

...from previous page

```
BT382:  q
BU382:  q
BV382:  q
BW382:  q
BX382:  q
BY382:  q
BT383:  {INDICATE}{BRANCH \m}
BU383:  {INDICATE}{BRANCH \m}
BV383:  {INDICATE}{BRANCH \m}
BW383:  {INDICATE}{BRANCH \m}
BX383:  {INDICATE}{BRANCH \m}
BY383:  {INDICATE}{BRANCH \m}
```

The above entries are the same as those used to create the first Schedule A #1 line chart graphics submenu, except that the two rows of entries are bar rather than line chart specifications.

The tb entries in row 372 specify the graph to be a bar chart rather than line chart; the cfan entries in row 376 indicate that neither lines nor symbols need be invoked due to the fact that the graphing to be done is in a bar rather than a line chart format.

As usual, test the submenu before proceeding to the next section. Figure 14.6 displays the output of the submenu when the 1SALR (salary expenditures) option is selected.

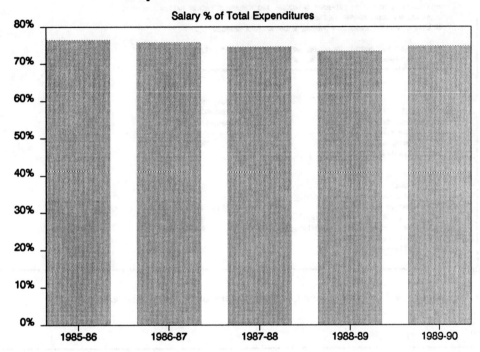

Department of Public Works

Salary % of Total Expenditures

Figure 14.6   *Sample # 1 Bar Graph of Schedule R: Salary % of Total Expenditures*

SECONDARY GRAPHICS
SUBMENUS: SCHEDULE R #2 LINE CHART

The Schedule R #2 line chart graphics submenu (see Figure 14.7) obtains its data from the Schedule R Data Table: % Annual Expenditure Change Factors (see Figure 14.8).

```
AH1:  [W45]  'SCHEDULE R:  SUMMARY OF ACTUAL AND REQUESTED BUDGET RATIOS        MENU
1LINE_GRAPHR  2BAR_GRAPHR  3LINE_GRAPH  4BAR_GRAPH
DO LINE GRAPHS OF SCHEDULE R ANNUAL % EXPENDITURE CHANGES
                              AH                  AI
1    SCHEDULE R:  SUMMARY OF ACTUAL AND REQUESTED BUDGET RATIOS
2    UNIT:  Department of Public Works
3    ================================================
4
5
6                                         % Total Exp
7                                         1985-86
8    Personal Services:                   Actual
9      Man Years
10     Salaries                           78.57%
11     Benefits                           0.00%
12
13   Supporting Services:
14     Travel                             3.96%
15     Telephone Tolls and Rental         0.79%
16     Postage                            3.40%
17     Rent - State Owned Buildings       0.57%
18     Rent - Privately Owned Buildings   0.37%
19     Building Improvements              0.01%
20     Utility Charges                    0.01%
```

Figure 14.7   # 2 Line Graphics Submenu Option for Schedule R

```
                              AH                  AI          AJ          AK
132  SCHEDULE R DATA TABLE:  % ANNUAL EXPENDITURE CHANGE FACTORS
133  UNIT:   DEPARTMENT OF PUBLIC WORKS
134  ================================================
135
136
137                                       1986-87     1987-88     1988-89
138
139
140  Man Years                            2.04%       1.00%       2.87%
141  Salaries                             2.04%       1.00%       4.02%
142  Travel                               0.00%      -8.57%       1.50%
143  Telephone                            4.89%       7.48%       0.00%
144  Postage                             15.00%       1.45%       7.94%
145  Capital Outlay                      85.58%     185.38%      63.73%
146  Total                                2.96%       2.73%       5.70%
147
148
149
150
151  ================================================
```

Figure 14.8   Schedule R Data Table: % Annual Expenditure Change Factors

AL	AM	AN	AO	AP	AQ	AR
						II
						II
━━━━━━━━━━━━━━						II
						II
1989-90						II
						II
						II
1.92%						II
7.15%						II
14.89%						II
0.00%						II
0.06%						II
-38.92%						II
5.18%						II
						II
						II
━━━━━━━━━━━━━━						II

Cell Listing: Figure 14.8

Enter the following listing to construct the table in Figure 14.8.

```
AH109: [W45] 'SCHEDULE R DATA TABLE: ANNUAL % OF TOTAL EXPENDITURE
             FACTORS
AR109: [W2] |||
AH110: [W45] 'UNIT:  DEPARTMENT OF PUBLIC WORKS
AR110: [W2] |||
AH111: [W45] \=
AI111: [W15] \=
AJ111: [W15] \=
AK111: [W13] \=
AL111: [W13] \=
AM111: [W13] \=
AN111: [W13] \=
AO111: [W13] \=
AP111: [W13] \=
AQ111: [W13] \=
AR111: [W2] |||
AR112: [W2] |||
AR113: [W2] |||
AI114: [W15] ^1985-86
AJ114: [W15] ^1986-87
AK114: [W13] ^1987-88AL114: [W13] ^1988-89
AM114: [W13] ^1989-90
AR114: [W2] |||
AR115: [W2] |||
AR116: [W2] |||
AH117: [W45] 'Salaries
AI117: (P2) U [W15] (AI10)
AJ117: (P2) U [W15] (AJ10)
AK117: (P2) U [W13] (AL10)
AL117: (P2) U [W13] (AN10)
AM117: (P2) U [W13] (AP10)
AR117: [W2] |||
AH118: [W45] 'Travel
AI118: (P2) U [W15] (AI14)
AJ118: (P2) U [W15] (AJ14)
AK118: (P2) U [W13] (AL14)
AL118: (P2) U [W13] (AN14)
```

continued...

...from previous page

```
AM118: (P2) U [W13] (AP14)
AR118: [W2] |||
AH119: [W45] 'Telephone
AI119: (P2) U [W15] (AI15)
AJ119: (P2) U [W15] (AJ15)
AK119: (P2) U [W13] (AL15)
AL119: (P2) U [W13] (AN15)
AM119: (P2) U [W13] (AP15)
AR119: [W2] |||
AH120: [W45] 'Postage
AI120: (P2) U [W15] (AI16)
AJ120: (P2) U [W15] (AJ16)
AK120: (P2) U [W13] (AL16)
AL120: (P2) U [W13] (AN16)
AM120: (P2) U [W13] (AP16)
AR120: [W2] |||
AH121: [W45] 'Capital Outlay
AI121: (P2) U [W15] (AI40)
AJ121: (P2) U [W15] (AJ40)
AK121: (P2) U [W13] (AL40)
AL121: (P2) U [W13] (AN40)
AM121: (P2) U [W13] (AP40)
AR121: [W2] |||
AH122: [W45] 'Other
AI122: (P2) U [W15] 1-@SUM(AI117..AI121)
AJ122: (P2) U [W15] 1-@SUM(AJ117..AJ121)
AK122: (P2) U [W13] 1-@SUM(AK117..AK121)
AL122: (P2) U [W13] 1-@SUM(AL117..AL121)
AM122: (P2) U [W13] 1-@SUM(AM117..AM121)
AR122: [W2] |||
AR123: [W2] |||
AR124: [W2] |||
AR125: [W2] |||
AR126: [W2] |||
AR127: [W2] |||
AR128: [W2] |||
AR129: [W2] |||
AR130: [W2] |||
AH131: [W45] \=
```

continued...

...from previous page

```
AI131:  [W15]  \=
AJ131:  [W15]  \=
AK131:  [W13]  \=
AL131:  [W13]  \=
AM131:  [W13]  \=
AN131:  [W13]  \=
AO131:  [W13]  \=
AP131:  [W13]  \=
AQ131:  [W13]  \=
AR131:  [W2]   |||
```

To begin creating the submenu, move the cursor to cell BT565, and give the range BT565..BT565 the name TLINE2; this is the MENUCALL reference name designated in cell BU348 and is required for activating Schedule R's #2 line chart graphics submenu. Then, make the following entries to construct the submenu:

Cell   **Macro Entry**

```
BS386:  RLINE2=
BT386:  1TOTR
BU386:  2MAN_YRSR
BV386:  3SALR
BW386:  4TRAVR
BX386:  5TELR
BY386:  6POSTR
BZ386:  7CAP_OUTLAYR
BT387:  TOTAL ANNUAL % EXPENDITURE CHANGE
BU387:  MAN YEARS ANNUAL % EXPENDITURE CHANGE
BV387:  SALARY ANNUAL % EXPENDITURE CHANGE
BW387:  TRAVEL ANNUAL % EXPENDITURE CHANGE
BX387:  TELEPHONE ANNUAL % EXPENDITURE CHANGE
BY387:  POSTAGE ANNUAL % EXPENDITURE CHANGE
BZ387:  CAPITAL OUTLAY ANNUAL % EXPENDITURE CHANGE
BT388:  {INDICATE WAIT}{CALC}{PANELOFF}{WINDOWSOFF}
BV388:  {INDICATE WAIT}{CALC}{PANELOFF}{WINDOWSOFF}
BW388:  {INDICATE WAIT}{CALC}{PANELOFF}{WINDOWSOFF}
BX388:  {INDICATE WAIT}{CALC}{PANELOFF}{WINDOWSOFF}
```

continued...

...from previous page

```
BY388: {INDICATE WAIT}{CALC}{PANELOFF}{WINDOWSOFF}
BZ388: {INDICATE WAIT}{CALC}{PANELOFF}{WINDOWSOFF}
BT389: /grg
BU389: /grg
BV389: /grg
BW389: /grg
BX389: /grg
BY389: /grg
BZ389: /grg
BT390: tl
BU390: tl
BV390: tl
BW390: tl
BX390: tl
BY390: tl
BZ390: tl
BT391: aAI146.AL146~
BU391: aAI140.AL140~
BV391: aAI141.AL141~
BW391: aAI142.AL142~
BX391: aAI143.AL143~
BY391: aAI144.AL144~
BZ391: aAI145.AL145~
BT392: xAI137.AL137~
BU392: xAI137.AL137~
BV392: xAI137.AL137~
BW392: xAI137.AL137~
BX392: xAI137.AL137~
BY392: xAI137.AL137~
BZ392: xAI137.AL137~
BT393: o
BU393: o
BV393: o
BW393: o
BX393: o
BY393: o
BZ393: o
BT394: cfab
BU394: cfab
```

continued...

...from previous page

```
BV394: cfab
BW394: cfab
BX394: cfab
BY394: cfab
BZ394: cfab
BT395: qsyfp0~q
BU395: qsyfp0~q
BV395: qsyfp0~q
BW395: qsyfp0~q
BX395: qsyfp0~q
BY395: qsyfp0~q
BZ395: qsyfp0~q
BT396: tfDepartment of Public Works~
BU396: tfDepartment of Public Works~
BV396: tfDepartment of Public Works~
BW396: tfDepartment of Public Works~
BX396: tfDepartment of Public Works~
BY396: tfDepartment of Public Works~
BZ396: tfDepartment of Public Works~
BT397: tsTotal Annual % Exp. Change~
BU397: tsMan Years Annual % Exp. Change~
BV397: tsSalary Annual % Exp. Change~
BW397: tsTravel Annual % Exp. Change~
BX397: tsTelephone Annual % Exp. Change~
BY397: tsPostage Annual % Exp. Change~
BZ397: tsCapital Outlay Annual % Exp.  Change~
BT398: q
BU398: q
BV398: q
BW398: q
BY398: q
BZ398: q
BT399: v
BU399: v
BV399: v
BW399: v
BX399: v
BY399: v
BZ399: v
```

continued...

...from previous page

```
BT400:  q
BU400:  q
BV400:  q
BW400:  q
BX400:  q
BY400:  q
BZ400:  q
BT401:  {INDICATE}{BRANCH \m}
BU401:  {INDICATE}{BRANCH \m}
BV401:  {INDICATE}{BRANCH \m}
BW401:  {INDICATE}{BRANCH \m}
BX401:  {INDICATE}{BRANCH \m}
BY401:  {INDICATE}{BRANCH \m}
BZ401:  {INDICATE}{BRANCH \m}
```

The range specifications in the first and X data ranges of the submenu (rows 391 and 392) refer to data located in the Schedule R Data Table: % Annual Expenditure Change Factors. These data consist of select between-years expenditure object postings from Schedule R.

Test the Schedule R #2 line graphics submenu and its supporting data table to see if they function properly before moving to the next section to construct the second Schedule R bar graphics submenu. Figure 14.9 displays the line chart that is drawn when the 3SALR option is selected from the submenu.

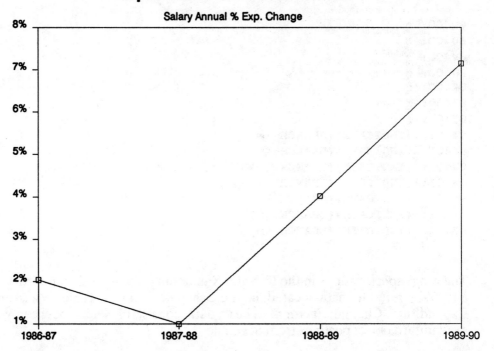

Figure 14.9   *Sample # 2 Line Graph of Schedule R: Salary Annual % Expenditures Change*

SECONDARY GRAPHICS
SUBMENUS: SCHEDULE R #2 BAR CHART

Move the cursor to cell BT404, and give the range BT404..BT404 the name RBAR2. Naming this range links the Schedule R #2 bar chart graphics submenu (see Figure 14.10) with the MENUCALL command in cell BV348 of the main Schedule R graphics menu.

```
AH1: [W45] 'SCHEDULE R: SUMMARY OF ACTUAL AND REQUESTED BUDGET RATIOS      MENU
1LINE_GRAPHR  2BAR_GRAPHR  3LINE_GRAPH  4BAR_GRAPH
DO LINE GRAPHS OF SCHEDULE R ANNUAL % EXPENDITURE CHANGES
                          AH                     AI
1   SCHEDULE R: SUMMARY OF ACTUAL AND REQUESTED BUDGET RATIOS
2   UNIT: Department of Public Works
3   ═══════════════════════════════════════════════
4
5
6                                           % Total Exp
7                                           1985-86
8   Personal Services:                      Actual
9      Man Years
10     Salaries                              76.57%
11     Benefits                               0.00%
12
13  Supporting Services:
14     Travel                                 3.96%
15     Telephone Tolls and Rental             0.79%
16     Postage                                3.40%
17     Rent - State Owned Buildings           0.57%
18     Rent - Privately Owned Buildings       0.37%
19     Building Improvements                  0.01%
20     Utility Charges                        0.01%
```

Figure 14.10   *# 2 Bar Graphics Submenu Option for Schedule R*

Next, to construct the submenu in Figure 14.10, make the following entries:

Cell   **Macro Entry**

BS404: RBAR2=
BT404: 1TOTR
BU404: 2MAN_YRSR
BV404: 3SALR
BW404: 4TRAVR
BX404: 5TELR
BY404: 6POSTR
BZ404: 7CAP_OUTLAYR
BT405: TOTAL ANNUAL % EXPENDITURE CHANGE
BU405: MAN YEARS ANNUAL % EXPENDITURE CHANGE
BV405: SALARY ANNUAL % EXPENDITURE CHANGE
BW405: TRAVEL ANNUAL % EXPENDITURE CHANGE
BX405: TELEPHONE ANNUAL % EXPENDITURE CHANGE

continued...

...from previous page

```
BY405: POSTAGE ANNUAL % EXPENDITURE CHANGE
BZ405: CAPITAL OUTLAY ANNUAL % EXPENDITURE CHANGE
BT406: {INDICATE WAIT}{CALC}{PANELOFF}{WINDOWSOFF}
BV406: {INDICATE WAIT}{CALC}{PANELOFF}{WINDOWSOFF}
BW406: {INDICATE WAIT}{CALC}{PANELOFF}{WINDOWSOFF}
BX406: {INDICATE WAIT}{CALC}{PANELOFF}{WINDOWSOFF}
BY406: {INDICATE WAIT}{CALC}{PANELOFF}{WINDOWSOFF}
BZ406: {INDICATE WAIT}{CALC}{PANELOFF}{WINDOWSOFF}
BT407: /grg
BU407: /grg
BV407: /grg
BW407: /grg
BX407: /grg
BY407: /grg
BZ407: /grg
BT408: tb
BU408: tb
BV408: tb
BW408: tb
BX408: tb
BY408: tb
BZ408: tb
BT409: aAI146.AL146~
BU409: aAI140.AL140~
BV409: aAI141.AL141~
BW409: aAI142.AL142~
BX409: aAI143.AL143~
BY409: aAI144.AL144~
BZ409: aAI145.AL145~
BT410: xAI137.AL137~
BU410: xAI137.AL137~
BV410: xAI137.AL137~
BW410: xAI137.AL137~
BX410: xAI137.AL137~
BY410: xAI137.AL137~
BZ410: xAI137.AL137~
BT411: o
BU411: o
BV411: o
BW411: o
```

continued...

...from previous page

```
BX411: o
BY411: o
BZ411: o
BT412: cfan
BU412: cfan
BV412: cfan
BW412: cfan
BX412: cfan
BY412: cfan
BZ412: cfan
BT413: qsyfp0~q
BU413: qsyfp0~q
BV413: qsyfp0~q
BW413: qsyfp0~q
BX413: qsyfp0~q
BY413: qsyfp0~q
BZ413: qsyfp0~q
BT414: tfDepartment of Public Works~
BU414: tfDepartment of Public Works~
BV414: tfDepartment of Public Works~
BW414: tfDepartment of Public Works~
BX414: tfDepartment of Public Work~
BY414: tfDepartment of Public Works~
BZ414: tfDepartment of Public Works~
BT415: tsTotal Annual % Exp. Change~
BU415: Man Years Annual % Exp. Change~
BV415: tsSalary Annual % Exp. Change~
BW415: tsTravel Annual % Exp. Change~
BX415: tsTelephone Annual % Exp. Change~
BY415: tsPostage Annual % Exp. Change~
BZ415: tsCapital Outlay Annual % Exp. Change~
BT416: q
BU416: q
BV416: q
BW416: q
BX416: q
BY416: q
BZ416: q
BT417: v
```

continued...

...from previous page

```
BU417:  v
BV417:  v
BW417:  v
BX417:  v
BY417:  v
BZ417:  v
BT418:  q
BU418:  q
BV418:  q
BW418:  q
BX418:  q
BY418:  q
BZ418:  q
BT419:  {INDICATE}{BRANCH \m}
BU419:  {INDICATE}{BRANCH \m}
BV419:  {INDICATE}{BRANCH \m}
BW419:  {INDICATE}{BRANCH \m}
BX419:  {INDICATE}{BRANCH \m}
BY419:  {INDICATE}{BRANCH \m}
BZ419:  {INDICATE}{BRANCH \m}
```

Test the Schedule R #2 bar graphics submenu to see if it functions properly before moving to the next section. Figure 14.11 displays the bar chart that is produced when the 3SALR option is selected from the submenu.

Department of Public Works

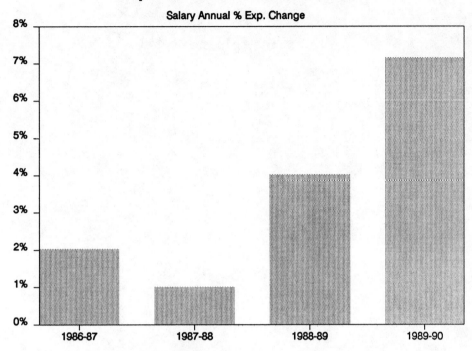

*Figure 14.11   Sample # 2 Bar Graph of Schedule R: Salary Annual %
Expenditures Change*

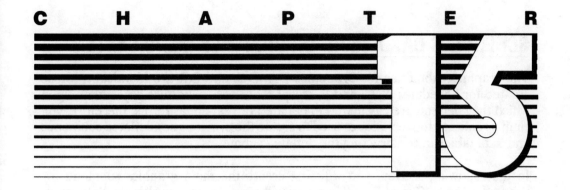

SECONDARY DEFLATED DATA MENUS AND SCHEDULE DA GRAPHICS

SCHEDULES DA, DC, AND DR GRAPHICS MENU SYSTEM

The graphics submenus for Schedules DA, DC, and DR are identical to those created for Schedules A, C, and R except that the expenditure object data upon which they depend are calculated in deflated or real dollar terms; therefore, you simply replicate the techniques used to create the previous nondeflated submenus and data tables in constructing the deflated submenus.

In the following section, you will first create the main graphics submenu for Schedules DA, DC, and DR. Then, you will create, where applicable, data tables and their cell locations before constructing the individual graphics submenus. The range names/locations of all submenus for deflated schedules will then be listed. As with previous submenus, you will name each submenu before creating its macros. Each deflated schedule submenu will be displayed sequentially followed by its cell/macro entries. Finally, a sample graph will be drawn of deflated salary expenditures. Make the entries necessary to construct the main graphics submenu for Schedules DA, DC, and DR.

The main submenu for graphics was displayed in Chapter 12 (see Figure 12.1). Before constructing the remaining graphics submenus, move the cursor to the cells designated below, and name the eight ranges for two other levels of graphics submenus that are associated with the main graphics submenu. The first level contains the main submenus named DAGRAPH, DCGRAPH, and DRGRAPH; the second level submenus are named DALINE, DABAR, DAPIE, DRLINE, and DRBAR.

Cell	**Range Name**
BS422..BS422:	DAGRAPH
BT427..BT422:	DALINE
BT444..BT444:	DABAR
BT462..BT462:	DAPIE
BS479..BS479:	DCPIE
BS496..BS496:	DRGRAPH
BT501..BT501:	DRLINE
BT518..BT518:	DRBAR

After naming the two levels of submenus, to construct the main graphics submenus for Schedules DA, DC, and DR and their respective submenus, make the entries listed in the subsections that follow.

SECONDARY GRAPHICS
SUBMENUS: SCHEDULE DA MAIN SUBMENU

The main graphics submenu for Schedule DA is displayed on 1-2-3's command line in Figure 15.1.

```
AA65: [W45] ^SCHEDULE DA:  SUMMARY OF ACTUAL AND DEFLATED REQUESTED EXPENDI MENU
LINE_GRAPHDA   BAR_GRAPHDA   PIE_GRAPHDA
DO LINE GRAPHS OF SCHEDULE DA
                              AA                    AB          AC
65   SCHEDULE DA:  SUMMARY OF ACTUAL AND DEFLATED REQUESTED EXPENDITURES
66   UNIT:  Department of Public Works
67   ======================================================================
68                        Deflator Factor:        4.20
69
70
71                                             1985-86     1986-87
72   Personal Services:                        Actual      Actual
73     Man Years                                    98         100
74     Salaries                              1,352,400   1,380,000
75     Benefits                                      0           0
76
77   Supporting Services:
78     Travel                                   70,000      70,000
79     Telephone Tolls and Rental               14,000      14,657
80     Postage                                  60,000      69,000
81     Rent - State Owned Buildings             10,000      10,000
82     Rent - Privately Owned Buildings          6,600       6,600
83     Building Improvements                       100         100
84     Utility Charges                             250         250
```

Figure 15.1   #1 Line Graphics Submenu Option for Schedule DA

To construct the submenu, make the following entries:

Cell	Macro Entry
BR422:	DAGRAPH=
BS422:	LINE_GRAPHDA
BT422:	BAR_GRAPHDA
BU422:	PIE_GRAPHDA
BS423:	DO LINE GRAPHS OF SCHEDULE DA
BT423:	DO BAR GRAPHS OF SCHEDULE DA
BU423:	DO PIE GRAPHS OF SCHEDULE DA
BS424:	{MENUCALL DALINE}
BT424:	{MENUCALL DABAR}
BU424:	{MENUCALL DAPIE}

SECONDARY GRAPHICS SUBMENUS: SCHEDULE DA LINE CHART

The line chart graphics submenu is displayed on 1-2-3's command line in Figure 15.2.

```
AA65: [W45] ^SCHEDULE DA:  SUMMARY OF ACTUAL AND DEFLATED REQUESTED EXPENDI MENU
1TOTDA 2SALDA 3TRAVDA 4TELDA 5POSTDA 6CAP_OUTLAYDA
TOTAL DEFLATED EXPENDITURES
                         AA                  AB          AC
65  SCHEDULE DA:  SUMMARY OF ACTUAL AND DEFLATED REQUESTED EXPENDITURES
66  UNIT:  Department of Public Works
67  ==================================================================
68                     Deflator Factor:          4.20
69
70
71                                       1985-86     1986-87
72  Personal Services:                   Actual      Actual
73      Man Years                            98         100
74      Salaries                      1,352,400   1,380,000
75      Benefits                              0           0
76
77  Supporting Services:
78      Travel                           70,000      70,000
79      Telephone Tolls and Rental       14,000      14,657
80      Postage                          60,000      69,000
81      Rent - State Owned Buildings     10,000      10,000
82      Rent - Privately Owned Buildings  6,600       6,600
83      Building Improvements               100         100
84      Utility Charges                     250         250
```

Figure 15.2 　*Schedule DA Submenu Options for Graphing Individual Objects of Expenditure*

To construct the submenu, make the following entries:

Cell   **Macro Entry**

```
BS427:  DALINE=
BT427:  1TOTDA
BU427:  2SALDA
BV427:  3TRAVDA
BW427:  4TELDA
BX427:  5POSTDA
BY427:  6CAP_OUTLAYDA
BT428:  TOTAL DEFLATED EXPENDITURES
BU428:  SALARY DEFLATED EXPENDITURES
BV428:  TRAVEL DEFLATED EXPENDITURES
BW428:  TELEPHONE DEFLATED EXPENDITURES
BX428:  POSTAGE DEFLATED EXPENDITURES
BY428:  CAPITAL OUTLAY DEFLATED EXPENDITURES
BT429:  {INDICATE WAIT}{CALC}{PANELOFF}{WINDOWSOFF}
BU429:  {INDICATE WAIT}{CALC}{PANELOFF}{WINDOWSOFF}
BV429:  {INDICATE WAIT}{CALC}{PANELOFF}{WINDOWSOFF}
BW429:  {INDICATE WAIT}{CALC}{PANELOFF}{WINDOWSOFF}
BX429:  {INDICATE WAIT}{CALC}{PANELOFF}{WINDOWSOFF}
BY429:  {INDICATE WAIT}{CALC}{PANELOFF}{WINDOWSOFF}
BT430:  /grg
BU430:  /grg
BV430:  /grg
BW430:  /grg
BX430:  /grg
BY430:  /grg
BT431:  tl
BU431:  tl
BV431:  tl
BW431:  tl
BX431:  tl
BY431:  tl
BT432:  aAB106.AF106~
BU432:  aAB74.AF74~
BV432:  aAB78.AF78~
BW432:  aAB79.AF79~
BX432:  aAB80.af80~
```

continued...

...from previous page

```
BY432: aAB104.AF104~
BT433: xAB71.AF71~
BU433: xAB71.AF71~
BV433: xAB71.AF71~
BW433: xAB71.AF71~
BX433: xAB71.AF71~
BY433: xAB71.AF71~
BT434: o
BU434: o
BV434: o
BW434: o
BX434: o
BY434: o
BT435: cfab
BU435: cfab
BV435: cfab
BW435: cfab
BX435: cfab
BY435: cfab
BT436: q
BU436: q
BV436: q
BW436: q
BX436: q
BY436: q
BT437: tfDepartment of Public Works~
BU437: tfDepartment of Public Works~
BV437: tfDepartment of Public Works~
BW437: tfDepartment of Public Works~
BX437: tfDepartment of Public Works~
BY437: tfDepartment of Public Works~
BT438: tsDeflated Total Expenditures~
BU438: tsDeflated Salary Expenditures~
BV438: tsDeflated Travel Expenditures~
BW438: tsDeflated Telephone Expenditures~
BX438: tsDeflated Postage Expenditures~
BY438: tsDeflated Capital Outlay Expenditures~
BT439: q
BU439: q
```

continued...

...from previous page

```
BV439: q
BW439: q
BX439: q
BY439: q
BT440: v
BU440: v
BV440: v
BW440: v
BX440: v
BY440: v
BT441: q
BU441: q
BV441: q
BW441: q
BX441: q
BY441: q
BT442: {INDICATE}{BRANCH \m}
BU442: {INDICATE}{BRANCH \m}
BV442: {INDICATE}{BRANCH \m}
BW442: {INDICATE}{BRANCH \m}
BX442: {INDICATE}{BRANCH \m}
BY442: {INDICATE}{BRANCH \m}
```

Test the submenu before you read the next section. Figure 15.3 displays the graph that is drawn when the LINE_GRAPH and 2SALDA options are selected from the first two secondary submenus, respectively.

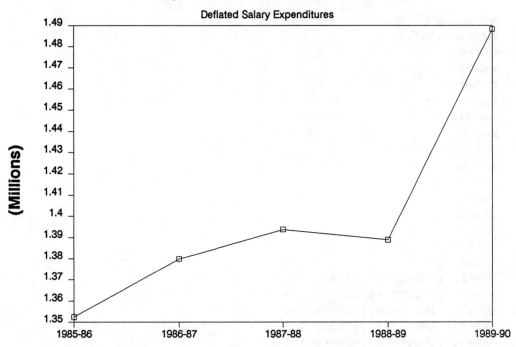

Department of Public Works

Figure 15.3   *Sample # 1 Line Graph of Schedule DA: Deflated Salary Expenditures*

SECONDARY GRAPHICS
SUBMENUS: SCHEDULE DA BAR CHART

To construct the Schedule DA bar chart graphics submenu, make the following entries:

Cell   Macro Entry

```
BS444:  DABAR=
BT444:  1TOTDA
BU444:  2SALDA
BV444:  3TRAVDA
BW444:  4TELDA
BX444:  5POSTDA
BT445:  TOTAL DEFLATED EXPENDITURES
BU445:  SALARY DEFLATED EXPENDITURES
BV445:  TRAVEL DEFLATED EXPENDITURES
BW445:  TELEPHONE DEFLATED EXPENDITURES
BX445:  POSTAGE DEFLATED EXPENDITURES
BY445:  CAPITAL OUTLAY DEFLATED EXPENDITURES
BT446:  {INDICATE WAIT}{CALC}{PANELOFF}{WINDOWSOFF}
BU446:  {INDICATE WAIT}{CALC}{PANELOFF}{WINDOWSOFF}
BV446:  {INDICATE WAIT}{CALC}{PANELOFF}{WINDOWSOFF}
BW446:  {INDICATE WAIT}{CALC}{PANELOFF}{WINDOWSOFF}
BX446:  {INDICATE WAIT}{CALC}{PANELOFF}{WINDOWSOFF}
BY446:  {INDICATE WAIT}{CALC}{PANELOFF}{WINDOWSOFF}
BT447:  /grg
BU447:  /grg
BV447:  /grg
BW447:  /grg
BX447:  /grg
BY447:  /grg
BT448:  tb
BU448:  tb
BV448:  tb
BW448:  tb
BX448:  tb
BY448:  tb
BT449:  aAB106.AF106~
BU449:  aAB74.AF74~
BV449:  aAB78.AF78~
BW449:  aAB79.AF79~
BX449:  aAB80.AF80~
BY449:  aAB104.AF104~
BT450:  xAB71.AF71~
BU450:  xAB71.AF71~
```

continued...

...from previous page

```
BV450: xAB71.AF71~
BW450: xAB71.AF71~
BX450: xAB71.AF71~
BY450: xAB71.AF71~
BT451: o
BU451: o
BV451: o
BW451: o
BX451: o
BY451: o
BT452: cfan
BU452: cfan
BV452: cfan
BW452: cfan
BX452: cfan
BY452: cfan
BT453: q
BU453: q
BV453: q
BW453: q
BX453: q
BY453: q
BT454: tfDepartment of Public Works~
BU454: tfDepartment of Public Works~
BV454: tfDepartment of Public Works~
BW454: tfDepartment of Public Works~
BX454: tfDepartment of Public Works~
BY454: tfDepartment of Public Works~
BT455: tsDeflated Total Expenditures~
BU455: tsDeflated Salary Expenditures~
BV455: tsDeflated Travel Expenditures~
BW455: tsDeflated Telephone Expenditures~
BX455: tsDeflated Postage Expenditures~
BY455: tsDeflated Capital Outlay Expenditures~
BT456: q
BU456: q
BV456: q
BW456: q
BX456: q
```

continued...

...from previous page

```
BY456:  q
BT457:  v
BU457:  v
BV457:  v
BW457:  v
BX457:  v
BY457:  v
BT458:  q
BU458:  q
BV458:  q
BW458:  q
BX458:  q
BY458:  q
BT459:  {INDICATE}{BRANCH \m}
BU459:  {INDICATE}{BRANCH \m}
BV459:  {INDICATE}{BRANCH \m}
BW459:  {INDICATE}{BRANCH \m}
BX459:  {INDICATE}{BRANCH \m}
BY459:  {INDICATE}{BRANCH \m}
```

The Schedule DA bar chart graphics submenu is identical to the Schedule DA line chart graphics submenu — except for the entries in rows 448 and 452 where the b command specifies bar rather than line chart and the n command specifies that neither lines nor symbols should be drawn between data points.

Figure 15.4 shows the bar graph that results when the BAR_GRAPH and 2SALDA options are chosen from the first and second levels of the DA line graphics submenus, respectively.

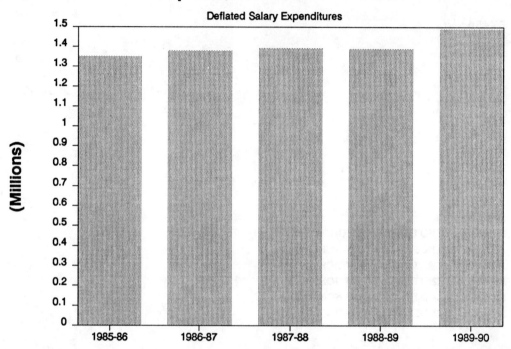

Figure 15.4   *Sample # 1 Bar Graph of Schedule DA: Deflated Salary Expenditures*

SECONDARY GRAPHICS SUBMENUS: SCHEDULE DA PIE CHART

The Schedule DA pie chart graphics submenu obtains its data from a data table, Schedule DA Data Table: Deflated Pie Chart Data (see Figure 15.5). For graphing purposes, the data in the table is posted from Schedule DA: Summary of Actual Deflated Requested Expenditures. Make the entries following Figure 15.5 to construct the data table before you construct the Schedule DA pie chart graphics submenu.

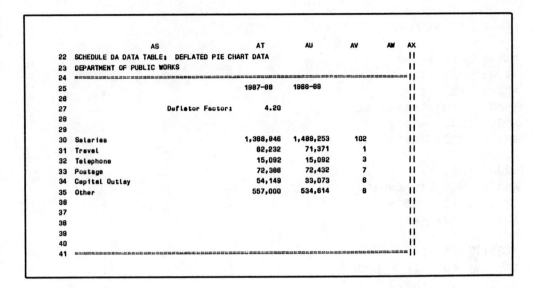

	AS	AT	AU	AV	AW	AX
22	SCHEDULE DA DATA TABLE: DEFLATED PIE CHART DATA					‖
23	DEPARTMENT OF PUBLIC WORKS					‖
24	===					‖
25		1987-88	1988-89			‖
26						‖
27	Deflator Factor:	4.20				‖
28						‖
29						‖
30	Salaries	1,388,946	1,488,253	102		‖
31	Travel	82,232	71,371	1		‖
32	Telephone	15,092	15,092	3		‖
33	Postage	72,386	72,432	7		‖
34	Capital Outlay	54,149	33,073	6		‖
35	Other	557,000	534,614	8		‖
36						‖
37						‖
38						‖
39						‖
40						‖
41	===					‖

Figure 15.5   *Schedule DA Data Table: Deflated Pie Chart Data*

Cell Listing: Figure 15.5

```
AS22: [W40] ^SCHEDULE DA DATA TABLE:  DEFLATED PIE CHART DATA
AU22: [W12] ^
AX22: [W2] \|
AS23: [W40] 'DEPARTMENT OF PUBLIC WORKS
AX23: [W2] \|
AS24: [W40] \=
AT24: [W12] \=
AU24: [W12] \=
AV24: \=
AW24: \=
AX24: [W2] \|
AT25: [W12] ^1987-88
AU25: [W12] ^1988-89
AX25: [W2] \|
AX26: [W2] \|
AS27: [W40] "Deflator Factor:
AT27: (F2) [W12] +$BZ$12
```

continued...

...from previous page

```
AX27: [W2] \|
AX28: [W2] \|
AX29: [W2] \|
AS30: [W40] 'Salaries
AT30: [W12] +AE74
AU30: [W12] +AF74
AV30: U 102
AX30: [W2] \|
AS31: [W40] 'Travel
AT31: [W12] +AE78
AU31: [W12] +AF78
AV31: U 1
AX31: [W2] \|
AS32: [W40] 'Telephone
AT32: [W12] +AE79
AU32: [W12] +AF79
AV32: U 3
AX32: [W2] \|
AS33: [W40] 'Postage
AT33: [W12] +AE80
AU33: [W12] +AF80
AV33: U 7
AX33: [W2] \|
AS34: [W40] 'Capital Outlay
AT34: [W12] +AE104
AU34: [W12] +AF104
AV34: U 6
AX34: [W2] \|
AS35: [W40] 'Other
AT35: [W12] +AE106-@SUM(AT30-AT34)
AU35: [W12] +AF106-@SUM(AU30-AU34)
AV35: U 8
AX35: [W2] \|
AX36: [W2] \|
AT37: [W12] ^
AX37: [W2] \|
AX38: [W2] \|
AX39: [W2] \|
AX40: [W2] \|
```

continued...

...from previous page

```
AS41:  [W40]  \=
AT41:  [W12]  \=
AU41:  [W12]  \=
AV41:  \=
AW41:  \=
AX41:  [W2]  \|
```

The Schedule DA pie chart graphics submenu (see Figure 15.6) graphs five expenditure change request categories (i.e., Salaries, Travel, Telephone, Capital Outlays, and Other expenditures) for the first and second biennial periods.

```
AA65:  [W45]  ^SCHEDULE DA:  SUMMARY OF ACTUAL AND DEFLATED REQUESTED EXPENDI MENU
1DA_SCH_1988-89  2DA_SCH_1989-90
DEFLATED SCHEDULE A, 1988-89:  SALARIES, TRAVEL, TELEPHONE,CAPITAL OUTLAYS, OTHE
                          AA              AB          AC
65  SCHEDULE DA:  SUMMARY OF ACTUAL AND DEFLATED REQUESTED EXPENDITURES
66  UNIT:  Department of Public Works
67  ===================================================================
68                          Deflator Factor:        4.20
69
70
71                                      1985-86      1986-87
72  Personal Services:                   Actual       Actual
73      Man Years                           98          100
74      Salaries                      1,352,400    1,380,000
75      Benefits                             0            0
76
77  Supporting Services:
78      Travel                          70,000       70,000
79      Telephone Tolls and Rental      14,000       14,857
80      Postage                         60,000       69,000
81      Rent - State Owned Buildings    10,000       10,000
82      Rent - Privately Owned Buildings 6,800        6,800
83      Building Improvements              100          100
84      Utility Charges                    250          250
```

Figure 15.6   Submenu Options for Graphing Schedule DA Pie Charts

To construct the submenu, make the following entries:

Cell	Macro Entry
BS462:	DAPIE=
BT462:	1DA_SCH_1988-89
BU462:	2DA_SCH_1989-90
BT463:	DEFLATED SCHEDULE A, 1988-89: SALARIES, TRAVEL, TELEPHONE , CAPITAL OUTLAYS, OTHER
BU463:	DEFLATED SCHEDULE A, 1989-90: SALARIES, TRAVEL, TELEPHONE , CAPITAL OUTLAYS, OTHER
BT464:	{INDICATE WAIT}{CALC}{PANELOFF}{WINDOWSOFF}
BU464:	{INDICATE WAIT}{CALC}{PANELOFF}{WINDOWSOFF}
BT465:	/grg
BU465:	/grg
BT466:	tp
BU466:	tp
BT467:	aAT30.AT35~
BU467:	aau30.au35~
BT468:	xAS30.AS35~
BU468:	xAS30.AS35~
BT469:	bAV30.AV35~
BU469:	bAV30.AV35~
BT470:	oc
BU470:	oc
BT471:	tfDepartment of Public Works~
BU471:	tfDepartment of Public Works~
BT472:	tsDeflated Relative Expenditure Share~
BU472:	tsDeflated Relative Expenditure Share~
BT473:	q
BU473:	q
BT474:	v
BU474:	v
BT475:	q
BU475:	q
BT476:	{INDICATE}{BRANCH \m}
BU476:	{INDICATE}{BRANCH \m}

Before proceeding to the next section, test the Schedule DA pie chart graphics submenu. Toggling the 1DA_SCH_1988-89 option results in the drawing of the graph displayed in Figure 15.7.

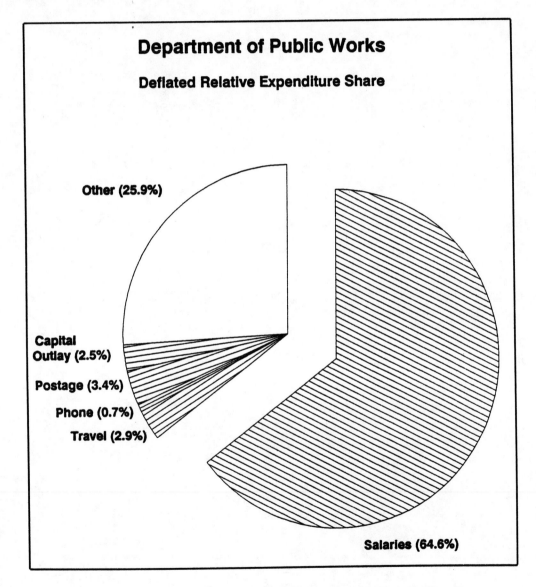

Figure 15.7   *Sample Pie Chart of Schedule DA: Individual Objects of Expenditure — First Biennium Data*

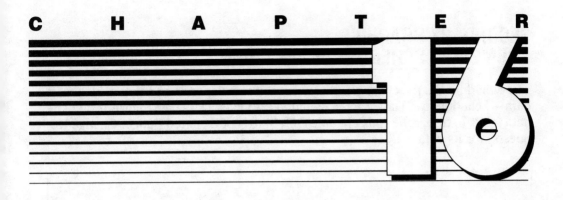

SCHEDULE DC GRAPHICS

SECONDARY GRAPHICS
SUBMENUS: SCHEDULE DC PIE CHART

The Schedule DC pie chart graphics submenu also depends on a data table for its data — Schedule DC Data Table: Deflated Pie Chart Data (see Figure 16.1). The data table, in turn, relies on Schedule DC (Matrix of Deflated Budget Change Requests) for its data.

```
                     AS              AT        AU        AV      AW  AX
 62  SCHEDULE DC DATA TABLE:  DEFLATED PIE CHART DATA                  ||
 63  DEPARTMENT OF PUBLIC WORKS                                        ||
 64  ==================================================================||
 65                                1987-88   1988-89                   ||
 66                                                                    ||
 67                   Deflator Factor:    4.20                         ||
 68                                                                    ||
 69                                                                    ||
 70  PC                           12,837    17,627        2           ||
 71  MI                          (27,064)  (13,412)       1           ||
 72  WC                           22,273    80,883      103           ||
 73  N&CS                         25,100    49,050        7           ||
 74  OC                            6,668    18,765        6           ||
 75  FF                           62,270    69,168        8           ||
 76                                                                    ||
 77                                                                    ||
 78                                                                    ||
 79                                                                    ||
 80                                                                    ||
 81  ==================================================================||
```

Figure 16.1   Schedule DC Data Table: Deflated Pie Chart Data

Cell Listing: Figure 16.1

Make the following entries to construct the data table before you construct the Schedule DC pie chart graphics submenu:

```
AS62:  [W40] ^SCHEDULE DC DATA TABLE:  DEFLATED PIE CHART DATA
AX62:  [W2] \|
AS63:  [W40] 'DEPARTMENT OF PUBLIC WORKS
AX63:  [W2] \|
AS64:  [W40] \=
AT64:  [W12] \=
```

continued...

...from previous page

```
AU64: [W12] \=
AV64: \=
AW64: \=
AX64: [W2] \|
AT65: [W12] ^1987-88
AU65: [W12] ^1988-89
AX65: [W2] \|
AX66: [W2] \|
AS67: (C0) [W40] "Deflator Factor:
AT67: (F2) [W12] +$BZ$12
AX67: [W2] \|
AX68: [W2] \|
AX69: [W2] \|
AS70: [W40] 'PC
AT70: [W12] +H86
AU70: [W12] +Q86
AV70: U 2
AX70: [W2] \|
AS71: [W40] 'MI
AT71: [W12] +I86
AU71: [W12] +R86
AV71: U 1
AX71: [W2] \|
AS72: [W40] 'WC
AT72: [W12] +J86
AU72: [W12] +S86
AV72: U 103
AX72: [W2] \|
AS73: [W40] 'N&CS
AT73: [W12] +K86
AU73: [W12] +T86
AV73: U 7
AX73: [W2] \|
AS74: [W40] 'OC
AT74: [W12] +L86
AU74: [W12] +U86
AV74: U 6
AX74: [W2] \|
AS75: [W40] 'FF
```

continued...

...from previous page

```
AT75: [W12] +M86
AU75: [W12] +V86
AV75: U 8
AX75: [W2] \|
AX76: [W2] \|
AT77: [W12] ^
AX77: [W2] \|
AX78: [W2] \|
AX79: [W2] \|
AX80: [W2] \|
AS81: [W40] \=
AT81: [W12] \=
AU81: [W12] \=
AV81: \=
AW81: \=
AX81: [W2] \|
```

After constructing the Schedule DC Data Table, make the following entries to create the Schedule DC pie chart graphics submenu (see Figure 16.2):

```
G45: [W45] ^ah65                                              MENU
1DC_SCH_1988-89  2DC_SCH_1989-90
DEFLATED SCHEDULE C, 1988-89: SALARIES, TRAVEL, TELEPHONE,CAPITAL OUTLAYS, OTHE
                        G                    H      I      J
45                      ah65
46  UNIT: Department of Public Works
47  ==========================================================
48              Deflator Factor:      4.20
49                                                      1988-
50  Change Categories                    PC     MI     WLC
51  --------------------------------------------------------
52  Personal Services:
53    Man Years
54    Salaries                          0  (39,518) 18,958
55    Benefits                          0      0      0
56                                      0      0      0
57  Supporting Services:                0      0      0
58    Travel                            0      0      0
59    Telephone Tolls and Rental        0      0      0
60    Postage                       3,832      0  1,494
61    Rent - State Owned Buildings   4,215      0      0
62    Rent - Privately Owned Buildings   0      0      0
63    Building Improvements             0      0      0
64    Utility Charges                   0      0      0
```

Figure 16.2   Submenu Options for Graphing Schedule DC Pie Charts

Cell	Macro Entry

```
BR479:  'DCPIE=
BS479:  ^1DC_SCH_1988-89
BT479:  ^2DC_SCH_1989-90
BS480:  'DEFLATED SCHEDULE C, 1988-89:  SALARIES, TRAVEL, TELEPHONE,
            CAPITAL OUTLAYS, OTHER
BT480:  'DEFLATED SCHEDULE C, 1989-90:  SALARIES, TRAVEL, TELEPHONE,
            CAPITAL OUTLAYS, OTHER
BS481:  '{INDICATE WAIT}{CALC}{PANELOFF}{WINDOWSOFF}
BT481:  '{INDICATE WAIT}{CALC}{PANELOFF}{WINDOWSOFF}
BS482:  '/grg
BT482:  '/grg
BS483:  'tp
BT483:  'tp
BS484:  'aAT76.AT81~
BT484:  'aAU76.AU81~
BS485:  ^xAS76.AS81~
BT485:  ^xAS76.AS81~
BS486:  'bAV76.AV81~
BT486:  'bAV76.AV81~
BS487:  'oc
BT487:  'oc
BS488:  ^tfDepartment of Public Works~
BT488:  ^tfDepartment of Public Works~
BS489:  ^tsDeflated 1988-89 Expenditures Increase~
BT489:  ^tsDeflated 1989-90 Expenditures Increase~
BS490:  'q
BT490:  'q
BS491:  'v
BT491:  'v
BS492:  'q
BT492:  'q
BS493:  ^{INDICATE}{BRANCH \m}
BT493:  ^{INDICATE}{BRANCH \m}
```

Test the Schedule DC pie chart graphics submenu before proceeding to the next section. Toggling 1DC_SCH_1988-89 causes the graph displayed in Figure 16.3 to be drawn.

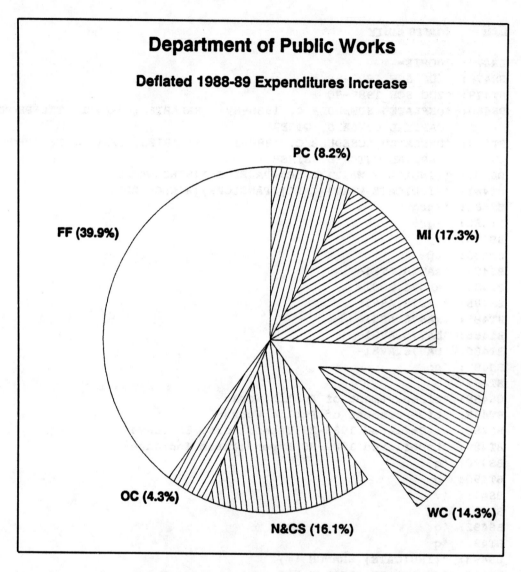

Figure 16.3   *Sample Pie Chart of Schedule DC: Individual Objects of Expenditure—First Biennium Data*

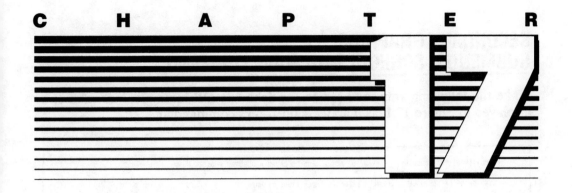

CHAPTER 17

SCHEDULE DR GRAPHICS

SECONDARY GRAPHICS
SUBMENUS: SCHEDULE DR MAIN SUBMENU

Make the following entries to create the Schedule DR main graphics submenu displayed in Figure 17.1, as it appears on 1-2-3's command line.

```
AH65: [W45] ^SCHEDULE DR:  SUMMARY OF ACTUAL AND DEFLATED REQUESTED BUDGET  MENU
LINE_GRAPHDR  BAR_GRAPHDR
LINE GRAPH OF SCHEDULE R ANNUAL % DEFLATED EXPENDITURE CHANGES
                          AH                          AI
65  SCHEDULE DR:  SUMMARY OF ACTUAL AND DEFLATED REQUESTED BUDGET RATIOS
66  UNIT:  Department of Public Works
67 ════════════════════════════════════════════════════════════════════
68                          Deflator Factor:        4.20
69
70                                        % Total Exp
71                                        1985-86
72  Personal Services:                     Actual
73     Man Years
74     Salaries                             76.57%
75     Benefits                              0.00%
76
77  Supporting Services:
78     Travel                                3.96%
79     Telephone Tolls and Rental            0.78%
80     Postage                               3.40%
81     Rent - State Owned Buildings          0.57%
82     Rent - Privately Owned Buildings      0.37%
83     Building Improvements                 0.01%
84     Utility Charges                       0.01%
```

Figure 17.1   Schedule DR Submenu Graphics Options

<u>**Cell**</u>   <u>**Macro Entry**</u>

BR496: DRGRAPH=
BS496: LINE_GRAPHDR
BT496: BAR_GRAPHDR
BS497: DP LINE GRAPH OF SCHEDULE R ANNUAL % DEFLATED EXPENDITURE
       CHANGES
BT497: DP BAR GRAPH OF SCHEDULE R ANNUAL % DEFLATED EXPENDITURE
       CHANGES
BS498: {MENUCALL DRLINE}
BT498: {MENUCALL DRBAR}

SECONDARY GRAPHICS
SUBMENUS: SCHEDULE DR LINE CHART

The line chart graphics submenu for Schedule DR depends on a data table for its data — Deflated Schedule R Data Table: % Annual Expenditure Change Factors (see Figure 17.2).

(See next page)

	AH	AI	AJ
175 DEFLATED SCHEDULE R DATA TABLE: % ANNUAL EXPENDITURE CHANGE FACTORS			
176 UNIT: DEPARTMENT OF PUBLIC WORKS			
177 ===			
178	Deflator Factor:	4.20%	
179			
180		1986-87	1987-88
181			
182			
183		2.04%	1.00%
184 Salaries		2.04%	1.00%
185 Travel		0.00%	-6.57%
186 Telephone		4.68%	7.48%
187 Postage		15.00%	1.45%
188 Capital Outlay		65.56%	185.38%
189 Total		2.96%	2.73%
190			
191			
192			
193			
194 ===			

Figure 17.2   Schedule DR Data Table: % Annual Expenditure Change Factors

AK	AL	AM	AN	AO	AP	AQ	AR

1988-89   1989-90

2.85%	1.84%
3.85%	6.85%
1.44%	14.07%
0.00%	0.00%
7.81%	0.06%
61.05%	-37.29%
1.26%	2.73%

Cell Listing: Figure 17.2

Make the following entries to create the data table before constructing the Schedule DR line chart graphics submenu:

```
AH175: [W45] 'DEFLATED SCHEDULE R DATA TABLE:   % ANNUAL EXPENDITURE
       CHANGE FACTORS
AR175: [W2] |||
AH176: [W45] 'UNIT:   DEPARTMENT OF PUBLIC WORKS
AR176: [W2] |||
AH177: [W45] \=
AI177: [W15] \=
AJ177: [W15] \=
AK177: [W13] \=
AL177: [W13] \=
AM177: [W13] \=
AN177: [W13] \=
AO177: [W13] \=
AP177: [W13] \=
AQ177: [W13] \=
AR177: [W2] |||
AH178: [W45] "Deflator Factor:
AI178: (P2) [W15] +BZ12*0.01
AR178: [W2] |||
AR179: [W2] |||
AI180: [W15] ^1986-87
AJ180: [W15] ^1987-88
AK180: [W13] ^1988-89
AL180: [W13] ^1989-90
AR180: [W2] |||
AR181: [W2] |||
AR182: [W2] |||
AI183: (P2) U [W15] +AI140
AJ183: (P2) U [W15] +AJ140
AK183: (P2) U [W13] +AK140*$BZ$13
AL183: (P2) U [W13] +AL140*$BZ$13
AR183: [W2] |||
AH184: [W45] 'Salaries
AI184: (P2) U [W15] +AI141
AJ184: (P2) U [W15] +AJ141
AK184: (P2) U [W13] +AK141*$BZ$13
AL184: (P2) U [W13] +AL141*$BZ$13
```

continued...

...from previous page

```
AR184: [W2] |||
AH185: [W45] 'Travel
AI185: (P2) U [W15] +AI142
AJ185: (P2) U [W15] +AJ142
AK185: (P2) U [W13] +AK142*$BZ$13
AL185: (P2) U [W13] +AL142*$BZ$13
AR185: [W2] |||
AH186: [W45] 'Telephone
AI186: (P2) U [W15] +AI143
AJ186: (P2) U [W15] +AJ143
AK186: (P2) U [W13] +AK143*$BZ$13
AL186: (P2) U [W13] +AL143*$BZ$13
AR186: [W2] |||
AH187: [W45] 'Postage
AI187: (P2) U [W15] +AI144
AJ187: (P2) U [W15] +AJ144
AK187: (P2) U [W13] +AK144*$BZ$13
AL187: (P2) U [W13] +AL144*$BZ$13
AR187: [W2] |||
AH188: [W45] 'Capital Outlay
AI188: (P2) U [W15] +AI145
AJ188: (P2) U [W15] +AJ145
AK188: (P2) U [W13] +AK145*$BZ$13
AL188: (P2) U [W13] +AL145*$BZ$13
AR188: [W2] |||
AH189: [W45] 'Total
AI189: (P2) U [W15] +AK106
AJ189: (P2) U [W15] +AM106
AK189: (P2) U [W13] +AO106
AL189: (P2) U [W13] +AM106
AR189: [W2] |||
AR190: [W2] |||
AR191: [W2] |||
AR192: [W2] |||
AR193: [W2] |||
AH194: [W45] \=
AI194: [W15] \=
AJ194: [W15] \=
AK194: [W13] \=
```

continued...

...from previous page

```
AL194:  [W13]  \=
AM194:  [W13]  \=
AN194:  [W13]  \=
AO194:  [W13]  \=
AP194:  [W13]  \=
AQ194:  [W13]  \=
AR194:  [W2]   \|
```

Next, make the following entries to construct the Schedule DR line graphics submenu displayed in Figure 17.3, as it appears on 1-2-3's command line:

```
AH65: [W45] ^SCHEDULE DR:  SUMMARY OF ACTUAL AND DEFLATED REQUESTED BUDGET  MENU
1TOTDR  2SALDR  3TRAVDR  4TELDR  5POSTDR  6CAP_OUTLAYDR
TOTAL ANNUAL % DEFLATED EXPENDITURE CHANGE
                          AH                         AI
   65  SCHEDULE DR:  SUMMARY OF ACTUAL AND DEFLATED REQUESTED BUDGET RATIOS
   66  UNIT:  Department of Public Works
   67  ================================================================
   68                         Deflator Factor:           4.20
   69
   70                                        % Total Exp
   71                                         1985-86
   72  Personal Services:                     Actual
   73     Man Years
   74     Salaries                             76.57%
   75     Benefits                              0.00%
   76
   77  Supporting Services:
   78     Travel                                3.96%
   79     Telephone Tolls and Rental            0.79%
   80     Postage                               3.40%
   81     Rent - State Owned Buildings          0.57%
   82     Rent - Privately Owned Buildings      0.37%
   83     Building Improvements                 0.01%
   84     Utility Charges                       0.01%
```

Figure 17.3 *Schedule DR Submenu Options for Graphing Individual Objects of Expenditure*

Cell   **Macro Entry**

```
BS501: DRLINE=
BT501: 1TOTDR
BU501: 2SALDR
BV501: 3TRAVDR
BW501: 4TELDR
BX501: 5POSTDR
BY501: 6CAP_OUTLAYDR
BT502: TOTAL ANNUAL % DEFLATED EXPENDITURE CHANGE
BU502: SALARY ANNUAL % DEFLATED EXPENDITURE CHANGE
BV502: TRAVEL ANNUAL % DEFLATED EXPENDITURE CHANGE
BW502: TELEPHONE ANNUAL % DEFLATED EXPENDITURE CHANGE
BX502: POSTAGE ANNUAL % DEFLATED EXPENDITURE CHANGE
BY502: CAPITAL OUTLAY ANNUAL % DEFLATED EXPENDITURE CHANGE
BT503: {INDICATE WAIT}{CALC}{PANELOFF}{WINDOWSOFF}
BU503: {INDICATE WAIT}{CALC}{PANELOFF}{WINDOWSOFF}
BV503: {INDICATE WAIT}{CALC}{PANELOFF}{WINDOWSOFF}
BW503: {INDICATE WAIT}{CALC}{PANELOFF}{WINDOWSOFF}
BX503: {INDICATE WAIT}{CALC}{PANELOFF}{WINDOWSOFF}
BY503: {INDICATE WAIT}{CALC}{PANELOFF}{WINDOWSOFF}
BT504: /grg
BU504: /grg
BV504: /grg
BW504: /grg
BX504: /grg
BY504: /grg
BT505: tl
BU505: tl
BV505: tl
BW505: tl
BX505: tl
BY505: tl
BT506: aAI189.AL189~
BU506: aAI184.AL184~
BV506: aAI185.AL185~
BW506: aAI186.AL186~
BX506: aAI187.AL187~
BY506: aAI188.AL188~
BT507: xAI180.AL180~
BU507: xAI180.AL180~
```

continued...

...from previous page

```
BV507: xAI180.AL180~
BW507: xAI180.AL180~
BX507: xAI180.AL180~
BY507: xAI180.AL180~
BT508: o
BU508: o
BV508: o
BW508: o
BX508: o
BY508: o
BT509: cfab
BU509: cfab
BV509: cfab
BW509: cfab
BX509: cfab
BY509: cfab
BT510: qsyfp0~q
BU510: qsyfp0~q
BV510: qsyfp0~q
BW510: qsyfp0~q
BX510: qsyfp0~q
BY510: qsyfp0~q
BT511: tfDepartment of Public Works~
BU511: tfDepartment of Public Works~
BV511: tfDepartment of Public Works~
BW511: tfDepartment of Public Works~
BX511: tfDepartment of Public Works~
BY511: tfDepartment of Public Works~
BT512: tsDeflated Total Annual % Exp. Change~
BU512: tsDeflated Salary Annual % Exp. Change~
BV512: tsDeflated Travel Annual % Exp. Change~
BW512: tsDeflated Telephone Annual % Exp. Change~
BX512: tsDeflated Postage Annual % Exp. Change~
BY512: tsDefl. Cap. Outlay Annual % Exp. Change~
BT513: q
BU513: q
BV513: q
BW513: q
BX513: q
```

continued...

...from previous page

```
BY513:  q
BT514:  v
BU514:  v
BV514:  v
BW514:  v
BX514:  v
BY514:  v
BT515:  q
BU515:  q
BV515:  q
BW515:  q
BX515:  q
BY515:  q
BT516:  {INDICATE}{BRANCH \m}
BU516:  {INDICATE}{BRANCH \m}
BV516:  {INDICATE}{BRANCH \m}
BW516:  {INDICATE}{BRANCH \m}
BX516:  {INDICATE}{BRANCH \m}
BY516:  {INDICATE}{BRANCH \m}
```

After making the above entries, test the submenu by toggling the 2SALDR option to create the graph displayed in Figure 17.4.

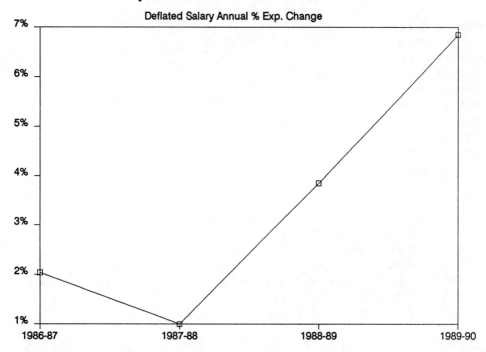

Department of Public Works

Figure 17.4   *Sample Line Graph of Schedule DR: Deflated Salary Annual %*
Expenditures Change

SECONDARY GRAPHICS
SUBMENUS: SCHEDULE DR BAR CHART

The Schedule DR bar chart graphics submenu (which looks the same as the
Schedule DR line chart graphics submenu when summoned to 1-2-3's command
line) depends on the same data table as the Schedule DR line chart graphics
submenu. Make the following entries to construct the submenu:

Cell	Macro Entry

BS518: DRBAR=
BT518: 1TOTDR
BU518: 2SALDR
BV518: 3TRAVDR
BW518: 4TELDR
BX518: 5POSTDR
BY518: 6CAP_OUTLAYDR
BT519: TOTAL ANNUAL % DEFLATED EXPENDITURE CHANGE
BU519: SALARY ANNUAL % DEFLATED EXPENDITURE CHANGE
BV519: TRAVEL ANNUAL % DEFLATED EXPENDITURE CHANGE
BW519: TELEPHONE ANNUAL % DEFLATED EXPENDITURE CHANGE
BX519: POSTAGE ANNUAL % DEFLATED EXPENDITURE CHANGE
BY519: CAPITAL OUTLAY ANNUAL % DEFLATED EXPENDITURE CHANGE
BT520: {INDICATE WAIT}{CALC}{PANELOFF}{WINDOWSOFF}
BU520: {INDICATE WAIT}{CALC}{PANELOFF}{WINDOWSOFF}
BV520: {INDICATE WAIT}{CALC}{PANELOFF}{WINDOWSOFF}
BW520: {INDICATE WAIT}{CALC}{PANELOFF}{WINDOWSOFF}
BX520: {INDICATE WAIT}{CALC}{PANELOFF}{WINDOWSOFF}
BY520: {INDICATE WAIT}{CALC}{PANELOFF}{WINDOWSOFF}
BT521: /grg
BU521: /grg
BV521: /grg
BW521: /grg
BX521: /grg
BY521: /grg
BT522: tb
BU522: tb
BV522: tb
BW522: tb
BX522: tb
BY522: tb
BT523: aAI189.AL189~
BU523: aAI184.AL184~
BV523: aAI185.AL185~
BW523: aAI186.AL186~
BX523: aAI187.AL187~
BY523: aAI188.AL188~
BT524: xAI180.AL180~
BU524: xAI180.AL180~

continued...

...from previous page

```
BV524: xAI180.AL180~
BW524: xAI180.AL180~
BX524: xAI180.AL180~
BY524: xAI180.AL180~
BT525: o
BU525: o
BV525: o
BW525: o
BX525: o
BY525: o
BT526: cfab
BU526: cfab
BV526: cfab
BW526: cfab
BX526: cfab
BY526: cfab
BT527: qsyfp0~q
BU527: qsyfp0~q
BV527: qsyfp0~q
BW527: qsyfp0~q
BX527: qsyfp0~q
BY527: qsyfp0~q
BT528: tfDepartment of Public Works~
BU528: tfDepartment of Public Works~
BV528: tfDepartment of Public Works~
BW528: tfDepartment of Public Works~
BX528: tfDepartment of Public Works~
BY528: tfDepartment of Public Works~
BT529: tsDeflated Total Annual % Exp. Change~
BU529: tsDeflated Salary Annual % Exp. Change~
BV529: tsDeflated Travel Annual % Exp. Change~
BW529: tsDeflated Telephone Annual % Exp. Change~
BX529: tsDeflated Postage Annual % Exp. Change~
BY529: tsDefl. Cap. Outlay Annual % Exp. Change~
BT530: q
BU530: q
BV530: q
BW530: q
BX530: q
```

continued...

...from previous page

```
BY530:  q
BT531:  v
BU531:  v
BV531:  v
BW531:  v
BX531:  v
BY531:  v
BT532:  q
BU532:  q
BV532:  q
BW532:  q
BX532:  q
BY532:  q
BT533:  {INDICATE}{BRANCH \m}
BU533:  {INDICATE}{BRANCH \m}
BV533:  {INDICATE}{BRANCH \m}
BW533:  {INDICATE}{BRANCH \m}
BX533:  {INDICATE}{BRANCH \m}
BY533:  {INDICATE}{BRANCH \m}
```

Test the submenu by toggling the 2SALDR option before proceeding to the next section. Figure 17.5 shows the graph that will be drawn.

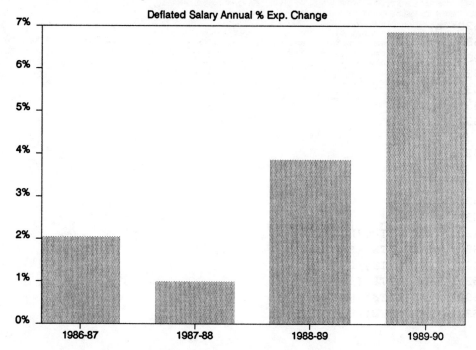

Department of Public Works

Figure 17.5   *Sample Bar Graph of Schedule DR: Deflated Salary Annual %*
Expenditures Change

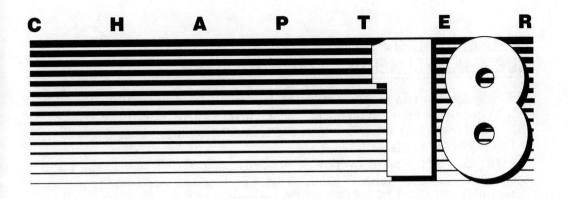

C H A P T E R

18

SCHEDULE T GRAPHICS

SECONDARY GRAPHICS SUBMENUS: SCHEDULE T MAIN SUBMENU

The Schedule T main graphics submenu is displayed in Figure 18.1. Five line graph options are featured on the menu: the first, 1_LINE_GRAPHT, results in the graphing of nondeflated actual and trend Schedule T data; the second, 2_LINE_GRAPHT, is deflated actual and trend Schedule T data; the third, 3_LINE_GRAPHT, is an overlay of nondeflated, deflated actual, and trend Schedule T data; the fourth, 4_LINE_GRAPHT, is actual, trend, and projection data; and the fifth, 5_LINE_GRAPHT, is an overlay of nondeflated/deflated actual, trend, and projection data.

```
AY88: [W45] ^SCHEDULE T: BUDGET TREND PROJECTION MODEL (ANNUAL (FIVE-YEAR   MENU
1_LINE_GRAPHT  2_LINE_GRAPHT  3_LINE_GRAPHT  4_LINE_GRAPHT  5_LINE_GRAPHT
DO LINE GRAPHS OF SCHEDULE T (NONDEFLATED)
                        AY                          AZ
88  SCHEDULE T: BUDGET TREND PROJECTION MODEL (ANNUAL (FIVE-YEAR AVERAGE) C
89  UNIT: Department of Public Works
90  =================================================================
91
92
93
94
95  Personal Services:
96      Man Years
97      Salaries
98      Benefits
99
100 Supporting Services:
101     Travel
102     Telephone Tolls and Rental
103     Postage
104     Rent - State Owned Buildings
105     Rent - Privately Owned Buildings
106     Building Improvements
107     Utility Charges
```

Figure 18.1   *Schedule T Main Graphics Submenu*

Move the cursor to cell BS536 and give the range BS536..BS536 the name TGRAPH. This range links the Schedule T submenu with the graphics MENUCALL command in cell BU270. Then, make the following entries to construct the main graphics menu for Schedule T:

<u>Cell</u>	<u>Macro Entry</u>
BR536:	TGRAPH=
BS536:	1_LINE_GRAPHT
BT536:	2_LINE_GRAPHT
BU536:	3_LINE_GRAPHT
BV536:	4_LINE_GRAPHT
BW536:	5_LINE_GRAPHT
BS537:	DO LINE GRAPHS OF SCHEDULE T (NONDEFLATED)
BT537:	DO LINE GRAPHS OF SCHEDULE T (DEFLATED)
BU537:	DO LINE GRAPHS OF SCHEDULE T (DEFLATED/NONDEFLATED COMPARED)
BV537:	DO LINE GRAPHS OF SCHEDULE T (TRENDS/PROJECTION)
BW537:	DO LINE GRAPHS OF SCHEDULE T (DEFLATED/NONDEFLATED COMPARED & TRENDS/PROJECTION)
BS538:	{MENUCALL TLINE1}
BT538:	{MENUCALL TLINE2}
BU538:	{MENUCALL TLINE3}
BV538:	{MENUCALL TLINE4}
BW538:	{MENUCALL TLINE5}

SECONDARY GRAPHICS
SUBMENUS: SCHEDULE T #1 LINE CHART

Before creating the Schedule T #1 line chart graphics submenu, you will construct a data table upon which it depends, the Schedule T Data Table: Budget Trend Requests (see Figure 18.2).

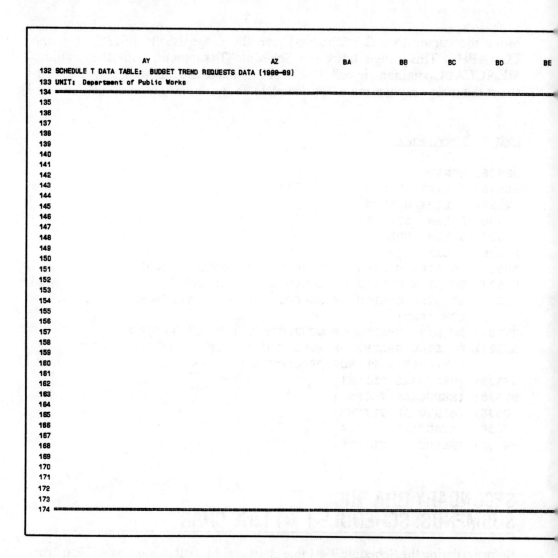

Figure 18.2   Schedule T Data Table: Budget Trend Request Data

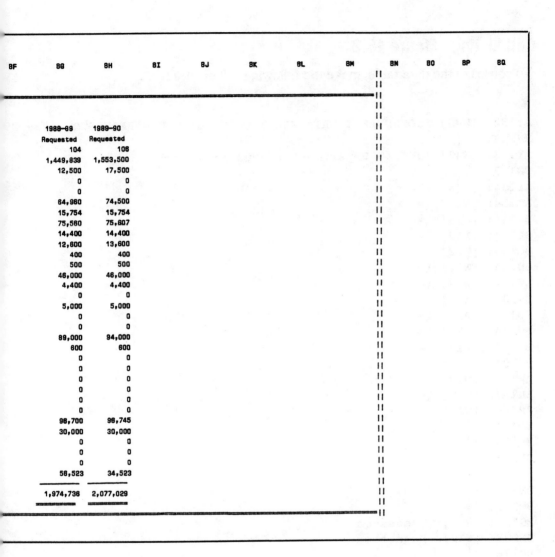

8F	8G	8H	8I	8J	8K	8L	8M	8N	8O	8P	8Q
	1988—89	1989—90									
	Requested	Requested									
	104	106									
	1,449,839	1,553,500									
	12,500	17,500									
	0	0									
	0	0									
	64,960	74,500									
	15,754	15,754									
	75,560	75,607									
	14,400	14,400									
	12,600	13,600									
	400	400									
	500	500									
	46,000	46,000									
	4,400	4,400									
	0	0									
	5,000	5,000									
	0	0									
	0	0									
	89,000	94,000									
	600	600									
	0	0									
	0	0									
	0	0									
	0	0									
	0	0									
	0	0									
	96,700	96,745									
	30,000	30,000									
	0	0									
	0	0									
	0	0									
	58,523	34,523									
	1,974,736	2,077,029									

Cell Listing: Figure 18.2

To construct the data table, make the following cell entries :

```
AY132: [W45] 'SCHEDULE T DATA TABLE:  BUDGET TREND REQUESTS (1988-89
BN132: '||
AY133: [W45] 'UNIT:  Department of Public Works
BN133: '||
AY134: [W45] '\=
AZ134: [W20] \=
BA134: [W15] \=
BB134: [W13] \=
BC134: [W12] \=
BD134: [W12] \=
BE134: [W12] \=
BF134: [W13] \=
BG134: [W12] \=
BH134: [W12] \=
BI134: [W12] \=
BJ134: [W12] \=
BK134: [W12] \=
BL134: [W12] \=
BM134: [W12] \=
BN134: '||
BN135: '||
BN136: '||
BG137: [W12] ^1988-89
BH137: [W12] ^1989-90
BN137: '||
BG138: [W12] ^Requested
BH138: [W12] ^Requested
BN138: '||
BG139: [W12] +AE9
BH139: [W12] +AF9
BN139: '||
BG140: [W12] +AE10
BH140: [W12] +AF10
BN140: '||
BG141: [W12] +AE11
BH141: [W12] +AF11
```

continued...

...from previous page

```
BN141:  '||
BG142:  [W12]  +AE12
BH142:  [W12]  +AF12
BN142:  '||
BG143:  [W12]  +AE13
BH143:  [W12]  +AF13
BN143:  '||
BG144:  [W12]  +AE14
BH144:  [W12]  +AF14
BN144:  '||
BG145:  [W12]  +AE15
BH145:  [W12]  +AF15
BN145:  '||
BG146:  [W12]  +AE16
BH146:  [W12]  +AF16
BN146:  '||
BG147:  [W12]  +AE17
BH147:  [W12]  +AF17
BN147:  '||
BG148:  [W12]  +AE18
BH148:  [W12]  +AF18
BN148:  '||
BG149:  [W12]  +AE19
BH149:  [W12]  +AF19
BN149:  '||
BG150:  [W12]  +AE20
BH150:  [W12]  +AF20
BN150:  '||
BG151:  [W12]  +AE21
BH151:  [W12]  +AF21
BN151:  '||
BG152:  [W12]  +AE22
BH152:  [W12]  +AF22
BN152:  '||
BG153:  [W12]  +AE23
BH153:  [W12]  +AF23
BN153:  '||
BG154:  [W12]  +AE24
BH154:  [W12]  +AF24
```

continued...

...from previous page

```
BN154:  '||
BG155:  [W12]  +AE25
BH155:  [W12]  +AF25
BN155:  '||
BG156:  [W12]  +AE26
BH156:  [W12]  +AF26
BN156:  '||
BG157:  [W12]  +AE27
BH157:  [W12]  +AF27
BN157:  '||
BG158:  [W12]  +AE28
BH158:  [W12]  +AF28
BN158:  '||
BG159:  [W12]  +AE29
BH159:  [W12]  +AF29
BN159:  '||
BG160:  [W12]  +AE30
BH160:  [W12]  +AF30
BN160:  '||
BG161:  [W12]  +AE31
BH161:  [W12]  +AF31
BN161:  '||
BG162:  [W12]  +AE32
BH162:  [W12]  +AF32
BN162:  '||
BG163:  [W12]  +AE33
BH163:  [W12]  +AF33
BN163:  '||
BG164:  [W12]  +AE34
BH164:  [W12]  +AF34
BN164:  '||
BG165:  [W12]  +AE35
BH165:  [W12]  +AF35
BN165:  '||
BG166:  [W12]  +AE36
BH166:  [W12]  +AF36
BN166:  '||
BG167:  [W12]  +AE37
```

continued...

...from previous page

```
BH167:  [W12]  +AF37
BN167:  '||
BG168:  [W12]  +AE38
BH168:  [W12]  +AF38
BN168:  '||
BG169:  [W12]  +AE39
BH169:  [W12]  +AF39
BN169:  '||
BG170:  [W12]  +AE40
BH170:  [W12]  +AF40
BN170:  '||
BG171:  [W12]  +AE41
BH171:  [W12]  +AF41
BN171:  '||
BG172:  [W12]  +AE42
BH172:  [W12]  +AF42
BN172:  '||
BG173:  [W12]  +AE43
BH173:  [W12]  "==========
BN173:  '||
AY174:  [W45]  \=
AZ174:  [W20]  \=
BA174:  [W15]  \=
BB174:  [W13]  \=
BC174:  [W12]  \=
BD174:  [W12]  \=
BE174:  [W12]  \=
BF174:  [W13]  \=
BG174:  [W12]  \=
BH174:  [W12]  \=
BI174:  [W12]  \=
BJ174:  [W12]  \=
BK174:  [W12]  \=
BL174:  [W12]  \=
BM174:  [W12]  \=
BN174:  '||
```

Next, move the cursor to cell BT541 and give the range BT541..BT541 the name **TLINE1**. This is the name of the Schedule T #1 line chart submenu (see Figure 18.3).

```
AY88: [W45] ^SCHEDULE T:  BUDGET TREND PROJECTION MODEL (ANNUAL (FIVE-YEAR  MENU
1TOTL  2MAN_YRSL  3SALL  4TRAVL  5TELL  6POSTL  7CAPL_OUTLL
TOTAL EXPENDITURE TRENDS
                          AY                          AZ
88   SCHEDULE T:  BUDGET TREND PROJECTION MODEL (ANNUAL (FIVE-YEAR AVERAGE) C
89   UNIT:  Department of Public Works
90   ==========================================================
91
92
93
94
95   Personal Services:
96       Man Years
97       Salaries
98       Benefits
99
100  Supporting Services:
101      Travel
102      Telephone Tolls and Rental
103      Postage
104      Rent - State Owned Buildings
105      Rent - Privately Owned Buildings
106      Building Improvements
107      Utility Charges
```

Figure 18.3   *Schedule T #1 Submenu Options for Graphing Individual Objects of Expenditure*

The cell and macro entries for constructing the submenu are as follows:

Cell	**Macro Entry**
BS541:	TLINE1=
BT541:	1TOTL
BU541:	2MAN_YRSL
BV541:	3SALL
BW541:	4TRAVL
BX541:	5TELL
BY541:	6POSTL
BZ541:	7CAPL_OUTLL

continued...

...from previous page

```
BT542:  TOTAL EXPENDITURE TRENDS
BU542:  MAN YEARS TRENDS
BV542:  SALARY EXPENDITURE TRENDS
BW542:  TRAVEL EXPENDITURE TRENDS
BX542:  TELEPHONE EXPENDITURE TRENDS
BY542:  POSTAGE EXPENDITURE TRENDS
BZ542:  CAPITAL OUTLAY EXPENDITURE TRENDS
BT543:  {INDICATE WAIT}{CALC}{PANELOFF}{WINDOWSOFF}
BU543:  {INDICATE WAIT}{CALC}{PANELOFF}{WINDOWSOFF}
BV543:  {INDICATE WAIT}{CALC}{PANELOFF}{WINDOWSOFF}
BW543:  {INDICATE WAIT}{CALC}{PANELOFF}{WINDOWSOFF}
BX543:  {INDICATE WAIT}{CALC}{PANELOFF}{WINDOWSOFF}
BY543:  {INDICATE WAIT}{CALC}{PANELOFF}{WINDOWSOFF}
BZ543:  {INDICATE WAIT}{CALC}{PANELOFF}{WINDOWSOFF}
BT544:  /grg
BU544:  /grg
BV544:  /grg
BW544:  /grg
BX544:  /grg
BY544:  /grg
BZ544:  /grg
BT545:  tl
BU545:  tl
BV545:  tl
BW545:  tl
BX545:  tl
BY545:  tl
BZ545:  tl
BT546:  aAZ41.BF41~
BU546:  aAZ8.BF8~
BV546:  aAZ9.BF9~
BW546:  aAZ13.BF13~
BX546:  aAZ14.BF14~
BY546:  aAZ15.BF15~
BZ546:  aAZ39.BF39~
BT547:  bAZ85.BF85~
BU547:  bAZ52.BF52~
BV547:  bAZ53.BF53~
BW547:  bAZ57.BF57~
```

continued...

...from previous page

```
BX547: bAZ58.BF58~
BY547: bAZ59.BF59~
BZ547: bAZ83.BF83~
BT548: cBA172.BH172~
BU548: cBA139.BH139~
BV548: cBA140.BH140~
BW548: cBA144.BH144~
BX548: cBA145.BH145~
BY548: cBA146.BH146~
BZ548: cBA170.BH170~
BT549: xAZ5.BH5~
BU549: xAZ5.BH5~
BV549: xAZ5.BH5~
BW549: xAZ5.BH5~
BX549: xAZ5.BH5~
BY549: xAZ5.BH5~
BZ549: xAZ5.BH5~
BT550: o
BU550: o
BV550: o
BW550: o
BX550: o
BY550: o
BZ550: o
BT551: cfabbbcb
BU551: cfabbbcb
BV551: cfabbbcb
BW551: cfabbbcb
BX551: cfabbbcb
BY551: cfabbbcb
BZ551: cfabbbcb
BT552: q
BU552: q
BV552: q
BW552: q
BX552: q
BY552: q
BZ552: q
BT553: laACTUAL~
```

continued...

...from previous page

```
BU553: laACTUAL˜
BV553: laACTUAL˜
BW553: laACTUAL˜
BX553: laACTUAL˜
BY553: laACTUAL˜
BZ553: laACTUAL˜
BT554: lbMOVING AVERAGE˜
BU554: lbMOVING AVERAGE˜
BV554: lbMOVING AVERAGE˜
BW554: lbMOVING AVERAGE˜
BX554: lbMOVING AVERAGE˜
BY554: lbMOVING AVERAGE˜
BZ554: lbMOVING AVERAGE˜
BT555: lcREQUEST˜
BU555: lcREQUEST˜
BV555: lcREQUEST˜
BW555: lcREQUEST˜
BX555: lcREQUEST˜
BY555: lcREQUEST˜
BZ555: lcREQUEST˜
BT556: tfDepartment of Public Works˜
BU556: tfDepartment of Public Works˜
BV556: tfDepartment of Public Works˜
BW556: tfDepartment of Public Works˜
BX556: tfDepartment of Public Works˜
BY556: tfDepartment of Public Works˜
BZ556: tfDepartment of Public Works˜
BT557: tsTotal Expenditure Trends˜
BU557: tsMan Years Trends˜
BV557: tsSalary Expenditure Trends˜
BW557: tsTravel Expenditure Trends˜
BX557: tsTelephone Expenditure Trends˜
BY557: tsPostage Expenditure Trends˜
BZ557: tsCapital Outlay Expenditure Trends˜
BT558: tx1981-88 TIME SERIES˜
BU558: tx1981-88 TIME SERIES˜
BV558: tx1981-88 TIME SERIES˜
BW558: tx1981-88 TIME SERIES˜
BX558: tx1981-88 TIME SERIES˜
```

continued...

...from previous page

```
BY558: tx1981-88 TIME SERIES~
BZ558: tx1981-88 TIME SERIES~
BT559: q
BU559: q
BV559: q
BW559: q
BX559: q
BY559: q
BZ559: q
BT560: v
BU560: v
BV560: v
BW560: v
BX560: v
BY560: v
BZ560: v
BT561: q
BU561: q
BV561: q
BW561: q
BX561: q
BY561: q
BZ561: q
BT562: {INDICATE}{BRANCH \m}
BU562: {INDICATE}{BRANCH \m}
BV562: {INDICATE}{BRANCH \m}
BW562: {INDICATE}{BRANCH \m}
BX562: {INDICATE}{BRANCH \m}
BY562: {INDICATE}{BRANCH \m}
BZ562: {INDICATE}{BRANCH \m}
```

The range entries in rows 547 and 548 are actual and trend data from (1) Schedules T and F Data Table: Summary of Actual Expenditures (1981-87) and (2) Schedule T Data Table: Three-Year Moving Average of Actual Expenditures (1981-88). They apply to the first and second data ranges of the Schedule T #1 line graph. The entries in rows 548 are data from the Schedule T Data Table: Budget Trend Requests (1988-89), which was just constructed. They apply to the third data range of the line graph. (The Schedules T and F Data Table was constructed in Chapter 8 — see Figure 8.2 — and, therefore, will not be redisplayed here.)

The empty cells in the ranges on row 548 are necessary to offset the location of data points and the lines between points that will be graphed when the Schedule T #1 line graphics submenu macros are activated.

The row 549 entries are found in the Schedules T and F Data Table: Summary of Actual Expenditures (1981-87). These entries are used to graph the x-axes of the Schedule T line graphs. Please note, however, that these data were not included in the data table when it was constructed in Chapter 8 because the data apply exclusively to the graphing requirements of submenus created in the current chapter. Now, make these data entries as follows:

Cell	Entry
AZ5:	81
BA5:	82
BB5:	83
BC5:	84
BD5:	85
BE5:	86
BF5:	87
BG5:	88
BH5:	89

The above data are abbreviated dates rather than full notations for each of the years 1981-89. You need to abbreviate the year notations because of scale/space limitations of the Schedule T line graphs. Because the abbreviated years are not necessary to the display requirements of the Schedule T and F Data Table, they are hidden in the schedule. Using 1-2-3's Range Format Hidden command, hide the range AZ5..BH5 before proceeding further.

As a result of the cfabbbcb commands in row 551, Schedule T line graphs are created in color; the commands also set the formats for all data ranges so that symbols will be inserted at each data point within each range and lines will be drawn between the data points.

None of the other cell entries for constructing the Schedule T #1 line graphics submenu involve new data entry techniques or result in effects that have not been explained or qualified in previous sections, so you can make all remaining cell entries at this time.

Figure 18.4 displays the results of choosing the 3SALL option from the Schedule T #1 line graphics menu.

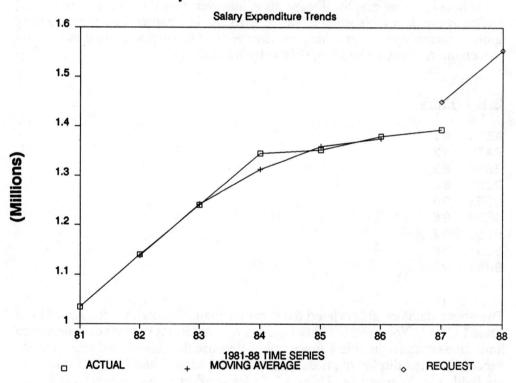

Figure 18.4   *Sample #1 Line Graph of Schedule T: Salary Expenditure Trends*

SECONDARY GRAPHICS SUBMENUS: SCHEDULE T #2 LINE CHART

The Schedule T #2 line chart submenu performs the same functions as the Schedule T #1 line graphics submenu except that expenditure data are deflated to real rather than current dollars. (The deflator value that is applied to the Schedule is the one that was most previously applied by the deflator macro created in Chapter 7.) The Schedule T #2 line graphics submenu depends on one data table — the Schedule T Data Table: Deflated Budget Trend Requests (1988-89) — on which the Schedule T #1 line graphics submenu does not depend (see Figure 18.5).

Cell Listing: Figure 18.5

Make the following entries to create the data table before creating the Schedule T #2 line graphics submenu:

```
AY175: [W45] 'SCHEDULE T DATA TABLE:  DEFLATED BUDGET TREND REQUESTS
       (1988-89)
BN175: '||
AY176: [W45] 'UNIT:  Department of Public Works
BN176: '||
AY177: [W45] \=
AZ177: [W20] \=
BA177: [W15] \=
BB177: [W13] \=
BC177: [W12] \=
BD177: [W12] \=
BE177: [W12] \=
BF177: [W13] \=
BG177: [W12] \=
BH177: [W12] \=
BI177: [W12] \=
BJ177: [W12] \=
BK177: [W12] \=
BL177: [W12] \=
BM177: [W12] \=
BN177: '||
AY178: [W45] "Deflator Factor:
AZ178: (P2) [W20] +BZ12*0.01
BN178: '||
```

continued after Figure 18.5...

	AY		AZ	BA	BB	BC	BD	BE
175	SCHEDULE T DATA TABLE: DEFLATED BUDGET TREND REQUESTS DATA (1988-89)							
176	UNIT: Department of Public Works							
177								
178		Deflator Factor:	4.20%					
179								
180								
181								
182								
183								
184								
185								
186								
187								
188								
189								
190								
191								
192								
193								
194								
195								
196								
197								
198								
199								
200								
201								
202								
203								
204								
205								
206								
207								
208								
209								
210								
211								
212								
213								
214								
215								
216								

Figure 18.5   Schedule T Data Table: Deflated Budget Trend Requests

8F	8G	8H	8I	8J	8K	8L	8M		8N	8O	8P	8Q
	1988-89	1989-90						‖				
	Requested	Requested						‖				
	104	106						‖				
	1,388,846	1,488,253						‖				
	11,975	16,785						‖				
								‖				
	62,232	71,371						‖				
	15,092	15,092						‖				
	72,386	72,432						‖				
	13,795	13,795						‖				
	12,071	13,029						‖				
	383	383						‖				
	479	479						‖				
	44,068	44,068						‖				
	4,215	4,215						‖				
	0	0						‖				
	4,790	4,790						‖				
	0	0						‖				
	0	0						‖				
	85,262	90,052						‖				
	575	575						‖				
	0	0						‖				
	0	0						‖				
	92,639	92,682						‖				
	28,740	28,740						‖				
	0	0						‖				
	54,149	33,073						‖				
	1,891,797	1,989,794						‖				

...from page 329

```
BG179: [W12] ^1988-89
BH179: [W12] ^1989-90
BN179: '||
BG180: [W12] ^Requested
BH180: [W12] ^Requested
BN180: '||
BG181: U [W12] 104
BH181: U [W12] 106
BN181: '||
BG182: (,0) U [W12] +AE10*($BZ$13)
BH182: (,0) U [W12] +AF10*($BZ$13)
BN182: '||
BG183: (,0) U [W12] +AE11*($BZ$13)
BH183: (,0) U [W12] +AF11*($BZ$13)
BN183: '||
BN184: '||
BN185: '||
BG186: (,0) U [W12] +AE14*($BZ$13)
BH186: (,0) U [W12] +AF14*($BZ$13)
BN186: '||
BG187: (,0) U [W12] +AE15*($BZ$13)
BH187: (,0) U [W12] +AF15*($BZ$13)
BN187: '||
BG188: (,0) U [W12] +AE16*($BZ$13)
BH188: (,0) U [W12] +AF16*($BZ$13)
BN188: '||
BG189: (,0) U [W12] +AE17*($BZ$13)
BH189: (,0) U [W12] +AF17*($BZ$13)
BN189: '||
BG190: (,0) U [W12] +AE18*($BZ$13)
BH190: (,0) U [W12] +AF18*($BZ$13)
BN190: '||
BG191: (,0) U [W12] +AE19*($BZ$13)
BH191: (,0) U [W12] +AF19*($BZ$13)
BN191: '||
BG192: (,0) U [W12] +AE20*($BZ$13)
BH192: (,0) U [W12] +AF20*($BZ$13)
BN192: '||
BG193: (,0) U [W12] +AE21*($BZ$13)
```

continued...

...from previous page

```
BH193: (,0) U [W12] +AF21*($BZ$13)
BN193: '||
BG194: (,0) U [W12] +AE22*($BZ$13)
BH194: (,0) U [W12] +AF22*($BZ$13)
BN194: '||
BG195: (,0) U [W12] +AE23*($BZ$13)
BH195: (,0) U [W12] +AF23*($BZ$13)
BN195: '||
BG196: (,0) U [W12] +AE24*($BZ$13)
BH196: (,0) U [W12] +AF24*($BZ$13)
BN196: '||
BG197: (,0) U [W12] +AE25*($BZ$13)
BH197: (,0) U [W12] +AF25*($BZ$13)
BN197: '||
BG198: (,0) U [W12] +AE26*($BZ$13)
BH198: (,0) U [W12] +AF26*($BZ$13)
BN198: '||
BG199: (,0) U [W12] +AE27*($BZ$13)
BH199: (,0) U [W12] +AF27*($BZ$13)
BN199: '||
BG200: (,0) U [W12] +AE28*($BZ$13)
BH200: (,0) U [W12] +AF28*($BZ$13)
BN200: '||
BN201: '||
BG202: (,0) U [W12] +AE30*($BZ$13)
BH202: (,0) U [W12] +AF30*($BZ$13)
BN202: '||
BG203: (,0) U [W12] +AE31*($BZ$13)
BH203: (,0) U [W12] +AF31*($BZ$13)
BN203: '||
BN204: '||
BN205: '||
BN206: '||
BG207: (,0) U [W12] +AE35*($BZ$13)
BH207: (,0) U [W12] +AF35*($BZ$13)
BN207: '||
BG208: (,0) U [W12] +AE36*($BZ$13)
BH208: (,0) U [W12] +AF36*($BZ$13)
BN208: '||
```

continued...

...from previous page

```
BG209:  (,0)  U  [W12]  +AE37*($BZ$13)
BH209:  (,0)  U  [W12]  +AF37*($BZ$13)
BN209:  '||
BN210:  '||
BN211:  '||
BG212:  (,0)  U  [W12]  +AE40*($BZ$13)
BH212:  (,0)  U  [W12]  +AF40*($BZ$13)
BN212:  '||
BG213:  (,0)  U  [W12]  "----------
BH213:  (,0)  U  [W12]  "----------
BN213:  '||
BG214:  (,0)  U  [W12]  +AE42*($BZ$13)
BH214:  (,0)  U  [W12]  +AF42*($BZ$13)
BN214:  '||
BG215:  (,0)  U  [W12]  "==========
BH215:  (,0)  U  [W12]  "==========
BN215:  '||
AY216:  [W45]  \=
AZ216:  [W20]  \=
BA216:  [W15]  \=
BB216:  [W13]  \=
BC216:  [W12]  \=
BD216:  [W12]  \=
BE216:  [W12]  \=
BF216:  [W13]  \=
BG216:  [W12]  \=
BH216:  [W12]  \=
BI216:  [W12]  \=
BJ216:  [W12]  \=
BK216:  [W12]  \=
BL216:  [W12]  \=
BM216:  [W12]  \=
BN216:  '||
```

Now that the data tables are complete, move the cursor to cell BT565 and name
the submenu by entering TLINE2 for the range BT565..BT565. Then, make the
following cell entries to create the Schedule T #2 graphics submenu (see Figure
18.6):

```
AY88: (W45) ^SCHEDULE T: BUDGET TREND PROJECTION MODEL (ANNUAL (FIVE-YEAR  MENU
1TOTL  2SALL  3TRAVL  4TELL  5POSTL  6CAPL_OUTLL
TOTAL DEFLATED EXPENDITURE TRENDS
                        AY                                AZ
88  SCHEDULE T: BUDGET TREND PROJECTION MODEL (ANNUAL (FIVE-YEAR AVERAGE) C
89  UNIT: Department of Public Works
90  ==========================================================================
91
92
93
94
95  Personal Services:
96     Man Years
97     Salaries
98     Benefits
99
100 Supporting Services:
101    Travel
102    Telephone Tolls and Rental
103    Postage
104    Rent - State Owned Buildings
105    Rent - Privately Owned Buildings
106    Building Improvements
107    Utility Charges
```

Figure 18.6　　*Schedule T #2 Submenu Options for Graphing Individual Objects of
Expenditure*

Cell　　Macro Entry

```
BS565:  'TLINE2=
BT565:  ^1TOTL
BU565:  ^2SALL
BV565:  ^3TRAVL
BW565:  ^4TELL
BX565:  ^5POSTL
BY565:  ^6CAPL_OUTLL
BT566:  ^TOTAL DEFLATED EXPENDITURE TRENDS
BU566:  ^SALARY DEFLATED EXPENDITURE TRENDS
BV566:  ^TRAVEL DEFLATED EXPENDITURE TRENDS
BW566:  ^TELEPHONE DEFLATED EXPENDITURE TRENDS
```

continued...

...from previous page

```
BX566:  ^POSTAGE DEFLATED EXPENDITURE TRENDS
BY566:  ^CAPITAL OUTLAY DEFLATED EXPENDITURE TRENDS
BT567:  '{INDICATE WAIT}{CALC}{PANELOFF}{WINDOWSOFF}
BU567:  '{INDICATE WAIT}{CALC}{PANELOFF}{WINDOWSOFF}
BV567:  '{INDICATE WAIT}{CALC}{PANELOFF}{WINDOWSOFF}
BW567:  '{INDICATE WAIT}{CALC}{PANELOFF}{WINDOWSOFF}
BX567:  '{INDICATE WAIT}{CALC}{PANELOFF}{WINDOWSOFF}
BY567:  '{INDICATE WAIT}{CALC}{PANELOFF}{WINDOWSOFF}
BT568:  '/grg
BU568:  '/grg
BV568:  '/grg
BW568:  '/grg
BX568:  '/grg
BY568:  '/grg
BT569:  'tl
BU569:  'tl
BV569:  'tl
BW569:  'tl
BX569:  'tl
BY569:  'tl
BT570:  ^aAZ41.BF41~
BU570:  ^aAZ9.BF9~
BV570:  ^aAZ13.BF13~
BW570:  ^aAZ14.BF14~
BX570:  ^aAZ15.BF15~
BY570:  ^aAZ39.BF39~
BT571:  'bAZ85.BF85~
BU571:  'bAZ53.BF53~
BV571:  'bAZ57.BF57~
BW571:  'bAZ58.BF58~
BX571:  'bAZ59.BF59~
BY571:  'bAZ83.BF83~
BT572:  ^cba214.bh214~
BU572:  ^cBA182.BH182~
BV572:  ^cBA186.BH186~
BW572:  ^cBA187.BH187~
BX572:  ^cBA188.BH188~
BY572:  ^cBA212.BH212~
BT573:  ^xAZ5.BH5~
```

continued...

...from previous page

```
BU573:  ^xAZ5.BH5~
BV573:  ^xAZ5.BH5~
BW573:  ^xAZ5.BH5~
BX573:  ^xAZ5.BH5~
BY573:  ^xAZ5.BH5~
BT574:  'o
BU574:  'o
BV574:  'o
BW574:  'o
BX574:  'o
BY574:  'o
BT575:  'cfabbbcb
BU575:  'cfabbbcb
BV575:  'cfabbbcb
BW575:  'cfabbbcb
BX575:  'cfabbbcb
BY575:  'cfabbbcb
BT576:  ^q
BU576:  ^q
BV576:  ^q
BW576:  ^q
BX576:  ^q
BY576:  ^q
BT577:  ^laACTUAL~
BU577:  ^laACTUAL~
BV577:  ^laACTUAL~
BW577:  ^laACTUAL~
BX577:  ^laACTUAL~
BY577:  ^laACTUAL~
BT578:  ^lbMOVING AVERAGE~
BU578:  ^lbMOVING AVERAGE~
BV578:  ^lbMOVING AVERAGE~
BW578:  ^lbMOVING AVERAGE~
BX578:  ^lbMOVING AVERAGE~
BY578:  ^lbMOVING AVERAGE~
BT579:  ^lc DEFL REQ~
BU579:  ^lc DEFL REQ~
BV579:  ^lc DEFL REQ~
BW579:  ^lc DEFL REQ~
```

continued...

...from previous page

```
BX579:  ^lc DEFL REQ~
BY579:  ^lc DEFL REQ~
BT580:  ^tfDepartment of Public Works~
BU580:  ^tfDepartment of Public Works~
BV580:  ^tfDepartment of Public Works~
BW580:  ^tfDepartment of Public Works~
BX580:  ^tfDepartment of Public Works~
BY580:  ^tfDepartment of Public Works~
BT581:  ^tsTotal Dfl. Expenditure Trends~
BU581:  ^tsSalary Dfl. Expenditure Trends~
BV581:  ^tsTravel Dfl. Expenditure Trends~
BW581:  ^tsTelephone Dfl. Expenditure Trends~
BX581:  ^tsPostage Dfl. Expenditure Trends~
BY581:  ^tsCapital Outlay Dfl. Expenditure Trends~
BT582:  ^tx1981-88 TIME SERIES~
BU582:  ^tx1981-88 TIME SERIES~
BV582:  ^tx1981-88 TIME SERIES~
BW582:  ^tx1981-88 TIME SERIES~
BX582:  ^tx1981-88 TIME SERIES~
BY582:  ^tx1981-88 TIME SERIES~
BT583:  'q
BU583:  'q
BV583:  'q
BW583:  'q
BX583:  'q
BY583:  'q
BT584:  'v
BU584:  'v
BV584:  'v
BW584:  'v
BX584:  'v
BY584:  'v
BT585:  'q
BU585:  'q
BV585:  'q
BW585:  'q
BX585:  'q
BY585:  'q
BT586:  ^{INDICATE}{BRANCH \m}
```

continued...

...from previous page

```
BU586: ^{INDICATE}{BRANCH \m}
BV586: ^{INDICATE}{BRANCH \m}
BW586: ^{INDICATE}{BRANCH \m}
BX586: ^{INDICATE}{BRANCH \m}
BY586: ^{INDICATE}{BRANCH \m}
```

Figure 18.7 displays the line graph that will be drawn when the 2SALL option is selected from the Schedule T #2 line graphics submenu.

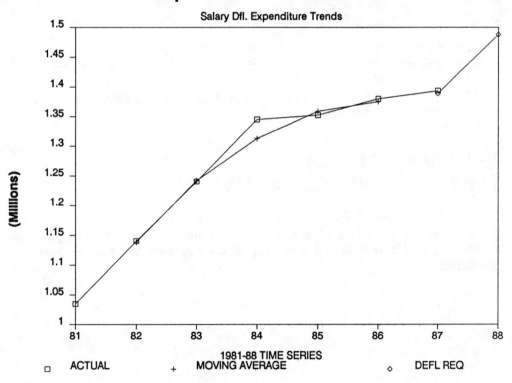

Figure 18.7   *Sample #2 Line Graph of Schedule T: Deflated Salary Expenditure Trends*

```
AY88; [W45] ^SCHEDULE T; BUDGET TREND PROJECTION MODEL [ANNUAL [FIVE-YEAR  MENU
1TOTL  2SALL  3TRAVL  4TELL  5POSTL  6CAPL_OUTLL
TOTAL DFL./NONDFL. EXPENDITURE TRENDS
                            AY                              AZ
88  SCHEDULE T; BUDGET TREND PROJECTION MODEL [ANNUAL [FIVE-YEAR AVERAGE] C
89  UNIT; Department of Public Works
90  ================================================================
91
92
93
94
95  Personal Services;
96      Man Years
97      Salaries
98      Benefits
99
100 Supporting Services;
101     Travel
102     Telephone Tolls and Rental
103     Postage
104     Rent - State Owned Buildings
105     Rent - Privately Owned Buildings
106     Building Improvements
107     Utility Charges
10-Aug-88  08;51 AM                      CMD       CALC
```

Figure 18.8   *Schedule T #3 Line Graph of Schedule T: Individual Objects of Expenditure*

SECONDARY GRAPHICS
SUBMENUS: SCHEDULE T #3 LINE CHART

Because the Schedule T #3 line graphics submenu (see Figure 18.8) overlays the nondeflated and deflated data graphed by Schedules T #3 and #4 line graphics submenus, it depends on all the data tables required by the previous two submenus.

Move the cursor to cell BT589 and name the submenu by creating the name TLINE3 for the range BT589..BT589. Then, construct the submenu by making the following entries:

Cell	Macro Entry
BS589:	'TLINE3=
BT589:	^1TOTL
BU589:	^2SALL
BV589:	^3TRAVL
BW589:	^4TELL
BX589:	^5POSTL
BY589:	^6CAPL_OUTLL
BT590:	^TOTAL DFL./NONDFL. EXPENDITURE TRENDS
BU590:	^SALARY DFL./NONDFL. EXPENDITURE TRENDS
BV590:	^TRAVEL DFL./NONDFL. EXPENDITURE TRENDS
BW590:	^TELEPHONE DFL./NONDFL. EXPENDITURE TRENDS
BX590:	^POSTAGE DFL./NONDFL EXPENDITURE TRENDS
BY590:	^CAPITAL OUTLAY DFL./NONDFL. EXPENDITURE TRENDS
BT591:	'{INDICATE WAIT}{CALC}{PANELOFF}{WINDOWSOFF}
BU991:	'{INDICATE WAIT}{CALC}{PANELOFF}{WINDOWSOFF}
BV591:	'{INDICATE WAIT}{CALC}{PANELOFF}{WINDOWSOFF}
BW591:	^{INDICATE WAIT}{CALC}{PANELOFF}{WINDOWSOFF}
BX591:	'{INDICATE WAIT}{CALC}{PANELOFF}{WINDOWSOFF}
BY591:	'{INDICATE WAIT}{CALC}{PANELOFF}{WINDOWSOFF}
BT592:	'/grg
BU592:	'/grg
BV592:	'/grg
BW592:	'/grg
BX592:	'/grg
BY592:	'/grg
BT593:	'tl
BU593:	'tl
BV593:	'tl
BW593:	'tl
BX593:	'tl
BY593:	'tl
BT594:	^aAZ41.BF41~
BU594:	^aAZ9.BF9~
BV594:	^aAZ13.BF13~

continued...

...from previous page

```
BW594:  ^aAZ14.BF14~
BX594:  ^aAZ15.BF15~
BY594:  ^aAZ39.BF39~
BT595:  'bAZ85.BF85~
BU595:  'bAZ53.BF53~
BV595:  'bAZ57.BF57~
BW595:  'bAZ58.BF58~
BX595:  'bAZ59.BF59~
BY595:  'bAZ83.BF83~
BT596:  ^cBA172.BH172~
BU596:  ^cBA140.BH140~
BV596:  ^cBA144.BH144~
BW596:  ^cBA145.BH145~
BX596:  ^cBA146.BH146~
BY596:  ^cBA170.BH170~
BT597:  ^dBA214.BH214~
BU597:  ^dBA182.BH182~
BV597:  ^dBA186.BH186~
BW597:  ^dBA187.BH187~
BX597:  ^dBA188.BH188~
BY597:  ^dBA212.BH212~
BT598:  ^xAZ5.BH5~
BU598:  ^xAZ5.BH5~
BV598:  ^xAZ5.BH5~
BW598:  ^xAZ5.BH5~
BX598:  ^xAZ5.BH5~
BY598:  ^xAZ5.BH5~
BT599:  'o
BU599:  'o
BV599:  'o
BW599:  'o
BX599:  'o
BY599:  'o
BT600:  'cfabbbcb
BU600:  'cfabbbcb
BV600:  'cfabbbcb
BW600:  'cfabbbcb
BX600:  'cfabbbcb
```

continued...

...from previous page

```
BY600:  'cfabbbcb
BT601:  ^q
BU601:  ^q
BV601:  ^q
BW601:  ^q
BX601:  ^q
BY601:  ^q
BT602:  ^laACTUAL~
BU602:  ^laACTUAL~
BV602:  ^laACTUAL~
BW602:  ^laACTUAL~
BX602:  ^laACTUAL~
BY602:  ^laACTUAL~
BT603:  ^lbMOV AVG~
BU603:  ^lbMOV AVG~
BV603:  ^lbMOV AVG~
BW603:  ^lbMOV AVG~
BX603:  ^lbMOV AVG~
BY603:  ^lbMOV AVG~
BT604:  'lcREQ~
BU604:  'lcREQ~
BV604:  'lcREQ~
BW604:  'lcREQ~
BX604:  'lcREQ~
BY604:  'lcREQ~
BT605:  'ld DEFL REQ~
BU605:  'ld DEFL REQ~
BV605:  'ld DEFL REQ~
BW605:  'ld DEFL REQ~
BX605:  'ld DEFL REQ~
BY605:  'ld DEFL REQ~
BT606:  ^tfDepartment of Public Works~
BU606:  ^tfDepartment of Public Works~
BV606:  ^tfDepartment of Public Works~
BW606:  ^tfDepartment of Public Works~
BX606:  ^tfDepartment of Public Works~
BY606:  ^tfDepartment of Public Works~
BT607:  ^tsTotal Dfl./Nondfl. Expenditure Trends~
```

continued...

...from previous page

```
BU607: ^tsSalary Dfl./Nondfl. Expenditure Trends~
BV607: ^tsTravel Dfl./Nondfl. Expenditure Trends~
BW607: ^tsTelephone Dfl./Nondfl. Exp. Trends~
BX607: ^tsPostage Dfl./Nondfl. Expenditure Trends~
BY607: ^tsCapital Outlay Dfl./Nondfl. Exp. Trends~
BT608: ^tx1981-88 TIME SERIES~
BU608: ^tx1981-88 TIME SERIES~
BV608: ^tx1981-88 TIME SERIES~
BW608: ^tx1981-88 TIME SERIES~
BX608: ^tx1981-88 TIME SERIES~
BY608: ^tx1981-88 TIME SERIES~
BT609: 'q
BU609: 'q
BV609: 'q
BW609: 'q
BX609: 'q
BY609: 'q
BT610: 'v
BU610: 'v
BV610: 'v
BW610: 'v
BX610: 'v
BY610: 'v
BT611: 'q
BU611: 'q
BV611: 'q
BW611: 'q
BX611: 'q
BY611: 'q
BT612: ^{INDICATE}{BRANCH \m}
BU612: ^{INDICATE}{BRANCH \m}
BV612: ^{INDICATE}{BRANCH \m}
BW612: ^{INDICATE}{BRANCH \m}
BX612: ^{INDICATE}{BRANCH \m}
BY612: ^{INDICATE}{BRANCH \m}
```

Figure 18.9 displays the graph that will be drawn when the 2SALL option is selected from the Schedule T #3 line graphics submenu.

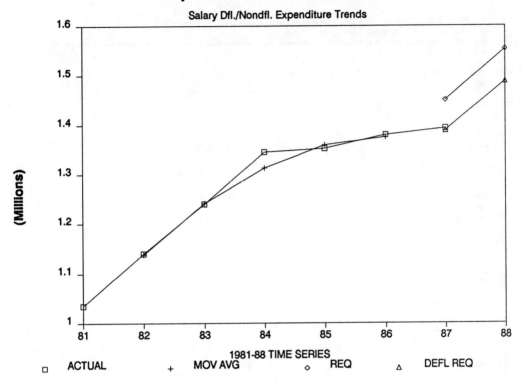

Department of Public Works

Salary Dfl./Nondfl. Expenditure Trends

Figure 18.9   Sample #3 Line Graph of Schedule

SECONDARY GRAPHICS
SUBMENUS: SCHEDULE T #4 LINE CHART

The cell entries and techniques for creating the Schedule T #4 line graphics submenu are the same as for the previously created Schedule T line graphics submenus—except for row 623, which obtains its data from Schedule T Data Table: Projected Requests (1988-89). (See Figure 18.10.)

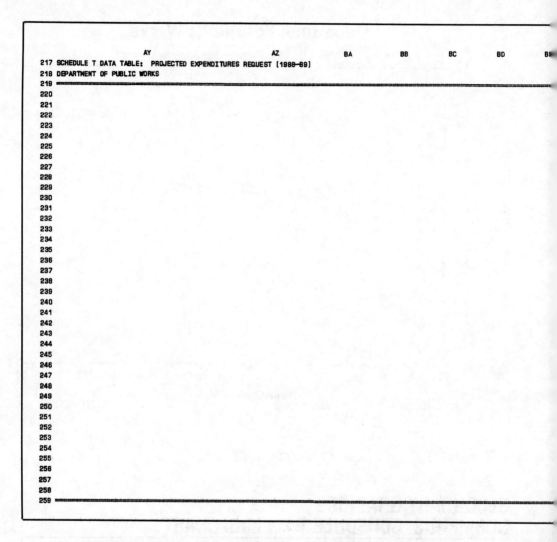

	AY	AZ	BA	BB	BC	BD	B
217	SCHEDULE T DATA TABLE: PROJECTED EXPENDITURES REQUEST (1988-89)						
218	DEPARTMENT OF PUBLIC WORKS						
219							
220							
221							
222							
223							
224							
225							
226							
227							
228							
229							
230							
231							
232							
233							
234							
235							
236							
237							
238							
239							
240							
241							
242							
243							
244							
245							
246							
247							
248							
249							
250							
251							
252							
253							
254							
255							
256							
257							
258							
259							

Figure 18.10   Schedule T Data Table: Projected Expenditure Requests

BF	BG	BH	BI	BJ	BK	BL	BM	BN	BO	BP	BQ

	PROJECTED REQUEST 1988-89	PROJECTED REQUEST 1989-90
	1,451,788	1,512,142
	0	0
	64,809	65,628
	16,289	16,801
	73,943	76,107
	10,475	10,972
	6,956	7,332
	583	791
	629	782
	48,479	51,092
	4,103	4,209
	0	0
	7,990	7,980
	0	0
	0	0
	245,439	717,145
	637	676
	0	0
	1,578	1,578
	282,275	847,649
	41,311	47,407
	0	0
	53,295	82,273
	———	———
	1,987,217	2,113,843
	=====	=====

347

This data table, in turn, depends on the Schedule T: Budget Trend Projection Model for its data. Make the following entries to create the data table before constructing the Schedule T #4 line graphics submenu:

Cell Listing: Figure 18.10

```
AY217: [W45] ^SCHEDULE T DATA TABLE:  PROJECTED REQUESTS (1988-89)
BN217: '||
AY218: [W45] 'DEPARTMENT OF PUBLIC WORKS
BN218: '||
AY219: [W45] \=
AZ219: [W20] \=
BA219: [W15] \=
BB219: [W13] \=
BC219: [W12] \=
BD219: [W12] \=
BE219: [W12] \=
BF219: [W13] \=
BG219: [W12] \=
BH219: [W12] \=
BI219: [W12] \=
BJ219: [W12] \=
BK219: [W12] \=
BL219: [W12] \=
BM219: [W12] \=
BN219: '||
BN220: '||
BG221: [W12] ^PROJECTED
BH221: [W12] ^PROJECTED
BN221: '||
BG222: [W12] ^REQUEST
BH222: [W12] ^REQUEST
BN222: '||
BG223: [W12] ^1988-89
BH223: [W12] ^1989-90
BN223: '||
BN224: '||
BG225: (,0) [W12] (BA97*BF9)+BF9
BH225: [W12] (BA97*BB97)+BB97
```

continued...

...from previous page

```
BN225: '||
BG226: (,0) [W12] (BA98*BF10)+BF10
BH226: [W12] (BA98*BB98)+BB98
BN226: '||
BN227: '||
BN228: '||
BG229: (,0) [W12] (BA101*BF13)+BF13
BH229: [W12] (BA101*BB101)+BB101
BN229: '||
BG230: (,0) [W12] (BA102*BF14)+BF14
BH230: [W12] (BA102*BB102)+BB102
BN230: '||
BG231: (,0) [W12] (BA103*BF15)+BF15
BH231: [W12] (BA103*BB103)+BB103
BN231: '||
BG232: (,0) [W12] (BA104*BF16)+BF16
BH232: [W12] (BA104*BB104)+BB104
BN232: '||
BG233: (,0) [W12] (BA105*BF17)+BF17
BH233: [W12] (BA105*BB105)+BB105
BN233: '||
BG234: (,0) [W12] (BA106*BF18)+BF18
BH234: [W12] (BA106*BB106)+BB106
BN234: '||
BG235: (,0) [W12] (BA107*BF19)+BF19
BH235: [W12] (BA107*BB107)+BB107
BN235: '||
BG236: (,0) [W12] (BA108*BF20)+BF20
BH236: [W12] (BA108*BB108)+BB108
BN236: '||
BG237: (,0) [W12] (BA109*BF21)+BF21
BH237: [W12] (BA109*BB109)+BB109
BN237: '||
BG238: (,0) [W12] (BA110*BF22)+BF22
BH238: [W12] (BA110*BB110)+BB110
BN238: '||
BG239: (,0) [W12] (BA111*BF23)+BF23
BH239: [W12] (BA111*BB111)+BB111
BN239: '||
```

continued...

...from previous page

```
BG240: (,0) [W12] (BA112*BF24)+BF24
BH240: [W12] (BA112*BB112)+BB112
BN240: '||
BG241: (,0) [W12] (BA113*BF25)+BF25
BH241: [W12] (BA113*BB113)+BB113
BN241: '||
BG242: (,0) [W12] (BA114*BF26)+BF26
BH242: [W12] (BA114*BB114)+BB114
BN242: '||
BG243: (,0) [W12] (BA115*BF27)+BF27
BH243: [W12] (BA115*BB115)+BB115
BN243: '||
BN244: '||
BG245: (,0) [W12] (BA117*BF29)+BF29
BH245: [W12] (BA117*BB117)+BB117
BN245: '||
BG246: (,0) [W12] (BA118*BF30)+BF30
BH246: [W12] (BA118*BB118)+BB118
BN246: '||
BN247: '||
BN248: '||
BN249: '||
BG250: (,0) [W12] (BA122*BF34)+BF34
BH250: [W12] (BA122*BB122)+BB122
BN250: '||
BG251: (,0) [W12] (BA123*BF35)+BF35
BH251: [W12] (BA123*BB123)+BB123
BN251: '||
BG252: (,0) [W12] (BA124*BF36)+BF36
BH252: [W12] (BA124*BB124)+BB124
BN252: '||
BN253: '||
BN254: '||
BG255: (,0) [W12] (BA127*BF39)+BF39
BH255: [W12] (BA127*BB127)+BB127
BN255: '||
BG256: (,0) [W12] "----------
BH256: (,0) [W12] "----------
BN256: '||
```

continued...

...from previous page

```
BG257: (,0) [W12] (BA129*BF41)+BF41
BH257: [W12] (BA129*BB129)+BB129
BN257: '||
BG258: [W12] "=========
BH258: [W12] "=========
BN258: '||
AY259: [W45] \=
AZ259: [W20] \=
BA259: [W15] \=
BB259: [W13] \=
BC259: [W12] \=
BD259: [W12] \=
BE259: [W12] \=
BF259: [W13] \=
BG259: [W12] \=
BH259: [W12] \=
BI259: [W12] \=
BJ259: [W12] \=
BK259: [W12] \=
BL259: [W12] \=
BM259: [W12] \=
BN259: '||
```

The Schedule T #4 line chart submenu is displayed in Figure 18.11.

```
AY88: [W45] ^SCHEDULE T: BUDGET TREND PROJECTION MODEL [ANNUAL [FIVE-YEAR  MENU
1TOTL  2SALL  3TRAVL  4TELL  5POSTL  6CAPL_OUTLL
TOTAL EXPENDITURE TRENDS/PROJECTION
                        AY                            AZ
88  SCHEDULE T: BUDGET TREND PROJECTION MODEL [ANNUAL [FIVE-YEAR AVERAGE] C
89  UNIT: Department of Public Works
90  =======================================================================
91
92
93
94
95  Personal Services:
96      Man Years
97      Salaries
98      Benefits
99
100 Supporting Services:
101     Travel
102     Telephone Tolls and Rental
103     Postage
104     Rent - State Owned Buildings
105     Rent - Privately Owned Buildings
106     Building Improvements
107     Utility Charges
```

*Figure 18.11   Schedule T #5 Option for Graphing Individual Objects
of Expenditure*

To construct the submenu, make the following entries:

Cell	**Macro Entry**
BS615:	'TLINE4=
BT615:	^1TOTL
BU615:	^2SALL
BV615:	^3TRAVL
BW615:	^4TELL
BX615:	^5POSTL
BY615:	^6CAPL_OUTLL
BT616:	^TOTAL EXPENDITURE TRENDS/PROJECTION
BU616:	^SALARY EXPENDITURE TRENDS/PROJECTION
BV616:	^TRAVEL EXPENDITURE TRENDS/PROJECTION
BW616:	^TELEPHONE EXPENDITURE TRENDS/PROJECTION
BX616:	^POSTAGE EXPENDITURE TRENDS/PROJECTION
BY616:	^CAPITAL OUTLAY EXPENDITURE TRENDS/PROJECTION

continued...

...from previous page

```
BT617:  '{INDICATE WAIT}{CALC}{PANELOFF}{WINDOWSOFF}
BU617:  '{INDICATE WAIT}{CALC}{PANELOFF}{WINDOWSOFF}
BV617:  '{INDICATE WAIT}{CALC}{PANELOFF}{WINDOWSOFF}
BW617:  ^{INDICATE WAIT}{CALC}{PANELOFF}{WINDOWSOFF}
BX617:  '{INDICATE WAIT}{CALC}{PANELOFF}{WINDOWSOFF}
BY617:  '{INDICATE WAIT}{CALC}{PANELOFF}{WINDOWOFF}
BT618:  '/grg
BU618:  '/grg
BV618:  '/grg
BW618:  '/grg
BX618:  '/grg
BY618:  '/grg
BT619:  'tl
BU619:  'tl
BV619:  'tl
BW619:  'tl
BX619:  'tl
BY619:  'tl
BT620:  ^aAZ41.BF41~
BU620:  ^aAZ9.BF9~
BV620:  ^aAZ13.BF13~
BW620:  ^aAZ14.BF14~
BX620:  ^aAZ15.BF15~
BY620:  ^aAZ39.BF39~
BT621:  'bAZ85.BF85~
BU621:  'bAZ53.BF53~
BV621:  'bAZ57.BF57~
BW621:  'bAZ58.BF58~
BX621:  'bAZ59.BF59~
BY621:  'bAZ83.BF83~
BT622:  ^cBA172.BH172~
BU622:  ^cBA140.BH140~
BV622:  ^cBA144.BH144~
BW622:  ^cBA145.BH145~
BX622:  ^cBA146.BH146~
BY622:  ^cBA170.BH170~
BT623:  ^dBA257.BH257~
BU623:  ^dBA225.BH225~
BV623:  ^dBA229.BH229~
```

continued...

...from previous page

```
BW623:  ^dBA230.BH230~
BX623:  ^dBA231.BH231~
BY623:  ^dBA255.BH255~
BT624:  ^xAZ5.BH5~
BU624:  ^xAZ5.BH5~
BV624:  ^xAZ5.BH5~
BW624:  ^xAZ5.BH5~
BX624:  ^xAZ5.BH5~
BY624:  ^xAZ5.BH5~
BT625:  'o
BU625:  'o
BV625:  'o
BW625:  'o
BX625:  'o
BY625:  'o
BT626:  'cfabbbcb
BU626:  'cfabbbcb
BV626:  'cfabbbcb
BW626:  'cfabbbcb
BX626:  'cfabbbcb
BY626:  'cfabbbcb
BT627:  ^q
BU627:  ^q
BV627:  ^q
BW627:  ^q
BX627:  ^q
BY627:  ^q
BT628:  ^laACT~
BU628:  ^laACTUAL~
BV628:  ^laACTUAL~
BW628:  ^laACTUAL~
BX628:  ^laACTUAL~
BY628:  ^laACTUAL~
BT629:  ^lbMOV AVG~
BU629:  ^lbMOV AVG~
BV629:  ^lbMOV AVG~
BW629:  ^lbMOV AVG~
BX629:  ^lbMOV AVG~
BY629:  ^lbMOV AVG~
```

continued...

...from previous page

```
BT630: 'lcRQ~
BU630: 'lcREQ~
BV630: 'lcREQ~
BW630: 'lcREQ~
BX630: 'lcREQ~
BY630: 'lcREQ~
BT631: ^ld PROJ REQ~
BU631: ^ld PROJ REQ~
BV631: ^ld PROJ REQ~
BW631: ^ld PROJ REQ~
BX631: ^ld PROJ REQ~
BY631: ^ld PROJ REQ~
BT632: ^tfDepartment of Public Works~
BU632: ^tfDepartment of Public Works~
BV632: ^tfDepartment of Public Works~
BW632: ^tfDepartment of Public Works~
BX632: ^tfDepartment of Public Works~
BY632: ^tfDepartment of Public Works~
BT633: ^tsTotal Expenditure Trends/Projection~
BU633: ^tsSalary Expenditure Trends/Projection~
BV633: ^tsTravel Expenditure Trends/Projection~
BW633: ^tsTelephone Exp. Trends/Projection~
BX633: ^tsPostage Expenditure Trends/Projection~
BY633: ^tsCapital Outlay Exp. Trends/Projection~
BT634: ^tx1981-88 TIME SERIES~
BU634: ^tx1981-88 TIME SERIES~
BV634: ^tx1981-88 TIME SERIES~
BW634: ^tx1981-88 TIME SERIES~
BX634: ^tx1981-88 TIME SERIES~
BY634: ^tx1981-88 TIME SERIES~
BT635: 'q
BU635: 'q
BV635: 'q
BW635: 'q
BX635: 'q
BY635: 'q
BT636: 'v
BU636: 'v
BV636: 'v
```

continued...

...from previous page

```
BW636:  'v
BX636:  'v
BY636:  'v
BT637:  'q
BU637:  'q
BV637:  'q
BW637:  'q
BX637:  'q
BY637:  'q
BT638:  ^{INDICATE}{BRANCH \m}
BU638:  ^{INDICATE}{BRANCH \m}
BV638:  ^{INDICATE}{BRANCH \m}
BW638:  ^{INDICATE}{BRANCH \m}
BX638:  ^{INDICATE}{BRANCH \m}
BY638:  ^{INDICATE}{BRANCH \m}
```

Figure 18.12 displays the line graph that is drawn when the 2SALL option is selected from the Schedule T #4 line graphics submenu.

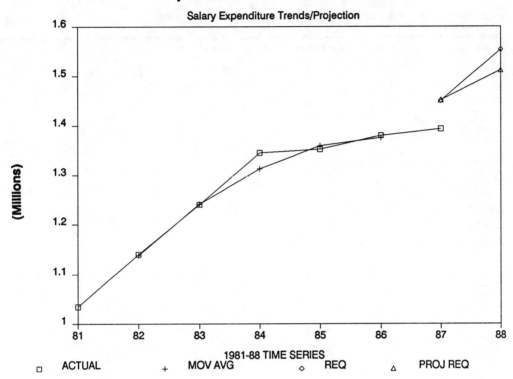

Department of Public Works

Figure 18.12   Sample #4 Line Graph of Schedule T: Salary Deflated/Nondeflated Expenditure Trends/Projection

SECONDARY GRAPHICS
SUBMENUS: SCHEDULE T #5 LINE CHART

The Schedule T #5 line graphics submenu depends on Schedule T Data Table: Deflated Projected Requests (1988-89) for its data (see Figure 18.13). These are the same data that appear in Schedule T Data Table: Projected Requests (1988-89) except that the data have been deflated to real rather than current dollars.

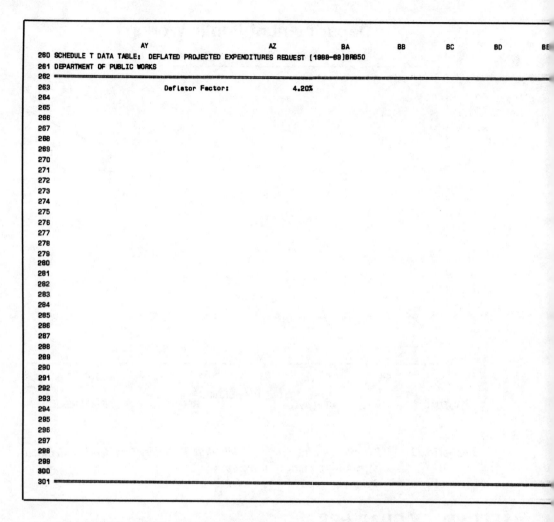

Figure 18.13   Schedule T Data Table

BF	BG	BH	BI	BJ	BK	BL	BM	BN	BO	BP	BQ

	PROJECTED 1988–89 REQUEST	PROJECTED 1989–90 REQUEST
	1,390,791	1,448,632
	0	0
	62,087	62,871
	15,586	16,095
	70,837	74,827
	10,035	10,511
	6,664	7,024
	539	758
	603	759
	48,443	48,947
	3,931	4,032
	0	0
	7,654	7,645
	0	0
	0	0
	235,130	687,025
	610	648
	0	0
	1,512	1,512
	270,419	812,048
	39,576	45,415
	0	0
	51,056	78,818
	1,903,754	2,025,062

359

The only entries in the Schedule T #5 line graphics submenu that do not have counterparts in one of the Schedule T submenus are those in row 651, which are data from the data table. These entries are data posted to the Schedule T Data Table (Deflated Projected Requests, [1988-89], which is from the Schedule Data Table: Projected Requests [1988-89]) and subsequently deflated. Create the deflated data table now by making the following entries before constructing the Schedule T #5 line graphics submenu.

Cell Listing: Figure 18.13

```
AY260: [W45] ^SCHEDULE T DATA TABLE:   DEFLATED PROJECTED REQUESTS
       (1988-89)
BN260: '||
AY261: [W45] 'DEPARTMENT OF PUBLIC WORKS
BN261: '||
AY262: [W45] \=
AZ262: [W20] \=
BA262: [W15] \=
BB262: [W13] \=
BC262: [W12] \=
BD262: [W12] \=
BE262: [W12] \=
BF262: [W13] \=
BG262: [W12] \=
BH262: [W12] \=
BI262: [W12] \=
BJ262: [W12] \=
BK262: [W12] \=
BL262: [W12] \=
BM262: [W12] \=
BN262: '||
AY263: [W45] "Deflator Factor:
AZ263: (P2) [W20] +BZ12*0.01
BN263: '||
BG264: [W12] ^PROJECTED
BH264: [W12] ^PROJECTED
BN264: '||
BG265: [W12] ^1988-89
BH265: [W12] ^1989-90
BN265: '||
BG266: [W12] ^REQUEST
```

continued...

...from previous page

```
BH266:  [W12]  ^REQUEST
BN266:  '||
BG267:  [W12]  +BG225*$BZ$13
BH267:  [W12]  +BH225*$BZ$13
BN267:  '||
BG268:  [W12]  +BG226*$BZ$13
BH268:  [W12]  +BH226*$BZ$13
BN268:  '||
BN269:  '||
BN270:  '||
BG271:  [W12]  +BG229*$BZ$13
BH271:  [W12]  +BH229*$BZ$13
BN271:  '||
BG272:  [W12]  +BG230*$BZ$13
BH272:  [W12]  +BH230*$BZ$13
BN272:  '||
BG273:  [W12]  +BG231*$BZ$13
BH273:  [W12]  +BH231*$BZ$13
BN273:  '||
BG274:  [W12]  +BG232*$BZ$13
BH274:  [W12]  +BH232*$BZ$13
BN274:  '||
BG275:  [W12]  +BG233*$BZ$13
BH275:  [W12]  +BH233*$BZ$13
BN275:  '||
BG276:  [W12]  +BG234*$BZ$13
BH276:  [W12]  +BH234*$BZ$13
BN276:  '||
BG277:  [W12]  +BG235*$BZ$13
BH277:  [W12]  +BH235*$BZ$13
BN277:  '||
BG278:  [W12]  +BG236*$BZ$13
BH278:  [W12]  +BH236*$BZ$13
BN278:  '||
BG279:  [W12]  +BG237*$BZ$13
BH279:  [W12]  +BH237*$BZ$13
BN279:  '||
BG280:  [W12]  +BG238*$BZ$13
BH280:  [W12]  +BH238*$BZ$13
```

continued...

...from previous page

```
BN280:  '||
BG281:  [W12]  +BG239*$BZ$13
BH281:  [W12]  +BH239*$BZ$13
BN281:  '||
BG282:  [W12]  +BG240*$BZ$13
BH282:  [W12]  +BH240*$BZ$13
BN282:  '||
BG283:  [W12]  +BG241*$BZ$13
BH283:  [W12]  +BH241*$BZ$13
BN283:  '||
BG284:  [W12]  +BG242*$BZ$13
BH284:  [W12]  +BH242*$BZ$13
BN284:  '||
BG285:  [W12]  +BG243*$BZ$13
BH285:  [W12]  +BH243*$BZ$13
BN285:  '||
BN286:  '||
BG287:  [W12]  +BG245*$BZ$13
BH287:  [W12]  +BH245*$BZ$13
BN287:  '||
BG288:  [W12]  +BG246*$BZ$13
BH288:  [W12]  +BH246*$BZ$13
BN288:  '||
BN289:  '||
BN290:  '||
BN291:  '||
BG292:  [W12]  +BG250*$BZ$13
BH292:  [W12]  +BH250*$BZ$13
BN292:  '||
BG293:  [W12]  +BG251*$BZ$13
BH293:  [W12]  +BH251*$BZ$13
BN293:  '||
BG294:  [W12]  +BG252*$BZ$13
BH294:  [W12]  +BH252*$BZ$13
BN294:  '||
BN295:  '||
BN296:  '||
BG297:  [W12]  +BG255*$BZ$13
BH297:  [W12]  +BH255*$BZ$13
```

continued...

...from previous page

```
BN297:  '||
BG298:  [W12]  "----------
BH298:  [W12]  "----------
BN298:  '||
BG299:  [W12]  +BG257*$BZ$13
BH299:  [W12]  +BH257*$BZ$13
BN299:  '||
BG300:  [W12]  "=========
BH300:  [W12]  "=========
BN300:  '||
AY301:  [W45]  \=
AZ301:  [W20]  \=
BA301:  [W15]  \=
BB301:  [W13]  \=
BC301:  [W12]  \=
BD301:  [W12]  \=
BE301:  [W12]  \=
BF301:  [W13]  \=
BG301:  [W12]  \=
BH301:  [W12]  \=
BI301:  [W12]  \=
BJ301:  [W12]  \=
BK301:  [W12]  \=
BL301:  [W12]  \=
BM301:  [W12]  \=
BN301:  '||  20
```

```
AY88: [W45] ^SCHEDULE T:  BUDGET TREND PROJECTION MODEL [ANNUAL [FIVE-YEAR  MENU
1TOTL  2SALL  3TRAVL  4TELL  5POSTL  6CAPL_OUTLL
TOTAL DFL./NONDFL. EXPENDITURE TRENDS/PROJECTION
                        AY                          AZ
88  SCHEDULE T:  BUDGET TREND PROJECTION MODEL [ANNUAL [FIVE-YEAR AVERAGE] C
89  UNIT:  Department of Public Works
90  ═══════════════════════════════════════════════════════════
91
92
93
94
95  Personal Services:
96      Man Years
97      Salaries
98      Benefits
99
100 Supporting Services:
101     Travel
102     Telephone Tolls and Rental
103     Postage
104     Rent - State Owned Buildings
105     Rent - Privately Owned Buildings
106     Building Improvements
107     Utility Charges
```

Figure 18.14   Schedule T #5 Options for Graphing Individual Objects
of Expenditure

Before creating the Schedule T #5 graphics submenu (see Figure 18.14), name
the submenu by moving the cursor to cell BT641 and creating the name TLINE5
for the range BT641..BT641. Then, make the following entries to construct the
Schedule T #5 line graphics submenu:

Cell   **Macro Entry**

BS641: 'TLINE5=
BT641: ^1TOTL
BU641: ^2SALL
BV641: ^3TRAVL
BW641: ^4TELL
BX641: ^5POSTL
BY641: ^6CAPL_OUTLL
BT642: ^TOTAL DFL./NONDFL. EXPENDITURE TRENDS/PROJECTION
BU642: ^SALARY DFL./NONDFL. EXPENDITURE TRENDS/PROJECTION
BV642: ^TRAVEL DFL./NONDFL. EXPENDITURE TRENDS/PROJECTION

continued...

...from previous page

```
BW642:  ^TELEPHONE DFL./NONDFL. EXPENDITURE TRENDS/PROJECTION
BX642:  ^POSTAGE DFL./NONDFL EXPENDITURE TRENDS/PROJECTION
BY642:  ^CAP. OUTLAY DFL./NONDFL EXPENDITURE TRENDS/PROJECTION
BT643:  '{INDICATE WAIT}{CALC}{PANELOFF}{WINDOWSOFF}
BU643:  '{INDICATE WAIT}{CALC}{PANELOFF}{WINDOWSOFF}
BV643:  '{INDICATE WAIT}{CALC}{PANELOFF}{WINDOWSOFF}
BW643:  ^{INDICATE WAIT}{CALC}{PANELOFF}{WINDOWSOFF}
BX643:  '{INDICATE WAIT}{CALC}{PANELOFF}{WINDOWSOFF}
BY643:  '{INDICATE WAIT}{CALC}{PANELOFF}{WINDOWSOFF}
BT644:  '/grg
BU644:  '/grg
BV644:  '/grg
BW644:  '/grg
BX644:  '/grg
BY644:  '/grg
BT645:  'tl
BU645:  'tl
BV645:  'tl
BW645:  'tl
BX645:  'tl
BY645:  'tl
BT646:  ^aAZ41.BF41~
BU646:  ^aAZ9.BF9~
BV646:  ^aAZ13.BF13~
BW646:  ^aAZ14.BF14~
BX646:  ^aAZ15.BF15~
BY646:  ^aAZ39.BF39~
BT647:  'bAZ85.BF85~
BU647:  'bAZ53.BƵ53~
BV647:  'bAZ57.BF57~
BW647:  'bAZ58.BF58~
BX647:  'bAZ59.BF59~
BY647:  'bAZ83.BF83~
BT648:  ^cBA172.BH172~
BU648:  ^cBA140.BH140~
BV648:  ^cBA144.BH144~
BW648:  ^cBA145.BH145~
BX648:  ^cBA146.BH146~
BY648:  ^cBA170.BH170~
```

continued...

...from previous page

```
BT649:  ^dBA214.BH214~
BU649:  ^dBA182.BH182~
BV649:  ^dBA186.BH186~
BW649:  ^dBA187.BH187~
BX649:  ^dBA188.BH188~
BY649:  ^dBA212.BH212~
BT650:  ^eBA257.BH257~
BU650:  ^eBA225.BH225~
BV650:  ^eBA229.BH229~
BW650:  ^eBA230.BH230~
BX650:  ^eBA231.BH231~
BY650:  ^eBA255.BH255~
BT651:  ^fBA299.BH299~
BU651:  ^fBA267.BH267~
BV651:  ^fBA271.BH271~
BW651:  ^fBA272.BH272~
BX651:  ^fBA273.BH273~
BY651:  ^fBA297.BH297~
BT652:  ^xAZ5.BH5~
BU652:  ^xAZ5.BH5~
BV652:  ^xAZ5.BH5~
BW652:  ^xAZ5.BH5~
BX652:  ^xAZ5.BH5~
BY652:  ^xAZ5.BH5~
BT653:  'o
BU653:  'o
BV653:  'o
BW653:  'o
BX653:  'o
BY653:  'o
BT654:  'cfabbbcb
BU654:  'cfabbbcb
BV654:  'cfabbbcb
BW654:  'cfabbbcb
BX654:  'cfabbbcb
BY654:  'cfabbbcb
BT655:  ^q
BU655:  ^q
BV655:  ^q
```

continued...

...from previous page

```
BW655:  ^q
BX655:  ^q
BY655:  ^q
BT656:  ^laAC~
BU656:  ^laAC~
BV656:  ^laAC~
BW656:  ^laAC~
BX656:  ^laAC~
BY656:  ^laAC~
BT657:  ^lbM AV~
BU657:  ^lbM AV~
BV657:  ^lbM AV~
BW657:  ^lbM AV~
BX657:  ^lbM AV~
BY657:  ^lbM AV~
BT658:  'lcRQ~
BU658:  'lcRQ~
BV658:  'lcRQ~
BW658:  'lcRQ~
BX658:  'lcRQ~
BY658:  'lcRQ~
BT659:  ^ldDF RQ~
BU659:  ^ldDF RQ~
BV659:  ^ldDF RQ~
BW659:  ^ldDF RQ~
BX659:  ^ldDF RQ~
BY659:  ^ldDF RQ~
BT660:  ^lePJ RQ~
BU660:  ^lePJ RQ~
BV660:  ^lePJ RQ~
BW660:  ^lePJ RQ~
BX660:  ^lePJ RQ~
BY660:  ^lePJ RQ~
BT661:  ^lfDF PJ~
BU661:  ^lfDF PJ~
BV661:  ^lfDF PJ~
BW661:  ^lfDF PJ~
BX661:  ^lfDF PJ~
BY661:  ^lfDF PJ~
```

continued...

...from previous page

```
BT662: ^tfDepartment of Public Works~
BU662: ^tfDepartment of Public Works~
BV662: ^tfDepartment of Public Works~
BW662: ^tfDepartment of Public Works~
BX662: ^tfDepartment of Public Works~
BY662: ^tfDepartment of Public Works~
BT663: ^tsTotal Dfl./Nondfl. Exp. Trends/Proj.~
BU663: ^tsSalary Dfl./Nondfl. Exp. Trends/Proj.~
BV663: ^tsTravel Dfl./Nondfl. Exp. Trends/Proj.~
BW663: ^tsTel. Dfl./Nondfl. Exp. Trends/Proj.~
BX663: ^tsPostage Dfl./Nondfl. Exp. Trends/Proj.~
BY663: ^tsCp. Otl. Dfl./Nondfl. Exp. Trends/Proj.~
BT664: ^tx1981-88 TIME SERIES~
BU664: ^tx1981-88 TIME SERIES~
BV664: ^tx1981-88 TIME SERIES~
BW664: ^tx1981-88 TIME SERIES~
BX664: ^tx1981-88 TIME SERIES~
BY664: ^tx1981-88 TIME SERIES~
BT665: 'q
BU665: 'q
BV665: 'q
BW665: 'q
BY665: 'q
BT666: 'v
BU666: 'v
BV666: 'v
BW666: 'v
BX666: 'v
BY666: 'v
BT667: 'q
BU667: 'q
BV667: 'q
BW667: 'q
BX667: 'q
BY667: 'q
BT668: ^{INDICATE}{BRANCH \m}
BU668: ^{INDICATE}{BRANCH \m}
BV668: ^{INDICATE}{BRANCH \m}
BW668: ^{INDICATE}{BRANCH \m}
BX668: ^{INDICATE}{BRANCH \m}
BY668: ^{INDICATE}{BRANCH \m}
```

Figure 18.15 displays the graph that will be drawn when the 2SALL option is selected from Schedule T #5 line graphics submenu.

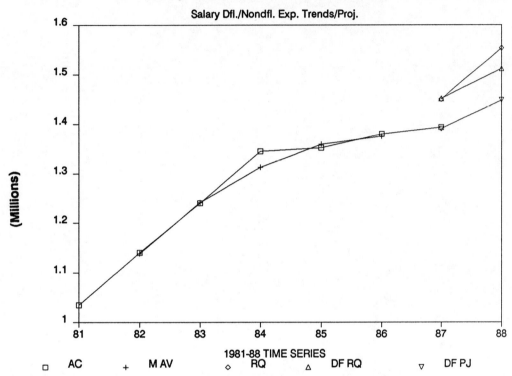

Department of Public Works

Figure 18.15   *Sample #4 Line Graph of Schedule T: Salary Deflated/Nondeflated Expenditure Trends/Projection*

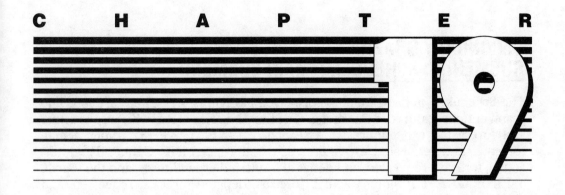

C H A P T E R

19

SCHEDULE F GRAPHICS

SECONDARY GRAPHICS SUBMENUS: SCHEDULE F MAIN SUBMENU

The Schedule F main submenu is displayed in Figure 19.1. There are four line graph options featured in this menu. The first, 1_LINE_GRAPHF, graphs actual and forecasted expenditures; the second, 2_LINE_GRAPHF, graphs actual, forecast, and requested expenditures; the third, 3_LINE_GRAPHF, graphs actual, forecast, requested, and deflated requested expenditures; and the fourth, 4_LINE_GRAPHF, graphs actual, forecast, deflated forecast, requested, and deflated requested expenditures.

```
AY302: [W45] 'SCHEDULE F: BUDGET FORECAST (EXPONENTIAL SMOOTHING) MODEL (# MENU
1_LINE_GRAPHF  2_LINE_GRAPHF  3_LINE_GRAPHF  4_LINE_GRAPHF
DO LINE GRAPHS OF SCHEDULE F ACTUAL/FORECAST
                          AY                      AZ
302 SCHEDULE F: BUDGET FORECAST (EXPONENTIAL SMOOTHING) MODEL (#000)
303 UNIT: DEPARTMENT OF PUBLIC WORKS
304 ========================================================================
305
306                                Weight=           1.6
307
308                                              1981-82
309   Man Years Actual                             85.0
310   Man Years Forecast                           85.0
311   Man Years Error Factor                        0.0
312   Salaries Actual                            1034.6
313   Salaries Forecast                          1034.6
314   Salaries Error Factor                         0.0
315   Travel Actual                               58.4
316   Travel Forecast                             58.4
317   Travel Error Factor                           0.0
318   Telephone Tolls and Rental Actual            12.6
319   Telephone Tolls and Rental Forecast          12.6
320   Telephone Tolls and Rental Error Factor       0.0
321   Postage Actual                              55.1
```

Figure 19.1   Schedule F Main Graphics Submenu

Move the cursor to cell BS671 and give the range BS671..BS671 the name FGRAPH. This links the Schedule F graphics submenu with the MENUCALL command in cell BV270 of the main graphics menu. Make the following entries to construct the Schedule F main graphics menu:

Cell   **Macro Entry**

```
BR671:  'FGRAPH=
BS671:  ^1_LINE_GRAPHF
BT671:  ^2_LINE_GRAPHF
BU671:  ^3_LINE_GRAPHF
BV671:  ^4_LINE_GRAPHF
BS672:  ^DO LINE GRAPHS OF SCHEDULE F ACTUAL/FORECAST
BT672:  ^DO LINE GRAPHS OF SCHEDULE F ACTUAL/FORECAST/REQ.
BU672:  ^DO LINE GRAPHS OF SCHEDULE F ACTUAL/FORECAST/REQ./DEFL REQ.
BV672:  ^DO LINE GRAPHS OF SCHEDULE F ACTUAL/FORECAST/DFL FORECAST
        /REQ/DFL REQ
BS673:  ^{MENUCALL FLINE1}
BT673:  ^{MENUCALL FLINE2}
BU673:  ^{MENUCALL FLINE3}
BV673:  ^{MENUCALL FLINE4}
```

The four sections that immediately follow provide step-by-step instructions for creating the four Schedule F line graphics submenus. Proceed now to the first of the sections to create the Schedule F #1 line graphics submenu.

SECONDARY GRAPHICS SUBMENUS: SCHEDULE F #1 LINE CHART

Before creating the Schedule F #1 line chart submenu (see Figure 19.2), move the cursor to cell BT676 and give the range BT676..BT676 the name FLINE1. This links the submenu to the Schedule F main graphics menu. Next, make the entries that follow Figure 19.2 to construct the Schedule F #1 line graphics menu.

```
AY302: [W45] 'SCHEDULE F: BUDGET FORECAST [EXPONENTIAL SMOOTHING] MODEL [$ MENU
1TOTL  2MAN_YRSL  3SALL  4TRAVL  5TELL  6POSTL  7CAPL_OUTLL
TOTAL EXPENDITURES FORECAST
                         AY                          AZ
302 SCHEDULE F:  BUDGET FORECAST [EXPONENTIAL SMOOTHING] MODEL [$000)
303 UNIT:  DEPARTMENT OF PUBLIC WORKS
304 ======================================================
305
306                              Weight=              1.8
307
308                                           1981-82
309  Man Years Actual                           85.0
310  Man Years Forecast                         85.0
311  Man Years Error Factor                      0.0
312  Salaries Actual                          1034.6
313  Salaries Forecast                        1034.6
314  Salaries Error Factor                       0.0
315  Travel Actual                              58.4
316  Travel Forecast                            58.4
317  Travel Error Factor                         0.0
318  Telephone Tolls and Rental Actual          12.6
319  Telephone Tolls and Rental Forecast        12.6
320  Telephone Tolls and Rental Error Factor     0.0
321  Postage Actual                             55.1
```

Figure 19.2   *Schedule F #1 Submenu Options for Graphing Individual Objects of Expenditure*

Cell   Macro Entry

BS676: 'FLINE1=

BT676: ^1TOTL

BU676: ^2MAN_YRSL

BV676: ^3SALL

BW676: ^4TRAVL

BX676: ^5TELL

BY676: ^6POSTL

BZ676: ^7CAPL_OUTLL

BT677: ^TOTAL EXPENDITURES FORECAST

BU677: ^MAN YEARS FORECAST

BV677: ^SALARY EXPENDITURES FORECAST

BW677: ^TRAVEL EXPENDITURES FORECAST

BX677: ^TELEPHONE EXPENDITURES FORECAST

BY677: ^POSTAGE EXPENDITURES FORECAST

BZ677: ^CAPITAL OUTLAY EXPENDITURES FORECAST

BT678: '{INDICATE WAIT}{CALC}{PANELOFF}{WINDOWSOFF}

BU678: '{INDICATE WAIT}{CALC}{PANELOFF}{WINDOWSOFF}

continued...

...from previous page

```
BV678:  '{INDICATE WAIT}{CALC}{PANELOFF}{WINDOWSOFF}
BW678:  '{INDICATE WAIT}{CALC}{PANELOFF}{WINDOWSOFF}
BX678:  ^{INDICATE WAIT}{CALC}{PANELOFF}{WINDOWSOFF}
BY678:  '{INDICATE WAIT}{CALC}{PANELOFF}{WINDOWSOFF}
BZ678:  '{INDICATE WAIT}{CALC}{PANELOFF}{WINDOWSOFF}
BT679:  '/grg
BU679:  '/grg
BV679:  '/grg
BW679:  '/grg
BX679:  '/grg
BY679:  '/grg
BZ679:  '/grg
BT680:  'tl
BU680:  'tl
BV680:  'tl
BW680:  'tl
BX680:  'tl
BY680:  'tl
BZ680:  'tl
BT681:  ^aAZ327.BF327~
BU681:  ^aAZ309.BF309~
BV681:  ^aAZ312.BF312~
BW681:  ^aAZ315.BF315~
BX681:  ^aAZ318.BF318~
BY681:  ^aAZ321.BF321~
BZ681:  ^aAZ324.BF324~
BT682:  'bAZ328.BG328~
BU682:  'bAZ310.BG310~
BV682:  'bAZ313.BG313~
BW682:  'bAZ316.BG316~
BX682:  'bAZ319.BG319~
BY682:  'bAZ322.BG322~
BZ682:  'bAZ325.BG325~
BS683:  ^
BT683:  ^xAZ5.BH5~
BU683:  ^xAZ5.BH5~
BV683:  ^xAZ5.BH5~
BW683:  ^xAZ5.BH5~
BX683:  ^xAZ5.BH5~
```

continued...

...from previous page

```
BY683: ^xAZ5.BH5~
BZ683: ^xAZ5.BH5~
BT684: 'o
BU684: 'o
BV684: 'o
BW684: 'o
BX684: 'o
BY684: 'o
BZ684: 'o
BT685: ^syinqty(Millions)~
BU685: ^syinqty(Millions)~
BV685: ^syinqty(Millions)~
BW685: ^syinqty(Millions)~
BX685: ^syinqty(Millions)~
BY685: ^syinqty(Millions)~
BZ685: ^syinqty(Millions)~
BT686: 'cfabbb
BU686: 'cfabbb
BV686: 'cfabbb
BW686: 'cfabbb
BX686: 'cfabbb
BY686: 'cfabbb
BZ686: 'cfabbb
BT687: ^q
BU687: ^q
BV687: ^q
BW687: ^q
BX687: ^q
BY687: ^q
BZ687: ^q
BT688: ^laACTUAL~
BU688: ^laACTUAL~
BV688: ^laACTUAL~
BW688: ^laACTUAL~
BX688: ^laACTUAL~
BY688: ^laACTUAL~
BZ688: ^laACTUAL~
BT689: ^lbEXPON. SMOOTHING~
BU689: ^lbEXPON. SMOOTHING~
```

continued...

...from previous page

```
BV689:  ^lbEXPON. SMOOTHING~
BW689:  ^lbEXPON. SMOOTHING~
BX689:  ^lbEXPON. SMOOTHING~
BY689:  ^lbEXPON. SMOOTHING~
BZ689:  ^lbEXPON. SMOOTHING~
BT690:  ^tfDepartment of Public Works~
BU690:  ^tfDepartment of Public Works~
BV690:  ^tfDepartment of Public Works~
BW690:  ^tfDepartment of Public Works~
BX690:  ^tfDepartment of Public Works~
BY690:  ^tfDepartment of Public Works~
BZ690:  ^tfDepartment of Public Works~
BT691:  ^tsActual Total Exp./Forecast~
BU691:  ^tsActual Man Years/Forecast~
BV691:  ^tsActual Salary Exp./Forecast~
BW691:  ^tsActual Travel Exp./Forecast~
BX691:  ^tsActual Telephone Exp./Forecast~
BY691:  ^tsActual Postage Exp./Forecast~
BZ691:  ^tsActual Capital Outlay Exp./Forecast~
BT692:  ^tx1981-88 FORECAST~
BU692:  ^tx1981-88 FORECAST~
BV692:  ^tx1981-88 FORECAST~
BW692:  ^tx1981-88 FORECAST~
BX692:  ^tx1981-88 FORECAST~
BY692:  ^tx1981-88 FORECAST~
BZ692:  ^tx1981-88 FORECAST~
BT693:  'q
BU693:  'q
BV693:  'q
BW693:  'q
BX693:  'q
BY693:  'q
BZ693:  'q
BT694:  'v
BU694:  'v
BV694:  'v
BW694:  'v
BX694:  'v
BY694:  'v
```

continued...

...from previous page

```
BZ694:  'v
BT695:  'q
BU695:  'q
BV695:  'q
BW695:  'q
BX695:  'q
BY695:  'q
BZ695:  'q
BT696:  ^{INDICATE}{BRANCH \m}
BU696:  ^{INDICATE}{BRANCH \m}
BV696:  ^{INDICATE}{BRANCH \m}
BW696:  ^{INDICATE}{BRANCH \m}
BX696:  ^{INDICATE}{BRANCH \m}
BY696:  ^{INDICATE}{BRANCH \m}
BZ696:  ^{INDICATE}{BRANCH \m}
```

The data in rows 681 and 682 of the Schedule F #1 line graphics submenu are actual and forecast data, respectively, and are located in Schedule F: Budget Forecast (Exponential Smoothing) Model. The data in row 683 are hidden, abbreviated dates located in the Schedule T & F Data Table.

The only entries in the submenu that you haven't seen while creating other submenus and that require elaboration at this point are the syinqty (Millions) 1-2-3 macro command entries located in row 685. Reviewing them each in turn, you will see that the s command prompts you to select a scaling option; the y command sets the scaling function on the y-axis; the i command is an indicator option that prompts you either to allow or suppress the scale indicator; the n entry enables the "no scale indicator" option; the q command quits the current submenu and returns the cursor to the graph menu; the t command prompts for the specification of graph title or axis title lines; the y command specifies the y-axis as the axis for which a title will be entered; and the (Millions) entry is the title you specify for the y-axis of the Schedule F #1 line graphics submenu.

As usual, test the submenu before proceeding to the next section. Selecting the 3SALL option from the Schedule F #1 line graphics menu causes the graph displayed in Figure 19.3 to be drawn.

Department of Public Works

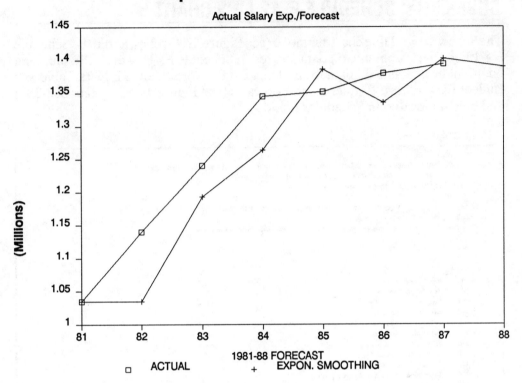

Figure 19.3   *Sample #1 Line Graph of Schedule F: Actual Salary Expenditures/Forecast*

SECONDARY GRAPHICS
SUBMENUS: SCHEDULE F #2 LINE CHART

The Schedule F #2 line chart submenu (see Figure 19.4) relies, as did the Schedule F #1 line chart submenu, on data located in Schedule F. However, the submenu additionally depends on data located in a data table, Schedule F Data Table #2: Budget Expenditure Requests and Forecasts (see Figure 19.5 on pages 382-383) and on data located in Schedules F and A.

```
AY302: [W45] 'SCHEDULE F:  BUDGET FORECAST (EXPONENTIAL SMOOTHING) MODEL (# MENU
1TOTL  2MAN_YRSL  3SALL  4TRAVL  5TELL  6POSTL  7CAPL_OUTLL
TOTAL EXPENDITURES FORECAST/REQUEST
                          AY                        AZ
302 SCHEDULE F:  BUDGET FORECAST (EXPONENTIAL SMOOTHING) MODEL (#000)
303 UNIT:  DEPARTMENT OF PUBLIC WORKS
304 ================================================================
305
306                              Weight=            1.6
307
308                                             1981-82
309  Man Years Actual                             85.0
310  Man Years Forecast                           85.0
311  Man Years Error Factor                        0.0
312  Salaries Actual                            1034.6
313  Salaries Forecast                          1034.6
314  Salaries Error Factor                         0.0
315  Travel Actual                                58.4
316  Travel Forecast                              58.4
317  Travel Error Factor                           0.0
318  Telephone Tolls and Rental Actual            12.6
319  Telephone Tolls and Rental Forecast          12.6
320  Telephone Tolls and Rental Error Factor       0.0
321  Postage Actual                               55.1
```

Figure 19.4   *Schedule F #2 Submenu Options for Graphing Individual Objects of Expenditure*

Before creating the Schedule F #2 line graphics submenu, construct Schedule F Data Table #2 by making the following entries.

Cell Listing: Figure 19.5

```
AY383: [W45] 'SCHEDULE F DATA TABLE 2:  BUDGET EXPENDITURE REQUESTS AND
             FORECASTS ($000)
BN383: '||
AY384: [W45] 'UNIT:  DEPARTMENT OF PUBLIC WORKS
BN384: '||
AY385: [W45] \=
AZ385: [W20] \=
BA385: [W15] \=
BB385: [W13] \=
BC385: [W12] \=
BD385: [W12] \=
BE385: [W12] \=
BF385: [W13] \=
BG385: [W12] \=
BH385: [W12] \=
BI385: [W12] \=
BJ385: [W12] \=
BK385: [W12] \=
BL385: [W12] \=
BM385: [W12] \=
BN385: '||
BN386: '||
BN387: '||
BF388: (T) [W13] ^1987-88
BG388: (T) [W12] ^1988-89
BN388: '||
BF389: [W13] ^ACTUAL
BG389: [W12] ^REQUEST
BN389: '||
AY390: [W45] '   Man Years Actual
BF390: [W13] +BF309
BG390: [W12] +AE9
BN390: '||
AY391: [W45] '   Man Years Forecast
BN391: '||
```

continued on page 384...

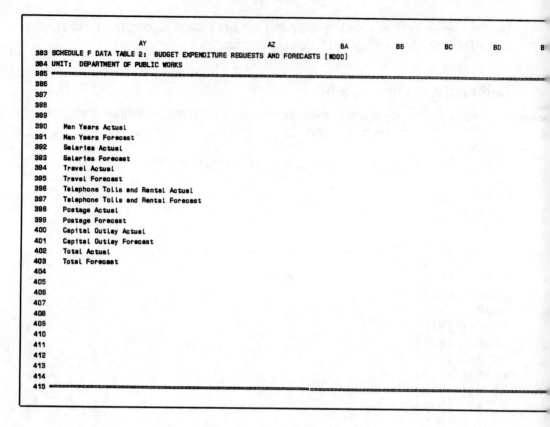

AY   AZ   BA   BB   BC   BD   B

383 SCHEDULE F DATA TABLE 2: BUDGET EXPENDITURE REQUESTS AND FORECASTS (\$000)
384 UNIT: DEPARTMENT OF PUBLIC WORKS
385
386
387
388
389
390 Man Years Actual
391 Man Years Forecast
392 Salaries Actual
393 Salaries Forecast
394 Travel Actual
395 Travel Forecast
396 Telephone Tolls and Rental Actual
397 Telephone Tolls and Rental Forecast
398 Postage Actual
399 Postage Forecast
400 Capital Outlay Actual
401 Capital Outlay Forecast
402 Total Actual
403 Total Forecast
404
405
406
407
408
409
410
411
412
413
414
415

Figure 19.5   *Schedule F Data Table: Budget Expenditure Requests and Forecasts*

BF	BG	BH	BI	BJ	BK	BL	BM		BN	BO	BP	BQ

1987-88 ACTUAL	1988-89 REQUEST
101	104
1393.8	1449.8
64.0	85.0
15.8	15.8
70.0	75.6
34.5	56.5
1868.2	1974.7

...from page 381

```
AY392: [W45] '   Salaries Actual
BF392: (F1) [W13] +BF312
BG392: (F1) [W12] +AE10/1000
BN392: '||
AY393: [W45] '   Salaries Forecast
BN393: '||
AY394: [W45] '   Travel Actual
BF394: (F1) [W13] +BF315
BG394: (F1) [W12] +AE14/1000
BN394: '||
AY395: [W45] '   Travel Forecast
BN395: '||
AY396: [W45] '   Telephone Tolls and Rental Actual
BF396: (F1) [W13] +BF318
BG396: (F1) [W12] +AE15/1000
BN396: '||
AY397: [W45] '   Telephone Tolls and Rental Forecast
BN397: '||
AY398: [W45] '   Postage Actual
BF398: (F1) [W13] +BF321
BG398: (F1) [W12] +AE16/1000
BN398: '||
AY399: [W45] '   Postage Forecast
BN399: '||
AY400: [W45] '   Capital Outlay Actual
BF400: (F1) [W13] +BF324
BG400: (F1) [W12] +AE40/1000
BN400: '||
AY401: [W45] '   Capital Outlay Forecast
BN401: '||
AY402: [W45] '   Total Actual
BF402: (F1) [W13] +BF327
BG402: (F1) [W12] +AE42/1000
BN402: '||
AY403: [W45] '   Total Forecast
BN403: '||
BN404: '||
BN405: '||
BN406: '||
```

continued...

...from previous page

```
BN407:  '||
BN408:  '||
BN409:  '||
BN410:  '||
BN411:  '||
BN412:  '||
BN413:  '||
BN414:  '||
AY415:  [W45] \=
AZ415:  [W20] \=
BA415:  [W15] \=
BB415:  [W13] \=
BC415:  [W12] \=
BD415:  [W12] \=
BE415:  [W12] \=
BF415:  [W13] \=
BG415:  [W12] \=
BH415:  [W12] \=
BI415:  [W12] \=
BJ415:  [W12] \=
BK415:  [W12] \=
BL415:  [W12] \=
BM415:  [W12] \=
BN415:  '||
```

The Schedule F #2 line chart submenu entries are similar to those of the previously constructed Schedule F #1 submenu. Move the cursor to cell BT699, and give the range BT699..BT699 the name FLINE2. To construct the submenu, make the following entries:

Cell   Macro Entry

```
BS699:  'FLINE2=
BT699:  ^1TOTL
BU699:  ^2MAN_YRSL
BV699:  ^3SALL
BW699:  ^4TRAVL
BX699:  ^5TELL
BY699:  ^6POSTL
BZ699:  ^7CAPL_OUTLL
BT700:  ^TOTAL EXPENDITURES FORECAST/REQUEST
```

continued...

...from previous page

```
BU700:  ^MAN YEARS FORECAST/REQUEST
BV700:  ^SALARY EXPENDITURES FORECAST/REQUEST
BW700:  ^TRAVEL EXPENDITURES FORECAST/REQUEST
BX700:  ^TELEPHONE EXPENDITURES FORECAST/REQUEST
BY700:  ^POSTAGE EXPENDITURES FORECAST/REQUEST
BZ700:  ^CAPITAL OUTLAY EXPENDITURES FORECAST/REQUEST
BT701:  '{INDICATE WAIT}{CALC}{PANELOFF}{WINDOWSOFF}
BU701:  '{INDICATE WAIT}{CALC}{PANELOFF}{WINDOWSOFF}
BV701:  '{INDICATE WAIT}{CALC}{PANELOFF}{WINDOWSOFF}
BW701:  '{INDICATE WAIT}{CALC}{PANELOFF}{WINDOWSOFF}
BX701:  ^{INDICATE WAIT}{CALC}{PANELOFF}{WINDOWSOFF}
BY701:  '{INDICATE WAIT}{CALC}{PANELOFF}{WINDOWSOFF}
BZ701:  '{INDICATE WAIT}{CALC}{PANELOFF}{WINDOWSOFF}
BT702:  '/grg
BU702:  '/grg
BV702:  '/grg
BW702:  '/grg
BX702:  '/grg
BY702:  '/grg
BZ702:  '/grg
BT703:  'tl
BU703:  'tl
BV703:  'tl
BW703:  'tl
BX703:  'tl
BY703:  'tl
BZ703:  'tl
BT704:  ^aAZ327.BF327~
BU704:  ^aAZ309.BF309~
BV704:  ^aAZ312.BF312~
BW704:  ^aAZ315.BF315~
BX704:  ^aAZ318.BF318~
BY704:  ^aAZ321.BF321~
BZ704:  ^aAZ324.BF324~
BT705:  'bAZ328.BG328~
BU705:  'bAZ310.BG310~
BV705:  'bAZ313.BG313~
BW705:  'bAZ316.BG316~
BX705:  'bAZ319.BG319~
BY705:  'bAZ322.BG322~
BZ705:  'bAZ325.BG325~
```

continued...

...from previous page

```
BT706:  ^caz402.bg402~
BU706:  ^cAZ390.BG390~
BV706:  ^cAZ392.BG392~
BW706:  ^cAZ394.BG394~
BX706:  ^cAZ396.BG396~
BY706:  ^cAZ398.BG398~
BZ706:  ^cAZ400.BG400~
BT707:  ^xAZ5.BH5~
BU707:  ^xAZ5.BH5~
BV707:  ^xAZ5.BH5~
BW707:  ^xAZ5.BH5~
BX707:  ^xAZ5.BH5~
BY707:  ^xAZ5.BH5~
BZ707:  ^xAZ5.BH5~
BT708:  'o
BU708:  'o
BV708:  'o
BW708:  'o
BX708:  'o
BY708:  'o
BZ708:  'o
BT709:  ^syinqty(Millions)~
BU709:  ^syinqty(Millions)~
BV709:  ^syinqty(Millions)~
BW709:  ^syinqty(Millions)~
BX709:  ^syinqty(Millions)~
BY709:  ^syinqty(Millions)~
BZ709:  ^syinqty(Millions)~
BT710:  'cfabbb
BU710:  'cfabbb
BV710:  'cfabbb
BW710:  'cfabbb
BX710:  'cfabbb
BY710:  'cfabbb
BZ710:  'cfabbb
BT711:  ^q
BU711:  ^q
BV711:  ^q
BW711:  ^q
```

continued...

...from previous page

```
BX711: ^q
BY711: ^q
BZ711: ^q
BT712: ^laACTUAL~
BU712: ^laACTUAL~
BV712: ^laACTUAL~
BW712: ^laACTUAL~
BX712: ^laACTUAL~
BY712: ^laACTUAL~
BZ712: ^laACTUAL~
BT713: ^lbEXPON. SMOOTHING~
BU713: ^lbEXPON. SMOOTHING~
BV713: ^lbEXPON. SMOOTHING~
BW713: ^lbEXPON. SMOOTHING~
BX713: ^lbEXPON. SMOOTHING~
BY713: ^lbEXPON. SMOOTHING~
BZ713: ^lbEXPON. SMOOTHING~
BT714: ^lcREQUEST~
BU714: ^lcREQUEST~
BV714: ^lcREQUEST~
BW714: ^lcREQUEST~
BX714: ^lcREQUEST~
BY714: ^lcREQUEST~
BZ714: ^lcREQUEST~
BT715: ^tfDepartment of Public Works~
BU715: ^tfDepartment of Public Works~
BV715: ^tfDepartment of Public Works~
BW715: ^tfDepartment of Public Works~
BX715: ^tfDepartment of Public Works~
BY715: ^tfDepartment of Public Works~
BZ715: ^tfDepartment of Public Works~
BT716: ^tsActual Total Exp./Forecast/Req.~
BU716: ^tsActual Man Years/Forecast/Req.~
BV716: ^tsActual Salary Exp./Forecast/Req.~
BW716: ^tsActual Travel Exp./Forecast/Req.~
BX716: ^tsActual Telephone Exp./Forecast/Req.~
BY716: ^tsActual Postage Exp./Forecast/Req.~
BZ716: ^tsActual Capital Outlay Exp./Forecast/Req.~
BT717: ^tx1981-88 FORECAST~
```

continued...

...from previous page

```
BU717:  ^tx1981-88 FORECAST~
BV717:  ^tx1981-88 FORECAST~
BW717:  ^tx1981-88 FORECAST~
BX717:  ^tx1981-88 FORECAST~
BY717:  ^tx1981-88 FORECAST~
BZ717:  ^tx1981-88 FORECAST~
BT718:  'q
BU718:  'q
BV718:  'q
BW718:  'q
BX718:  'q
BY718:  'q
BZ718:  'q
BT719:  'v
BU719:  'v
BV719:  'v
BW719:  'v
BX719:  'v
BY719:  'v
BZ719:  'v
BT720:  'q
BU720:  'q
BV720:  'q
BW720:  'q
BX720:  'q
BY720:  'q
BZ720:  'q
BT721:  ^{INDICATE}{BRANCH \m}
BU721:  ^{INDICATE}{BRANCH \m}
BV721:  ^{INDICATE}{BRANCH \m}
BW721:  ^{INDICATE}{BRANCH \m}
BX721:  ^{INDICATE}{BRANCH \m}
BY721:  ^{INDICATE}{BRANCH \m}
BZ721:  ^{INDICATE}{BRANCH \m}
```

Like the Schedule F #1 line graphics submenu entries, the submenu entries in rows 704 and 705 rely on Schedule F for data. The entries in row 706, however, are dependent on data located in Schedule F Data Table #2. Note that the data located in the table are dependent on Schedules F and A.

Figure 19.6 displays the graph that is drawn when you select the 3SALL option from the Schedule F #2 line graphics submenu.

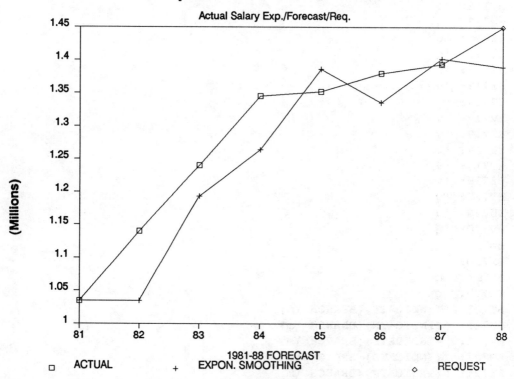

Figure 19.6   *Sample #2 Line Graph of Schedule F: Actual Salary Expenditures/Forecast/Request*

SECONDARY GRAPHICS
SUBMENUS: SCHEDULE F #3 LINE CHART

The Schedule F #3 line chart submenu (see Figure 19.7) depends on still another
data table for its data, Schedule F Data Table 3: Deflated Budget Expenditure
Requests and Deflated Forecasts. The data table (see Figure 19.8), in turn,
depends on Schedule F for its data. Create the table now by making the entries
following Figure 19.8.

```
AY302: [W45] 'SCHEDULE F:  BUDGET FORECAST [EXPONENTIAL SMOOTHING] MODEL [$ MENU
1TOTL  3SALL  4TRAVL  5TELL  6POSTL  7CAPL_OUTLL
TOTAL EXPENDITURES FORECAST/REQUEST/DFL. REQUEST
                          AY                        AZ
302 SCHEDULE F:  BUDGET FORECAST [EXPONENTIAL SMOOTHING] MODEL [$000)
303 UNIT:  DEPARTMENT OF PUBLIC WORKS
304 ===========================================================
305
306                             Weight=            1.6
307
308                                             1981-82
309   Man Years Actual                            85.0
310   Man Years Forecast                          85.0
311   Man Years Error Factor                       0.0
312   Salaries Actual                           1034.6
313   Salaries Forecast                         1034.6
314   Salaries Error Factor                        0.0
315   Travel Actual                               58.4
316   Travel Forecast                             58.4
317   Travel Error Factor                          0.0
318   Telephone Tolls and Rental Actual           12.6
319   Telephone Tolls and Rental Forecast         12.6
320   Telephone Tolls and Rental Error Factor      0.0
321   Postage Actual                              55.1
```

Figure 19.7   *Schedule F #3 Submenu Options for Graphing Individual Objects of
Expenditure*

	AY	AZ	BA	BB	BC	BD	BE
416 SCHEDULE F DATA TABLE 3: DEFLATED BUDGET EXPENDITURE REQUESTS AND DEFLATED FORECASTS [$000]							
417 UNIT: DEPARTMENT OF PUBLIC WORKS							
418							
419	Deflator Factor:	4.20%					
420							
421							
422							
423							
424							
425 Salaries Actual							
426 Salaries Forecast		991	991	1,150	1,210	1,333	1,
427 Travel Actual							
428 Travel Forecast		56	56	59	62	66	
429 Telephone Tolls and Rental Actual							
430 Telephone Tolls and Rental Forecast		12	12	13	14	13	
431 Postage Actual							
432 Postage Forecast		53	53	50	48	53	
433 Capital Outlay Actual							
434 Capital Outlay Forecast		6	6	6	6	7	
435 Total Actual							
436 Total Forecast		1,214	1,214	1,375	1,441	1,575	1,
437							
438							
439							
440							
441							
442							
443							
444							
445							
446							
447							
448							

Figure 19.8   Schedule F Data Table 3: Deflatable Budget

BF	BG	BH	BI	BJ	BK	BL	BM	BN	BO	BP	BQ
1987-88	1988-89										
ACTUAL	REQUEST										
1,335	1388.9										
1,349	1,327										
61.3	62.2										
67	58										
15.1	15.1										
14											
67.1	72.4										
88	87										
33.1	54.1										
16	54										
1789.7	1891.8										
1,733	1,822										

Cell Listing: Figure 19.8

```
AY416: [W45] 'SCHEDULE F DATA TABLE 3:  DEFLATED BUDGET EXPENDITURE
              REQUESTS AND DEFLATED FORECASTS ($000)
BN416: '||
AY417: [W45] 'UNIT:  DEPARTMENT OF PUBLIC WORKS
BN417: '||
AY418: [W45] \=
AZ418: [W20] \=
BA418: [W15] \=
BB418: [W13] \=
BC418: [W12] \=
BD418: [W12] \=
BE418: [W12] \=
BF418: [W13] \=
BG418: [W12] \=
BH418: [W12] \=
BI418: [W12] \=
BJ418: [W12] \=
BK418: [W12] \=
BL418: [W12] \=
BM418: [W12] \=
BN418: '||
AY419: [W45] "Deflator Factor:
AZ419: (P2) [W20] +BZ12*0.01
BN419: '||
BN420: '||
BF421: (T) [W13] ^1987-88
BG421: (T) [W12] ^1988-89
BN421: '||
BF422: [W13] ^ACTUAL
BG422: [W12] ^REQUEST
BN422: '||
BN423: '||
BN424: '||
AY425: [W45] '   Salaries Actual
BF425: [W13] +BF312*$BZ$13
BG425: (F1) [W12] +AE10/1000*($BZ$13)
BN425: '||
AY426: [W45] '   Salaries Forecast
AZ426: [W20] +AZ313*$BZ$13
```

continued...

...from previous page

```
BA426: [W15] +BA313*$BZ$13
BB426: [W13] +BB313*$BZ$13
BC426: [W12] +BC313*$BZ$13
BD426: [W12] +BD313*$BZ$13
BE426: [W12] +BE313*$BZ$13
BF426: [W13] +BF313*$BZ$13
BG426: [W12] +BG313*$BZ$13
BN426: '||
AY427: [W45] '   Travel Actual
BF427: (F1) [W13] +BF315*$BZ$13
BG427: (F1) [W12] +AE14/1000*($BZ$13)
BN427: '||
AY428: [W45] '   Travel Forecast
AZ428: [W20] +AZ316*$BZ$13
BA428: [W15] +BA316*$BZ$13
BB428: [W13] +BB316*$BZ$13
BC428: [W12] +BC316*$BZ$13
BD428: [W12] +BD316*$BZ$13
BE428: [W12] +BE316*$BZ$13
BF428: [W13] +BF316*$BZ$13
BG428: [W12] +BG316*$BZ$13
BN428: '||
AY429: [W45] '   Telephone Tolls and Rental Actual
BF429: (F1) [W13] +BF318*$BZ$13
BG429: (F1) [W12] +AE15/1000*($BZ$13)
BN429: '||
AY430: [W45] '   Telephone Tolls and Rental Forecast
AZ430: [W20] +AZ319*$BZ$13
BA430: [W15] +BA319*$BZ$13
BB430: [W13] +BB319*$BZ$13
BC430: [W12] +BC319*$BZ$13
BD430: [W12] +BD319*$BZ$13
BE430: [W12] +BE319*$BZ$13
BF430: [W13] +BF319*$BZ$13
BN430: '||
AY431: [W45] '   Postage Actual
BF431: (F1) [W13] +BF321*$BZ$13
BG431: (F1) [W12] +AE16/1000*($BZ$13)
BN431: '||
```

continued...

...from previous page

```
AY432: [W45]  '    Postage Forecast
AZ432: [W20]  +AZ322*$BZ$13
BA432: [W15]  +BA322*$BZ$13
BB432: [W13]  +BB322*$BZ$13
BC432: [W12]  +BC322*$BZ$13
BD432: [W12]  +BD322*$BZ$13
BE432: [W12]  +BE322*$BZ$13
BF432: [W13]  +BF322*$BZ$13
BG432: [W12]  +BG322*$BZ$13
BN432: '||
AY433: [W45]  '    Capital Outlay Actual
BF433: (F1) [W13]  +BF324*$BZ$13
BG433: (F1) [W12]  +AE40/1000*($BZ$13)
BN433: '||
AY434: [W45]  '    Capital Outlay Forecast
AZ434: [W20]  +AZ325*$BZ$13
BA434: [W15]  +BA325*$BZ$13
BB434: [W13]  +BB325*$BZ$13
BC434: [W12]  +BC325*$BZ$13
BD434: [W12]  +BD325*$BZ$13
BE434: [W12]  +BE325*$BZ$13
BF434: [W13]  +BF325*$BZ$13
BG434: [W12]  +BG325*$BZ$13
BN434: '||
AY435: [W45]  '    Total Actual
BF435: (F1) [W13]  +BF327*$BZ$13
BG435: (F1) [W12]  +AE42/1000*($BZ$13)
BN435: '||
AY436: [W45]  '    Total Forecast
AZ436: [W20]  +AZ328*$BZ$13
BA436: [W15]  +BA328*$BZ$13
BB436: [W13]  +BB328*$BZ$13
BC436: [W12]  +BC328*$BZ$13
BD436: [W12]  +BD328*$BZ$13
BE436: [W12]  +BE328*$BZ$13
BF436: [W13]  +BF328*$BZ$13
BG436: [W12]  +BG328*$BZ$13
BN436: '||
BN437: '||
```

continued...

...from previous page

```
BN438:  '||
BN439:  '||
BN440:  '||
BN441:  '||
BN442:  '||
BN443:  '||
BN444:  '||
BN445:  '||
BN446:  '||
BN447:  '||
AY448:  [W45]  \=
AZ448:  [W20]  \=
BA448:  [W15]  \=
BB448:  [W13]  \=
BC448:  [W12]  \=
BD448:  [W12]  \=
BE448:  [W12]  \=
BF448:  [W13]  \=
BG448:  [W12]  \=
BH448:  [W12]  \=
BI448:  [W12]  \=
BJ448:  [W12]  \=
BK448:  [W12]  \=
BL448:  [W12]  \=
BM448:  [W12]  \=
BN448:  '||
```

Move the cursor to cell BT724 and give the range BT724..BT724 the name FLINE3 to link the Schedule F #3 line graphics submenu to the main Schedule F graphics menu. Then, make the following entries to construct the Schedule F #3 line chart submenu:

Cell	**Macro Entry**
BS724:	'FLINE3=
BT724:	^1TOTL
BU724:	^3SALL

continued...

...from previous page

```
BV724:  ^4TRAVL
BW724:  ^5TELL
BX724:  ^6POSTL
BY724:  ^7CAPL_OUTLL
BT725:  ^TOTAL EXPENDITURES FORECAST/REQUEST/DFL. REQUEST
BU725:  ^SALARY EXPENDITURES FORECAST/REQUEST/DFL. REQUEST
BV725:  ^TRAVEL EXPENDITURES FORECAST/REQUEST/DFL. REQUEST
BW725:  ^TELEPHONE EXPENDITURES FORECAST/REQUEST/DFL. REQUEST
BX725:  ^POSTAGE EXPENDITURES FORECAST/REQUEST/DFL. REQUEST
BY725:  ^CAPITAL OUTLAY EXPENDITURES FORECAST/REQUEST/DFL. REQUEST
BT726:  '{INDICATE WAIT}{CALC}{PANELOFF}{WINDOWSOFF}
BU726:  '{INDICATE WAIT}{CALC}{PANELOFF}{WINDOWSOFF}
BV726:  '{INDICATE WAIT}{CALC}{PANELOFF}{WINDOWSOFF}
BW726:  ^{INDICATE WAIT}{CALC}{PANELOFF}{WINDOWSOFF}
BX726:  '{INDICATE WAIT}{CALC}{PANELOFF}{WINDOWSOFF}
BY726:  '{INDICATE WAIT}{CALC}{PANELOFF}{WINDOWSOFF}
BT727:  '/grg
BU727:  '/grg
BV727:  '/grg
BW727:  '/grg
BX727:  '/grg
BY727:  '/grg
BT728:  'tl
BU728:  'tl
BV728:  'tl
BW728:  'tl
BX728:  'tl
BY728:  'tl
BT729:  ^aAZ327.BF327~
BU729:  ^aAZ312.BF312~
BV729:  ^aAZ315.BF315~
BW729:  ^aAZ318.BF318~
BX729:  ^aAZ321.BF321~
BY729:  ^aAZ324.BF324~
BT730:  'bAZ328.BG328~
BU730:  'bAZ313.BG313~
BV730:  'bAZ316.BG316~
BW730:  'bAZ319.BG319~
BX730:  'bAZ322.BG322~
```

continued...

...from previous page

```
BY730:  'bAZ325.BG325~
BT731:  ^cAZ402.BG402~
BU731:  ^cAZ392.BG392~
BV731:  ^cAZ394.BG394~
BW731:  ^cAZ396.BG396~
BX731:  ^cAZ398.BG398~
BY731:  ^cAZ400.BG400~
BT732:  ^dAZ435.BG435~
BU732:  ^dAZ425.BG425~
BV732:  ^dAZ427.BG427~
BW732:  ^dAZ429.BG429~
BX732:  ^dAZ431.BG431~
BY732:  ^dAZ433.BG433~
BT733:  ^xAZ5.BH5~
BU733:  ^xAZ5.BH5~
BV733:  ^xAZ5.BH5~
BW733:  ^xAZ5.BH5~
BX733:  ^xAZ5.BH5~
BY733:  ^xAZ5.BH5~
BT734:  'o
BU734:  'o
BV734:  'o
BW734:  'o
BX734:  'o
BY734:  'o
BT735:  ^syinqty(Millions)~
BU735:  ^syinqty(Millions)~
BV735:  ^syinqty(Millions)~
BW735:  ^syinqty(Millions)~
BX735:  ^syinqty(Millions)~
BY735:  ^syinqty(Millions)~
BT736:  'cfabbb
BU736:  'cfabbb
BV736:  'cfabbb
BW736:  'cfabbb
BX736:  'cfabbb
BY736:  'cfabbb
BT737:  ^q
BU737:  ^q
```

continued...

...from previous page

```
BV737:  ^q
BW737:  ^q
BX737:  ^q
BY737:  ^q
BT738:  ^laACTUAL~
BU738:  ^laACTUAL~
BV738:  ^laACTUAL~
BW738:  ^laACTUAL~
BX738:  ^laACTUAL~
BY738:  ^laACTUAL~
BT739:  ^lbEX SMTH~
BU739:  ^lbEX SMTH~
BV739:  ^lbEX SMTH~
BW739:  ^lbEX SMTH~
BX739:  ^lbEX SMTH~
BY739:  ^lbEX SMTH~
BT740:  ^lcREQUEST~
BU740:  ^lcREQUEST~
BV740:  ^lcREQUEST~
BW740:  ^lcREQUEST~
BX740:  ^lcREQUEST~
BY740:  ^lcREQUEST~
BT741:  ^ldDF RQ~
BU741:  ^ldDF RQ~
BV741:  ^ldDF RQ~
BW741:  ^ldDF RQ~
BX741:  ^ldDF RQ~
BY741:  ^ldDF RQ~
BT742:  ^tfDepartment of Public Works~
BU742:  ^tfDepartment of Public Works~
BV742:  ^tfDepartment of Public Works~
BW742:  ^tfDepartment of Public Works~
BX742:  ^tfDepartment of Public Works~
BY742:  ^tfDepartment of Public Works~
BT743:  ^tsAc. Tot. Exp./Forecast/Req./Df. Req.~
BU743:  ^tsAc. Salary Exp./Forecast/Req./Df. Req.~
BV743:  ^tsAc. Travel Exp./Forecast/Req./Df. Req.~
BW743:  ^tsAc. Tel. Exp./Forecast/Req./Df. Req.~
BX743:  ^tsAc. Postage Exp./Forecast/Req./Df. Req.~
```

continued...

...from previous page

```
BY743:  ^tsAc. Cp. Otl. Exp./Forecast/Req./Df. Req.~
BT744:  ^tx1981-88 FORECAST~
BU744:  ^tx1981-88 FORECAST~
BV744:  ^tx1981-88 FORECAST~
BW744:  ^tx1981-88 FORECAST~
BX744:  ^tx1981-88 FORECAST~
BY744:  ^tx1981-88 FORECAST~
BT745:  'q
BU745:  'q
BV745:  'q
BW745:  'q
BX745:  'q
BY745:  'q
BT746:  'v
BU746:  'v
BV746:  'v
BW746:  'v
BX746:  'v
BY746:  'v
BT747:  'q
BU747:  'q
BV747:  'q
BW747:  'q
BX747:  'q
BY747:  'q
BT748:  ^{INDICATE}{BRANCH \m}
BU748:  ^{INDICATE}{BRANCH \m}
BV748:  ^{INDICATE}{BRANCH \m}
BW748:  ^{INDICATE}{BRANCH \m}
BX748:  ^{INDICATE}{BRANCH \m}
BY748:  ^{INDICATE}{BRANCH \m}
```

This completes the construction of the Schedule F #3 line chart submenu. Figure 19.9 displays the graph that is drawn when the 3SALL option is selected from the submenu.

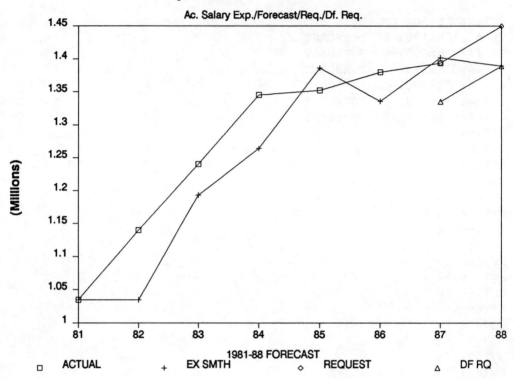

Department of Public Works

Ac. Salary Exp./Forecast/Req./Df. Req.

1981-88 FORECAST

□   ACTUAL   +   EX SMTH   ◇   REQUEST   △   DF RQ

Figure 19.9   *Sample #3 Line Graph of Schedule F: Actual Salary*
Expenditures/Forecast/Request/Deflated Request

SECONDARY GRAPHICS SUBMENUS: SCHEDULE F #4 LINE CHART

As your first step in creating the Schedule F #4 line graphics submenu (see Figure 19.10), move the cursor to BT751 and give the range BT751..BT751 the name FLINE4. Then, make the cell entries following Figure 19.10 to construct the submenu.

```
AY302: [W45] 'SCHEDULE F:  BUDGET FORECAST (EXPONENTIAL SMOOTHING) MODEL (# MENU
1TOTL  3SALL  4TRAVL  5TELL  6POSTL  7CAPL_OUTLL
TOTAL EXPENDITURES FORECAST/DFL. FORECAST/REQUEST/DFL. REQUEST
                        AY                       AZ
302 SCHEDULE F:  BUDGET FORECAST (EXPONENTIAL SMOOTHING) MODEL ($000)
303 UNIT:  DEPARTMENT OF PUBLIC WORKS
304 ============================================================
305
306                          Weight=            1.8
307
308                                          1981-82
309  Man Years Actual                          85.0
310  Man Years Forecast                        85.0
311  Man Years Error Factor                     0.0
312  Salaries Actual                         1034.8
313  Salaries Forecast                       1034.6
014  Salaries Error Factor                      0.0
315  Travel Actual                             58.4
316  Travel Forecast                           58.4
317  Travel Error Factor                        0.0
318  Telephone Tolls and Rental Actual         12.8
319  Telephone Tolls and Rental Forecast       12.6
320  Telephone Tolls and Rental Error Factor    0.0
321  Postage Actual                            55.1
```

Figure 19.10   *Schedule F #4 Submenu Options for Graphing Individual Objects of Expenditures*

Cell   Macro Entry

BT751: ^1TOTL
BU751: ^3SALL
BV751: ^4TRAVL
BW751: ^5TELL
BX751: ^6POSTL
BY751: ^7CAPL_OUTLL
BT752: ^TOTAL EXPENDITURES FORECAST/DFL. FORECAST/REQUEST/DFL.
        REQUEST
BU752: ^SALARY EXPENDITURES FORECAST/DFL. FORECAST/REQUEST/DFL.
        REQUEST
BV752: ^TRAVEL EXPENDITURES FORECAST/DFL. FORECAST/REQUEST/DFL.
        REQUEST
BW752: ^TELEPHONE EXPENDITURES FORECAST/DFL. FORECAST/REQUEST/D
        FL. REQUEST
BX752: ^POSTAGE EXPENDITURES FORECAST/DFL. FORECAST/REQUEST/DFL.
        REQUEST
BY752: ^CAPITAL OUTLAY EXPENDITURES FORECAST/DFL. FORECAST/REQUEST
        /DFL. REQUEST

continued...

...from previous page

```
BT753:  '{INDICATE WAIT}{CALC}{PANELOFF}{WINDOWSOFF}
BU753:  '{INDICATE WAIT}{CALC}{PANELOFF}{WINDOWSOFF}
BV753:  '{INDICATE WAIT}{CALC}{PANELOFF}{WINDOWSOFF}
BW753:  ^{INDICATE WAIT}{CALC}{PANELOFF}{WINDOWSOFF}
BX753:  '{INDICATE WAIT}{CALC}{PANELOFF}{WINDOWSOFF}
BY753:  '{INDICATE WAIT}{CALC}{PANELOFF}{WINDOWSOFF}
BT754:  '/grg
BU754:  '/grg
BV754:  '/grg
BW754:  '/grg
BX754:  '/grg
BY754:  '/grg
BT755:  'tl
BU755:  'tl
BV755:  'tl
BW755:  'tl
BX755:  'tl
BY755:  'tl
BT756:  ^aAZ327.BF327~
BU756:  ^aAZ312.BF312~
BV756:  ^aAZ315.BF315~
BW756:  ^aAZ318.BF318~
BX756:  ^aAZ321.BF321~
BY756:  ^aAZ324.BF324~
BT757:  'bAZ328.BG328~
BU757:  'bAZ313.BG313~
BV757:  'bAZ316.BG316~
BW757:  'bAZ319.BG319~
BX757:  'bAZ322.BG322~
BY757:  'bAZ325.BG325~
BT758:  ^cAZ402.BG402~
BU758:  ^cAZ392.BG392~
BV758:  ^cAZ394.BG394~
BW758:  ^cAZ396.BG396~
BX758:  ^cAZ398.BG398~
BY758:  ^cAZ400.BG400~
BT759:  ^dAZ435.BG435~
BU759:  ^dAZ425.BG425~
BV759:  ^dAZ427.BG427~
```

continued...

...from previous page

```
BW759:  ^dAZ429.BG429~
BX759:  ^dAZ431.BG431~
BY759:  ^dAZ433.BG433~
BT760:  ^eAZ436.BG436~
BU760:  ^eAZ426.BG426~
BV760:  ^eAZ428.BG428~
BW760:  ^eAZ430.BG430~
BX760:  ^eAZ432.BG432~
BY760:  ^eAZ434.BG434~
BT761:  ^xAZ5.BH5~
BU761:  ^xAZ5.BH5~
BV761:  ^xAZ5.BH5~
BW761:  ^xAZ5.BH5~
BX761:  ^xAZ5.BH5~
BY761:  ^xAZ5.BH5~
BT762:  'o
BU762:  'o
BV762:  'o
BW762:  'o
BX762:  'o
BY762:  'o
BT763:  ^syinqty(Millions)~
BU763:  ^syinqty(Millions)~
BV763:  ^syinqty(Millions)~
BW763:  ^syinqty(Millions)~
BX763:  ^syinqty(Millions)~
BY763:  ^syinqty(Millions)~
BT764:  'cfabbb
BU764:  'cfabbb
BV764:  'cfabbb
BW764:  'cfabbb
BX764:  'cfabbb
BY764:  'cfabbb
BT765:  ^q
BU765:  ^q
BV765:  ^q
BW765:  ^q
BX765:  ^q
BY765:  ^q
```

continued...

...from previous page

```
BT766: ^laAC~
BU766: ^laAC~
BV766: ^laAC~
BW766: ^laAC~
BX766: ^laAC~
BY766: ^laAC~
BT767: ^lbEX SMTH~
BU767: ^lbEX SMTH~
BV767: ^lbEX SMTH~
BW767: ^lbEX SMTH~
BX767: ^lbEX SMTH~
BY767: ^lbEX SMTH~
BT768: ^lcRQ~
BU768: ^lcRQ~
BV768: ^lcRQ~
BW768: ^lcRQ~
BX768: ^lcRQ~
BY768: ^lcRQ~
BT769: ^ldDF RQ~
BU769: ^ldDF RQ~
BV769: ^ldDF RQ~
BW769: ^ldDF RQ~
BX769: ^ldDF RQ~
BY769: ^ldDF RQ~
BT770: ^leDF EX SMTH-
BU770: ^leDF EX SMTH-
BV770: ^leDF EX SMTH~
BW770: ^leDF EX SMTH~
BX770: ^leDF EX SMTH~
BY770: ^leDF EX SMTH~
BT771: ^tfDepartment of Public Works~
BU771: ^tfDepartment of Public Works~
BV771: ^tfDepartment of Public Works~
BW771: ^tfDepartment of Public Works~
BX771: ^tfDepartment of Public Works~
BY771: ^tfDepartment of Public Works~
BT772: ^tsActual Total Exp./Forecast/Req.~
BU772: ^tsActual Salary Exp./Forecast/Req.~
BV772: ^tsActual Travel Exp./Forecast/Req.~
```

continued...

...from previous page

```
BW772: ^tsActual Telephone Exp./Forecast/Req.~
BX772: ^tsActual Postage Exp./Forecast/Req.~
BY772: ^tsActual Capital Outlay Exp./Forecast/Req.~
BT773: ^tx1981-88 FORECAST~
BU773: ^tx1981-88 FORECAST~
BV773: ^tx1981-88 FORECAST~
BW773: ^tx1981-88 FORECAST~
BX773: ^tx1981-88 FORECAST~
BY773: ^tx1981-88 FORECAST~
BT774: 'q
BU774: 'q
BV774: 'q
BW774: 'q
BX774: 'q
BY774: 'q
BT775: 'v
BU775: 'v
BV775: 'v
BW775: 'v
BX775: 'v
BY775: 'v
BT776: 'q
BU776: 'q
BV776: 'q
BW776: 'q
BX776: 'q
BY776: 'q
BT777: ^{INDICATE}{BRANCH \m}
BU777: ^{INDICATE}{BRANCH \m}
BV777: ^{INDICATE}{BRANCH \m}
BW777: ^{INDICATE}{BRANCH \m}
BX777: ^{INDICATE}{BRANCH \m}
BY777: ^{INDICATE}{BRANCH \m}
```

You don't need to create special data tables for the Schedule F #4 line chart submenu because that submenu depends on the same data tables as the Schedule F #3 line chart submenu. The only difference between the two submenus is that the Schedule F #4 submenu line graphs include deflated forecast data overlays in addition to the current expenditure forecasts and current and deflated expenditure requests.

Figure 19.11 displays the graph that is drawn when the 3SALL option is selected from the Schedule F #4 line graphics submenu.

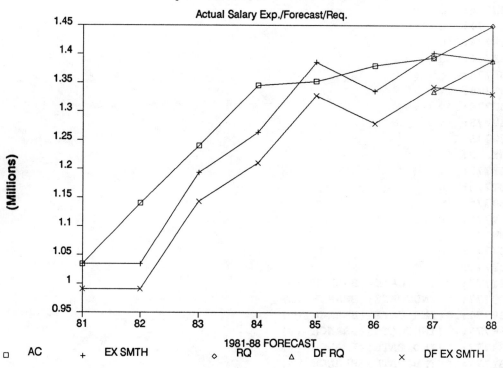

Figure 19.11   *Sample #4 Line Graph of Schedule F: Actual Salary Expenditure/Forecast/Request/Deflated Request/Deflated Forecast*

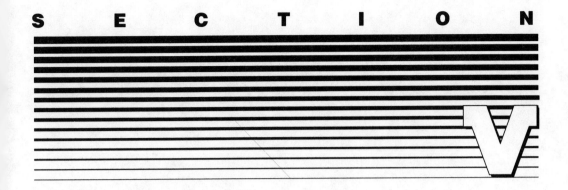

WORKSHEET APPLICATION PRINTING AND PRINTING TO FILE

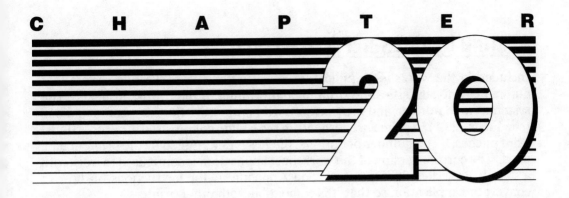

C H A P T E R

20

MAIN PRINT/PRINT TO FILE MENUS AND SCHEDULES A/DA PRINTING

SETTING UP USER-DEFINED MENUS

Included in the worksheet application is a Print and Print To File system that automates and simplifies the printing and printing to file of spreadsheets. The system is menu-driven and provides you with options on the 1-2-3 command line (see Figure 20.1) to print spreadsheets in pica, elite, compressed, or proportional print pitches. (The number of optional pitches is determined by the printer being used. The current version of the worksheet application is configured to work with a C.Itoh Prowriter 8085 printer. See Appendix A for instructions on how to convert the application so that it is compatible with other printers.)

```
AA1: [W45] ^SCHEDULE A:  SUMMARY OF ACTUAL AND REQUESTED EXPENDITURES        MENU
A_SCHs  B_SCHs  C_SCH  Rs/T/F_SCHs  WINDOWS  GRAPH  PRINT/FILE  DATA_TABLES
PRINT SCHEDULES/SET FONTS/PRINT TO FILE
                        AA                      AB          AC
1    SCHEDULE A:  SUMMARY OF ACTUAL AND REQUESTED EXPENDITURES
2    UNIT:  Department of Public Works
3    ==================================================================
4
5
6
7                                          1985-86     1986-87
8    Personal Services:                    Actual      Actual
9       Man Years                              98         100
10      Salaries                        1,352,400   1,380,000
11      Benefits                                0           0
12
13   Supporting Services:
14      Travel                             70,000      70,000
15      Telephone Tolls and Rental         14,000      14,657
16      Postage                            60,000      69,000
17      Rent - State Owned Buildings       10,000      10,000
18      Rent - Privately Owned Buildings    6,600       6,600
19      Building Improvements                 100         100
20      Utility Charges                       250         250
10-Aug-88  08:54 AM              CMD       CALC
```

Figure 20.1   Main Menu Options for Print/Print to File

MAIN PRINT MENU

Begin by expanding the main menu of the worksheet application to include the following cell entries:

Cell   Macro Entry

BX4: ^PRINT/FILE
BX5: ^PRINT SCHEDULES/SET FONTS/PRINT TO FILE
BX6: ^{MENUCALL PRIN/FIL}{MENUBRANCH MENU}

The cell BX4 entry PRINT/FILE is the main Print submenu option, which activates the Print/Print to File submenu. The Print/Print to File submenu is located on the first level of the secondary submenu print system. Before making the entries to create that submenu, move the cursor to cell BQ84, and give the range BQ84..BQ84 the name PRIN/FIL. This range name is referenced in the {MENUCALL PRIN/FIL} command located in cell BX6 and activates the Print/Print to File submenu.

MAIN PRINT/PRINT TO FILE SUBMENU

Figure 20.2 displays the Print/Print to File submenu.

```
AA1: [W45] ^^SCHA                                          MENU
PRINT  FILE_PRINT
PRINT SCHEDULES/SET FONTS
                       AA                    AB          AC
1                          ^SCHA
2    UNIT: Department of Public Works
3    ================================================================
4
5
6
7                                         1985-86     1986-87
8    Personal Services:                   Actual      Actual
9        Man Years                             98         100
10       Salaries                       1,352,400   1,380,000
11       Benefits                               0           0
12
13   Supporting Services:
14       Travel                            70,000      70,000
15       Telephone Tolls and Rental        14,000      14,657
16       Postage                           60,000      69,000
17       Rent - State Owned Buildings      10,000      10,000
18       Rent - Privately Owned Buildings   6,600       6,600
19       Building Improvements                100         100
20       Utility Charges                      250         250
```

Figure 20.2   *Main Submenu Print/Print to File Options*

Make the following entries to construct the submenu:

Cell   **Macro Entry**

```
BP84:  ^PRIN/FIL=
BQ84:  ^PRINT
BR84:  ^FILE_PRINT
BQ85:  ^PRINT SCHEDULES/SET FONTS
BR85:  ^PRINT SCHEDULES TO FILE
BQ86:  ^{MENUCALL PRINT}{MENUBRANCH MENU}
BR86:  ^{MENUCALL FILE}{MENUBRANCH MENU}
```

The same techniques used in previous chapters to construct submenus are used in this chapter to construct submenus. The PRINT submenu option activates the MENUCALL PRINT command that shifts the cursor to the Print submenu. Move the cursor to cell BQ89, and give the range BQ89..BQ89 the name PRINT to name the Print submenu. In the next section, you will begin constructing the submenu.

SECONDARY PRINT/PRINT TO FILE SUBMENUS: PRINT

The Print submenu is displayed in Figure 20.3.

```
AA1: [W45] ^*SCHA                                          MENU
A_SCHs  B_SCHs  C_SCH  R_SCH  T_SCH  F_SCH
PRINT SCHEDULE As
                        AA              AB          AC
1                       *SCHA
2       UNIT:  Department of Public Works
3       ========================================================
4
5
6
7                                       1985-86     1986-87
8       Personal Services:              Actual      Actual
9           Man Years                        98         100
10          Salaries                  1,352,400   1,380,000
11          Benefits                          0           0
12
13      Supporting Services:
14          Travel                       70,000      70,000
15          Telephone Tolls and Rental   14,000      14,657
16          Postage                      60,000      69,000
17          Rent - State Owned Buildings 10,000      10,000
18          Rent - Privately Owned Buildings 6,600   6,600
19          Building Improvements           100         100
20          Utility Charges                 250         250
```

Figure 20.3   *Submenu Budget Schedule Print Options*

Make the following entries to construct the submenu:

Cell   Macro Entry

BQ89: 'PRINT=
BR89: ^A_SCHs
BS89: ^B_SCHs
BT89: ^C_SCH
BU89: ^R_SCH
BV89: ^T_SCH
BW89: ^F_SCH
BR90: ^PRINT SCHEDULE As
BS90: ^PRINT SCHEDULE Bs
BT90: ^PRINT SCHEDULE Cs
BU90: ^PRINT SCHEDULE R
BV90: ^PRINT SCHEDULE T
BW90: ^PRINT SCHEDULE F
BR91: ^{MENUCALL SCHAP}

continued...

...from previous page

```
BS91:  ^{MENUCALL SCHBP}
BT91:  ^{MENUCALL SCHCP}
BU91:  ^{MENUCALL SCHRP}
BV91:  ^{MENUCALL T}
BW91:  ^{MENUCALL F}
```

Row 89 arrays all schedule options for printing purposes, and row 91 includes the names of the Print submenus that coincide with each option. Before constructing the individual Print submenu options, make the following entries to create the range names for the two levels of each of the Print submenus:

<u>Cell</u>	<u>Range Name</u>
BS93:	SCHAP
BT98:	SCHAPA
BT111:	SCHDAPA
BS124:	SCHBP
BS137:	SCHCP
BT142:	SCHCPC
BT155:	SCHDCPC
BS168:	SCHRP
BT173:	SCHRPR
BT186:	SCHDRPR

SECONDARY PRINT/PRINT TO FILE SUBMENUS: SCHEDULE A/DA SUBMENU

The Schedule A/DA main Print submenu is displayed in Figure 20.4.

```
AA1: [W45] ^*SCHA                                    MENU
A_SCH  DA_SCH
PRINT SCHEDULE As
                          AA              AB        AC
1                        *SCHA
2       UNIT:  Department of Public Works
3       ==================================================================
4
5
6
7                                        1985-86    1986-87
8       Personal Services:               Actual     Actual
9          Man Years                          98        100
10         Salaries                    1,352,400  1,380,000
11         Benefits                            0          0
12
13      Supporting Services:
14         Travel                         70,000     70,000
15         Telephone Tolls and Rental     14,000     14,657
16         Postage                        60,000     89,000
17         Rent - State Owned Buildings   10,000     10,000
18         Rent - Privately Owned Buildings 6,600      6,600
19         Building Improvements             100        100
20         Utility Charges                   250        250
```

Figure 20.4   *Main Print Submenu Options for Schedules A/DA*

To construct the Schedule A/DA main Print submenu (see Figure 20.4), make the following entries:

Cell   Macro Entry

```
BR93:  'SCHAP=
BS93:  ^A_SCH
BT93:  ^DA_SCH
BS94:  ^PRINT SCHEDULE As
BT94:  ^GO TO SCHEDULE DA (DEFLATED SCHEDULE A)
BS95:  ^{MENUCALL SCHAPA}
BT95:  ^{MENUCALL SCHDAPA}
```

The submenu provides two schedule options, A_SCH for printing Schedule A and DA_SCH for printing Schedule DA. The next two sections cover construction of these second-level Print submenus.

SECONDARY PRINT/PRINT TO FILE SUBMENUS: SCHEDULE A PRINT SUBMENU

Make the following entries to create the Schedule A Print submenu (see Figure 20.5):

```
AA1: [W45] ^*SCHA                                         MENU
PICA PITCH  ELITE PITCH  COMPRESS PITCH  PROPORTIONAL PITCH
PRINT SCHEDULE A IN PICA MODE
                    AA                    AB        AC
1                   *SCHA
2    UNIT: Department of Public Works
3    ═══════════════════════════════════════════════════
4
5
6
7                                         1985-86   1986-87
8    Personal Services:                   Actual    Actual
9       Man Years                              98       100
10      Salaries                        1,352,400 1,380,000
11      Benefits                                0         0
12
13   Supporting Services:
14      Travel                             70,000    70,000
15      Telephone Tolls and Rental         14,000    14,657
16      Postage                            60,000    69,000
17      Rent - State Owned Buildings       10,000    10,000
18      Rent - Privately Owned Buildings    6,600     6,600
19      Building Improvements                 100       100
20      Utility Charges                       250       250
```

Figure 20.5   Print Submenu Options for Schedule A: Pica, Elite, Compress, Proportional Pitches

Cell   Macro Entry

```
BS98:  'SCHAPA=
BT98:  ^PICA PITCH
BU98:  ^ELITE PITCH
BV98:  ^COMPRESS PITCH
BW98:  ^PROPORTIONAL PITCH
BT99:  ^PRINT SCHEDULE A IN PICA MODE
BU99:  ^PRINT SCHEDULE A IN ELITE MODE
BV99:  ^PRINT SCHEDULE A IN COMPRESS MODE
BW99:  ^PRINT SCHEDULE A IN PROPORTIONAL MODE
BT100: '{CALC}
BU100: '{CALC}
```

continued...

...from previous page

```
BV100:  '{CALC}
BW100:  '{CALC}
BT101:  ^{PANELOFF}
BU101:  ^{PANELOFF}
BV101:  ^{PANELOFF}
BW101:  ^{PANELOFF}
BT102:  '/ppcaomr180~q
BU102:  '/ppcaomr180~q
BV102:  '/ppcaomr180~q
BW102:  '/ppcaomr180~q
BT103:  ^rSCHA~
BU103:  ^rSCHA~
BV103:  ^rSCHA~
BW103:  ^rSCHA~
BT104:  ^os{ECS}s\027\078~q
BU104:  ^os{ECS}s\027\069~q
BV104:  ^os{ECS}s\027\081~q
BW104:  ^os{ECS}s\027\080~q
BT105:  ^ag
BU105:  ^ag
BV105:  ^ag
BW105:  ^ag
BT106:  ^rBLANK~
BU106:  ^rBLANK~
BV106:  ^rBLANK~
BW106:  ^rBLANK~
BT107:  ^os{ECS}s\027\078~q
BU107:  ^os{ECS}s\027\078~q
BV107:  ^os{ECS}s\027\078~q
BW107:  ^os{ECS}s\027\078~q
BT108:  ^{BRANCH \m}
BU108:  ^{BRANCH \m}
BV108:  ^{BRANCH \m}
BW108:  ^{BRANCH \m}
```

The {CALC} commands in row 100 recalculate the worksheet before printing any of the specified spreadsheets. The /pp command combinations in row 102 output a range to the printer. The c and a commands reset all print settings to their default values. The o command prepares for the setting of print options. The m, r, and 180 commands set the right margin to 180. The q command quits the current submenu level of 1-2-3 and returns to the previous submenu level. The r command specifies the range to print. In this case, the range to print is the range named SCHA, the name given Schedule A in Chapter 2. The command following SCHA activates the range.

The o and s commands specify the printer setup strings, which vary across the range of cells between BT104 and BX104. The {ECS} entry cancels any previous setup string that may have been entered, and the s command that follows reinvokes the prompt for entry of the printer setup string. Each of the strings that appears in the macro corresponds with the print pitch specified for the respective columns. For example, \027\078 is the print code required by the C column.

The C. Itoh Prowriter printer normally prints in pica pitch (the default pitch). The print codes \027\069, \027\081, and \027\080 cause the printer to print in elite, compress, and proportional pitches, respectively.

The a command resets the top of page, thus alleviating the need to manually realign the printer, and the g command instructs the printer to begin printing.

The r{BLANK} command combinations in row 106 eliminate any previously defined ranges to be printed before the os{ECS}s\027\078q commands in row 107 are invoked. The latter command combinations reset the printer to the default (pica) pitch mode.

The remaining Print submenus are similar to those already constructed except that they require different schedule options and range names, depending on which schedules are to be printed. Make the entries in the following sections to construct the first and second levels of the remaining Print submenus.

SECONDARY PRINT/PRINT TO FILE SUBMENUS: SCHEDULE DA PRINT SUBMENU

The Schedule DA Print submenu is displayed in Figure 20.6.

```
AA1: [W45] ^SCHEDULE A:  SUMMARY OF ACTUAL AND REQUESTED EXPENDITURES        MENU
PICA PITCH  ELITE PITCH  COMPRESS PITCH  PROPORTIONAL PITCH
PRINT SCHEDULE A IN PICA MODE
                         AA                   AB          AC
  1   SCHEDULE A:  SUMMARY OF ACTUAL AND REQUESTED EXPENDITURES
  2   UNIT: Department of Public Works
  3   =========================================================
  4
  5
  6
  7                                      1985-86     1986-87
  8   Personal Services:                 Actual      Actual
  9      Man Years                            98         100
 10      Salaries                      1,352,400   1,380,000
 11      Benefits                              0           0
 12
 13   Supporting Services:
 14      Travel                           70,000      70,000
 15      Telephone Tolls and Rental       14,000      14,657
 16      Postage                          60,000      69,000
 17      Rent - State Owned Buildings     10,000      10,000
 18      Rent - Privately Owned Buildings  6,600       6,600
 19      Building Improvements               100         100
 20      Utility Charges                     250         250
```

Figure 20.6   *Print Submenu Options for Schedules B: Pica, Elite, Compress,*
Proportional Pitches

Make the following entries to construct the Schedule DA Print submenu:

Cell   Macro Entry

BS111: ' SCHDAPA=
BT111: ^PICA PITCH
BU111: ^ELITE PITCH
BV111: ^COMPRESS PITCH
BW111: ^PROPORTIONAL PITCH
BT112: ^PRINT DEFLATED SCHEDULE A IN PICA MODE
BU112: ^PRINT DEFLATED SCHEDULE A IN ELITE MODE
BV112: ^PRINT DEFLATED SCHEDULE A IN COMPRESS MODE
BW112: ^PRINT DEFLATED SCHEDULE A IN PROPORTIONAL MODE
BT113: ' {CALC}
BU113: ' {CALC}
BV113: ' {CALC}
BW113: ' {CALC}
BT114: ^{PANELOFF}

continued...

...from previous page

```
BU114:  ^{PANELOFF}
BV114:  ^{PANELOFF}
BW114:  ^{PANELOFF}
BT115:  '/ppcaomr180~q
BU115:  '/ppcaomr180~q
BV115:  '/ppcaomr180~q
BW115:  '/ppcaomr180~q
BT116:  ^rSCHDA~
BU116:  ^rSCHDA~
BV116:  ^rSCHDA~
BW116:  ^rSCHDA~
BT117:  ^os{ECS}s\027\078~q
BU117:  ^os{ECS}s\027\069~q
BV117:  ^os{ECS}s\027\081~q
BW117:  ^os{ECS}s\027\080~q
BT118:  ^ag
BU118:  ^ag
BV118:  ^ag
BW118:  ^ag
BT119:  ^rBLANK~
BU119:  ^rBLANK~
BV119:  ^rBLANK~
BW119:  ^rBLANK~
BT120:  ^os{ECS}s\027\078~q
BU120:  ^os{ECS}s\027\078~q
BV120:  ^os{ECS}s\027\078~q
BW120:  ^os{ECS}s\027\078~q
BT121:  ^{BRANCH \m}
BU121:  ^{BRANCH \m}
BV121:  ^{BRANCH \m}
BW121:  ^{BRANCH \m}
```

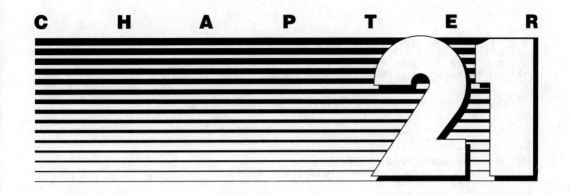

CHAPTER 21

SCHEDULES B PRINTING

SECONDARY PRINT/PRINT TO FILE
SUBMENUS: SCHEDULES B PRINT SUBMENU

The Schedules B Print submenu is displayed in Figure 21.1.

```
A82: [W35] ^SCHEDULE B:  BUDGET CHANGE DESCRIPTION                          MENU
PICA PITCH  ELITE PITCH  COMPRESS PITCH  PROPORTIONAL PITCH
PRINT SCHEDULE Bs IN PICA MODE
                        A              B        C        D        E
82   SCHEDULE B:  BUDGET CHANGE DESCRIPTION
83
84   UNIT:  Department of Public Works
85
86   1. Categories of Budget Change:
87
88      -X-Price Change                  ——New and Changed Services
89
90      ——Methods Improvement            ——Other Continuing
91
92      ——Workload Change                ——Full Financing
93
94   2. Fiscal Effect:
95
96                               1988-89  1989-90
97   MAJOR OBJECT EXPENDITURES    AMOUNT REQUESTED      REFERENCE
98
99      Postage                   4,000    4,000         [1]
100     Rent - State Owned Buildings  4,400    4,400     [2]
101     Data Processing Contr. Service  5,000   10,000   [3]
```

Figure 21.1   *Print Submenu Options for Schedules B: Pica, Elite, Compress,*
Proportional Pitches

To construct the Schedules B Print submenu, make the following entries:

Cell   **Macro Entry**

BR124: ' SCHBP=
BS124: ^PICA PITCH
BT124: ^ELITE PITCH
BU124: ^COMPRESS PITCH
BV124: ^PROPORTIONAL PITCH
BS125: ^PRINT SCHEDULE Bs IN PICA MODE
BT125: ^PRINT SCHEDULE Bs IN ELITE MODE
BU125: ^PRINT SCHEDULE Bs IN COMPRESS MODE

continued...

...from previous page

```
BV125: ^PRINT SCHEDULE Bs IN PROPORTIONAL MODE
BS126: '{CALC}
BT126: '{CALC}
BU126: '{CALC}
BV126: '{CALC}
BS127: ^{PANELOFF}
BT127: ^{PANELOFF}
BU127: ^{PANELOFF}
BV127: ^{PANELOFF}
BS128: '/ppcaomr180~q
BT128: '/ppcaomr180~q
BU128: '/ppcaomr180~q
BV128: '/ppcaomr180~q
BS129: ^rSCHB~
BT129: ^rSCHB~
BU129: ^rSCHB~
BV129: ^rSCHB~
BS130: ^os{ESC}s\027\078~q
BT130: ^os{ESC}s\027\069~q
BU130: ^os{ESC}s\027\081~q
BV130: ^os{ESC}s\027\080~q
BS131: ^ag
BT131: ^ag
BU131: ^ag
BV131: ^ag
BS132: ^rBLANK~
BT132: ^rBLANK~
BU132: ^rBLANK~
BV132: ^rBLANK~
BS133: ^os{ESC}s\027\078~q
BT133: ^os{ESC}s\027\078~q
BU133: ^os{ESC}s\027\078~q
BV133: ^os{ESC}s\027\078~q
BS134: ^{M/BRANCH \m}
BT134: ^{M/BRANCH \m}
BU134: ^{M/BRANCH \m}
BV134: ^{M/BRANCH \m}
```

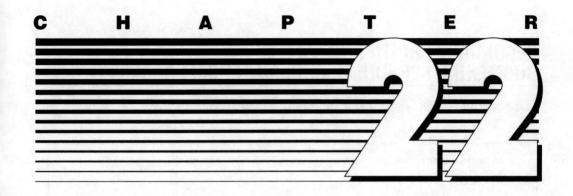

SCHEDULES C/DC PRINTING

SECONDARY PRINT/PRINT TO FILE
SUBMENUS: SCHEDULES C/DC MAIN PRINT SUBMENU

The Schedule C/DC main Print submenu is displayed in Figure 22.1.

```
G1: [W45] 'SCHEDULE C: MATRIX OF BUDGET CHANGE REQUESTS              MENU
C_SCH  DC_SCH
PRINT SCHEDULE C
                    G                      H      I      J
 1   SCHEDULE C: MATRIX OF BUDGET CHANGE REQUESTS
 2   UNIT: Department of Public Works
 3   ==============================================================
 4
 5                                                       1988-
 6   Change Categories                   PC     MI      WLC
 7   ──────────────────────────────────────────────────────────
 8   Personal Services:
 9      Man Years
10      Salaries                               (41,250) 19,789
11      Benefits
12
13   Supporting Services:
14      Travel
15      Telephone Tolls and Rental
16      Postage                        4,000           1,560
17      Rent - State Owned Buildings   4,400
18      Rent - Privately Owned Buildings
19      Building Improvements
20      Utility Charges
```

Figure 22.1 *Main Print Submenu Options for Schedules C/DC*

To construct the Schedule C/DC main Print submenu, make the following entries:

Cell   Macro Entry

```
BBR137:  'SCHCP=
BS137:   ^C_SCH
BT137:   ^DC_SCH
BS138:   ^PRINT SCHEDULE C
BT138:   ^PRINT SCHEDULE DC
BS139:   ^{MENUCALL SCHCPC}
BT139:   ^{MENUCALL SCHDCPC}
```

SECONDARY PRINT/PRINT TO FILE SUBMENUS: SCHEDULE C PRINT SUBMENU

The Schedule C Print submenu is displayed in Figure 22.2.

```
G1: [W45] 'SCHEDULE C: MATRIX OF BUDGET CHANGE REQUESTS              MENU
PICA PITCH  ELITE PITCH  COMPRESS PITCH  PROPORTIONAL PITCH
PRINT SCHEDULE C IN PICA MODE
                        G                   H       I      J
 1   SCHEDULE C: MATRIX OF BUDGET CHANGE REQUESTS
 2   UNIT: Department of Public Works
 3   ===========================================================
 4
 5                                                       1988-
 6   Change Categories                  PC      MI      WLC
 7   -----------------------------------------------------------
 8   Personal Services:
 9      Man Years
10      Salaries                               [41,250] 19,789
11      Benefits
12
13   Supporting Services:
14      Travel
15      Telephone Tolls and Rental
16      Postage                        4,000            1,560
17      Rent - State Owned Buildings   4,400
18      Rent - Privately Owned Buildings
19      Building Improvements
20      Utility Charges
```

Figure 22.2   *Print Submenu Options for Schedule C: Pica, Elite, Compress, Proportional Pitches*

To construct the Schedule C Print submenu, make the following entries:

Cell	Macro Entry
BS142:	'SCHCPC=
BT142:	^PICA PITCH
BU142:	^ELITE PITCH
BV142:	^COMPRESS PITCH
BW142:	^PROPORTIONAL PITCH
BT143:	^PRINT SCHEDULE C IN PICA MODE
BU143:	^PRINT SCHEDULE C IN ELITE MODE
BV143:	^PRINT SCHEDULE C IN COMPRESS MODE

continued...

...from previous page

```
BW143:  ^PRINT SCHEDULE C IN PROPORTIONAL MODE
BT144:  '{CALC}
BU144:  '{CALC}
BV144:  '{CALC}
BW144:  '{CALC}
BT145:  ^{PANELOFF}
BU145:  ^{PANELOFF}
BV145:  ^{PANELOFF}
BW145:  ^{PANELOFF}
BT146:  '/ppcaomr180~q
BU146:  '/ppcaomr180~q
BV146:  '/ppcaomr115~q
BW146:  '/ppcaomr180~q
BT147:  ^rSCHC~
BU147:  ^rSCHC~
BV147:  ^rSCHC~
BW147:  ^rSCHC~
BT148:  ^os{ESC}s\027\078~q
BU148:  ^os{ESC}s\027\069~q
BV148:  ^os{ESC}s\027\081~q
BW148:  ^os{ESC}s\027\080~q
BT149:  ^ag
BU149:  ^ag
BV149:  ^ag
BW149:  ^ag
BT150:  ^rBLANK~
BU150:  ^rBLANK~
BV150:  ^rBLANK~
BW150:  ^rBLANK~
BT151:  ^os{ESC}s\027\078~q
BU151:  ^os{ESC}s\027\078~q
BV151:  ^os{ESC}s\027\078~q
BW151:  ^os{ESC}s\027\078~q
BT152:  ^{BRANCH \m}
BU152:  ^{BRANCH \m}
BV152:  ^{BRANCH \m}
BW152:  ^{BRANCH \m}
```

SECONDARY PRINT/PRINT TO FILE
SUBMENUS: SCHEDULE DC PRINT SUBMENU

The Schedule DC Print submenu is displayed in Figure 22.3.

```
G45: [W45] ^ah65                                          MENU
PICA PITCH  ELITE PITCH  COMPRESS PITCH  PROPORTIONAL PITCH
PRINT DEFLATED SCHEDULE C IN PICA MODE
                        G              H      I      J
45                      ah65
46  UNIT:  Department of Public Works
47  ==================================================================
48                      Deflator Factor:     4.20
49                                                  1988-
50  Change Categories                       PC     MI     WLC
51  ----------------------------------------------------------------
52  Personal Services:
53    Man Years
54    Salaries                              0  [39,518]  18,958
55    Benefits                              0      0      0
56                                          0      0      0
57  Supporting Services:                    0      0      0
58    Travel                                0      0      0
59    Telephone Tolls and Rental            0      0      0
60    Postage                           3,832      0  1,494
61    Rent - State Owned Buildings      4,215      0      0
62    Rent - Privately Owned Buildings      0      0      0
63    Building Improvements                 0      0      0
64    Utility Charges                       0      0      0
```

Figure 22.3   *Print Submenu Options for Schedule DC: Pica, Elite, Compress,*
                Proportional Pitches

To construct the Schedule DC Print submenu, make the following entries:

Cell	Macro Entry
BS155:	'SCHDCPC=
BT155:	^PICA PITCH
BU155:	^ELITE PITCH
BV155:	^COMPRESS PITCH
BW155:	^PROPORTIONAL PITCH
BT156:	^PRINT DEFLATED SCHEDULE C IN PICA MODE
BU156:	^PRINT DEFLATED SCHEDULE C IN ELITE MODE

continued...

...from previous page

```
BV156:  ^PRINT DEFLATED SCHEDULE C IN COMPRESS MODE
BW156:  ^PRINT DEFLATED SCHEDULE C IN PROPORTIONAL MODE
BT157:  '{CALC}
BU157:  '{CALC}
BV157:  '{CALC}
BW157:  '{CALC}
BT158:  ^{PANELOFF}
BU158:  ^{PANELOFF}
BV158:  ^{PANELOFF}
BW158:  ^{PANELOFF}
BT159:  '/ppcaomr180~q
BU159:  '/ppcaomr180~q
BV159:  '/ppcaomr115~q
BW159:  '/ppcaomr180~q
BT160:  ^rSCHDC~
BU160:  ^rSCHDC~
BV160:  ^rSCHDC~
BW160:  ^rSCHDC~
BT161:  ^os{ESC}s\027\078~q
BU161:  ^os{ESC}s\027\069~q
BV161:  ^os{ESC}s\027\081~q
BW161:  ^os{ESC}s\027\080~q
BT162:  ^ag
BU162:  ^ag
BV162:  ^ag
BW162:  ^ag
BT163:  ^rBLANK~
BU163:  ^rBLANK~
BV163:  ^rBLANK~
BW163:  ^rBLANK~
BT164:  ^os{ESC}s\027\078~q
BU164:  ^os{ESC}s\027\078~q
BV164:  ^os{ESC}s\027\078~q
BW164:  ^os{ESC}s\027\078~q
BT165:  ^{BRANCH \m}
BU165:  ^{BRANCH \m}
BV165:  ^{BRANCH \m}
BW165:  ^{BRANCH \m}
```

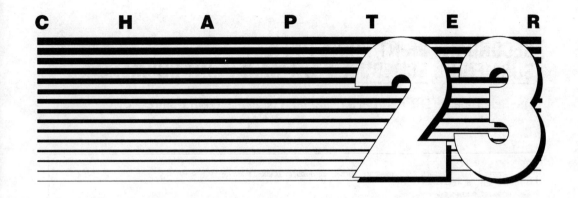

SCHEDULES R/DR PRINTING

SECONDARY PRINT/PRINT TO FILE
SUBMENUS: SCHEDULE R/DR MAIN PRINT SUBMENU

The Schedule R/DR main Print submenu is displayed in Figure 23.1.

```
AH1: [W45] 'SCHEDULE R:  SUMMARY OF ACTUAL AND REQUESTED BUDGET RATIOS        MENU
R_SCH  DR_SCH
PRINT SCHEDULE R
                            AH                          AI
   1   SCHEDULE R:  SUMMARY OF ACTUAL AND REQUESTED BUDGET RATIOS
   2   UNIT:  Department of Public Works
   3   ================================================================
   4
   5
   6                                                  % Total Exp
   7                                                  1985-86
   8   Personal Services:                             Actual
   9      Man Years
  10      Salaries                                     78.57%
  11      Benefits                                      0.00%
  12
  13   Supporting Services:
  14      Travel                                        3.96%
  15      Telephone Tolls and Rental                    0.79%
  16      Postage                                       3.40%
  17      Rent - State Owned Buildings                  0.57%
  18      Rent - Privately Owned Buildings              0.37%
  19      Building Improvements                         0.01%
  20      Utility Charges                               0.01%
```

Figure 23.1   Main Print Submenu Options for Schedules R/DR

To construct the Schedule R/DR main Print submenu, make the following entries:

Cell   Macro Entry

BR168: 'SCHRP=
BS168: ^R_SCH
BT168: ^DR_SCH
BS169: ^PRINT SCHEDULE R
BT169: ^GO TO SCHEDULE DR (DEFLATED SCHEDULE R)
BS170: ^{MENUCALL SCHRPR}
BT170: ^{MENUCALL SCHDRPR}

SECONDARY PRINT/PRINT TO FILE SUBMENUS: SCHEDULE R PRINT SUBMENU

The Schedule R Print submenu is displayed in Figure 23.2.

```
AH1: [W45] 'SCHEDULE R: SUMMARY OF ACTUAL AND REQUESTED BUDGET RATIOS      MENU
PICA PITCH  ELITE PITCH  COMPRESS PITCH  PROPORTIONAL PITCH
PRINT SCHEDULE R IN PICA MODE
                          AH                      AI
1   SCHEDULE R: SUMMARY OF ACTUAL AND REQUESTED BUDGET RATIOS
2   UNIT: Department of Public Works
3   ==========================================================
4
5
6                                              % Total Exp
7                                              1985-86
8   Personal Services:                         Actual
9       Man Years
10      Salaries                               78.57%
11      Benefits                               0.00%
12
13  Supporting Services:
14      Travel                                 3.96%
15      Telephone Tolls and Rental             0.79%
16      Postage                                3.40%
17      Rent - State Owned Buildings           0.57%
18      Rent - Privately Owned Buildings       0.37%
19      Building Improvements                  0.01%
20      Utility Charges                        0.01%
```

Figure 23.2   *Print Submenu Options for Schedule R: Pica, Elite, Compress,*
Proportional Pitches

To construct the Schedule R Print submenu, make the following entries:

Cell   Macro Entry

```
BS173:  'SCHRPR=
BT173:  ^PICA PITCH
BU173:  ^ELITE PITCH
BV173:  ^COMPRESS PITCH
BW173:  ^PROPORTIONAL PITCH
BT174:  ^PRINT SCHEDULE R IN PICA MODE
BU174:  ^PRINT SCHEDULE R IN ELITE MODE
BV174:  ^PRINT SCHEDULE R IN COMPRESS MODE
BW174:  ^PRINT SCHEDULE R IN PROPORTIONAL MODE
```

continued...

...from previous page

```
BT175:  '{CALC}
BU175:  '{CALC}
BV175:  '{CALC}
BW175:  '{CALC}
BT176:  ^{PANELOFF}
BU176:  ^{PANELOFF}
BV176:  ^{PANELOFF}
BW176:  ^{PANELOFF}
BT177:  '/ppcaomr180~q
BU177:  '/ppcaomr180~q
BV177:  '/ppcaomr124~q
BW177:  '/ppcaomr180~q
BT178:  ^rSCHR~
BU178:  ^rSCHR~
BV178:  ^rSCHR~
BW178:  ^rSCHR~
BT179:  ^os{ESC}s\027\078~q
BU179:  ^os{ESC}s\027\069~q
BV179:  ^os{ESC}s\027\081~q
BW179:  ^os{ESC}s\027\080~q
BT180:  ^ag
BU180:  ^ag
BV180:  ^ag
BW180:  ^ag
BT181:  ^rBLANK~
BU181:  ^rBLANK~
BV181:  ^rBLANK~
BW181:  ^rBLANK~
BT182:  ^os{ESC}s\027\078~q
BU182:  ^os{ESC}s\027\078~q
BV182:  ^os{ESC}s\027\078~q
BW182:  ^os{ESC}s\027\078~q
BT183:  ^{BRANCH \m}
BU183:  ^{BRANCH \m}
BV183:  ^{BRANCH \m}
BW183:  ^{BRANCH \m}
```

SECONDARY PRINT/PRINT TO FILE
SUBMENUS: SCHEDULE DR PRINT SUBMENU

The Schedule DR Print submenu is displayed in Figure 23.3.

```
AH65: [W45] ^SCHEDULE DR:  SUMMARY OF ACTUAL AND DEFLATED REQUESTED BUDGET  MENU
PICA PITCH  ELITE PITCH  COMPRESS PITCH  PROPORTIONAL PITCH
PRINT DEFLATED SCHEDULE R IN PICA MODE
                        AH                      AI
65  SCHEDULE DR:  SUMMARY OF ACTUAL AND DEFLATED REQUESTED BUDGET RATIOS
66  UNIT:  Department of Public Works
67  ==============================================================
68                      Deflator Factor:          4.20
69
70                                       % Total Exp
71                                       1985-86
72  Personal Services:                   Actual
73      Man Years
74      Salaries                         76.57%
75      Benefits                         0.00%
76
77  Supporting Services:
78      Travel                           3.96%
79      Telephone Tolls and Rental       0.79%
80      Postage                          3.40%
81      Rent - State Owned Buildings     0.57%
82      Rent - Privately Owned Buildings 0.37%
83      Building Improvements            0.01%
84      Utility Charges                  0.01%
```

Figure 23.3   *Print Submenu Options for Schedule DR: Pica, Elite, Compress,*
Proportional Pitches

To construct the Schedule DR Print submenu, make the following entries:

Cell	Macro Entry
BS186:	' SCHDRPR=
BT186:	^PICA PITCH
BU186:	^ELITE PITCH
BV186:	^COMPRESS PITCH
BW186:	^PROPORTIONAL PITCH
BT187:	^PRINT DEFLATED SCHEDULE R IN PICA MODE
BU187:	^PRINT DEFLATED SCHEDULE A IN ELITE MODE
BV187:	^PRINT DEFLATED SCHEDULE A IN COMPRESS MODE

continued...

...from previous page

```
BW187: ^PRINT DEFLATED SCHEDULE A IN PROPORTIONAL MODE
BT188: '{CALC}
BU188: '{CALC}
BV188: '{CALC}
BW188: '{CALC}
BT189: ^{PANELOFF}
BU189: ^{PANELOFF}
BV189: ^{PANELOFF}
BW189: ^{PANELOFF}
BT190: '/ppcaomr180~q
BU190: '/ppcaomr180~q
BV190: '/ppcaomr124~q
BW190: '/ppcaomr180~q
BT191: ^rSCHDR~
BU191: ^rSCHDR~
BV191: ^rSCHDR~
BW191: ^rSCHDR~
BT192: ^os{ESC}s\027\078~q
BU192: ^os{ESC}s\027\069~q
BV192: ^os{ESC}s\027\081~q
BW192: ^os{ESC}s\027\080~q
BT193: ^ag
BU193: ^ag
BV193: ^ag
BW193: ^ag
BT194: ^rBLANK~
BU194: ^rBLANK~
BV194: ^rBLANK~
BW194: ^rBLANK~
BT195: ^os{ESC}s\027\078~q
BU195: ^os{ESC}s\027\078~q
BV195: ^os{ESC}s\027\078~q
BW195: ^os{ESC}s\027\078~q
BT196: ^{BRANCH \m}
BU196: ^{BRANCH \m}
BV196: ^{BRANCH \m}
BW196: ^{BRANCH \m}
```

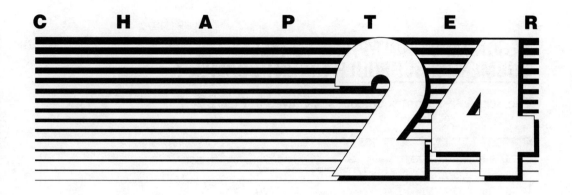

SCHEDULE T PRINTING

SECONDARY PRINT/PRINT TO FILE SUBMENUS: SCHEDULE T PRINT SUBMENU

The Schedule T Print submenu is displayed in Figure 24.1.

```
AY88: [W45] ^SCHEDULE T:  BUDGET TREND PROJECTION MODEL [ANNUAL [FIVE-YEAR  MENU
PICA PITCH  ELITE PITCH  COMPRESS PITCH  PROPORTIONAL PITCH
PRINT SCHEDULE T IN PICA MODE
                        AY                              AZ
 88  SCHEDULE T:  BUDGET TREND PROJECTION MODEL [ANNUAL [FIVE-YEAR AVERAGE] C
 89  UNIT:  Department of Public Works
 90  ==================================================================
 91
 92
 93
 94
 95  Personal Services:
 96      Man Years
 97      Salaries
 98      Benefits
 99
100  Supporting Services:
101      Travel
102      Telephone Tolls and Rental
103      Postage
104      Rent - State Owned Buildings
105      Rent - Privately Owned Buildings
106      Building Improvements
107      Utility Charges
```

Figure 24.1   *Print Submenu Options for Schedule T: Pica, Elite, Compress,*
                  Proportional Pitches

To construct the Schedule T Print submenu, make the following entries:

<u>**Cell**</u>   <u>**Macro Entry**</u>

BR211: 'SCHTP=
BS211: ^PICA PITCH
BT211: ^ELITE PITCH
BU211: ^COMPRESS PITCH
BV211: ^PROPORTIONAL PITCH
BS212: ^PRINT SCHEDULE T IN PICA MODE
BT212: ^PRINT SCHEDULE T IN ELITE MODE

continued...

...from previous page

```
BU212:  ^PRINT SCHEDULE T IN COMPRESS MODE
BV212:  ^PRINT SCHEDULE T IN PROPORTIONAL MODE
BS213:  '{CALC}
BT213:  '{CALC}
BU213:  '{CALC}
BV213:  '{CALC}
BS214:  '/ppcaomr180~q
BT214:  '/ppcaomr180~q
BU214:  '/ppcaomr124~q
BV214:  '/ppcaomr180~q
BS215:  ^rSCHT~
BT215:  ^rSCHT~
BU215:  ^rSCHT~
BV215:  ^rSCHT~
BS216:  ^os{ESC}s\027\078~q
BT216:  ^os{ESC}s\027\069~q
BU216:  ^os{ESC}s\027\081~q
BV216:  ^os{ESC}s\027\080~q
BS217:  ^ag
BT217:  ^ag
BU217:  ^ag
BV217:  ^ag
BS218:  ^rBLANK~
BT218:  ^rBLANK~
BU218:  ^rBLANK~
BV218:  ^rBLANK~
BS219:  ^os{ESC}s\027\078~q
BT219:  ^os{ESC}s\027\078~q
BU219:  ^os{ESC}s\027\078~q
BV219:  ^os{ESC}s\027\078~q
BS220:  ^{BRANCH \m}
BT220:  ^{BRANCH \m}
BU220:  ^{BRANCH \m}
BV220:  ^{BRANCH \m}
```

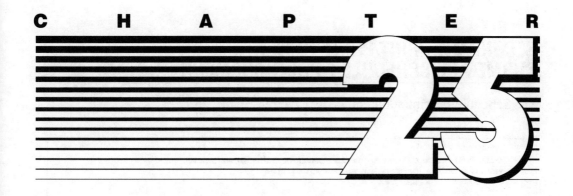

SCHEDULE F PRINTING

SECONDARY PRINT/PRINT TO FILE
SUBMENUS: SCHEDULE F PRINT SUBMENU

The Schedule F Print submenu is displayed in Figure 25.1.

```
AY302: [W45] 'SCHEDULE F:  BUDGET FORECAST [EXPONENTIAL SMOOTHING] MODEL [$ MENU
PICA PITCH  ELITE PITCH  COMPRESS PITCH  PROPORTIONAL PITCH
PRINT SCHEDULE F IN PICA MODE
                           AY                        AZ
302 SCHEDULE F:  BUDGET FORECAST [EXPONENTIAL SMOOTHING] MODEL [$000)
303 UNIT:  DEPARTMENT OF PUBLIC WORKS
304 ═══════════════════════════════════════════════════════
305
306                            Weight=          1.6
307
308                                          1981-82
309  Man Years Actual                          85.0
310  Man Years Forecast                        85.0
311  Man Years Error Factor                     0.0
312  Salaries Actual                         1034.6
313  Salaries Forecast                       1034.6
314  Salaries Error Factor                      0.0
315  Travel Actual                             58.4
316  Travel Forecast                           58.4
317  Travel Error Factor                        0.0
318  Telephone Tolls and Rental Actual         12.6
319  Telephone Tolls and Rental Forecast       12.6
320  Telephone Tolls and Rental Error Factor    0.0
321  Postage Actual                            55.1
```

Figure 25.1   Print Submenu Options for Schedule F

To construct the Schedule F Print submenu, make the following entries:

Cell   **Macro Entry**

BR199: 'F=
BS199: ^PICA PITCH
BT199: ^ELITE PITCH
BU199: ^COMPRESS PITCH
BV199: ^PROPORTIONAL PITCH
BS200: ^PRINT SCHEDULE F IN PICA MODE
BT200: ^PRINT SCHEDULE F IN ELITE MODE
BU200: ^PRINT SCHEDULE F IN COMPRESS MODE

continued...

...from previous page

```
BV200:  ^PRINT SCHEDULE F IN PROPORTIONAL MODE
BS201:  '{CALC}
BT201:  '{CALC}
BU201:  '{CALC}
BV201:  '{CALC}
BS202:  '/ppcaomr180~q
BT202:  '/ppcaomr180~q
BU202:  '/ppcaomr124~q
BV202:  '/ppcaomr180~q
BS203:  ^rSCHF~
BT203:  ^rSCHF~
BU203:  ^rSCHF~
BV203:  ^rSCHF~
BS204:  ^os{ESC}s\027\078~q
BT204:  ^os{ESC}s\027\069~q
BU204:  ^os{ESC}s\027\081~q
BV204:  ^os{ESC}s\027\080~q
BS205:  ^ag
BT205:  ^ag
BU205:  ^ag
BV205:  ^ag
BS206:  ^rBLANK~
BT206:  ^rBLANK~
BU206:  ^rBLANK~
BV206:  ^rBLANK~
BS207:  ^os{ESC}s\027\078~q
BT207:  ^os{ESC}s\027\078~q
BU207:  ^os{ESC}s\027\078~q
BV207:  ^os{ESC}s\027\078~q
BS208:  ^{BRANCH \m}
BT208:  ^{BRANCH \m}
BU208:  ^{BRANCH \m}
BV208:  ^{BRANCH \m}
```

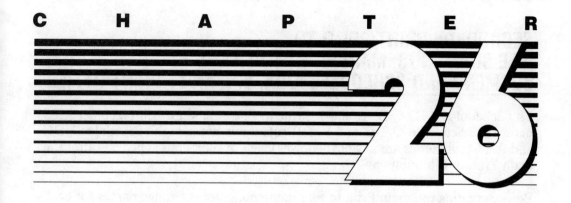

C H A P T E R

26

SECONDARY PRINT/PRINT TO FILE SUBMENUS AND SCHEDULES A/DA, B, T AND F PRINTING TO FILE

SECONDARY PRINT/PRINT TO FILE SUBMENUS: MAIN PRINT TO FILE SUBMENU AND SCHEDULES A/DA, B, T, AND F PRINT TO FILE

The Schedules A/DA, B, T, and F Print to File submenus will be constructed before the Schedule C/DC and R/DR submenus because the Schedule C/DC and R/DR submenus are located on lower levels of submenus appearing after the main Print to File submenu.

Before creating the main Print to File submenu, enter the range names for each of the Print to File submenus in accordance with the following names and cell locations:

Cell	Range Name
BR223:	FILE
BS230:	FPMA
BT234:	FPA
BT238:	FPDA
BS242:	FPMC
BT247:	FPC
BT251:	FPDC
BS255:	FPMR
BT259:	FPR
BT263:	FPDR

Next, to construct the main Print to File submenu and print to file Schedules B, T, and F (see Figure 26.1), make the entries that follow Figure 26.1.

```
AA1: [W45] ^^SCHA                                               MENU
A_SCHs  B_SCHs  C_SCHs  R_SCHs  T_SCH  F_SCH
PRINT SCHEDULE As TO FILE
                        AA                  AB          AC
1                       ^^SCHA
2      UNIT:  Department of Public Works
3      ===================================================
4
5
6
7                                       1985-86     1986-87
8      Personal Services:               Actual      Actual
9          Man Years                        98         100
10         Salaries                  1,352,400   1,380,000
11         Benefits                          0           0
12
13     Supporting Services:
14         Travel                       70,000      70,000
15         Telephone Tolls and Rental   14,000      14,657
16         Postage                      60,000      69,000
17         Rent - State Owned Buildings 10,000      10,000
18         Rent - Privately Owned Buildings 6,600    6,600
19         Building Improvements           100         100
20         Utility Charges                 250         250
```

Figure 26.1   Submenu Budget Schedule Print to File Options

Cell   Macro Entry

BQ223: 'FILE=
BR223: ^A_SCHs
BS223: 'B_SCHs
BT223: ^C_SCHs
BU223: ^R_SCHs
BV223: ^T_SCH
BW223: ^F_SCH
BR224: ^PRINT SCHEDULE As TO FILE
BS224: ^PRINT SCHEDULE Bs TO FILE
BT224: ^PRINT SCHEDULE Cs TO FILE
BU224: ^PRINT SCHEDULE Rs TO FILE
BV224: ^PRINT SCHEDULE T TO FILE
BW224: ^PRINT SCHEDULE F TO FILE
BR225: ^{MENUCALL FPMA}
BS225: ^{INDICATE WAIT}
BT225: ^{MENUCALL FPMC}
BU225: ^{MENUCALL FPMR}

continued...

...from previous page

```
BV225:  ^{INDICATE WAIT}
BW225:  ^{INDICATE WAIT}
BS226:  ^{CALC}{PANELOFF}{WINDOWSOFF}
BV226:  ^{CALC}{PANELOFF}{WINDOWSOFF}
BW226:  ^{CALC}{PANELOFF}{WINDOWSOFF}
BS227:  ^/pfSCHB~{ESC 6}/pfSCHB~rcarSCHB~gcaq
BV227:  '/pfSCHT~{ESC 6}/pfSCHT~rcarSCHT~gcaq
BW227:  '/pfSCHF~{ESC 6}/pfSCHF~rcarSCHF~gcaq
BS228:  ^{INDICATE}{BRANCH \m}
BV228:  ^{INDICATE}{BRANCH \m}
BW228:  ^{INDICATE}{BRANCH \m}
```

The commands and techniques used to create the Print to File submenus are basically the same as those entered in the earlier Print submenu sections, with the exception of the macro command combinations found in row 227. The /pfSCHB~{ESC 6}/pfSCHB~ portion of the /pfSCHB~{ESC 6}/pfSCHB~rcarSCHB~gcaq command combination initiates 1-2-3's print to file command and then enters the range name of the file to be printed; in the current example, the SCHB~ command is entered as the name of the file. After entering the spreadsheet name, you must enter Esc six times with the {ESC 6} command and then repeat the /pfSCHB~ command because the sequence of commands required by 1-2-3 for printing to file varies depending on whether the file name has been entered previously. For example, the first time a file name is entered after the /pf command, 1-2-3 requires you to specify the appropriate spreadsheet range to be printed to file; however, once a file name has been entered after the /pf command and has been printed to file, if you later want to print to file the same file name, 1-2-3 requires that you indicate whether to Cancel or Replace the file name previously entered for printing to file instead of prompting for the appropriate range name as it does the first time a file name is entered. Entering the /pfSCHB~ command and cancelling it with the series of Esc commands in effect tricks 1-2-3 into thinking that the SCHB file name has been printed to file. The initial macro command for printing to file, /pf, can then be repeated, the command SCHB~ reentered, and 1-2-3 will then consistently require you to choose the Replace command option before entering the remaining command sequence, carSCHB~gcaq.

The ca command combination resets all previously entered print settings to default values. The rSCHB~ combination enters the range name to be printed to file SCHB, which happens to be the range name for the Schedules B that was specified in Chapter 4. The g command prints the specified range name, the ca command combination again resets all print settings to default values, and the q command quits 1-2-3's Print to File submenu.

The types of macro commands in the remaining Print to File submenus have been discussed in earlier sections of the book, so they will not be covered in this chapter. In the next section, you will make the entries to create the menu system for printing to file Schedules A and DA.

SECONDARY PRINT/PRINT TO FILE SUBMENUS: SCHEDULES A/DA PRINT TO FILE SUBMENU

The Schedule A/DA main Print to File submenu is displayed in Figure 26.2.

```
AA1: [W45] ^*SCHA                                           MENU
A_SCH  DA_SCH
PRINT SCHEDULE A TO FILE
                        AA              AB          AC
1                       *SCHA
2    UNIT:  Department of Public Works
3    ============================================================
4
5
6
7                                    1985-86      1986-87
8    Personal Services:              Actual       Actual
9      Man Years                         98          100
10     Salaries                   1,352,400    1,380,000
11     Benefits                           0            0
12
13   Supporting Services:
14     Travel                        70,000       70,000
15     Telephone Tolls and Rental    14,000       14,657
16     Postage                       60,000       69,000
17     Rent - State Owned Buildings  10,000       10,000
18     Rent - Privately Owned Buildings 6,600      6,600
19     Building Improvements            100          100
20     Utility Charges                  250          250
```

Figure 26.2   *Main Print to File Submenu Options for Schedules A/DA*

To construct the Schedule A/DA main Print to File submenu, make the following entries:

Cell   **Macro Entry**

```
BR230:  'FPMA=
BS230:  ^A_SCH
BT230:  ^DA_SCH
BS231:  ^PRINT SCHEDULE A TO FILE
BT231:  ^PRINT SCHEDULE DA TO FILE
BS232:  ^{INDICATE WAIT}{CALC}{PANELOFF}{WINDOWSOFF}
BT232:  ^{INDICATE WAIT}{CALC}{PANELOFF}{WINDOWSOFF}
BS233:  '/pfSCHA~{ESC 6}/pfSCHA~rcarSCHA~gcaq
BT233:  '/pfSCHDA~{ESC 6}/pfSCHDA~rcarSCHDA~gcaq
BS234:  ^{INDICATE}{BRANCH \m}
BT234:  ^{INDICATE}{BRANCH \m}
```

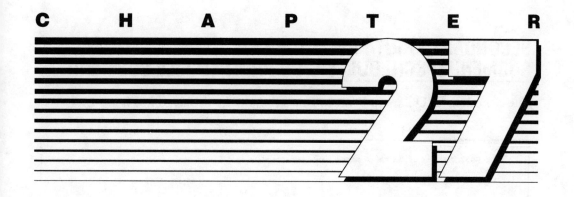

SECONDARY PRINT/PRINT TO FILE SUBMENUS AND SCHEDULES C/DC PRINTING TO FILE

SECONDARY PRINT/PRINT TO FILE
SUBMENUS: SCHEDULES C/DC PRINT TO FILE SUBMENU

The Schedule C/DC main Print to File submenu is displayed in Figure 27.1.

```
G1: [W45] 'SCHEDULE C: MATRIX OF BUDGET CHANGE REQUESTS                    MENU
C_SCH  DC_SCH
PRINT SCHEDULE C TO FILE
                        G                        H      I      J
1    SCHEDULE C: MATRIX OF BUDGET CHANGE REQUESTS
2    UNIT:  Department of Public Works
3    ==========================================================================
4
5                                                                  1988-
6    Change Categories                          PC     MI     WLC
7    _____
8    Personal Services:
9       Man Years
10      Salaries                                     (41,250) 19,789
11      Benefits
12
13   Supporting Services:
14      Travel
15      Telephone Tolls and Rental
16      Postage                                4,000         1,560
17      Rent - State Owned Buildings           4,400
18      Rent - Privately Owned Buildings
19      Building Improvements
20      Utility Charges
```

Figure 27.1   Main Print to File Submenu Options for Schedules C/DC

To construct the Schedule C/DC main Print to File submenu, make the following entries:

Cell   **Macro Entry**

```
BR242:  'FPMC=
BS242:  ^C_SCH
BT242:  ^DC_SCH
BS243:  ^PRINT SCHEDULE C TO FILE
BT243:  ^PRINT SCHEDULE DC TO FILE
BS244:  ^{INDICATE WAIT}{CALC}{PANELOFF}{WINDOWSOFF}
BT244:  ^{INDICATE WAIT}{CALC}{PANELOFF}{WINDOWSOFF}
BS245:  '/pfSCHC~{ESC 6}/pfSCHC~rcarSCHC~gcaq
BT245:  '/pfSCHDC~{ESC 6}/pfSCHDC~rcarSCHDC~gcaq
BS246:  ^{INDICATE}{BRANCH \m}
BT246:  ^{INDICATE}{BRANCH \m}
```

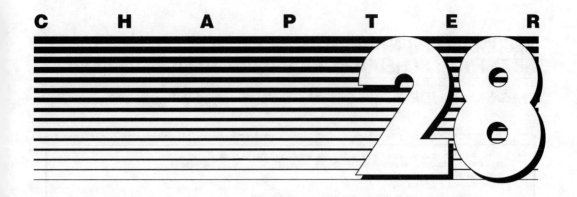

PRINT/PRINT TO FILE
SUBMENUS AND SCHEDULES R/DR
PRINTING TO FILE

SECONDARY PRINT/PRINT TO FILE
SUBMENUS: SCHEDULES R/DR PRINT TO FILE SUBMENU

The Schedule R/DR Print to File submenu is displayed in Figure 28.1.

```
AH1: [W45] 'SCHEDULE R:  SUMMARY OF ACTUAL AND REQUESTED BUDGET RATIOS     MENU
R_SCH  DR_SCH
PRINT SCHEDULE R TO FILE
                        AH                              AI
1   SCHEDULE R:  SUMMARY OF ACTUAL AND REQUESTED BUDGET RATIOS
2   UNIT:  Department of Public Works
3   ==================================================================
4
5
6                                          % Total Exp
7                                          1985-86
8   Personal Services:                     Actual
9      Man Years
10     Salaries                            76.57%
11     Benefits                            0.00%
12
13  Supporting Services:
14     Travel                              3.96%
15     Telephone Tolls and Rental          0.79%
16     Postage                             3.40%
17     Rent - State Owned Buildings        0.57%
18     Rent - Privately Owned Buildings    0.37%
19     Building Improvements               0.01%
20     Utility Charges                     0.01%
```

Figure 28.1   Main Print to File Submenu Options for Schedules R/DR

To construct the Schedule R/DR main Print to File submenu, make the following entries.

Cell   Macro Entry

```
BR255:  'FPMR=
BS255:  ^R_SCH
BT255:  ^DR_SCH
BS256:  ^PRINT SCHEDULE R TO FILE
BT256:  ^PRINT SCHEDULE DR TO FILE
BS257:  ^{INDICATE WAIT}{CALC}{PANELOFF}{WINDOWSOFF}
BT257:  ^{INDICATE WAIT}{CALC}{PANELOFF}{WINDOWSOFF}
BS258:  '/pfSCHR~{ESC 6}/pfSCHR~rcarSCHR~gcaq
BT258:  '/pfSCHDR~{ESC 6}/pfSCHDR~rcarSCHDR~gcaq
BS259:  ^{INDICATE}{BRANCH \m}
BT259:  ^{INDICATE}{BRANCH \m}
```

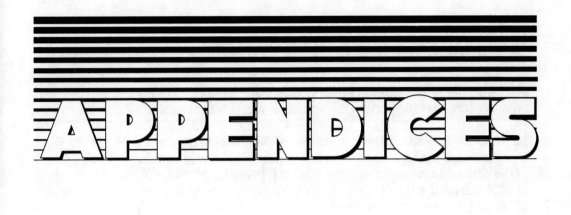

APPENDICES

APPENDIX A: CONSTRUCTION OF
OPTIONAL DATA TABLE MENU SYSTEMS

Following the instructions in this appendix will enable you to construct an optional menu system that facilitates the process of locating data tables.

Move to cell BR780, and give the range BR780..BR780 the name GRAPHT. This is the location of the second level of the data table menu system or the first level of the data table submenu system. The {MENUBRANCH GRAPHT} command in BX6 causes the flow of the macro to return to the main menu once execution of submenu functions is finished.

Use the same techniques for constructing the data table submenus that you used in Chapter 10 to construct the submenus for getting around in the worksheet application. First, name the following cell ranges:

Cell	Range Name
BR785:	ASPIEM
BS790:	APIEM
BR794:	PIEDDA
BR798:	CSPIEM
BS803:	CPIEM
BS807:	DCPIEM
BR811:	RSGRAPH
BS816:	RGRAPHM1
BS820:	RGRAPHM2
BS824:	DRGRAPHM1
BR832:	FSGRAPH
BS837:	FGRAPHM1
BS841:	FGRAPH2
BS845:	FGRAPH3
BR849:	TSGRAPH
BS854:	TGRAPH1
BS858:	TGRAPH2
BS862:	TGRAPH3
BS865:	TGRAPH4
BS868:	TGRAPH5
BS871:	TGRAPH6

These range names direct the data table submenu macros to lower levels of the submenu system.

Next, make the following entries to complete the construction of the optional data table menu system.

Cell Listing: Appendix A

```
BX4:    ^DATA_TABLES
BX5:    ^GO TO GRAPH TABLES
BX6:    ^{MENUCALL GRAPHT}
BX4:    ^DATA_TABLES
BX5:    ^GO TO GRAPH TABLES
BX6:    ^{MENUCALL GRAPHT}
BQ780:  'GRAPHT=
BR780:  ^AGRAPH_TABLEs
BS780:  ^CGRAPH_TABLEs
BR781:  ^GO TO AGRAPH DATA TABLES
BS781:  ^GO TO CGRAPH DATA TABLES
BR782:  ^{MENUCALL AsPIEM}
BS782:  ^{MENUCALL CsPIEM}
BQ785:  'AsPIEM=
BR785:  ^AGRAPH_TABLE
BS785:  ^DAGRAPH_TABLE
BR786:  ^TABLE A PIE CHART DATA
BS786:  ^TABLE DA PIE CHART DATA (DEFLATED)
BR787:  ^{APIEM}
BS787:  ^{DAPIEM}
BR790:  'APIEM=
BS790:  ^{GOTO}PIEDA~
BS791:  ^{BRANCH \m}
BR794:  'DAPIEM=
BS794:  ^{GOTO}PIEDDA~
BS795:  ^{BRANCH \m}
BQ798:  'CsPIEM=
BR798:  ^CGRAPH_TABLE
BS798:  ^DCGRAPH_TABLE
BR799:  ^TABLE C PIE CHART DATA
BS799:  ^TABLE DC PIE CHART DATA (DEFLATED)
```

continued...

...from previous page

```
BR800:  ^{CPIEM}
BS800:  ^{DCPIEM}
BR803:  'CPIEM=
BS803:  ^{GOTO}PIEDC~
BS804:  ^{BRANCH \m}
BR807:  'DCPIEM=
BS807:  ^{GOTO}PIEDDC~
BS808:  ^{BRANCH \m}
BQ811:  'RsGRAPH=
BR811:  ^1RGRAPH_TABLE
BS811:  ^2RGRAPH_TABLE
BR812:  ^TABLE R ANNUAL % OF TOTAL EXPENDITURES DATA
BS812:  ^TABLE R ANNUAL % EXPENDITURE CHANGES DATA
BR813:  ^{RGRAPHM1}
BS813:  ^{RGRAPHM2}
BR816:  'RGRAPHM1=
BS816:  ^{GOTO}RGRAPH1~
BS817:  ^{BRANCH \m}
BR820:  'RGRAPHM2=
BS820:  ^{GOTO}RGRAPH2~
BS821:  ^{BRANCH \m}
BR824:  'DRGRAPHM1=
BS824:  ^{GOTO}DRGRAPH1~
BS825:  ^{BRANCH \m}
BQ832:  'FsGRAPH=
BR832:  ^1FGRAPH_TABLE
BS832:  ^2FGRAPH_TABLE
BR833:  ^F TABLE 1 MEAN-SQUARED ERROR MODEL
BS833:  ^F TABLE 2 BUDGET EXPENDITURE REQUESTS ($000)
BR834:  ^{FGRAPHM1}
BS834:  ^{FGRAPHM2}
BR837:  'FGRAPHM1=
BS837:  ^{GOTO}FGRAPH1~
BS838:  ^{BRANCH \m}
BR841:  'FGRAPHM2=
BS841:  ^{GOTO}FGRAPH2~
BS842:  ^{BRANCH \m}
BR845:  'FGRAPHM3=
BS845:  ^{GOTO}FGRAPH3~
```

continued...

...from previous page

```
BS846:  ^{BRANCH \m}
BQ849:  'TsGRAPH=
BR849:  ^1TGRAPH_TBL
BS849:  ^2TGRAPH_TBL
BR850:  ^TABLE T AND F SUMMARY OF ACTUAL EXPENDITURES DATA (1981-87)
BS850:  ^TABLE T THREE-YEAR MOVING AVERAGE DATA (1981-87)
BR851:  ^{TGRAPHM1}
BS851:  ^{TGRAPHM2}
BR854:  'TGRAPHM1=
BS854:  ^{GOTO}TGRAPH1~
BS855:  ^{BRANCH \m}
BR858:  'TGRAPHM2=
BS858:  ^{GOTO}TGRAPH2~
BS859:  ^{BRANCH \m}
BR862:  'TGRAPHM3=
BS862:  ^{GOTO}TGRAPH3~
BS863:  ^{BRANCH \m}
BR865:  ^TGRAPHM4=
BS865:  ^{GOTO}TGRAPH4~
BS866:  ^{BRANCH \m}
BR868:  ^TGRAPHM5=
BS868:  ^{GOTO}TGRAPH5~
BS869:  ^{BRANCH \m}
BR871:  ^TGRAPHM6=
BS871:  ^{GOTO}TGRAPH6~
BS872:  ^{BRANCH \m}
```

APPENDIX B: INSTRUCTIONS FOR USING OTHER PRINTERS

The printing macros that appear in the worksheet application automate the print codes of a C.Itoh Prowriter 8510 printer. You will need to adjust the printing macros if you want to use another printer. Substitute new print codes under each of the printing macro options that currently appear on the application (pica, elite, proportional, compress).

For example, to substitute the print code for compress pitch used by the IBM Proprinter for that used by the Prowriter 8510 printer, you would change the entry in cell BV104 from

```
^os{ESC}s\027\081~q
```

to

```
os{ESC}s\027\015~q
```

and the entry in cell BV107 from

```
os{ESC}s\027\078~q
```

to

```
os{ESC}\027\018~q
```

If the printer you will use does not feature the four fonts or pitches available to the C.Itoh Prowriter — for example, if the proportional pitch is not available on your printer — you will need to erase the proportional print macro from the worksheet application. If, on the other hand, the printer you use allows fonts or pitches that currently are not available in the worksheet application, and if you want access to a font or pitch in addition to those currently available, you will need to insert space for it in the application and enter a print macro (copy and revise a macro already in place or enter a new one) that is comparable to those already available and that includes the new print code. Also, you must configure 1-2-3 for a print driver that corresponds to the printer you use.

APPENDIX C: CONSTRUCTION OF MACRO FOR REMOVING ZEROS FROM SCHEDULE DC

When you construct Schedule DC, zeros will occur in its cells if data are not posted to them from Schedule C. Of course, you can suppress zeros throughout the worksheet application, using 1-2-3's /Worksheet /Global /Zero command; however, it you prefer to enter and retain certain zero entries but not others, the following macro will erase any errant zeros that appear in Schedule DC. Before you begin making the entries to construct the macro, move the cursor to cell BZ155 and identify the macro by giving the range BZ155..BZ155 the name \z. Next, give the range BZ..BZ the name NEXTCOL and the range BZ166 the name END. Then, enter @NA in cell H89, and copy the entry to the range H89..W89. Next, hide the contents of range H89..W89, using 1-2-3's /Range Format Hidden command. Move the cursor to cell X89, and enter 99999. With the cursor resting in cell X89, hide the 99999 entry. You can now begin constructing the macro by making the following entries:

Cell   Macro Entry

```
BY155:  '\z=
BZ155:  ^{INDICATE WAIT}{GOTO}H54~
BZ156:  '/rncHERE~~
BZ157:  ^{IF @ISNA(HERE)}{BRANCH NEXTCOL}
BZ158:  ^{IF HERE=0}/re~
BZ159:  ^{IF HERE=99999}{BRANCH END}
BZ160:  '/rndHERE~~
BZ161:  '{DOWN}
BZ162:  ^{BRANCH BZ156}
BY163:  'nextcol=
BZ163:  '/rndHERE~~
BZ164:  ^{UP 32}{RIGHT}
BZ165:  ^{BRANCH BZ156}
BY166:  'END=
BZ166:  '/rndHERE~~
BZ167:  ^{GOTO}H85~"--------~/c~.{RIGHT 5}~
BZ168:  ^{GOTO}O85~"--------~
BZ169:  ^{GOTO}Q85~"--------~/c~.{RIGHT 5}~
BZ170:  ^{GOTO}X85~"--------~
BZ171:  ^{INDICATE}{ESC}
BZ172:  ^{BEEP 0}{BEEP 3}{BEEP 0}{BEEP 3}{BEEP 0}{BEEP 3}{BEEP 0}
BZ173:  ^{GOTO}G45~
BZ174:  '{QUIT}
```

The entry in cell BZ155, in addition to invoking the WAIT indicator in the upper right corner of 1-2-3's command line, moves the cursor to cell H54 in Schedule DC. Cell BZ156 creates the range name HERE in the range H54..H54. Cell BZ57 determines whether the value of the entry in cell H54 is @NA. If that value is @NA (signifying that the end of the column has been reached), then the macro proceeds to cell BZ163, which you previously named NEXTCOL; the range named HERE (H54..H54) is deleted at that point, the cursor moves to the top of the next column of Schedule DC, and a new range named HERE is created (the first entry in the next column). If a zero rather than an @NA entry is encountered in the cell, the entry in cell BZ158 requires that it be erased. If, on the other hand, the value of the cell is 99999 (signifying that the final entry in Schedule DC has been reached), the macro branches to cell BZ163, which you previously named END. When that location is reached, the entries in the range BZ167..BZ170 create underscore lines for each column of Schedule DC before discontinuing the macro after invoking the entries in the range BZ171..BZ174. When the macro invokes the entry in cell BZ159, if the cursor does not encounter the 99999 entry, the range you previously named HERE is deleted; the cursor then moves down the column to the next cell entry and loops back to cell BZ156, where the process of eliminating zeros and checking to see if the end of the spreadsheet has been reached repeats itself.

A

Alt/D macro, 22, 108-109
Alt/E exponential smoothing macro, 21, 191-193
Alt/M macro, 200-206, 223
Alt/W weighting macro, 21, 188-189
Alt/Z zero removal macro, 101, 465-466

C

calculation mode, 20

D

data tables
    design concept, 18
    Alt/D macro, 22, 108-109
    Alt/E exponential smoothing macro, 21, 182-185, 191-193
    optional menu system, 200, 458-461
    Schedule A Pie Chart, 227-228,

E

exponential smoothing model, 182-185
exponential smoothing weight, 21, 182-185, 188-189

G

graphics
    features, 23
    main graphics menu, 214-215
    main graphics submenu, 215-217
    Schedule A
        bar chart, 224-226
        exploding pie chart wedges, 227

Schedule T
   # 1 line chart, 314, 322-328
   # 2 line chart, 314, 299, 335-339
   # 3 line chart, 314, 340-347
   # 4 line chart, 314, 351-357
   # 5 line chart, 314, 364-369
      budget trend request data table, 315-321
      deflated projected expenditurer equest data table, 357-363
      deflated budget trend request data table, 329-335
      main graphics submenu, 314-315
      projected expenditure request data table, 345-351

L

line-item format x

M

major menu macros
   Alt/M macro, 200-206, 223
   graphics, 215-216
   locating spreadsheets, 200-206
   window splitting option, 208-211
   print/print to file, 23, 412-413
   optional data tables, 200, 458-461
mean-squared error, 21, 182

O

objective of expenditures format, x

P

print/print to file budget schedules
   C.Itoh Proprinter 8510 print codes, 420
   IBM Proprinter print codes, 463
   main menu options, 23, 412-413
   main print submenu, 414-416

R

S

Schedule T annual compound growth rate factor, 150, 154
  projected expenditure requests formula, 154-155

W

what-if analysis, x, 18, 215
window splitting macro, 209-211
worksheet application features, x-xii